THE SONG
OF HELLAS

By M.A. Soupios

KLIDARITHMOS

Pubished by
Klidarithmos
27 B Stournara st.
Athens, 106 82
Greece

Tel. 210-52.37.635
Fax: 210-52.37.677
email: orders@klidarithmos.gr
Web side: http://www.klidarithmos.gr

ISBN: 960-209-786-8

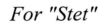

For "Stet"

Contents

ACKNOWLEDGMENTS

This project came to fruition only with the support of a large and diverse number of family, friends, and colleagues. My wife, Linda, and our children---Alex, Nick and Athena--can legitimately be deemed co-authors of this volume. Their love and encouragement sustained me in ways they do not begin to understand.

Next, I give thanks to a core of extraordinary teachers with whom I have had the privilege of studying over the years. These include Jack Culpepper (St. Lawrence); Lawrence Ritt (C.W. Post); Philip Phenix (Columbia); David Nyberg and George Hourani (SUNY Buffalo); and Francis Canavan (Fordham).

I have been blessed as well with a throng of wonderful friends whose loyalty and laughter have lightened my heart and refreshed my spirit in innumerable ways. Among others, I am indebted to Noble and Mary Smith, Paul DiMarco, Ray and Joan Scannell, Ed and Dale Dick, Rich and Gwen Shear, Rich and Carol Shields, Kevin and Debra Fitzgerald, Steve Kwintner, and Harold Reilly.

There have also been a number of "facilitators" throughout the span of my career who made possible the sort of opportunities that result in unpayable debts. In particular, these include David Newton, Rosalie Levine, and Mary Lai. Be it hoped this work will confirm the faith they placed in me.

My colleagues at C.W. Post have been an inestimable source of inspiration and insight over the years—many were also generous enough to read part or all of the manuscript during various stages of its development. Accordingly, I extend my deep appreciation to Stan Jarolem, Bob ("The Mummy") Brier, Roger

Goldstein, Mori Watanabe, Julian Mates, Arthur Coleman, and Bob Reidy. Above all, I am under extraordinary obligation to the dedicatee of this volume. Although this splendid curmudgeon has paid Charon his fee, his memory will always burn brightly in my heart and mind.

Finally, several individuals proved to be of invaluable technical support throughout the course of this project. Special thanks to my trusted typist Patricia Abbondondolo, to our departmental secretary Barbara Zahra, and to research librarian Louis Pisha. In addition, I acknowledge the energy and insight of my graduate assistant, Diana Poulos.

Preface

The most impressive feature of the modern era is its astonishing record of scientific and technological achievement. These triumphs have altered all contemporary life, allowing each of us to engage routinely in activities which a century ago would have been the stuff of dreams. One affect of these accomplishments, however, has been a strong tendency to view modernity in ahistorical terms, as enjoying a moment without parallel, precedent, or even foundation. Not surprisingly, this perspective has encouraged a tendency to assert that the past is no longer capable of speaking to the present. According to this view the ancients, including the Greeks, cannot possibly be pertinent to the modern world given the massive disjunctures of time and place. After all, what possible affinities could exist between a people who prospered 2500 years ago and a civilization that has landed men on the moon and solved the riddle of the double helix?

Two aspirations are contained in the pages of this book. First, an effort is made to present an assessment of the contributions to Western Civilization made by the Greeks in areas such as science, art, politics, and philosophy. Next, there is a suggestion that the Greeks may yet be serviceable to modernity, that certain of their insights and approaches may still illumine the human condition. This is not to suggest the Greeks devised some canonic template valid for all time. No ancient people can furnish us with a ready supply of answers—not even those most responsible for lending the West the bulk of its unique culture. But what the Greeks are able to do is remind us that truth must be pursued regardless of inconvenience or controversy; that the Good, the True, and the Beautiful are mysteriously coextensive; and, above all, that a child-like wonder is humanity's greatest virtue.

These are the crucial attitudes requisite for a vibrant culture. They allow a people to rub the dust from their eyes, enabling a view of life that is clear and whole. As such, they collectively constitute a life strategy that no society, however advanced technologically, can afford to ignore. It is for these reasons that we must continue to keep faith with our Hellenic patrimony. Failure in this matter would not only involve cultural dereliction, in the end it would contribute to an abandonment of culture itself.

Chapter I

The Spell of Homer

"The best men choose one thing rather than all else:
everlasting fame among mortal men" —Heraclitus

Introduction

Historians of ancient civilization deserve our respect and sympathy. They are routinely faced with the formidable and often painful task of unlocking the mysteries of the past--in many instances, the very distant past. A challenge such as this is compounded significantly for cultural historians, who are called upon to reconstruct not only the factual framework of vanished civilizations, but to penetrate the thought-world of ancient peoples as well. In other words, their job does not end with the establishment of key chronologies or with the identification of some pivotal event or personality. We also expect these researchers to access the "mind" of their subjects, to somehow envision and experience life as others did centuries earlier--all this, while remaining vigilant against that scholarly virus, anachronism!

Students of ancient Greece are confronted with all of these obstacles. Even though the Hellenes represent a more explicit link to Western civilization than do any other ancient people, they nevertheless seem at many points alien, confusing, impenetrable. Fortunately in the case of Hellas, we have a powerful ally in our efforts to decode the enigmas fostered by massive discontinuities of time and culture. This ally's name is Homer and by investigating the path he established, by endeavoring to grasp the lessons and paradigms he offers in epic verse, we enlist the services of a guide with unrivaled credentials in our efforts to negotiate the labyrinth that is ancient Greece.

Homer enjoys a rank and status in Hellenic civilization difficult for modern students to comprehend. The record of his impact suggests an influence typically reserved for a great statesman, prophet, or lawgiver, rather than a "mere" poet. Still, works such as the Odyssey, and particularly the Iliad, served as the fount of Greek *paideia* (culture, learning) for more than a thousand years. They endowed the Greeks with a sense of cultural unity and presented a common code of values inexhaustibly operative in Hellenic society long after the demise of Mycenean civilization (Grote I:433-34). The explanation for this continuous impact is that Homer was the central pivot around which the whole of Greek education was organized (Marrou xiv). Accordingly, one Homeric commentator of the late first century B.C. describes the poet's verses as the "mother's milk" upon which all children were nourished. The description is apt. Homer dominates the cultural horizon of Greece because his message is not simply aesthetic; first and foremost the purpose of a work like the Iliad is pedagogic. Its aim is to serve as an aphoristic treasury, a kind of "tribal encyclopedia" (Havelock 1963, 165) including strongly idealized portraits of heroic *arete* (virtue). The epic's ultimate aim is to instill and inspire, entertainment is an incidental concern. That these larger cultural objectives, the normative elements of Homer, are embedded in a poetic medium of incomparable beauty and richness lends greater force to the instruction.

In short, Homer became the unequaled shaper of Greek life and Greek character (Jaeger 1:36). Wherever Hellenic influence spread—from Marseilles to India, from the Dnieper to the Nile—there too was Homer. The testimony of the ancients themselves makes all of this abundantly clear: Xenophanes of Colophon said of Homer, "all have learned from him;" the great tragedian Aeschylus observed that his tragedies were but "slices from Homer's banquet;" Plato, despite a spirited critique in the Republic, still describes Homer as "the poet wise in all things;" Xenophon in his Symposium (3.5) refers to a young man named Niceratus who can recite both the Iliad and Odyssey by heart having been encouraged to memorize the works by his father who wanted him to be "a good man;" the historian Arrian relates how Alexander the Great actively sought to emulate the exploits of Homer's heroes, particularly Achilles;[*] the architectural historian Vitruvius describes the life of a poet named Zoilus who came to Alexandria and attacked the works of Homer for which the King, Ptolemy, sentenced him to death for parricide (Homer being the father of all poets).

The roster of devotional anecdotes is endless—all testify to the high station Homer and his works enjoyed throughout the Greek world. It should also be noted that a strong claim can be made as well for Homer as the father of Latin letters, specifically as a result of his influence upon Virgil. At Rome too, Homer was the core curriculum for more than five centuries (Scott 120).

Troy—Fact or Fiction?

With few exceptions (e.g. Anaxagoras), the ancients seem to have been convinced of the Trojan War's historicity. For the typi-

---

[*] A good example being the spectacular funeral games staged by Alexander to mark the death of his friend Hephaestion, just as Achilles had done for Patroclus (7.14).

cal Greek of the classical period, the Homeric epic was not a fic-
tional account of a bygone era, but a poetic recollection of ancestral
heroism involving real men and real struggles. The Greeks understood themselves as the descendants of great champions who em-
barked from Mycenean, Tiryns, Orchomenus, Pylos, etc. to make
war upon Priam's city. Alexander was not considered naïve in
claiming direct ancestry from Achilles (Arrian 1.11), nor were the
Caesars in tracing their pedigree back to the Trojan hero, Aeneas
(Horace 4:15: 30-31).

The strength of these convictions regarding Troy's facticity is
also seen in the hallowed treatment extended the alleged site. Upon
crossing into Asia, Alexander immediately traveled inland to the
area acknowledged by the ancients as Troy and offered sacrifice at
the shrine of Athena where he also dedicated his personal armor
and took in exchange weapons believed to have been preserved
from the ancient conflict. In addition, he traveled several miles further, probably southwest, to an area known today as Besik Tepe, to
place a wreath on a mound believed to have been the burial site of
Achilles (Arrian 1.12). The ancients recorded a similar episode earlier in 480 B.C. as Xerxes was preparing to invade Europe.
Herodotus (7.40) tells us the Great King had a strong desire to see
Troy, and that he sacrificed a thousand oxen at the site to the Trojan Athena and had the magi offer libations of wine to the great
heroes of old who had fought at Ilium. There is also a tradition that
Julius Caesar planned to move his capital from Rome to Troy—
Horace refers to a Roman aspiration to "renew the roofs of ancestral Troy!" (3.3.59), but speaks of a thwarting vindictiveness on the
part of the gods—especially Juno (Hera). Even during the Christian
era (4th century A.D.), the lure and legend of Troy remained strong.
Before turning his attention to Constantinople, there is some evi-

dence that Constantine had first tried to build his new city on the Sigeum ridge at Troy (Wood 31).

It is clear then that the Greeks, and not merely the Greeks, were convinced of the Trojan War's authenticity. Indeed, they were so certain of the event, they offered some intriguingly precise chronological speculations. Doulis of Samos claims the battle took place in 1334 B.C. Herodotus cites 1250 B.C. Eratosthenes, the chief librarian at Alexandria, proposes 1184 B.C. as the legitimate date. And perhaps most remarkable of all, a slab of Parian marble brought to England by the Ambassador of Charles I to the Ottoman Court, claims the sack of Troy occurred on 5 June 1209 B.C. (Wood 28)!

Despite a rising tide of skepticism, a small band of romantics, adventurers, and Grecophiles stubbornly maintained that Homer was much more than simply a weaver of poetic fictions; that he was instead the great oral historian of his race. Among this dreamy-eyed minority, pride of place is given Heinrich Schliemann (1822-1890), the man whose name has become synonymous with the archeological "rediscovery" of Ilium. At a site in modern-day Turkey known as Hissarlik (meaning "place of the fort"), Schliemann conducted six excavations between 1870-1890 and claimed to have located the exact site of the fabled city. In addition to this project, Schliemann dug extensively at Mycenae, Orchomenos, and Tiryns. Some of his finds, such as the "mask of Agamemnon" and the "Jewels of Helen" became international sensations and guaranteed their discoverer's place in archeological history.

Schliemann's work at Hissarlik was continued by Wilhelm Dorpfeld and Carl Blagen, both of whom applied more rigorous standards of scientific archeology to the mysteries of the site. Their discoveries, as well as a few very recent determinations constitute the prevailing core of archeological belief regarding the historicity of Priam's city. Here is where we stand currently. The mound excavated at Hissarlik is a very ancient and highly stratified site. At least nine major layers have been unearthed representing a time span from 3000 B.C. to the end of the Roman Empire. Mycenean artifacts, including a significant number of Greek weapons—arrowheads, knives, axes, lanceheads—many with excellent mainland (Greece) parallels, have been discovered at the site. In addition, Hittite diplomatic records unearthed at Boghaz Koy clearly indicate Mycenean (Greek) activity in western Anatolia within the time frame presumed by the epic (Wood 175). Based on evidence such as this, many experts now believe the Troy of which Homer sang is located somewhere between strata vi and viiA. Many difficulties remain however, and we must concede that the unequivocal evidence we seek regarding the veracity of the Trojan saga probably lies beyond our grasp (see Finley 1979, Appendix II).

The Living Voice

If the events described by Homer have any foundation in fact, they would have occurred toward the end of the Mycenean period—13th - 12th century B.C.. It should be remembered, however, that the poem's composition probably did not receive its unique Homeric stamp until four hundred years later. Accordingly, a distinction must be made between the world described in the poem and the world in which the heroic events receive the poetic formulation with which we are familiar. Regarding the latter, there is one preeminently significant factor that must be recognized; most Greeks of Homer's time were illiterate or at best, semi-literate. With the collapse of Mycenean civilization, brought on by the Dorian incursions, the use of Linear B script ceased. This means that from roughly 1100 B.C. until the late 8th century B.C., the Greeks were without an alphabet (Havelock 1978, 9). The situation changes when the Greeks adopt Phoenician letters around 750 - 725 B.C., adding vowels and several new consonants to the semitic script creating thereby the first fully phonetic alphabet (Logan 40).

The importance of all this for our purposes lies in the fact that the Iliad was originally the product of oral composition and probably did not assume textual status (at Athens first) until the 6th century B.C.. The research of Milman Parry (see A. Parry 1987) and others demonstrated Homer's reliance upon a venerable oral tradition that received its uniquely Homeric attributes at about the same time the Greeks were reestablishing their letters. In short, Homer was probably a singer of songs, not a writer of verse.

What are the distinctions, in terms of historical impact, between an acoustic culture and a literary culture? It is very likely that our contemporary reliance upon written and visual forms of communication make it difficult for the modern mind to grasp many of the distinguishing characteristics of oral culture. This may be particularly true in the case of ancient Greece where orality is strongly entrenched, and remains the dominant communicative mode long after literacy has been reestablished (Harris 29). Indeed, with few exceptions, it seems the Greeks read most everything aloud (see Knox 1968, 435 and Svenbro 18). With these limitations in mind, we can proceed to speak of an "oral state of mind" operating among the Greeks (Havelock 1963, 42). In the context of Homer, the phrase implies a direct and passionate association between the recited poem and the reciter; a psychological and emotional involvement bordering on personal identity. The skillfully constructed rhythms and formulas contained in a work such as the Iliad serve as powerful mimetic instruments facilitating recall. They also function as a sort of cerebral script, an invisible writing that forge strong links between the poem and the listener (Havelock 1963, 141). In other words, a person reciting the Iliad's embassy scene (Bk 9) in some sense experiences the rage and indignation of Achilles in a manner distinct from a person who merely reads the episode silently.

This is a pivotal point to the extent it may explain how a poem could have served as the cultural foundation for ancient Greece for more than a millennium. It may also explain how the values of the Homeric warriors remained living precepts centuries after their utility had faded.

Warrior Ethos—The Code of Honor

Homer's world represents a zone of transition—a place where eye was supplanting ear and where the polis had replaced Mycenean feudalism. But what of the world depicted in the Iliad; what of the life code governing the existence of heroic figures such as Achilles, Odysseus, Hector, and Agamemnon? The credo of these warriors can be reduced to four fundamental and cognate propositions. First, an almost pathological obsession with *timē* (honor) defined in terms of public esteem. Second, an agonistic (competitive) instinct that colors every facet of heroic existence. Third, a fierce determination to expunge dishonor or shame by whatever means necessary. And finally, a quest for glory that outranks life itself on the scale of Homeric values.

Honor is an all-pervasive and continuous objective of the Homeric warrior. Its maintenance, expansion, or restoration is an abiding personal concern pursued by virtually every figure in the Iliad. In fact, the quest for honor and the expunging of its negative corollary (shame), is a thematic thread lending structure and unity to the entire poem: Hera and Athena must restore their honor after their defeat in the contest with Aphrodite; Menelaus must undo the shame associated with Paris' abduction and violation of Helen; above all, Achilles demands honor from Agamemnon who denies him his captive trophy and in the same spirit, must extract blood vengeance from Hector who strips him of his dearest friend.

For the modern mind this preoccupation with *timē* seems strange and difficult to comprehend on at least two levels. First, our value priorities have evolved along lines different than those espoused by the Iliad's warrior chieftains. Money, influence, political authority have, to a considerable degree, directed our interests and energies. Thus, in the modern value climate, calls to "honor," to doing the "honorable" thing, all too often collide with what are deemed more "realistic" and "prudential" priorities. In many respects, honor today has assumed the status of an archaic abstraction—it is certainly not a value for which most would be willing to lay down their lives. But this is precisely what the Iliad tends to indicate. Indeed, the famous choice of Achilles explicitly prescribes such sacrifice (Iliad 9.410-416).

In addition to this axiological gulf, there is also a fundamental psychological disparity complicating our understanding of the Homeric honor code. Modern man has a personal, inner life that places him at considerable distance from the Homeric heroes. In terms of character, decision making, assessments of worth, he operates under the aegis of an internal dynamic generally absent from the likes of Achilles, Odysseus, or Agamemnon. This is not to suggest that the social environment exercises no influence upon the modern individual—the sway of sociological forces is now thoroughly acknowledged. Still, there is a kind of "interiority," a certain complexity and depth present in the modern psyche that can, at least in principle, maintain some degree of autonomy against the mandates of the social setting. It is this autonomous capacity that appears to be generally lacking in Homer's characters. These are not "inner-directed" figures; Freud would have had little work among the Myceneans.[*] Social psychologists, on the other hand, would have had a wealth of material to examine.

What is being suggested here is that the Homeric code of honor was only related in part to self-contained endeavor by a given hero. A major dimension of honorific attributions in the Iliad involves public commendation. Great deeds must be witnessed, more, they must be acknowledged in some collective fashion as "great." What the Greeks called *demou phatis*, or public opinion, was a vital ingredient in the general ecology of warrior life. In this social milieu humility is a largely unknown and unpracticed social grace; no Homeric hero can afford to keep his light under a bushel. This explains why flyting, a boastful declaration of one's excellence, is a pervasive feature of the Iliad (e.g., 3.43-51, 6.882, 11.39). A man must, in addition to bold actions, declare his greatness to the world to have it properly recognized and recorded. This is important because social standing, the manner in which one is perceived by society, is a prime factor in defining personal character. In other words, for Homeric man, public persona is synonymous with consciousness; there is little behind the mask, (see MacIntyre, chpt. 10).[†]

---

[*] Although this has not prevented some from attempting to apply modern psychological analysis to the Iliad. See MacCary (1982) and Van Nortwick (1992).

[†] Here, too, some qualification is in order. There are some scholars, particularly certain German authorities (e.g. Snell 1953 and Frankel 1975) who stress the external determinants of heroic conduct to a point where there is virtually no volitional dynamic operating in Homer's champions. This is incorrect. While the heroes portrayed in the Iliad may not possess fully evolved character states along modern lines, it is wrong to reduce them to armor-clad marionettes. Achilles is not an empty husk; he participates in a wide-range of inner experience, including rage, sorrow, vengefulness and reconciliation. In addition, there is evidence of analytical activity (Iliad 9.315-325).

The push and pull of public opinion then, constitutes the chief source of behavioral impulse among Homeric warriors. Social imagery, and the need to conform to that imagery, exercises a powerful influence in this world. Accordingly, there is a radically extended notion of "significant other" operating in the Iliad. Diomedes is not only concerned about what his fellow Acheans will say if he withdraws from battle. He is also troubled about the opportunity for boasting this will afford Hector (8.152-6)!

In sum, the Iliad's heroes are propelled principally by external social forces. When an Achilles engages in some action, martial or otherwise, the underlying motivation is typically linked to the norms and expectations of the social setting. His paramount concern is not related, to use a jaded phrase from our own times, to "feeling good about himself." The determinant standards operating here in the late bronze age are "outside" of the individual. Achilles must be concerned with the assessments of his peers because it is their opinions, not some inner consciousness, that will determine his sense of dignity and worth.

The Agonistic Spirit

The Achean warrior is a man possessed of what might be described as a jealous and unforgiving soul. This is necessarily the case given a social system in which honor is assigned based on competitive achievement. Nietzsche (1982, 32-39) identifies this agonistic passion as the true essence of Hellenism as opposed to the rationalistic "swindle" prescribed by Plato (see also Burckhardt 114). The testimony of both Homer and Hesiod tends to support much of Nietzsche's claim. Further credence has been lent by what has became a standard text on the subject, A.W.H. Adkins' Merit and Responsibility. Adkins draws an important distinction between what he calls the "competitive virtues" versus the "cooperative virtues," noting that the former category remains dominant throughout all of Greek history. Despite certain objections registered recently by some scholars (see Cairns 1993 and Long 1970), the general assessment of Greek society presented by Adkins remains fundamentally sound.

This is a world in which competitive excellence operates along exclusive, hierarchic lines. Only one brow can don the laurel wreath; also-rans receive little solace in the zero-sum honor economy of this culture. The agonistic flavor of the environment is clearly illustrated by a comparison with New Testament teaching. In the gospel of Luke we encounter a brief "Homeric" moment as the disciples argue as to who among their rank is the greatest. The debate ends abruptly with Jesus saying, "For the one who is least among you is the one who is the greatest" (9:46). Nothing could be more contrary to the tone and spirit of the Iliad, or for that matter, to Greek culture in general, than this teaching.[*]

In contrast to this self-effacing instruction, we find Peleus bidding his son, Achilles, farewell as he departs for war with an admonition to "excel all others" (11.783 cf. 6.208 and 12.310-328). Elsewhere in the Iliad we hear warriors vaunting their superiority over slain adversaries with unsavory zeal (e.g., 16.745); and we are told of athletic contests between comrades that escalate rapidly into potentially murderous confrontations (23.477-492, 565-585, and 730-737).

---

[*] Given the competitive nature of Greek society, it is not surprising that aid to the poor and hapless was sporadic at best. We know that war orphans were sometimes raised by the state and that food allowances were occasionally extended to the needy (Aristotle, Ath. Const. 49.4), but, in general, the Greeks display little compassion for the less fortunate; Zeus may have been the protector of strangers, but he typically turned his back on those incapable of fending for themselves (see Hands 1968). By comparison, Yahweh was remarkably benign (Lev. 19.9, Deut. 24.19-21, Ruth 2.5-7, etc.).

Centuries after Homer's poetic achievement, the agonistic spirit persists unabated in both application and intensity. The polis remains an environment entirely committed to competitive endeavor—the games, the theater, public recitation, artistic production—all reflect the ancient combativeness of the agon. Some have argued that this zeal for competition elevated human accomplishment to heights unmatched before or since. This may be true. But it is also true that the spirit of contest worked a terrible mischief within the social fabric of the Greek world.[*] In great measure, it explains the persistent inability of the Greeks, except under the most exigent circumstances (e.g., the Persian Wars), to make common cause. Here, too, lies the explanation for that peculiar violence that continuously lurks just beneath the surface of the polis' fragile decorum. It may even constitute a portion of the explanation behind the outrages committed at places like Corcyra and Melos (Thucydides 2.81 and 5.117).

Shame Culture

The opening lines of the Iliad make reference to the "pains thousandfold" brought upon the Acheans by the anger of Achilles. The source of his anger is *aidos* (shame).

Agamemnon has humiliated the foremost warrior at Troy by denying him his *geras* (booty) the captive woman, Briseis, and doing so publicly before the assembled host. In the Mycenean world, this outrage against the *timē* of Achilles constitutes both a cardinal sin and a capital offense—were it not for Athena's intervention, Agamemnon would have died on the spot (1.194-200).

---

[*] As Bowra notes (34), "The desire to excel feeds on the humiliation of others, and Greek individuals and cities alike slaked their ambitions in this way."

Eventually, the son of Atreus will recant his violation of the *charis* convention, a code of reciprocal gifts and acknowledgments aimed at counteracting the centrifugal tendencies of this highly volatile environment (MacLachlan 13). He will blame *atē* (god induced blindness) for his misconduct, a sort of "psychic intervention" (Dodds 5) that robs a man of his better judgment, but excuses will not assuage the sense of dishonor experienced by the great champion. Achilles resumes fighting only after Hector has killed his beloved comrade Patroclus. In other words, only the instinct for revenge can quench the fiery outrage produced by the earlier disgrace. In the meantime Achilles relishes the misfortunes of his former comrades; their lacerations are salve for his wounded honor. Viewed through a modern lens the conduct of both Agamemnon and Achilles seems childish, mutually disadvantageous, and potentially destructive of the entire enterpise, viz., the sack of Troy. But in a society where public esteem and maintenance of "face" is as essential as food and drink, affronting Achilles as if he were some "dishonored vagabond" goes well beyond a simple breach of warrior etiquette. It is a transgression that calls into question the very essence of Achilles' being and is therefore intolerable. Within the context of this shame-driven society, Achilles is entitled to his *menis* (god-like wrath); more, he is justified in seeking redress.

Although Achilles' ire is implacable and constitutes what, in later dramatic terms, would be called a tragic flaw, one gets the distinct impression from reading Homer that under analogous circumstances any of the heroes would have acted similarly. Indeed, shame is one of the epic's primary motifs. It is the reason why Hector cannot avail himself of the safety afforded by the walls of his city; better to face Achilles and die with glory than endure the shame and accusations of the people (22.98-110). Not even the pitiful urgings of his parents can stay Hector's determination to avoid shame (22.37-90).

Shame is also portrayed in the <u>Iliad</u> as a powerful exhortative device. As the horror of battle begins to erode combative resolve, fear of shame is invoked as a means of stiffening the spines of the fighters. This is the strategy employed by Sarpedon as he attempts to rally his Lykian comrades against the assaults of Patroclus (16.422).

Again, Homer uses the figure of Alexandros (Paris) as a means of dichotomizing the glorious and shameful hero. In his direct confrontation with Menelaos in Book III, Alexandros shrinks back into the safety of the Trojan host truckling in the presence of the man he has wronged.[*] Hector's reaction to his brother's shameful behavior illustrates the sort of ridicule a man could expect in response to unheroic conduct. He observes, among other things, that it would be _____ if he (Alexandros) had never been born and that justice in _____ "a mantle of flying stones" for a man like

cultural gravity of themes such as honor, shame _____ e remains the all-important concept of kleos _____ on, these are all part of a tightly connected _____ , contest, and shame tend to flow in and o _____ with reflexive ease. But glory as an object of warrio _____ distinctive. It alone implies an enduring

---

[*] Alexandros' cowardice also receives subtle punctuation through his choice of weapons. The bow is a low status instrument in the protocols of Greek warfare because it relieves a man of the burden of having to fight "in the front ranks," face to face (see Euripides, <u>Heracles</u> 157-163 and Hanson 15).

quality that tends to set it apart from the rest of Homer's axiology. Honor involves the securing of some finite acknowledgment, an accolade worn for a day. Winning honor is an important achievement to be sure, but it is one whose luster fades rapidly. By its very nature, it must be seen as an evanescent commodity.

Glory, on the other hand, defies temporal parameter. Once attained, it allows its possessor to stand beyond the bitter reality of time according its recipient a status that defiantly transcends pyre and grave.

The special salience the concept of *kleos* held for the Greeks—not merely Homer's Hellenes, but for all Greeks throughout Hellenic history—is directly related to what they saw as the dreadful brevity of human existence. Death is the omnipresent horizon of epic poetry in general, and of the Iliad in particular. But Homer's treatment of the subject is different from most other presentations in the sense that his does not glorify death. Although the Iliad ascribes great importance to the idea of dying for noble cause, the brilliant light cast by glorious sacrifice is never allowed to outshine the fundamental hatefulness of the "bronze sleep." Human life is always referred to as something "sweet," "dear," "precious"; death is spoken of in terms of the "hateful darkness."

The opening lines of the epic reflect this emphasis. The poet announces from the outset that he is going to sing of the sufferings associated with war—how multitudes are sent down to the House of Hades and how the supple flesh of young men is converted to glut for dogs and birds (1.1-5). For Homer, death is a sorrowful dissolution, it is never romanticized. His description of the god Ares (the god of War) might have consisted of glowing characterizations and inspiring epithets. Instead, Ares is described as "man-slaughtering, blood-stained" (5.455), and even Zeus is made to express contempt for him, referring to Ares as "most hateful of all gods" (5.890).[*]

Similarly, the famous Shield of Achilles is not used by Homer to extol the virtues of slaughter despite its deadly associations. The scenes depicted on the Shield include laughter, music, dance, and a general celebration of life's many joys (18.490-6 cf. the Shield of Heracles in Hesiod 144-163). In short, while the central action of the Iliad revolves around combat, death is never extolled by Homer; Zeus is nowhere portrayed as Odin, nor is Olympus offered as the Greek Valhalla.

Why then do men fight? Why do they risk reduction to ash and urn if the horrors of death are so evident? Part of the explanation lies in the warrior code itself; the good man is expected to maintain his heroic bearing even unto the grave—death being a capstone expression of one's honor. But there is more to Homer's treatment of death than simple compliance with heroic ethos. The Iliad suggests that death, notwithstanding its bleak and frightful essence, presents men with a certain opportunity as ephemeral creatures. Specifically, Homer is conversant with one of life's great ironies, viz. that confronting the ugly absurdity of human finitude can lend richness and meaning to human existence. It is for this reason perhaps that we are all drawn to one degree or another to the mystery of death. It has the ability to plunge us deep within ourselves compelling us to explore levels of our being that would otherwise remain untapped—a poignancy of the death enigma that did not escape Hegel.[†]

---

[*] Among the Romans, Mars enjoyed an important and ubiquitous cult, but among the Greeks, the god of war received little homage (Finley 1991, 130).

[†] In the Phenomenology, Hegel discusses the life affirming combat between "self" and "other," "The relationship of both self-consciousnesses is in this way so constituted that they prove themselves and each other through a life-and-death struggle. They

All this represents part of the warrior's "wisdom"—the fateful recognition that challenging death is a necessary part of life's adventure and that denial of this challenge is more than cowardice, it is theft of our potential to attain full humanity. These points can be traced in the development of the Iliad's greatest hero. The Achilles of Book XXIV is not the same man encountered earlier in Book IX; the sulking child of the embassy scene has been matured by the death of his friend, the slaying of his enemy, and the awareness of his own impending demise. He learns much through the course of the poem and death is his stern instructor. Homer's intent then is not to praise death itself but rather man's response to death—this being the core of Homeric humanism. The Iliad proclaims that courage, endurance, and dignity are often shadowed by grief and misery. By accepting death as a companion in life's journey, the warriors of the Iliad transcend their mortality.

It is specifically this desire to conquer death, to achieve something enduring, that explains the special place *kleos* enjoyed among the Greeks. Eschatologically speaking, the Hellenes afforded themselves little by way of paradisal solace. Homer's image of Hades is forbidding; dank and dreary, with pallid shades existing in permanent torpor. The haunting words of Achilles' ghost offered in the Odyssey (11.490-93) lend full measure to the bitter existence awaiting us beyond this world.[*]

Faced with a lifeless eternity in which "heaven" as we understand that term is unattainable, the Greeks had *kleos* as a surrogate. Nothing can avert the sad transience of this life, but the despair of

---

must enter into this struggle, for they must bring their certainty of themselves, the certainty of being for themselves, to the level of objective truth, and make this a fact both in the case of the other and in their own case as well" (232-3).

[*] "Better, I say, to break sod as a farm hand for some poor country man, on iron rations, than lord it over all the exhausted dead."

human impermanence is mitigated by the immortality conferred by remembrance. Homer's warriors seek the everlasting via the sword; each attempts to perform deeds that will echo in eternity. This is the message offered by Sarpedon, (12.322-328) as he explains the necessity of heroic combat and the glory that it yields; by this means alone men gain immortality. By risking death on the field of battle, a man earns glory and places his name on the lips of posterity. In this manner we cease to be merely a "generation of leaves," becoming instead the object of song securing thereby the only immortality our kind can anticipate.

Glory then, enjoys a redemptive significance in the Iliad, functioning as part of a warrior beatitude that defends against the grave. There is little doubt that *kleos* figures prominently in Achilles' decision to exchange his *nostos* (safe homecoming) in favor of everlasting reputation (9.410-416) and equally without question, it remains a powerful cultural precept throughout all of Greek history.

Homeric Continuities

The Iliad is a great poetic incantation that holds Hellenic culture in its spell for centuries. Thus, despite a separation of roughly eight hundred years between the world depicted by Homer and the classical era, we nevertheless find the old standards substantially operative in the time of Socrates and beyond. This continuity exists in great measure because of the role "mythical exemplars" played in Greek civilization (Kirk 291). Works such as the Iliad were more than poetry, they were a kind of moral catechism through which a specific core of behavioral paradigms were instilled and perpetuated. As we have seen, the heroic value system was not particularly pacific—by its very nature it tended to call forth the competitive juices which often included the poisons of ambition, jealousy,

31

envy, and violence. These toxins were more easily managed in the organizational context presented by Mycenean sociology; the loosely configured social structures of the bronze age dissipated much of the violent potential. As the Greeks develop the new, more highly condensed social forms associated with the polis, however, the ongoing operation of Homeric values present grave obstacles to cooperative endeavor (see Gouldner 13-17). Everywhere—from the athletic fields, to the agora, to the courts and assemblies—the hegemony of Homeric axiology continued to function, often in virulently unsublimated form. In a sense, the entire culture operated under the aegis of an "Achilles complex;" the sword had been sheathed, but the instinct for its use remained very strong.

The problems attached to such continuities are well illustrated by the moral code of classical Greece. By comparison with modern standards, Greek ethics seem shallow and disturbingly devoid of theoretical foundations. Kantian "duty" along with universalizing precepts such as the "categorical imperative" are generally absent from Hellenic morality. Instead we find a kind of moral minimalism operating, in which a crude and rather one-dimensional utility serves as the standard of propriety. Here, only results have value. The entire question of intentionality, a critical dimension of modern moral systems, remains unconsidered. Few distinctions exist between premeditated, accidental, or justifiable actions—someone or something must always be held responsible. This explains the presence at Athens of a remarkable court assigned the task of adjudicating cases in which animals or inanimate objects had caused death (see Plato Laws 873e, Demonsthenes Aristocrates 76, and Parker 117).

Not surprisingly, the idea of guilt also appears to be generally missing from the classical scene. To the extent that the concept of "guilt" denotes the presence of some internalized standard, a capacity to experience a sense of wrongdoing even while unobserved by others, it is fair to say the Greeks experienced very few pangs of conscience. Like their Homeric ancestors, the Hellenes of the historical period remain closely attached to the "shame" standard with its all-important public criterion of "what people say." In such an environment, morality is chiefly procedural and remains largely unattached to states of inner-consciousness. Some counter-tendencies will eventually emerge such as the moral discipline prescribed by the Pythagoreans and the religiously inspired code developed in Orphism. Above all, there is the moral revolution proffered by Socrates (e.g., Crito 45-49). For the most part, however, the Greeks remain wedded to the old ways.

A related field in which the Homeric residue manifests itself lies in the area of conflict resolution. In the Iliad strife is not resolved by negotiation. The futility of such an approach is powerfully conveyed in the embassy scene of Book IX where Achilles belligerently maintains his enmity toward Agamemnon, despite valid arguments presented by his comrades. When his beloved tutor Phoinix, a man whom Achilles addresses as "my father," also counsels reconciliation, Achilles responds, "It does not become you to love this man (Agamemnon), for fear you turn hateful to me, who love you. It should be your pride with me to hurt whoever shall hurt me" (9.614-15). Here we encounter a clear expression of the Hellenic talion that commands Greek loyalty for centuries, i.e., the duty to "help one's friends and harm one's enemies."[*] Conspicuously absent from the one-dimensional logic underlying this code is any transcending standard of "right" or "justice" by which discord can be definitively resolved. Instead, the talion invites an ongoing cycle

---

[*] Archilochus, Solon, Theognis, Pindar, and Simonides all make reference in their poetry to this grudging logic of "helping friends and harming enemies."

of wrong being returned for wrong, leading to an infinite regress of conflict. Under these conditions, not even jurisprudence provides a meaningful remedy. In essence, the courts become the talion by other means, functioning as little more than a legalized system of revenge. Socrates recognizes the solution to this dilemma when he argued that it was better to suffer evil than to do it (Gorgias 469), but his proposal, a heterodoxy that flies in the face of a still vibrant Homeric value system, is poorly received.

Envy is another problematic legacy of the Homeric world that continued to bedevil Hellas in historic times. The universal quest for honor distinguishing Greek society, coupled with a correspondingly intense competitiveness, made envy an integral and accepted feature of the Hellenic code of conduct.[*] Greek mythology lent specific credence to envious sentiments. Had not Peleus, the father of Achilles, killed his own brother, envious of the preference shown him by their father (Apollodorus 3.12.6)? Did not Daedalus murder Talos, consumed by envy over the latter's invention of the saw and compass (Ovid 8.236-59)? And from Homer, the most well-known and powerful example of all, the morbid envy of Ajax toward Odysseus generated by his denial of Achilles' armor (Odyssey 11.512-565).

The same attitudes may also explain certain political phenomena. Ostracism, for example, may in fact mirror the spirit of envy on a societal-wide scale; banishment as a collective expression of democracy's ill-feeling toward the exceptional individual. Plutarch

---

[*] Public achievement in the Greek world was not admired as much as it was resented which explains why few eminent men went unpunished. Correspondingly, the Greeks took a dark delight in witnessing the misfortune of their enemies and rivals. The German term *schadenfreude* equates well with the malicious gloating in which the Greeks commonly engaged (on the matter of envy see Thucydides 2.35 and 3.84; Isocrates 9.6).

argues specifically that this was the explanation for democratic Athens' expulsion of the likes of Aristides and Themistocles (7.2 and 22.3). Nor did the political relevance of envy, its potentials for disruption and faction, escape the notice of Plato who notes the necessity of counteracting its effects in his Cretan city (Laws 679b-c).[*]

Certain aspects of the Homeric shame standard also continue to operate in classical times. As noted earlier, in the Iliad martial victory per se is often not an adequate prize for the great champions. In addition, the victor seeks to augment his triumph by arrogantly ridiculing the vanquished foe. This "vaunting"[†] is a standard feature of the major battle scenes, one of the better illustrations being the bitter sarcasm heaped upon Kebriones by Patroclus. As the former's lifeless body tumbles from a chariot, Patrolcus jeeringly likens him to an acrobat and an oyster diver (16.745). It is not enough, in other words, to simply kill a man in battle; one must also mock and strut.

This readiness to pour gratuitous insult upon a slain or helpless opponent, to compound victory with verbal shaming, does not cease with the passing of Mycenean civilization. Echoes of the ancient vaunt remain strong and clear in later day Athens, so much so that special legislation is passed to punish those guilty of arrogantly shaming an adversary. Our knowledge of these laws, the so-called

---

[*] The spirit of envy among the Hellenes even involves the employ of occult practice to damage one's opponent. The use of *defixiones* (binding spells) as a means of securing advantage in a competitive situation is merely a theurgic extension of the agon-envy creed of the Greeks (see Faraone 1991).

[†] Vaunting may appear to be little more than a brutal expression of warrior culture but the practice may indeed hold a deeper significance. To fade from the memory of men is to be wiped from the slate of existence. Accordingly, fame and glory were critically important for the Greeks and from this perspective, the vaunt was more than a victory shout. It affirmed and extended one's very existence.

graphe hybreos, stems chiefly from a speech prepared by the fourth century orator Demosthenes entitled, Against Meidias and from several comedic references in Aristophanes (Clouds 1296-9, Wasps 1417-1441, Birds 1021-1055). The fact that they proved necessary suggests the serious dilemma posed by the constancy of Homeric values. In a society where public esteem and the maintenance of personal honor persist as prime determinants of social status, no individual can afford to be mocked.[*] On the other hand, no society can tolerate the violent disruptions engendered by those seeking honorific redress. Acts of shaming and the reciprocal attempts to restore honor by those shamed, represented more than a petty inconvenience to the polis. As Aristotle was aware, these squabbles could escalate into large-scale disorders, up to and including civil war (Politics 5.2.4, also Fisher 498).

Are we to conclude then that the Greeks of the classical era were helpless against the vestigial prescriptions set down by Homer centuries before? Was the sense of reverence and fidelity felt for the great epics so compelling that it precluded any opportunity for critical assessment? Those well-schooled in classical literature would surely respond in the negative. They might point, for example, to certain statements among the pre-Socratics (e.g. Xenophanes and Heraclitus) or to the famous disapproval of Homer registered by Plato in the Republic (386c-38a, 388a-b, 389d-e, 390e, 391a-c, etc.). Similarly, it would be difficult to imagine someone

---

[*] It is important to note that our modern understanding of "hubris," i.e. excessive pride or arrogance, conveys only a portion of the original Greek meaning. Here, Aristotle (Rhet. 2.2) should be our guide when he observes that hubris is a kind of insult aimed at disgracing the opponent for the pleasure and sense of superiority enjoyed in so doing. In other words, for the Greeks the true essence of hubris was the infliction of shame and humiliation upon one's opponent.

endowed with Aristotle's critical sense reflexively acquiescing to poetic mandates.

A closer examination of the relevant material however, reveals a surprising loyalty on the part of both thinkers to the Homeric patrimony. At times this allegiance is obvious and direct; on other occasions, it appears in more subtle, perhaps unconscious form. On some level then, even for Plato and Aristotle, Homeric values operate reflexively. The unexamined life, as Socrates argues, may not be worth living, but one cannot examine what one does not perceive. And given the fact that Homer had become so integral to the spiritual landscape of Hellas, not even Plato and Aristotle can fully conceptualize a distinction between being "Homeric" and being Greek.

Several of the Platonic dialogues illustrate the point. The Apology presents an Athenian legal proceeding that unfolds along Homeric lines. Specifically, it is Socrates' *aristeia*, a combative assertion of manly courage reminiscent, *mutatis mutandis*, of the Iliad's great warrior *agons*. Indeed, during his verbal assault against the Athenian jury, Socrates expressly likens himself to Achilles (28c-d) and cites the Iliad (18.88-121) as a source of principled truth in matters of courage.

In this same context the Crito also echoes the themes and action of the Iliad. Crito and others have made arrangements for Socrates to escape the death sentence imposed by the court. Friends wait to receive Socrates in Thessaly where he can live out his final years in peace (45a-c). In short, Socrates is presented with a concrete choice between life and death in the same way Achilles is accorded a choice in the Iliad (9.410-418) between a brief but glorious life

versus a long and inconspicuous one back in the land of his fathers—Thessaly.[*]

Significantly, some of the strongest Homeric imagery in the Platonic corpus is found in the very dialogue in which Plato offers his
most stringent criticism of the poet—Republic. Here, Plato presents
his famous portrait of the *Callipolis* (good city) which includes a
vigorous condemnation of Homer on both moral and epistemological grounds. Nevertheless, even here Plato's scheme reveals its
substantial loyalty to the Iliad's aristocratic ideology. The critique
of democracy, the proposed system of social stratification, the
definition of justice, the call for the states' meritocratic organization, all point to the constancy of Homeric values in Plato's
thought.

These perspectives are particularly important in assessing
Plato's ideas about the ruling elite. Statesmen in the ideal society
are not selected by popular mandate, nor are they chosen by party
affiliation. Instead, Plato certifies his leadership corps through a
process of intellectualized combat, a kind of agon of the mind, the
survivors of which are entrusted with political authority. Plato may
offer a stylus in place of the spear of Cheiron, but he retains the
ancient agonistic spirit as a necessary and pervasive feature of the
best state. Is not the philosopher-king a "champion" born of contest, an Achilles with brains?[†]

---

[*] Given Plato's craft and cunning as literary artist, it may well be that there is little
subliminal about these Homeric allusions. What Plato may be doing is consciously
attempting to fuse the identities of the Iliad's greatest hero and Athens' greatest
thinker as part of his effort to exonerate and ennoble the image and memory of Socrates. This logic seems less applicable to the Republic, however, where Plato seems
genuinely incapable of escaping the orbit of Homer's influence.

[†] Nietzsche (1971, 81) argued that dialectic was simply a new artistic form of the
ancient agon.

Similar observations also hold for Plato's most illustrious student. In his ethical theory, for instance, Aristotle displays a consistent loyalty to much of Homer's aristocratic code. He speaks admiringly of the *megalopsuche* (magnanimous man), an individual committed to a life of personal honor and manly pride (N.E. 4.3-4, also Jaeger 1:11-12, 34). Similarly, Aristotle applauds the role of courage and nobility in human affairs (N.E. 3.8), arguing that honor is the best of all external goods (N.E. 4.3). In addition, he endorses traditional Greek assessments of Achilles as the paradigm of "highmindedness" defined as intolerance for dishonor (Post. An. 2.13.15-30).

The same Homeric perspective is operative in Aristotle's political analysis. The concept of distributive justice, a key feature of the Politics, is at its core an aristocratic scheme in which offices and honors are dispensed by the state in accordance with the merit of individual citizens. Explicit here is Aristotle's rejection of the un-Homeric system of justice advocated by democratic regimes, viz., that justice implies equality in all things for all people (3.5.8). This same distributive logic figures in Aristotle's assessment of party strife and revolutionary violence. He warns that failure to assign honors and dishonors in conformity to excellence engenders situations in which those slighted seek remedy by force (5.2.3-5). Needless to say, this observation and the social conditions prompting it are highly redolent of the Homeric creed.[*]

---

[*] Homeric continuities are also evident on the Greek stage. Sophocles' Ajax is acutely concerned with the mockery of his enemies (Lines 367, 382, 454, 961, and 969) as is Euripdes' Medea (Lines 383, 404, 797, 1049, 1355, and 1362) and in Antigone the heroine is not only dedicated to securing glory (Line 547), she willingly embraces her demise in a manner reminiscent of Achilles (Line 506).

Conclusion

Just as a man cannot escape his shadow, so too the Greeks could not escape the influence of their first and greatest poet. Simply put, the Hellenes were in thrall to Homer and because of this, it is difficult, if not impossible, to overstate the impact a work such as the Iliad had in conditioning Hellenic consciousness. Virtually every concept, every value, every ideal evidenced by Greek culture was refracted through a Homeric lens to one degree or another. The passage of centuries does little to diminish this influence. Even the great thinkers of the fourth century B.C. still rely, consciously or unconsciously, upon the Homeric patrimony while conducting their philosophic enterprise. In fact, according to one noted scholar, the same fierce sense of pride and masculine privilege emblematic of the Homeric code continues to exist in Greece today (Knox 1993, 125)—Achilles in the plaka!

Poetic authority such as this is not easy for the contemporary mind to comprehend. As we seek to understand the factors that have shaped our world, we appeal to the lessons of thinkers such as Marx and Freud and focus upon economic, political, and psychological forces—we do not think of dactylic hexameter. Specifically, it is difficult for us to conceive of a social environment in which the economic, political, and psychological variables themselves are conditioned by poetic verse.

How was this possible? What explanation can be offered for the almost liturgical status Homer's verse enjoyed for a thousand years among the Greeks? There is no simple response to a question such as this, but perhaps part of the answer lies with the point made earlier regarding the acoustical nature of Hellenic civilization. In a world devoid of print media and telecommunications, the recited word assumes a dominion unlike anything for which there is a modern analogy. No radio or television broadcast today could possibly bear the same cultural weight enjoyed by Homeric recitations at the Panathenaic festival. Here, the work of a master poet functioned simultaneously as tribal history, gnomic codex, and admonitory treatise.

The peculiarities of oral culture aside, Homer's rank among the ancients must also be tied in some way to the spirit and context of the poems themselves. The analysis offered in this chapter focuses principally upon the Iliad and more specifically on the competitive virtues prescribed by that work. This was both fitting and necessary because as Simone Weil observes, the Iliad is most assuredly a "poem of might" (153-183). But there is another side to the epic, something beyond the carnage and savagery, the neglect of which does violence to both the greatness of the poem and its author. I refer to the generosity of Homer's humanistic vision, to his sensitive and insightful assessments of the human condition.

One of the truly exceptional features of the Iliad is its lack of ethno-provincial elements; Homer is a Greek, but he is no jingoist. To its credit, the poem displays a consistent capacity to avoid the partisan stereotyping one might expect. We see this in the portraits of the major protagonists; Achilles may be the greatest of champions, but the most attractive figure in the Iliad, the one for whom we feel greatest sympathy and affection, is Hector, a Trojan.[*] Homer's ultimate intent, therefore, must be something beyond merely extolling the military ardor of his ancestors. The ultimate message, despite the prominence of martial motif, may in fact have more to do with explicating the bonds of a common humanity evoked by man's universal fate as suffering creature.

---

[*] Hannah Arendt (51) observes that "impartiality" came into the world with Homer who applauds the deeds of the Trojans no less than the Achaeans.

This claim presumes a rather extraordinary sophistication on the part of a work composed more than seven hundred years before Christ. Nevertheless, the closing scene of the Iliad presents a new and lofty vision of heroism that substantially extends traditional meanings.* Here, Homer leaves behind the sanguineous side of heroic endeavor and focuses upon the unity between men forged by the bitter experience of loss. Although they are partisans of different worlds, Achilles and Priam come to share a mutual empathy that not only blurs the ugliness of their antagonism, it provides a new perspective on the meaning and priorities of life itself. In effect, Homer consciously blunts the brutal clarity of the agon by powerfully emphasizing the ultimate inefficacy of heroic violence—no victory can restore Patroclus to Achilles' side just as no amount of kingly power can quicken the limbs of a fallen son. The true and higher heroism is not something obtained in blood from another warrior. It involves instead, men sharing and suffering a common fate and doing so with grace and dignity. More, it entails a new courage allowing men to transcend the restrictive parameters of their tribal loyalties and unite in the bonds of a common humanity.

It is this unity, this spiritual alliance between victor and vanquished that reveals both the tragic futility of war and the full measure of Homer's genius. The Iliad supplies Hellas with a curriculum for the competitive virtues, but it also furnishes Western man with his first lessons in that unique aesthetic known as "humanism." In the end Homer denies the wreath to those who merely wield the sharp bronze and instead offers the hymn of praise to a humanity ennobled by its sorrows and receptive to the calls of a

---

* It has been suggested the closing scene of the Iliad is a later addition to the text, a view I do not share. The misery of human loss is a thematic constant in Homer.

larger brotherhood. Although many centuries separate Homer from the ideas expressed in Isocrates' Panegyricus or the instruction offered at Zeno's Porch, the seeds of cosmopolis, albeit nascent, are found here in the Iliad's final moments. For this reason, Homer is more than simply a poet of the Greeks, he is a poet to the world.

Chapter II

Dawn at Miletus

*"Men who love wisdom must be inquirers into
very many things indeed"* —*Heraclitus*

Introduction

In the 6th century B.C., three thinkers from the city-state of Miletus altered the course of world history forever and bestowed upon Western civilization one of its most distinctive features—the scientific spirit. The individuals in question, the so-called *physiologoi*, were Thales, Anaximander, and Anaximenes. Unfortunately, the extant literature from this period is pitiably scant. In fact, most scholars agree we have only one genuine fragment available, a line from Anaximander preserved by the 6th century A.D. commentator, Simplicius. As a result, we are forced to collect our impressions about these scientific pioneers from epitomists, compilers, doxographers, and excerpters which is to say, we must contend with a host of frustrating obstacles, including compressions, anachronisms, omissions, and tendentious contamination. Even so august a figure as Aristotle (along with his Peripatetic disciples) seems to have contributed substantially to the exegetical dilemma.[*]

Notwithstanding these formidable obstacles, a cautious reconstruction of the world-view presented by these thinkers is possible. In particular, we can identify three consistent elements of the Milesian ethos:

1) an omnivorous curiosity that audaciously demanded rational explanations from nature,
2) a conviction that the universe is an orderly and rational domain subject to human investigation, and
3) the rejection of theological elements and explanations.

Both Plato and Aristotle agree that philosophy begins in wonder (Theatetus 155d and Meta 1.2.9) and the natural philosophy of the Milesians was no exception to this rule. Indeed, one can sense an almost child-like enthusiasm in the words and thoughts attributed to these thinkers—precisely the sort of exuberance one might expect from Western thinkers as they began to deploy their minds in a

---

[*] There is considerable evidence that Aristotle and his followers (e.g., Theophrastus) are responsible for many confusions regarding the Milesian philosophers. For one thing, Aristotle consistently presents the doctrines of his predecessors in a more abstract light than 6th century thought was capable of generating. He does this in two ways. First, by foisting themes and issues onto the Presocratics which were never their concern or interest. A good example being Aristotle's theory of causation. Second, Aristotle tends to intrude his own highly technical vocabulary into Milesian assessments of nature where they have limited or dissimilar application. Terms such as *arche*, *apeiron*, and *stocheion* have all proven problematic in this sense. Also, the Metaphysics (1.10.2) makes clear Aristotle's belief that all philosophic antecedents among the Greeks are but a prelude to the ripened perspectives of his own system. This conviction is the source of a conceptual straitjacket that has confounded interpretive matters ever since. The point is well summarized by Harold Cherniss who notes, "The use to which in his writings Aristotle has put the Presocratic theories has not only perverted details but has also obliterated the problems these theories had to meet and obscured the relationship of the doctrines to one another" (404, also Heidel in Mourelatos 87-88. Cf. Guthrie in Furley and Allen 242-246).

new and unprecedented fashion. This same avidity is traceable in the expanse of their speculative ambitions. Unlike other ancient peoples whose scientific efforts were constrained by the dictates of a narrow utility, unlike modern science whose lens has become incurably fragmented and specialized, the Milesians display a remarkable breadth. They saw the "big picture" and attempted to explain nothing less than the operational logic of the entire cosmos. We see this clearly in the career of Anaximander who in a single lost work, Concerning Nature, sought to explain the beginnings of the universe, the conduct of heavenly bodies, the origins of life, meteorological phenomena, geography, etc. (Barnes 1:19). In short, the Milesian panorama included virtually every zone of nature, not for the sake of practical application or material benefit but for the sheer joy of knowing.

These global perspectives were supported by a single grand conviction, viz., that the world in which we live was a rational and orderly place and that nature would reward systematic investigation with insight and truth. The modern reader may find these propositions singularly unimpressive, but when such convictions are placed in historical/cultural context, they take on an entirely different significance. Ancient Eastern thought for example, had no equivalent conception of "nature" as intelligible order. The Chinese portrait of nature, heavily influenced by Taoist doctrines, depicts the cosmos in the following terms:

"The Tao of Heaven operates mysteriously and secretly; it has no fixed slope; it follows no definite rules; it is so great that you can never come to the end of it; it is so deep that you can never fathom it" (cited in Logan 52).

Scientifically speaking, this is intellectual surrender; a hoisting of white flags in the face of staggering complexity. But the Greeks saw nature very differently. While acknowledging the intimidating complexities of the world around them, they nevertheless believed that nature was something more than a vast kaleidoscope of random phenomena; that the manifold flux of experience was more superficial than real, and that an underlying order did exist. More importantly, from the very outset, Greek scientific thought attributed to man the requisite capacities to penetrate the mystery. Man, the rational animal, was capable of revealing the necessary, lawful, and predictable operations of an intelligible universe. The rest, as they say, is history.

What we discover here is a continuous effort on the part of the Milesians to rationalize nature, i.e., to extend the notion of "order" throughout the entire physical universe. Inherent in this ambition is a powerful sub-theme that bore an irresistible fruit later in the 5th and 4th centuries, viz., secularism. There is a fundamental incompatibility between the notion of scientific lawfulness and conventional Hellenic conceptions of divinity. It is precisely the gods who disregard and violate the regularities of nature upon which science depends; who arbitrarily intervene and disrupt the orderly sequence of phenomena. For these reasons "science" can only exist where the capricious involvement of gods and spirits is denied and it is this necessity that explains the Milesians' historic departure from the practices of priests, poets, and mythographers.

Science required that Marduk be deleted (Farrington 37), and the Milesians did this with remarkable thoroughness in the process of dismantling Hellas' traditional mytho-religious scaffolding. Actually, there were proto-rationalistic elements already operating in certain of the mythological tales such as those spun by Hesiod (see

Jaeger 12; Guthrie 1962, 1:28-29; Cornford 1967, 95-116).[*] Significantly, his portrayal of the gods places them "inside" nature, not outside or beyond the natural order. As a result, not only the gods' existence but their activities as well were seen as inseparably tied to natural processes. This proved to be a critically important move to the extent that placing divinity in the natural order allowed the Greeks to purge the world of miracles, magic, and Olympian fiat. This does not mean the Milesians no longer spoke of deities— Thales will still reason that "all things are full of gods" and Anaximenes will continue to claim that air is "divine." But these are in fact not theological declarations. The natural elements and processes described in religious terms have nothing to do with public cult. Indeed, there is so great a discontinuity between the natural forces described by these thinkers and the traditional pantheon that the very existence of the latter is rendered suspect by the former (Vlastos in Graham 1995, 1:10). In truth then, the Milesians take the term "divine" and drain it of any religious significance. For

---

[*] This rationalism, along with other evidence, has prompted certain scholars to conclude that logos emerged from mythos; that the magus gave birth to the scientist. The leading figures here are F.M. Cornford and the other members of the so-called "Cambridge School" who saw Milesian speculation as a form of "philosophical theology." There is some merit to their position. There are, for example, transitional figures such as Pherekydes of Syros who seem to span the world of Homer and Hesiod on the one hand, and Thales and Anaximander on the other (Schibli 134). Aristotle acknowledged the existence of such thinkers in the <u>Metaphysics</u> describing them as part myth-loving and part philosopher (see 1.2.10 and 14.4.5). In addition, the ideas attributed to the Milesians themselves suggest religious legacy; e.g., the concepts of moira, nemesis, and "soul-substance" are arguably present in early Ionian thought (see Cornford 1957, 10, 16-17, 54-55, 149; Davies 34). Still Cornford over-works his thesis, which is heavily reliant upon the now defunct theory of pre-logical consciousness proffered by Levy-Bruhl, just as John Burnet overstates his rebuttal of the Cambridge hypothesis (see for example, Burnet 13). In truth, the former was correct to affirm that Greek science evolved from pre-rational rudiments; the latter right to insist that Anaximander was something more than Hesiod in sheep's clothing.

them it is nothing more than a descriptive epithet; something equivalent to terms such as "ageless," "deathless," or "remarkable." This is why Aristophanes' description of the natural philosophers as atheists is fully legitimate, notwithstanding their reference to "gods." He correctly understood that through their efforts "air" and "vortex" had driven out Zeus (Clouds 378-79).

By asserting that nature can and must be viewed independently of the gods, the Milesians placed Western man on a new path. No longer would angry seas be seen as the work of Poseidon, nor thunderbolts an indication of Zeus' displeasure. Beginning here in the 6th century, for the first time in human history, man steps beyond the prohibitive dogma of received religious opinion and demands that theology yield to reason.

The Milesian World Picture

According to tradition, Thales is the patriarch of Milesian speculation. In truth, he is a dim figure about whom we can say very little with certainty. The ancients were themselves unclear on whether he composed any scientific treatises (Diogenes Laertius 1.23-24). What is available to us are a series of colorful stories which make Thales sound much more the folk-hero than the scientist. Herodotus tells us that he tried to organize the Ionians into a mutual defense league against impending Persian aggression (1.170). He is also described as a military engineer in the service of King Croesus, the father of Greek mathematics and astronomy, and as an absent-minded professor who nevertheless possesses a keen business acumen when he elects to apply himself to such matters (see Plato, Theat. 174a and Aristotle, Politics 1.4.5). Significantly, Thales' name appears routinely among the Greeks' legendary roster of wise-men, the proverbial Seven Sages (see Plato, <u>Protagoras</u> 343 and Plutarch, <u>Dinner of the Seven Wise Men</u>).

Despite the romantic flavor of these anecdotes, the ancient sources are definite in identifying Thales' thought as a new beginning, the first giant step toward a rational account of the world that rendered the gods supernumeraries. In other words, Thales was the first to abandon anthropomorphic and zoomorphic images and to speak of the origins of the world in terms of a natural substance. From this moment on, scientific cosmogony replaces divine procreation—there would be no further talk of "those born to wide Ouranos and Gaia."

Thales was a "monist;" i.e., he identified a single natural element as the progenitive source from which everything else originates. For Thales, this *arche*[*] or primordial "beginning" is water. Exactly how Thales arrived at this conclusion is not entirely clear. The idea may have stemmed from personal observation of the Nile's silting process, leading him to conclude that water produced land or, as Aristotle speculated, the explanation may lie in biological observation, viz.; the universal need for moisture among all living organisms (<u>Meta</u>. 1.3.5).

In all probability, however, Thales' identification of water as the *arche* is traceable to certain mythological traditions. We know that very ancient beliefs among the Greeks ascribed to water, particularly rivers, powerful generative properties (Onians 230; see also <u>Iliad</u> 14.8-9). Not surprisingly, similar ideas are also found in the

---

[*] Our assumption that Thales identified water as the *arche* depends almost entirely upon a key passage in Aristotle (<u>Meta</u> 1.3.6). Here, in accordance with the logic of his own thought, Aristotle seeks a single material cause as the foundation of all existing matter. He concludes, therefore, that Thales believed the earth and all its contents were somehow water when in fact the Milesian may have only asserted that the earth was originally derived from water (see Kirk, Raven and Schofield 88-91).

mythologies of the great river civilizations—Egypt and Mesopotamia (Kirk, Raven and Schofield 11). The chief Babylonian creation epic describes Apsu and Tiamat as the primeval waters upon which Marduk acts to create Sky and Earth. For the Egyptians, Nun is the chief water deity and oldest of the gods. Atum, the sun-god, emerges from this watery source and Geb (earth) was imagined to float on this same aboriginal liquid.

It should be noted that as a citizen of Miletus, Thales undoubtedly was exposed to the mythological traditions of the Eastern cultures. Miletus was a rich and powerful commercial state in the 6th century and the parent city of some ninety colonies, including the all-important site of Naucratis on the Nile delta (Lloyd in Daiches 1972, 385). Thales' description of water as the original source of the world, plus his assertion that earth floats on water (see Aristotle de Caelo 2.13 and Meta 1.3.5), correspond too closely to the Eastern myths to be mere coincidence. Still, the significance of Thales' observations lies not in what he may have borrowed from mythology but in what he rejected. As naïve and rudimentary as his scheme was, it was still an unprecedented first step in the demystification of the cosmos. In short, Thales' water is not a god, and as a result, the initial phase of nature's exorcism had begun.

The next figure on the list of pioneering Milesian thinkers is Anaximander. Unlike Thales for whom we have precious little concrete information, a more extensive and less idealized record exists for the theories and achievements of this man. Accordingly, some have identified Anaximander as the first genuinely philosophic-scientific mind in the Western tradition (Jaeger 23).

Without question, the most important and perplexing feature of Anaximander's world-view is the so-called *apeiron*. The exact meaning of this term has remained one of the most baffling questions in all of Greek philosophy. Even the ancient commentators display a certain diffidence toward the word. Aristotle, for instance, lists five possible meanings for *apeiron* and seems uncharacteristically reticent in his treatment of Anaximander (Physics 3.4. See also Classen 95). What does seem clear is that Anaximander departs significantly from the previous views of Thales and that his thought represents something more than the simple monism of his predecessor.

What then is the *apeiron*? One attempt to decode this term relies on etymological analysis. It is traditionally argued that the word is formed by combining the stem word *peras* (boundary or limit) with the alpha privative, creating thereby the term "boundless" or "limitless." More recently another view has been advanced suggesting the true stem as *perao*, meaning "traverse" which when combined with the negative compound yields the term "untraversable" or "inexhaustible" (see Kahn 1960, Appendix II and Barnes 1:36). Modern wordsmiths may find all this very interesting, but it does not take us very far in our efforts to decipher the term—indeed, a bewildering array of questions remain: Does the notion of "unlimited" refer to a spatial or temporal boundlessness? Do the Greeks of this period even possess an idea of "infinity" or is this a concept that emerges only later in the thought of philosophers such as Melissus and Zeno? Is the reference to "boundless" actually a description of the content of the *apeiron,* i.e. a qualitatively indeterminate mass of pre-cosmic "stuff"? Or does the term perhaps point to an inexhaustible stock of primordial material from which our world is concocted? Or could it be that the term actually denotes some endless cyclical process of generation and dissolution?

Questions such as these continue to vex scholars, but at least this much seems clear: The *apeiron* is the source of our world and many others* which are formed as a result of some mechanical motion that "separates out" (*apokrisis*) a series of contrary substances from within the *apeiron*. Some have suggested the motion in question is a form of vortex but this may in fact be a reading back into Anaximander of later ideas proposed by Anaxagoras. In any event, "hot" and "cold" were the first opposite components to be delineated in this fashion. The hot manifests itself as a sphere of flame surrounding an inner core of dense, cold matter "as bark surrounds a tree." The earth, which Anaximander describes as shaped like the drum of a column, is formed from this icy central core. In addition, small circles of fire detach from the larger celestial flame and are encapsulated in envelopes of air. These structures contain "breathing holes" from which jets of fire appear explaining what we see when observing the sun and the moon (for a possible Eastern connection here see West 89, 108-9). Periodic obstructions of these fiery passages explains the phenomena known as eclipses.

Unlike Thales, Anaximander proposed an entirely novel explanation for the earth's stablility involving a theory of celestial equilibrium. Apparently he reasoned that the earth was equidistant from everything else in the universe and that this centrality alone ensured our planet's fixed station—a logic hailed as one of the most remarkable achievements in the history of human speculation to the extent that it announced the first mathematically conceived notion of "cosmos" (see Popper in Furley and Allen 133 and Cornford

---

* This reference to multiple worlds is yet another matter of scholarly contention. The issue: Does Anaximander refer to a crowd of coexistent worlds or is he speaking of temporally successive worlds? It may be that much of this debate stems from anachronistic attribution. The idea of innumerable coexistent worlds is a view held by the later atomists that may have been read back into Milesian thought (see Guthrie 1962, 1:107-108 and Kirk, Raven and Schofield 122-126).

1952, 165. See also Plato, Phaedo 108e-109a and Tim. 62d).[*] By so arguing, Anaximander also avoided the logical dilemma to which Thales exposed himself, viz., if earth rested upon water, what did water rest upon (Aristotle, de Caelo 2.13)?

A conception of equilibrium or balance also figured prominently in Anaximander's doctrine of "cosmic justice." The key passage here is contained within the fragment ascribed to Anaximander himself:

> "And the source of coming to be for existing things is that into which destruction, too, happens according to necessity; for they pay penalty and retribution to each other for their injustice according to the assessment of Time..." (Kirk, Raven and Schofield 118).

Here Anaximander alludes to a continuous conflict between opposite elements in which an individual ingredient temporarily enjoys hegemony. This ascendancy represents an "injustice" toward the other substances which ends with the offending material being absorbed back into the *apeiron*. The assimilation reestablishes the cosmic equilibrium but over time another particular element arises to assert its sovereignty in a relentless cycle of offense and compensation.

---

[*] Another remarkable facet of Anaximander's thought concerns the statements attributed to him regarding the origins of human life. To some, these remarks have proto-Darwinian flavor but in fact Anaximander does not espouse an evolutionary system. He argued that a first generation of humans could not have survived on its own. Accordingly, humans must have originally developed in some protected state. Anaximander speculated that men were originally nurtured inside some fish-like creature until they were capable of caring for themselves and subsequent generations. It may be that he was analogizing from the conduct of the viviparous *galei* or dogfishes (see Aristotle, History of Animals 6.10.1-10 and Plutarch, Symposium 730e). The gods play no part in human origins—there is no Yahweh and no Adam for Anaximander.

It is clear from all this that Anaximander saw nature as a self-regulating system in which a uniform periodicity, a balancing of cosmic opposites, and a fundamental symmetry of parts serve as the governing mechanism of the universe (Kahn 1960, 229-230). These views eventually exercised a profound influence upon philosophers such as Empedocles and Parmenides and would even have an impact on medical doctrine (Vlastos in Graham 1:65 and Kahn 1960, 190-191). Here too, we find one of the earliest assertions of natural law theory—the idea that universal necessity embedded in nature itself continuously strives to establish *dike* among contentiously opposite elements. Again, the moral governance to which Anaximander eludes does not include supernatural agency of any kind; the warp and woof of this ceaseless adjudication remains both rational and naturalistic.

The final member of the Milesian triumvirate is Anaximenes who, in making "air" his *arche*, seems to return to the sort of material monism proposed earlier by Thales.[*] It is safe to say we will never know exactly why Anaximenes elected air as his originative source but two possibilities suggest themselves. First, this apparent reversion to a single, simple substance may reflect Anaximenes' logical dissatisfaction with the idea of the *apeiron*. To be "something" implies the possession of certain characteristics which Anaximander's "boundless" seems to lack by definition. Further, the idea of particular substances arising somehow from a nondescript mass of primal "stuff" may have suggested additional difficulties to Anaximenes.

Second, by choosing air as his *arche*, Anaximenes availed himself of some venerable and powerfully suggestive images long

---

[*] On the issue of Anaximene's presumed reversion to a material monist position see Taran (1970) and Fritz (1993).

prevalent among the ancient Greeks. From earliest times air had been linked in the Hellenic imagination to "soul" and to the very notion of life itself. Anaximenes not only accepted this affinity, he developed it further as did one of his 5th century followers, Diogenes of Apollonia. In the end, these views came to play an important role in later philosophy by influencing the ideas of both the Pythagoreans and Stoics.

According to Anaximenes' aeriomorphic scheme, the origins of everything we know—every material object and all forms of life—is the primordial air. His precise explanation of how air produces the manifold objects of our experience represents an important and entirely unprecedented explanation of physical alteration in nature. The secret, according to Anaximenes, lay in a process of condensation and rarefaction, i.e. compression of air produces progressively heavier, more solid matter while increasingly diffuse amounts of air resulted in fire. The earth, for example, was formed sequentially as air assumed greater degrees of density eventually resulting in soil and stone. A similar continuum in reverse explained the origins of heavenly bodies; the rarification into fire of moist vapors emitted from the earth produced the observable celestial entities. To explain the stablility of all these objects, including the earth, Anaximenes returned to the idea of physical support. The earth as well as the stars and planets were buoyed by cushions of air.

In assessing his contributions to the foundations of Greek science, Anaximenes has been credited with at least one major advance over previous thinkers. Specifically, he offered a simple, quantitatively based explanation for change and diversity in nature; the difference between water and earth is the amount of air contained in each substance. These were precocious thoughts for the 6th century B.C., all the more impressive for their anticipation of a central tenet of present-day science; viz., that qualitative distinctions in nature are often the result of quantitative variations. Still, we must maintain our historical bearings here. There is no mention in any of the views attributed to Anaximenes of an attempt to measure relative air densities. Although his thought points in the direction of a quantitative approach to nature, a hallmark of modern science, a genuine mathematizing of nature only begins in the Renaissance; for all his provocative theorizing, Anaximenes was still far from being a Greek Galileo.

Why the Greeks?

The world picture drawn by the Milesians, however opaque by modern standards, constituted something truly unprecedented in man's attempt to make sense of the universe. Simply put, they were thinkers of a different tribe. But why the Greeks? Why not some of the older Eastern cultures such as the Egyptians or Babylonians? Surely these civilizations possessed all of the preconditions necessary for the development of scientific thought—things like material prosperity and ample opportunity for leisured pursuits, sociopolitical stability, and a core of highly cultured citizens. In a chronological sense too, these peoples had more than enough time to develop scientific reasoning; by comparison, the Greeks were but children on the stage of history. Yet science, in the Greek sense of the word, the idea of unfettered theorizing on a global scale, the belief that nature itself can be made to yield its secrets without appeal to extra-rational entities, this understanding of science fails to appear in non-Hellenic cultures.

Perhaps the single most important explanation of how the Greeks initiated the rational analysis of nature lies in the role and status that Hellenic culture assigned its religious institutions. Many of the Eastern civilizations were essentially theocracies in which "official" schools, castes, doctrines, and texts dominated the conceptual horizon. Here the wise man was not a philosopher or scientist, he was a priest, scribe, or prophet, which meant that the marketplace of ideas was severely constricted by the dictates of religious orthodoxy. Accordingly, intellectual experimentation and the free play of human imagination were not encouraged. In these societies, innovation tended to equal heresy. An Egyptian physician, for example, deviating from the standard procedures laid down in the sacred medical texts was subject to the death penalty (Diodorus 1.82.3).

By their very nature, science and philosophy cannot prosper in an environment dominated by religious certainties. The essence of the investigative enterprise requires opportunity to doubt, question, debate, and analyze. It is precisely this dialectical quality of truth that is unappreciated, or worse, untolerated, in the great Eastern cultures. Matters were different with the Greeks. For one thing, there was no priestly or scribal corporation strategically placed in Hellenic society capable of controlling the content or flow of intellectual endeavor. There were, of course, numerous priests and priestesses, but these were attached to specific religious shrines (e.g., Delphi, Eleusis, Dodona, Didyma, etc.) and never constituted a societal-wide caste. In addition, the Greeks had no sacred, authoritative literature comparable to the Hebrew Bible or the Egyptian Book of the Dead—about the closest comparison here would be Homer. As a result, there were no binding doctrines or religious prescriptions capable of predetermining the substance and course of the mind's journey.

These and related points are well illustrated by a comparison of Greek and Egyptian medical documents. The vast majority of the latter are replete with the sort of superstitious quackery indicative of a general absence of scientific mentality (e.g., the Ebers papyrus). Even the more rational texts such as the Smith papyrus contain no explicit repudiation of magic. Nor is there any discussion or analysis of the nature and causes of disease (see Lloyd 1979, 231; 1991, 296; and 1970, 4). It should also be noted that thaumaturgical elements actually became more prevalent in Egyptian medicine as time went on (Majno 73).

The Hippocratic corpus, on the other hand, represents an entirely different mind set. Here the scientific spirit is not only apparent, it is acerbically proclaimed and defended. In the document entitled On Ancient Medicine, for instance, empty postulates and vague speculation are attacked as beneath the dignity of the true practitioner (1.20-27). A similar tone is taken in a treatise dealing with epilepsy, the so-called "sacred disease," where the author vehemently rejects divine causation and declares such ascriptions the product of human ignorance (The Sacred Disease 1.1-15). Again, in the Epidemics we encounter a series of remarkable clinical histories demonstrating the Hippocratic commitment to rigorous, scientifically based observation without reference to supernatural agency. There are simply no parallels for such outlooks and methods among the Egyptians, or for that matter, among any other ancient people.

The role of language must also be considered in our attempt to explain, "*Why the Greeks*?" At first glance, an investigation of linguistic factors may seem far afield of our efforts to explain the origins of Western science. In truth, however, the Hellenic tongue may have played a key role in the Milesian achievement. The formulation of complex thought systems such as those represented by philosophy can occur only in a culture where language is capable of bearing a certain conceptual weight (Havelock 1963, x). In this regard, not all languages display the same degree of philosophical adequacy (see Kahn 1966, 245). Here the Greeks were extremely fortunate. By adopting and modifying Phoenician script in the 8th century B.C., they successfully devised the world's first fully phonetic alphabet. This proved significant because phonetic systems tend to foster abstraction to a greater degree than pictographic systems (Logan 47; see also Havelock 1976 and Ong 1988). This probably accounts for the general absence of Western-style abstraction in Chinese culture. It also explains the means by which the Greeks were able to initiate a series of linguistic experiments traceable in the fragments of the early philosophers and scientists. What we discover here is a progressive manipulation of existing syntactical relationships designed to pull and extend meaning in the direction of greater abstraction (Havelock in Robb 21. See also Snell 226 and Burkhardt 278). Innovative grammatical usage also accompanies these changes. We increasingly detect a preference for neuter forms as opposed to the more animate masculine and feminine forms employed in mythological expression (Kahn 1960, 193).

The conceptual fruit of these linguistic developments, the idea without which the very notion of science might never have emerged among the Greeks, is reflected in the term *phusis* (nature). To the modern ear the word "nature" has become so commonplace that it is difficult to associate it with the sort of intellectual transformation being suggested. Still, the idea of nature was a major achievement of the Greek genius that has materially influenced the flow of Western speculation for the last twenty five centuries. Historically, the term had been employed by the Greeks in two ways: 1) to refer to the origin or beginning of a person or thing, 2) to indicate the character or quality of something (Beardslee 2). The Milesians expanded the meaning to include the idea of some internally determined dynamic as opposed to some process resulting from external cause (Guthrie 1:82-83). Conceived in these terms, the idea of nature helped to draw an increasingly clear distinction between intrinsically lawful processes versus supernatural whim. In other words, the conception of "nature" helped advance the view that the world operated in accordance with a determinable sequence of cause and effect inherent in the system itself. In a real sense, this logic helped to dethrone the gods, rendering them superfluous in man's quest to fathom the universe.

In addition to consigning divinity to the fringes of human imagination, the idea of nature also helped produce the analytical distance requisite for scientific investigation. In order to attain the insight they sought, the Presocratics needed to distinguish between the "knower" and the "things" to be known. As long as the human mind remains conceptually immersed in the natural environment, it lacks the capacity to assess its surroundings—presumably, if fish were scientists, the last thing they would discover would be water! What is required is a degree of Archimedean distance—the researcher needs to become a spectator and the subject of his investigation needs to become an object. It is specifically this "objectification" of nature which constitutes the necessary precondition of all scientific inquiry. The Presocratics, the Milesians in particular, were among the first to prescind themselves from the natural realm, to take themselves out of the equation so to speak, allowing an assessment of nature unlike anything that had come before. None of this could have occurred had the notion of *phusis*, i.e., nature as autonomous, lawful system not been available to the Greeks.

Finally, there are also reasons to believe that political institutions contributed to the Greeks' unique intellectual outlook. In his history of Rome, Gibbon observed that "...freedom is the first step to curiosity and knowledge" (3:714). The truth of this statement is borne out by the political organization known as the city-state. With the emergence of the polis in the 9th - 8th centuries B.C., the

Greeks initiated one of the most important social experiments in history, viz., the conversion of subjects into citizens. Even before the full realization of democracy in the 5th - 4th century,[*] the city-state had already distinguished itself as a largely deliberative organism where political debate and analysis stood at the center of public policy formation. Interestingly, this remained essentially the case even during the age of tyrants (7th - 6th centuries B.C.), as the career of Peisistratus suggests. Such experiences undoubtedly helped foster the critical skills and evaluative capacities essential to scientific and philosophical speculation. More, it surely instilled an appreciation for the conjectural and tentative nature of truth, for the idea that veracity and authoritative opinion are not necessarily allies.

Peculiarities of Greek Science

Before examining some of the oddities of Greek science, it is important to recognize the fluidity of the term "science" itself; to appreciate the manner in which cultural and historical factors have conditioned the principles, approaches, and purposes associated with this term. Without this diachronic perspective, the degree of factual accuracy contained in any comparative analysis is easily compromised. This is a particularly crucial point for our examination because so much of what we take for granted regarding scientific technique and aspiration would have been seen by the Greeks as misconceived and misdirected.

Aristotle affords us a glimpse of one important difference between ancient and modern science in the opening lines of his <u>Metaphysics</u>—"All men naturally desire knowledge." The message

---

[*] "Full" in the sense of the ancient, non-inclusive understanding of the term democracy.

here is important both for what is said and for what is omitted. Curiosity is a natural impulse·in man and it is this desire to know that propels the mind in its search for understanding. Conspicuously absent from this statement, and others like it, is any reference to utility or the satisfaction of material need. In general, the Greeks do not conceive of intellectual investigation as a means of enhancing their creature comforts. Men seek knowledge by their very nature and as an end in itself. According to this reasoning, scientific and philosophic reflection is, in some broad sense, an employment of human essence. Man, the cognitive creature, delights in the pursuit and acquisition of knowledge, not in the securing of extrinsic material advantage.

Implicit in these perspectives is a strong preference for the pure and theoretical sciences which the Greeks tended to pursue at the expense of the mechanical and practical arts (Landels 187 and Farrington 28-29). True wonderment for the Greeks lay in "theoria," not in invention.* For them, the human mind was never fully at home unless engaged in abstract/speculative activities. This explains the peculiar Hellenic affection for the mathematical sciences—especially geometry—which they pursued in a manner entirely distinct from the approach in oriental cultures. The spirit of Egyptian mathematics, for example, was entirely "applied" as we see from the Rhind papyrus (see Burnet 18-19). Nowhere in this

---

* A word about Chinese science. There is no question that China enjoyed an impressive technological superiority over Western science up until the Renaissance. The horse-harness, iron and steel technology, gun powder, paper, movable type, the magnetic compass, and mechanical clocks are all products of the Chinese genius. But the oriental sciences were entirely absorbed by issues of utility. Consequently, they never developed a critical philosophic approach to nature. They lacked, therefore, a theoretical framework capable of sustaining their inventive priorities long-term. This is why after the Renaissance, i.e., after the re-emergence of Greek mathematical approaches in Europe, China was entirely surpassed by Western science (see Needham 41).

text is there any suggestion of a system of mathematical proofs or of a progress toward scientifically conceived principles.[*] Instead, we find a consistent and all-absorbing attachment to utility—a feature of Egyptian culture noted with disdain by Plato (Rep. 435e and Laws 747b-c cf. Rep. 527a). Indeed, according to Herodotus, geometry itself was conceived originally by the Egyptians as a practical device for the recalculation of boundary lines after the annual Nile floodings (2.109-110).

The same sort of distinctions can be drawn between Greek and Babylonian astronomy. There is no question that the Greeks were heavily indebted to the East with regard to descriptive astronomy. Over the centuries the Babylonians had amassed an impressive array of observational data. But this information was not gathered in response to scientific curiosity. The spirit underlying its accumulation was entirely practical, specifically to forecast certain celestial episodes, aid in calendrical adjustments, and to assist in omen astrology (Dicks 169). At no time did the Babylonians pass beyond a purely computational phase in their astrological investigations. This explains why there was no move to assess the nature and causes of various celestial events; no attempt to construct a synoptic view of the cosmos as a whole; and above all, no effort to develop and apply mathematical models to heavenly phenomena. Geometrical modeling remains unknown among the Babylonians until the Seleucid period, i.e., until it is introduced by the Greeks in the late 4th century B.C..

Not surprisingly, the Greek love of abstraction fostered a considerable neglect, and in some cases an outright contempt, for em-

---

[*] Leon Robin addresses this point—"Never, so far as we know, in all its centuries of existence, and even after coming into contact with the science of the Greeks, did Oriental science go beyond utilitarian interests and curiosity about details, to rise to pure speculation and the determination of principles" (32).

pirical methodologies, i.e., science based not on theory, but on observation. This does not mean that the Greeks were incapable of conducting investigations along inductive lines. Various treatises within the Hippocratic corpus provide clear evidence to the contrary (e.g., Epidemics II and III). Nonetheless, Hellenic preferences were strongly inclined toward abstraction which meant Greek science displayed some rather eccentric features. For one thing, the Greeks tended to "leap" to hypothesis prior to any reasonable accumulation of supportive data (see Lloyd 1991, 89). This meant that many of their theories simply lacked foundation in concrete fact. In short, the Greeks evidence a chronic impatience with inductive details and as a result, inconvenient empirical evidence was not allowed to get in the way of a "good" theory.

This sort of apriorism, for all its faults, made for some fascinating and often insightful speculation. We should remember that in a remarkably brief period of time the Greeks had recognized the earth as spherical, correctly diagnosed the mechanics of both lunar and solar eclipses, and arrived at the heliocentric conception of our planetary system. Simultaneously, however, their love of postulative approaches resulted in some extravagant distortions. The astronomical system proposed by Eudoxus, for example, may have satisfied Plato's admonition to "save the phenomena" but to do so required the use of a geometrical fiction involving 27 concentric circles (Lloyd 1989, 285 and 1991, 256)! In other words, Eudoxus saved the phenomena by ignoring them; by constructing a mathematical model that had little to do with physical reality.

This same pattern of preconception and empirical neglect typified Pythagorean astronomy, as proposed by Philolaus, where the existence of both a central fire (in addition to the sun) and a counter-earth known as the *antichthon* were insisted upon despite the absence of any observed evidence (see Aristotle de Caelo

2.13.15-30). Examples such as these lend considerable credibility to Daremberg's[*] famous quip that the Greeks explored nature with their eyes closed.

Another demarcation between modern and ancient science is the heavy Greek reliance upon analogies. A strong analogy remains a formidable mode of reasoning even today. But the Greeks display a special fascination for this sort of thinking and as a result, we find analogies employed in virtually every sphere of Hellenic thought. A particularly high percentage of the analogical models used by the Greeks are drawn from two areas—the biological and political domains. Vitalistic images, for example, stand behind the Milesian description of the cosmos as a living entity. Echoes of this idea continued to be heard down to the time of Plato and Aristotle and even into the Christian era as we see in the thought of Origen and Ambrose of Milan (Laws 886; Meta. 12.8.1-14; Scott 166).

But by far the most significant series of analogies tend to come from the political arena. The notion of an orderly, lawful universe, a central tenet of Greek science, was almost certainly based upon the model of a harmoniously organized state (see Kahn 1960, 223; Lloyd 1979, 247; Vlastos 1995, 1:107). Anaximander's theory of regulative-equilibrium has an obvious legalistic flavor that is no doubt related to the juridical environment of the polis. Similarly, the medical theories proposed by Alcmaeon, viz., that health is achieved by balancing opposing elements within the body (*isonomia*), is clearly indebted to social/political doctrine.

Despite his own use of analogies, Plato seems to have been among the first to question the validity of analogical reasoning. He was right to raise the issue. Analogies can be a fruitful source of stimulating and innovative ways to look at the world. But the ca-

---

[*] Charles V. Daremberg (1816-1872), a noted French medical historian.

pacity of analogies to embolden the mind, particularly among the Greeks, had a negative corollary. By their very nature, analogies tend to be inductively incomplete. They often fail to consider the full detail of the suggested parallelism, specifically ignoring the noncompliant aspects of the comparison. In addition, dogmatically employed analogies have a tendency to foster a premature closure of the investigative process. They encourage a sense of uncritical satisfaction even in cases where the logic is in fact simplistic or even fraudulent. All of which indicates that the heuristic function of analogies requires serious care and qualification—something the Greeks were prone to ignore.

A final word regarding scientific experimentation. Scholars have long noted the general absence of experimentation among the Greeks, identifying this deficiency as the most fundamental discontinuity between ancient and modern science. While there are indeed genuine shortcomings in this area, the Greeks did in fact conduct at least some experiments. We know, for instance that the existence of atmospheric pressure was demonstrated experimentally by both Empedocles and Anaxagoras and that the Pythagoreans engaged in acoustical research resulting in the discovery of the numerical ratios underlying the musical scale. Still, these efforts are probably best described as not much more than "flirtations" with experimental method. Nothing resembling genuine experimentation is seen among the Greeks until the Hippocratic physicians (5th century) and it is not until Aristotle that the systematic rules of scientific engagement receive nascent expression (Lloyd 1991, 116).

The reasons for this dearth of experimentation are not far to see. For one thing, the very notion of a hypothesis had an entirely different meaning among the Greeks. It was not a provisional conjecture awaiting testing and validation. Indeed, the Greeks were not the least bit hesitant or cautious in offering scientific postulates.

Their hypotheses were in essence narrative assertions that imply a degree of assuredness completely unparalleled in the modern use of the term. The point is, one does not test narratives (see Cornford in Needham and Pagel 9).

In addition, the focus of Greek scientific interests tended to negate any realistic possibility of experimental approaches. As we have noted, the Greeks, particularly the pre-Socratics, tended to ask the "big" questions. Their theories dealt chiefly with cosmogonic and cosmological issues for which experimental methods had little or no meaningful application. This was not simply a matter of technological inadequacy. It had to do more with the inherent untestability of certain types of theorizing. How does one design an experiment to demonstrate the origins of the universe (Gomperz 169-170)?

A final explanation for the paucity of Greek experimentation relates to certain habits of the Hellenic mind. Unlike modern scientists who approach nature as something to be carefully segmented, measured, and sequenced, the Greeks sought integration. Their primary interests lay in the formulation of grand, panoramic visions of the world. Why the Greeks brought this particular lens to their investigations cannot be known with certainty but is perhaps related to their deep reverence for mathematics. As Plato recognized, mathematics had a tendency to project the mind beyond the ceaseless flow of particular empirical events (Rep. 527a-c). Studies such as geometry may have helped instill a longing among the Greeks to grasp the larger, more permanent order of things, and to the extent that geometry became the Hellenic paradigm for all systematic knowing, the Greeks may have become correspondingly disinclined to trifle with activities involving mere phenomena (see Cornford in Neeham and Pagel 12).

Conclusion

Was Greek science really science? The answer to this question depends in great measure upon one's definition of "science." In modern times there has been a strong tendency to define science in terms of method; only those activities following a rigorously standardized order of experimental procedures are deemed scientific. So viewed, the Greek achievement is easily reduced to little more than a series of fertile intuitions—a science in swaddling clothes. But we must temper the tone of condescension 2500 years of scientific development has generated. Specifically, we must resist the tendency to project invidious comparisons along methodological lines upon the 6th century B.C.. To do so, is to engage in hopelessly distortive anachronism. More, it assigns modernity a definitive moment in history which arrogantly assumes future generations will not assess our scientific procedures in the same dismissive light that some choose to view the ancients today.

Perhaps it is best that methodology not be the focal point of these historical assessments. Method per se is not science and the roster of Hellenic achievements clearly demonstrates that, in some sense, "science" was born prior to the development of formal method. Long before there was anything approaching systematic scientific technique, the Greeks had already arrived at some amazing conclusions about our world: Xenophanes had begun to understand the concept of geological change; the Pythagoreans had hypothesized that the moon was not auto-candescent but instead derived its light from the sun; Leucippus and Democritus had proposed the atomic theory—twenty-five centuries before Boyle and Dalton; Praxagoras had discovered the diagnostic value of the human pulse; Aristarchus has asserted that the sun, not the earth, was at the center of our universe; and Eratosthenes had correctly calculated the earth's circumference to within a few hundred miles of the actual measurement. Clearly something of a scientific nature, something unprecedented in the history of mankind, was going on in ancient Greece with or without the methodological competencies we demand today. It seems appropriate, therefore, to employ some other criterion; something beyond the mechanics of methodology, as a better test of scientific merit. I propose that the underlying spirit or attitude that the Greeks brought to their enterprise be considered a truer test of their scientific mettle.

In this regard, a list of criteria set forth by G.S. Kirk is worth considering. Kirk suggests there are four conditions that must be met in order for an activity to be certified as genuinely scientific. First, is the object of the investigation approached in a rational and systematic fashion? Second, does the research seek a broad and generalized understanding of the subject matter? Third, is the inquiry unrestricted and wide-ranging? And fourth, are traditional positions and received opinions critically analyzed and rejected where appropriate (Kirk 1974, 289)? By these standards there can be no doubt. The Greeks, for all their methodological imperfections, despite their unbridled love of theory and their rash analogical reasoning, nevertheless qualify as the first legitimate scientists.

There remains, however, one additional obstacle, perhaps the most formidable of all, to any impartial and accurate assessment of Greek science. It is the Greeks' near total inattention to utility. The cultural sentiments mirrored by this disregard are grasped by the modern mind only with great difficulty because today any reference to "science" usually implies invention, cures, and profits. So much so, that the credibility of those not "doing" science in this fashion is automatically suspect.

Despite having been inspired in large measure by the revival of classical learning, the science of the Renaissance and post-

Renaissance period increasingly displayed an ethos entirely distinct from antiquity. The new spirit of scientific investigation receives its definitive expression in the writings of Francis Bacon who insists that the proper purpose of science is to dominate nature and to extract from her a bounty capable of "relieving" the human estate.[*] Given these pragmatic imperatives, Bacon became a loud and consistent critic of the ancients, particularly Aristotle, asserting that their wisdom was "fruitful of controversy but barren of works" (Bacon 8).

By comparison, Greek science was motivated by pure curiosity—the "fruit" sought in antiquity was almost entirely speculative.[†] There were no "Bensalemites" at Miletus, and Athens never developed into anything like a "Solomon's House," the Baconian think-tank described in the New Atlantis. In fact, the Greeks were generally satisfied to merely interrogate nature as opposed to subduing her, and they also displayed a similar quietism with regard to their material circumstance. Aristotle continually reminds us, for example, that life's priorities are not to be understood in economic or material terms; that the resources necessary for the good life are remarkably meager, and that these conditions had, for all intents and purposes, been satisfied by the polis (Politics 2.6.23; 3.5.10-11; 7.1.3-5; 7.12.4-5; also Athenaeus, Diepnosophists 511d).

Sentiments such as these bespeak a profound disparity between modern and ancient cultural objectives. Were he now alive to ana-

---

[*] Although as Kuhn notes, it would take several more centuries for the links between science and technology to be fully forged (see Kuhn 1971).

[†] A good illustration of this is seen in the activities of Heron of Alexandria (c. 100 A.D.). Long before James Watt, Heron had invented a crude "steam engine." But the idea of developing this mechanism into a truly functional, labor-saving device is never pursued. It remained for the Greeks a mere *thaumaton,* a fascinating gadget or toy and nothing more (see Cohen and Drabkin 254-55 and Landels 28-29).

lyze the creed of "growth" and "progress" animating so much of today's world, Aristotle would undoubtedly indict modernity for having allowed its frenzied zeal for more and more "fruit" to invert the relationship between means and ends, i.e., to confuse the marginally significant with the genuinely valuable. Above all, he would disapprove of making science in any way subservient to the whim of a consumer economy. From the Hellenic perspective any such arrangement would trivialize, if not stultify, man's most precious gift—his mind.

The point of all this is not to exonerate Aristotle and the Greeks from Bacon's criticisms—many of which were just and long overdue. Rather, it is to highlight the impropriety of dismissing as nonscientific those who fail to comply with the standards desiderated by the Baconian paradigm. More, it is to remind the modern student that it was the Greek passion for asking idle, "useless" questions that ultimately dissipated the mist of myth and superstition in the West. That it was this same love for matters useless[*] that enabled the Greeks to erect the essential framework by which modern science continues to be supported—something the Greeks achieved virtually *ab initio*. Finally, the purpose of assessing the scientific pedigree of the Hellenes is to affirm the fact that we are indeed the progeny of those original restless minds of the 6th century B.C.; that no blame should attach to the Greeks for having breathed the air of history in their own way; and that it was their irreverence, their child-like curiosity, and their dauntless will to know that first

---

[*] Love of matters useless continues to pay important, practical dividends. A good example being the impressive breakthroughs registered by the U.S. space program which have not only extended the boundaries of human exploration, but have also pioneered a host of technologies which, in the health care field alone, include the excimer lazer, new ocular screening systems, thermal video and ultra-sound imaging, microbial detection devices, advanced blood analyzers, etc. (see Gall and Plumberger 1992).

ignited the scientific spirit in man—all points well summarized by John Burnet's observation that the very term "science" means "thinking about the world in the Greek way"(v).

Chapter III

The Plastic Vision

"Beauty is truth, truth beauty—this is all ye know
on earth, and all ye need to know" —John Keats

Introduction

If one hundred randomly chosen, non-expert individuals were asked what first came to mind upon hearing the phrase, "Ancient Greece," a significant number would no doubt respond by referring to the major figures of Greek philosophy and literature—Homer, Socrates, and Plato, etc. Still others, perhaps the majority, would offer images of art and architecture. They might not know the precise chronology or even the correct names of such famous works as the Parthenon, Porch of the Maidens, or the Aphrodite of Melos, but their selection of these and other masterpieces would clearly express the undeniable truth that we tend to envision Hellenic civilization aesthetically.

As it turns out, this tendency to conjure aesthetic imagery at the mention of ancient Greece, however reflexive and unschooled it might be, is in truth a valid assessment of who and what the Greeks were as a people. The Hellenes were deeply moved by the "mystery of the beautiful" in a way beyond what is evident in any other ancient civilization. In fact, it can be argued that this aesthetic perspective was a universal cultural lens brought to bear by the Greeks on every facet of life. We find aesthetics reflected in their moral theory where the terms "good" and "beautiful" function synonymously; in the scientific speculation of the Ionian Greeks whose *arche* (first principle) presumes a harmonious and orderly "one" behind the flux of experience; in political theory where balance and proportion are seen as the key to social stability; and in medical doctrine where a measured equivalence (*isonomia*) between key bodily substances is requisite for good health.

All of which indicates that unlike modern man who has elected to cloister his art in museums and galleries, narrowing thereby the function of art to a kind of spectator sport, the Greeks made the aesthetic moment a ubiquitous feature of life. The painting, architecture, and statuary of ancient Greece were not intended as isolated amusements for a few connoisseurs—indeed, all Greek art was "public," private collections being virtually unknown until Roman times. These works were instead part of a conscious strategy to harness the culturally constructive energies of beauty. As such, the aesthetic activities of the Greeks became an integral part of *paideia* (education, enculturation); a conscious attempt to actualize the ideal in man.

In what follows, the major formulae and principles governing Greek art will be presented. First, however, a brief survey of the evolution of Greek art along with some of the exegetical issues surrounding that development.

The Evolution of Greek Art

The exemplary role of Greek art in Western culture naturally led scholars to scrutinize the various phases of its history and development. Of particular interest in this regard, given the radically unprecedented achievements of the classical period, was the search for origins: Was Greek art an autochthonous cultural phenomenon or were external forces operative at various points in the progression toward the high classical?

A key figure in the examination of this question was Johann Joachim Winckelmann (1717-1768), the father of German Classicism and the founder of modern art history. Winckelmann was an unqualified philhellene whose enthusiasm for everything Greek proved as normative as it was dogmatic. Indeed, Goethe, commenting on the influence of his scholarship, delcared the 18th century, "The Century of Winckelmann." In Winckelmann's opinion, the aesthetic accomplishments of the Greeks were an autonomous cultural development that manifested itself sequentially in a series of distinct artistic periods. This was not a notion unique to Winckelmann—similar ideas of phased evolution are also found in Vico, Turgot, Saint-Simon, and Comte, among others. What distinguishes Winckelmann is his attempt to apply this cyclical logic specifically to the history of art. So employed, this scheme suggests a steady progress of artistic maturation from primitive aniconic representations (wooden and stone objects without representative essence), to iconic forms (works with specific theistic identities), to full figural monuments portrayed in anthropomorphic terms (Winckelmann 1:196-8). Significantly, Winckelmann does not allow for foreign influence in the evolution of this art. While he does acknowledge the resemblance of Egyptian sculpture to works of the Greek archaic period, he specifically rejects the idea of imitation (1:199). This assertion is not based on some lack of familiarity with non-Hellenic art (Winckelmann's massive study, The History of Ancient Art, contains an extensive analysis of Egyptian, Persian, and Phoenician antecedents). What we find instead is simply a Hellenocentric bias; a series of factually unconfirmed assertions that collectively discredit what has been termed the "ancient model" (see Bernal 75-120), i.e., a belief espoused by the Greeks themselves, that many of their cultural foundations were derived from semitic sources, particularly Egypto-Phoenician. The archeological record, fragmented and uneven though it is in many respects, does indicate oriental influence in the development of Greece's plastic vision. But the interpretive "tyranny" of Winckelmann's Teuto-Hellenism simply denied this indebtedness. Among German intellectuals, these perspectives remained dominant well into the 19th century until challenged by the irreverent heterodoxies of men like Heine and Nietzsche (Bultler 5-7).

Modern research has successfully liberated itself from much of the polemical and tendentious thinking of the 18th and 19th centuries. Today, our understanding of the historical development of Greek art presents a far more balanced portrait of the inter-cultural relationships between Hellas and the Eastern peoples. We see this for instance in the manner in which contemporary art historians approach the foundations of Greek art. Most now begin their analysis with a consideration of the so-called Cycladic art of the early Bronze Age (c.3000 B.C.).

The term, "Cycladic" means, "those in a circle" referring to a cluster of small Aegean islands including Paros, Amorgos, Keros, and Naxos situated around Delos, the sacred island of Apollo. We know very little about the early inhabitants of these islands, but they were certainly not "Greeks" as we understand that designation and were most likely immigrants from Asia Minor (Richter 1987, 15 and Higgins 53).[*] Working with stone tools, primarily emery

---

[*] Renfrew (39) argues that the early inhabitants of the Cycladic Islands could have come either from western Anatolia or from mainland Greece, but Thucydides had no doubts—they were Carians (1.4 and 1.8).

and obsidian, these people created a series of fascinating figural sculptures, the most sophisticated occurring during the Keros-Syros period (2700-2200 B.C.).

Though of extreme antiquity, Cycladic art reflects an abstract, geometric quality which makes it appear intriguingly modern. The vast majority of the idols are small female representations carved in marble. They have almost always been retrieved from grave sites and the statues themselves are often executed in a manner suggesting funereal significance—reclining posture, arms folded over the chest, head tilted backward.

Apparently Cycladic art became quite popular with other groups living on the fringes of these islands. Large numbers of the sculptures were exported to Crete, and significant finds have also been made on mainland Greece, particularly in the vicinity of Attica. Experts now agree that the art of the Cyclades exercised an important influence on both the Minoans (Crete) and on the Helladic or Bronze Age culture of Greece (Getz-Preziosi 34).

As important as these foundational influences surely were upon the earliest developments of Greek art, of far greater significance was the "Orientalizing Revolution" of the 9th and 8th centuries B.C.. During this period East met West in a series of economic and cultural exchanges that proved pivotal to the future development of Hellas. Greek trading sites were well established at Al Mina on the Orantes River by the 9th century (Boardman 1988, 38-39). Footholds such as those in Asia Minor exposed the Greeks to a wide range of new artistic themes and motifs, especially Syrian and Phoenician; Hellenic art between the Geometric (900-720 B.C.) and Archaic periods (620-480 B.C.) clearly bespeaks such influence. It should also be noted, of course, that the Eastern peoples ventured west. This is particularly true of the ubiquitous Phoenicians who established commercial stations throughout the Mediterranean and may actually have circumnavigated the continent of Africa as early as 600 B.C. (Hyde 233).

The origins of monumental sculpture (i.e., large-scale statuary) among the Greeks is also related directly to oriental contacts. Herodotus tells us that before the reign of Psammetichos I, Egypt had been closed to foreign settlement, but in return for their service as mercenary troops, a group of Ionian Greeks and Carians were granted two parcels of land on opposite sides of the Nile (2.154). These arrangements provided the Greeks with a first-hand opportunity to study Egyptian culture, including their venerable artistic conventions. Not coincidentally, the first appearance of Greek monumental art occurs shortly after the establishment of these colonies in the mid-7th century B.C.

The specific works involved here are the so-called kouros/kore (male/female) figures of the Archaic period in Greek art. Even the most cursory analysis of these sculptures and their Egyptian prototypes illustrates an undeniable affinity. By far the most characteristic unifying feature is a strong sense of rigidity and tension: arms hanging straight at the sides of the body, feet positioned side by side or one foot slightly advanced, torso and head locked into a mechanical frontal stance. In addition, these works express a dominance of vertical axis obviating any suggestion of motion, all of which contribute to an almost two-dimensional quality in these figures (Buitron-Oliver 23).

With few exceptions, these canonical features of Egyptian art dominate Greek aesthetic standards for roughly two hundred years (Richter 1988, 1). About the only innovations made by the Greeks during this period were the formulaic use of male nudity and the elimination of the rear support struts typical of Egyptian sculpture

(Boardman 1993, 52).[*] The Egyptian hegemony was not to last however, and by the year 480 B.C. we discover a series of remarkable artistic innovations among the Greeks that formally announce the end of static effigy.

Few individual works of art can claim the sort of significance justly assigned the "Kritios Boy." Above all, it marks the precise moment of Greek artistic manumission from the frozen paradigms of Egypt. The lifeless, cubic monotony that had guided oriental taste for millennia was now consciously suppressed by the Greeks in favor of a new style that would become increasingly lively, accurate, and natural (Pollitt 1972, 43).

In particular, the Kritios Boy marks the beginning of kinesthetic experimentation among the Greeks, i.e the incorporation of movement into the aesthetic presentation. Unlike Egyptian works that remain eternally the children of the quarry, Greek sculpture now conveys an unprecedented energy and suppleness signaling the human form's historic emergence from its rocky chrysalis. Specifically, the Kritios Boy includes a series of subtle weight shifts as indicated by the asymmetry of shoulder stance and by the gentle tilting of the head. Traditional frontal posture is replaced by a bold reassignment of weight to the left leg anticipating the full contrapposto (in Greek, *chiasmus*) of Polyclitus' later masterpiece, the Doryphoros. Even the facial expression is altered, the archaic smile displaced by a new contemplative gaze. In short, by the early 5th century B.C., the Greeks rendered the icy idiom of Egypt obsolete. No longer will their statuary serve as symbols of human reality—the Greeks will now create "living" beings out of stone (Lullies 7).

The revolution in marble achieved by the Kritios Boy serves as a prelude to one of the most spectacular eras in human history—the

---

[*] In addition, the Greeks added that enigmatic grin known as the "archaic smile."

fifty-year period (*pentekontaetia*) that has come to be called the "Golden Age" of Greece. The outpouring of optimism and promise permeating the Greek world during these years, and particularly at Athens, was no doubt related to the triumph over Persian forces at Marathon, Salamis, and Plataea. Flushed by these victories, the Greeks experience an "exaltation of national sentiment" that nourish their achievements in literature, poetry, philosophy, politics, and art. Nowhere do the bright rays of this Hellenic summer shine more brilliantly than at Athens. Militarily secure and financially empowered as a result of her usurpation of the Delian League, the city of Pericles strides forth to meet its "High Destiny," and, in the process, indelibly alters the history of art (Buschor 10-11).

The reverence Western man has legitimately felt for the classical artistic achievement is based on a depressingly meager sampling of original works. In fact, the few undisputed originals from the 5th and 4th centuries B.C. are chiefly decorative pieces from various temples and were considered by the Greeks themselves as merely "architectural" (Gardner 80). Free-standing statuary, particularly works in bronze, enjoyed first rank in the protocols of Greek art. Tragically, many of the masterpieces of the great craftsmen fell victim to those dual monuments of human ignorance—the melting pot and the lime kiln. Consequently, the vast majority of what we see in our museums today are Roman copies of Greek originals, few of which presumably approach the splendor of their Hellenic antecedents.

Accordingly, our analysis of classical art is of necessity a composite enterprise in which a handful of original works (chiefly metopes, friezes, and pediment statuary), Roman representations, and references in Pliny and Pausanias, serve as components. On the technical side, the portrait presented collectively by these sources indicate an ongoing mastery of the human form including unparalleled attention to musculature and bodily proportion; a conscious attempt to transcend the "particular" by expressing the defining essence of a given character or subject (*ethos*); and an inspiring loftiness and serenity sometimes termed "Olympianism" by art historians. Two of the great masters of these hallmark features were Polyclitus, an Argive sculptor specializing in athletic presentation, and above all, the Athenian, Phidias. The latter, generally acknowledged as the impresario of the Periclean beautification project, also created several huge cult-statues including the chryselephantine Zeus at Olympia, one of the seven wonders of the ancient world, a work described by Pliny as unrivaled in the history of art (34.19.54 cf. Pausanias 5.11.9).

At the same time as these developments in the plastic arts were unfolding, major achievements were also being recorded in painting. Typically, when thinking of Greek art we tend to restrict ourselves to architecture and sculpture, forgetting that the Hellenes were also avid painters who typically painted their statues as well as various portions of their temples. This sort of conceptual neglect is understandable given the fact that time and the elements have been particularly harsh in denying us virtually all illustration of Greek pictorial art other than vase painting. This lack of legacy should not however obscure the fact that already by the second half of the 5th century, the Greeks displayed a firm command of foreshadowing, linear perspective, and color overlay techniques (Kuels 60). It should also be noted that the talents of the great masters of this medium—Apollodorus, Polygnotus, Zeuxis, Apelles, Protogenes—were widely acknowledged as comparable to the major artisans in other fields and that certain of their works became the stuff of legend, e.g. the painted portico of Athens, the murals at Delphi, the portrait of Alexander at the temple of Artemis (Ephesus), and the famous Aphrodite Anadyomene (Aphrodite Rising from the Sea), the thematic ancestor of Boticelli's "Birth of Venus." Indeed, by the 4th century, painting had become so much a part of Hellenic culture that it was included in the educational curriculum at Sicyon, a major center for this art form (Pliny 35.76-77 cf. Seneca Epist. 88.18). Painting terminology even finds its way into certain aspects of Plato's epistemological arguments (e.g. Phaedo 69b, Rep 365c, 583b, 602d).

Thus far, most of our assessment has centered on the grand style of the era known as the high classical. During the late classical era (4th century) many of the previous period's conventions continue but with important modifications. Two of the outstanding figures of this new era in Greek art are the virtuosi sculptors, Praxiteles (370-330 B.C.) and Lysippus (360-315 B.C.). The former is perhaps the most famous sculptor of all time among the Greeks (Gardner 140), much of his reputation being based upon an ability to convey tender sensuous quality in his work. This "softness" represents a distinct departure from the robust athleticism of the high classical period. No longer do we see the sharply contoured and mathematically precise musculature of a Polyclitus (see below), but are instead presented with visibly softer, less "taut" lines that lend a certain warmth and elasticity to the marble.

Although Praxiteles produced many highly acclaimed sculptures, none is more famous than the Knidian Aphrodite, a work described by Pliny as "known all over the world" (34.19.70). The original has long been lost, but excellent copies can be seen today at the Vatican Museum.

According to tradition, this statue had a famous model whose immodest reputation probably contributed to the work's fame. She was Phryne, a *hetaera* or concubine (who also posed for Apelles' painting of Aphrodite emerging from the sea), with whom Praxiteles was reportedly involved romantically. The work caused a sensation by displaying the goddess nude—a major break with 5th century proprieties. To the best of our knowledge there were no nude representations of female subjects prior to the 4th century. During the high classical period the Greeks used diaphanous drapery as a mechanism for revealing female anatomy (e.g., Nike fastening her sandal, Acropolis Museum, Athens). This allowed for the suggestion of nudity while still remaining within the parameters of Hellenic moral sensitivities. Praxiteles may have been one of the first to dispense with this strategy, a move apparently well received by the Greeks of his time. A clothed version of the same Aphrodite executed by Praxiteles for the citizens of Kos was reportedly far less popular.

In addition to portraying female nudity, the 4th century sculptors also initiated a series of stylistic experiments and in this regard Lysippus played a key role. In his day, Lysippus was acknowledged as the successor to the great athletic art produced by Polyclitus. Unlike his predecessor, however, Lysippus apparently preferred a sleeker, more sinewy musculature and as a result, he altered the famous canon of Polyclitus to lend his statuary a taller, less bulky appearance (Pliny 34.19.65, cf. Plato, Sophist 235 and Diodoros 1.98.7). Specifically, this alteration was accomplished by elongating the torso and reducing the head size. The effect is well seen in the Apoxyomenos (athlete scraping himself with a strigil), a favorite statue of the emperor Tiberius who had the original removed from the public baths to his bed chamber (Pliny 34.19.62), and particularly in the statue of Agias on display at the Delphi Museum.

Beyond these proportional innovations, Lysippus also experimented with sculptural scale. Among the more than 1,500 pieces he reportedly produced during his lifetime, there were enormous variations in size. We know, for example, that he was responsible for a colossal statue of Zeus at Tarentum that stood 40 cubits high (cubit = the length of the forearm or approximately 18 inches). Efforts such as these seem to have had a direct influence on the Rhodian School including Chares of Lindos who cast the famous Colossus of Rhodes. At the other extreme, we have examples of Lysippic "statuettes" such as the Heracles Epitrapezios (tabletop Heracles), a miniature piece less than 12 inches in height, a copy of which is on display in the British Museum.

Modifications of classical canonicity such as these suggest that Lysippus stood between two artistic epochs, that he was a transitional figure pointing toward a new era in Greek art. This observation is powerfully corroborated by the degree to which "pathos," a hallmark of Hellenistic art, comes to replace "ethos," a characteristic feature of the high classical. The art of the mid-5th century sought intentionally to mute the passions, to foster a sense of sublime repose befitting the dignity and grace of the gods. The works of the late classical period however, increasingly make provision for the role of emotion. Specifically, facial expression undergoes a dramatic transformation. The ethereal countenance characteristic of the Parthenon statuary is replaced by a new descriptive realism portrayed by arching eyebrows, parted lips, and expressive deep-set eyes. Lysippus and his older contemporary Skopas lead the way in these emotive innovations and in so doing, they serve as prelude to the Hellenistic period.

The "Hellenistic Age" refers to the period between Alexander's death (323 B.C.) and the absorption of Greece by Rome—typically marked by the latter's victory over the Achaean Confederacy (146 B.C.). The many sociopolitical transformations typifying this era are mirrored by a series of new artistic developments. For one thing, there is a dramatic expansion of portraiture art. During classical times there were very few examples of such work—the bust of Pericles by Kresilas is a rare and noted exception. During Alexander's lifetime however, this genre began to receive royal patronage, with certain master craftsmen receiving exclusive privilege, e.g. Lysippus enjoyed a sculptural monopoly vis-à-vis Alexander (Plutarch 1986, 3.4.1). Later, a host of powerful potentates—Ptolemies, Seleucids, Antigonids, Attalids—would sponsor a widescale expansion of such art, which reaches its peak at Rome where portrait sculpture was extremely popular.

Another new feature of Hellenistic art is the dramatic expansion of subject matter. Classical art generally restricted its repertoire to the lofty figures of mytho-religious traditions; these characters alone were deemed fit for artistic representation. In marked contrast, Hellenistic art is committed to representing the more banal rhythms of everyday life and as a result, a host of new figures crowd the aesthetic scene—statesmen, generals, poets, philosophers, orators. Along these same lines, the art of this period actively seeks to express the sentiment and experience of real people engaged in genuine life enterprise. On an unprecedented scale, the range of human emotions—joy, anger, despair, misery—are explored artistically where before only the serene majesty of the gods had been portrayed.

In sum, the Hellenistic period engenders an art that fundamentally alters the aesthetic landscape of Greece. In some sense, the movement from ethos to pathos was an inevitable corollary to a new *zeitgeist* that signaled the autumn of Hellenic civilization. This development should not imply however, that Hellenistic art is nothing more than the last gasp of a decadent culture. There is much here that is vivid, clever, often bold, but it remains part of an era governed chiefly by "artistic reminiscences" (Ridgway 7). In viewing these works, one has the distinct impression that the Greeks no longer trust themselves to attempt a representation of the spiritual;

they seem to be compelled as a result to represent everything else, including the mundane and the pedestrian. Would Polyclitus have committed his genius to creating a statue of a drunken old woman (Munich, Glyptothek)? Would Phidias have arranged the Parthenon frieze with the cluttered baroque of the Great Altar of Pergamum? Gone is the precisioned restraint and judiciously understated energies of the high classical.

Technically, these works remain thoroughly competent, but the artistic aspiration is now entirely different. The quest for the eternal has ended; the Hellenistic masters can no longer dream the Phidian dream.

The Principles of Greek Art

The evolution of Greek art was not a spontaneous growth lacking in pattern and value. From the outset, there were a series of recurring principles that guided and nurtured the development. One of the most important of those precepts involves the Hellenic need to impose order upon the flux of experience—a need to banish the chaotic, to dispel the irrational, to grasp the enduring reality in a world swirling with change (Pollitt 3). This instinct for cosmos (order) manifests itself continually in Hellenic culture. We see it embedded in Greek scientific thought, their language, and, in particular, it explains their adoration of mathematics, especially geometry. In the Hellenic pursuit of order, this discipline served as the supreme methodology because nothing more clearly revealed the hidden truth of the universe than the logic and system of the mathematical sciences. Pythagorean insistence that all of nature was "number" was not the idiosyncratic musing of an isolated sect (Heath 1:67-8). It expressed the "volksgeist" (spirit of the race) of the Greek peoples.

Beyond its significance as a means of probing the mystery of Being, mathematics was also seen by the Greeks as intimately related to beauty. This may sound like quite a leap to us, but unlike modern man who has compartmentalized his life into a collage of disjointed moments, the Greeks brought an integrated vision to life that specifically commingled ontological (being, existence) and axiological (value, worth) elements. The Real, the True, the Beautiful, and the Good were all, in some ultimate sense, consubstantial in the Greek imagination and the common thread uniting them was the "rational" which the Greeks understood chiefly in mathematic terms. This explains why Plato insists that measure and proportion are the true essence of beauty (Philebus 64e, Timeus 31c cf. Plotinus, Ennead 1.6.1), and why modern authorities often refer to a mathematical rhythm operating at the heart of Greek artistic expression (e.g., Bowra 154).

The idea that numbers somehow stood behind the mysteries of beauty is clearly illustrated by the concept of "symmetria." The term refers to the commensurability of parts within an artistic whole and specifically mandates the application of number, ratio, and proportion as central to aesthetic experience. The acknowledged master of this concept was Polyclitus who fashioned a series of sculptures consonant with the mathematical thinking of his age. One of his works, in particular, came to exemplify these premises beyond all others, and as such enjoyed canonical status in antiquity—the Doryphoros (spear-bearer). For years researchers have attempted to decode Polyclitus' formula in an effort to explain the wonderful symmetry and balance achieved by this work. A variety of explanations have been proposed, including a modular system, a fractional system, an arithmetic mean, a geometric mean, and the golden section (Moon 38).

Polyclitus' accomplishment, his ability to create faithful representations of the human form by employing abstract mathematical formulas, captures in a fundamental way, the essence of Greek aesthetic sensitivities. This accounts, no doubt, for both the Doryphoros' canonicity and for the fact that it became one of the most heavily replicated statues of antiquity. Moreover, the symmetrical perfection of such mathematically attuned works may also explain the extra-Hellenic appeal they enjoyed. Long after the close of Greece's classical era, standing figures of the Buddha displayed in Northern India continue to speak of their indebtedness to Polyclitus and the marriage of number and beauty (Boardman 397).

The role of mathematics in the creation of Greek art is not something the average viewer of a classical statue would find obvious. The subtlety with which science is blended with stone creates an impression so natural, so reflexive that the complex measurements and intensive calculations necessary to create the effect are entirely concealed. All of which testifies to an extraordinary sophistication of artistic technique among the Hellenes.

The use of number in Greek art reflects a keen aesthetic sense, but it does not indicate a slavish devotion to mathematical formula. The Greeks instinctively recognized that an art based exclusively on number would succeed only in producing a mechanical parody of beauty. For this reason, they demonstrate a consistent willingness to go beyond the constraints a complete mathematical accuracy would impose. In essence, the Greeks devised a series of measures that consciously depart from geometrical fact in order to preserve geometrical effect (see Goodyear 19), and in so doing, reveal the profundity of their aesthetic competence.

The tendencies to which I allude are best expressed in the meticulous optical adjustments the Greeks incorporated in their architecture. These are the so-called *alexemata* (compensations, better-ments) observable in many of the most famous surviving temples at Athens, Sunium, Corinth, Paestum, etc.. Careful measurement by modern scholars reveal these refinements in the stylobates (temple platforms), entablatures (upper portion of a temple including the frieze, cornica, and architrave), gables, and cellae (inner chambers of a temple). Perhaps the best known of these alterations is the gentle swelling (*entasis*) of the center portion of a column (see Vitruvius 3.3.13). Without this adaptation, the vertical line of the column would appear concave instead of straight resulting in a disruption of visual symmetry. What is important here is that this and similar variations in the pure mathematics of a given edifice are not the product of mason error or of settling; they are consciously conceived, systematically executed adjustments aimed at achieving premeditated aesthetic effects.

The motivation for embellishments such as these has traditionally been explained as an attempt to "correct" certain optical illusions that occur while viewing large architectural structures. It may also be that the Greeks engaged in these refinements for aesthetic reasons beyond the imperatives of visual correctness. For instance, it seems the Greeks harbored a certain distaste for perfectly straight lines which they found monotonous and dull (Penrose 107).[*] By incorporating a series of carefully calculated irregularities into their works, the Greeks could gently manipulate the eye, softening thereby the lines of their buildings, lending them a less rigid, more abstract quality. These adjustments may explain why Greek temples, notwithstanding their massiveness, convey "lightness" and "vibrancy" (Goodyear 87, 211), and why various experts ascribe

---

[*] Appearances notwithstanding, there is hardly a straight line to be found anywhere in the Parthenon.

"dynamic" and "lifelike" qualities to certain Greek architecture (see Mavrikios 224, in Bruno).

A second major principle of Greek art, and for that matter, of Greek civilization in general, is summarized by Protagoras, a 5th century sophist, who proclaims "Man is the measure of all things." This declaration bespeaks the "severely anthropocentric" orientation employed by the Greeks to distill everything in life to human terms and collaterally, to make man himself the locus of all value and worth. To a considerable degree, this humanistic narrative was uniquely Hellenic and constituted a major point of demarcation between Greek and non-Greek. At the same time, this human-centeredness also explains much about artistic approach and priority among the Hellenes.

This is why, for instance, nature is accorded little attention by Hellenic artists. No one who has been to Greece can fail to appreciate the natural splendor of the land—the brilliant sunrises, the rugged beauty of the mountains, the magnificent blue waters of the Aegean. Despite these stunning vistas, the depiction of nature is denied high priority in Hellenic aesthetics. This is not to suggest the Greeks were insensitive to natural beauty. The poetry of Alcman, Alcaeus, and Theocritus indicate otherwise, as does the care exercised by the Greeks in selecting sites for their shrines and temples (e.g. Sunium and Delphi). Still, the protocols of Greek art militate against assigning "landscape" high station in the aesthetic hierarchy. For the Hellene, the proper focus of art was man, and in some fundamental sense, man alone (Kitto 52; Pollitt 1972, 5; Carpenter 68; Bowra 147).[*]

---

[*] The beauty of nature is not ignored by the Greeks, but the central interest of their art was almost always the human form; nature served as the frame with man as the picture (Grube 269).

The humanistic ethos also explains why we find so little theriomorphic representation in Greek art (i.e., deities portrayed in animal form), notwithstanding its ubiquity among the older Eastern cultures. The Egyptians and Babylonians, for instance, saw nothing inappropriate in displaying the gods in this manner, but the Greeks apparently viewed such representation as unsavory or at least inconsistent with the dignity and honor of the gods. By the 8th century B.C. the Greeks abandon virtually all theriomorphic motifs replacing them with a thoroughly anthropomorphized scheme (Stewart 1:44).

The decision to employ the human form as the icon of divine essence was perhaps the greatest contribution of Greek art to world culture. For one thing, it announced a historic elevation of human status in which the godhead was humanized. Man alone, according to this depictive logic, was worthy of bearing the image of god. As a result, the gap between heaven and earth was narrowed; an anthropomorphised theology produced an apotheosized humanity. In other words, the gods were made more human, and men were made more divine. Moreover, by cloaking mankind in the mantle of divinity, the Greeks infused their art with an exhortative idealism that invited men to reach for heaven and appropriate their spiritual inheritance.

It is this idealism, beyond any other precept of Greek art that reveals the soul-landscape of the Hellenes. In particular, it is the art of the high classical era that reflects this principle with greatest force and purity, doing so in a variety of ways. On one level, the dictates of idealism were expressed negatively through the exclusion of any subjective, mercurial, and transitory elements. This is why Greek sculpture says so little about the age, rank, origin, and background of its subjects (Lullies 24). Instinctively, the Greeks seemed to have sensed the fundamental incompatibility of the particular and the ideal.

This same logic explains the Greek's general exclusion of "ornamental" art, such as that common to Arabic culture (Carpenter 46-7). The Greeks learned early that a key ingredient in the production of an ideal art was unencumbered simplicity. Repetitive detail and highly ornate patterns can become sources of visual dissonance that disrupt and fragment aesthetic experience. In contrast, the Greeks sought parsimony; their works were presented in a focused, uncomplicated fashion in an effort to minimize visual distraction. Undiluted display technique ensured both the thematic integrity of the work and the proper attunement of viewer attention.

These points illustrate what the ideal art of the Greeks was not. On the positive side, it can be said that Greek art was an attempt to transcend the spatiotemporal limitations of this world. In a real sense, the art produced during the high classical period reflects a generic aspiration. Its purpose was not to portray the singular or prosaic details of daily experience but rather the category or the class of which the particular object is but a limited and finite expression (Kantorowicz 53). By its very nature, this approach tends to obviate the peculiar irrelevancies of a precise subject or theme and elevates a work of art to ideal heights. It suggests a "discipline of the essential" that actively rejects any element of the artistic presentation that fails to point beyond itself in some important way (Ashmole 14 and Bowra 146).

A concomitant of this quest for the type form includes a concerted effort to escape the boundaries of time. For the Greeks, part of capturing the "truth" in art involved creating a chronologically defiant statement, i.e., an art capable of placing itself beyond the ephemeral restrictions of common routine capturing thereby the uniquely permanent substance of a given subject matter. This bias against the time-specific is powerfully reflected in the figural sculptures of the Parthenon where the limitations of temporal specificity are masterfully negated. Here, we see horsemen, gods, and combatants presented in their abiding, idealized essence. Indeed, the spirit of earthly detachment achieved in those works is so extraordinary that the figures assume an almost Platonic air—timeless, immutable, numinous.

Winckelmann attempted to summarize these and related qualities of Greek art for his generation by offering the famous evaluation, "noble simplicity and quiet grandeur" (Winckelmann 33, cf. Lessing 8). While his insistence that the Laocoon was the finest embodiment of these artistic properties continues to puzzle modern art historians, this should not obscure the fundamental legitimacy of his assessment. Winckelmann accurately perceived that classical art's ideal qualities endowed it with something more than sentient charm, viz., a mysterious capacity to infuse cold, lifeless marble with sublime vitality. It is precisely this ability to lend inert matter a metaphysical quality, to transfigure raw stone into something timeless, lofty, and good that explains our continued fascination with Hellenic art. Even those with no special sensitivities in this regard are often powerfully moved by these works because in some ultimate sense art such as this must be seen as a manifestation of the spirit, an epiphany of the holy in man. When possessed of these qualities, art has the ability to open us up, to penetrate the dull plainness encrusting our daily lives, and lubricate the secret recesses of the human soul. No art in history has stirred the interior life of man with greater skill or insight than that of the Greeks.

Conclusion

In describing their art the Greeks typically employed the term *agalma*, meaning "a thing to take pleasure in." It is certainly reasonable to assume that the Hellenes did indeed delight in their artistic achievements. But it would be a serious error to conclude that the chief aspiration of Hellenic art was the venting of some hedonic play impulse. The true meaning of Hellenic art, as indicated by the range and intensity with which aesthetic activity was pursued by the Greeks, must have involved something beyond mere amusement. A more accurate description of Greek art's true motives and ambitions is expressed by the phrase "spiritual enterprise."

In the largest sense, theirs was an art that sought to gather to itself heaven and earth, being and becoming, divine and mortal. It displayed a keen impatience with things fragmentary and inconstant and seemed committed from the outset to capturing the full sweep of life's mystery—the tragic, the joyous, the savage, the sweet. It had, in short, the courage and the insight to omit nothing significant from its repertoire and for this reason too it sought access to realms beyond this world. Such a path was natural for the Greeks who correctly perceived that all "great" art was a kind of revelation. For them, the truly beautiful was a shining of the ideal through the opacity of matter; a rendering in stone and metal of things unseen.

As powerful as the ethereal instincts of Greek art were however, they never resulted in some navel-gazing abandonment of the concrete realities of life. The rapture of beauty certainly lifted the Hellenic spirit to extraordinary heights but as the Greek soul took flight, Greek feet remained firmly planted. Evidence of this is found in the "utility" the Hellenes saw in beauty. Specifically, Greek civilization viewed the following proposition axiomatically:

beauty, truth, and goodness are fundamentally consubstantial. This amalgamative insight in which aesthetic, epistemological, and moral categories were integrated, led the Greeks to the conviction that art not only had the potential to delight, it could also enlighten and ennoble. To their lasting renown, the Greeks were not content with the mere recognition of this wisdom; they attempted to make it functional.

In particular, the Hellenes sensed a powerful relationship between character formation and beauty, which in turn explains their efforts to meld aesthetics and *paideia*. It is not a coincidence that in describing the well-formed gentleman, the Greeks used the word *kaloskagathos*, literally a "good and beautiful" person. Nor is it merely chance that the Greeks summarized a correct education in terms of aesthetic sensitivities—specifically a capacity to "love what is beautiful and hate what is ugly." In the hands of philosophers such as Plato and Aristotle these tendencies become part of an aggressive and carefully conceived program to conscript beauty as an agent for the advancement of culture. In fact, the role of the arts (including the performing arts) proposed by these thinkers is so integral to their theories of human nature, as well as to their sociopolitical formulas, that they can legitimately be designated "moral aestheticians" (Pollitt 1974, 10). The *orthi paideia* (true education) presented in Plato's Republic, for instance, reveals a critical reliance upon the arts. Only beautiful sights and sounds will ensure the soul's proper formation among those from whom the future philosophers-kings will be chosen (401 b-e, cf. Laws 654e, 812 b-c, Symposium 211 c). Aristotle too, expresses enthusiasm over the moral efficacy of the arts, an extensive analysis of which appears in Bk 8 of the Politics. Here, we are advised of art's powerful influence upon character with an admonition that the young must be

exposed only to those paintings, sculptures, and musical composi-
tions deemed morally edifying (8.7.35, cf. <u>Poetics</u> 1.2.2).

And how do these Hellenic perspectives correspond with the
aims and practices of modern art? More precisely, to what degree
can we speak of a classical legacy expressed in the work of today's
artists? Even the most cursory examination suggests profound discontinuities, disjunctures inadequately explained by the mere passage of time. Indeed, the notion of "legacy" itself seems out of
place in this regard. About the most one can legitimately speak of
here is a "residue" of the Hellenic. The startling number of schools,
movements, and "isms" crowding the contemporary aesthetic scene
illustrate the point. Whereas Greek art spoke in a pure and uniform
voice throughout most of its history, modern art expresses itself in
a wild profusion of techniques and styles—Fauvism, Cubism,
Dadaism, Surrealism, Abstract Expressionism, Pop Art, Op Art,
Neo-Expressionism, Superrealism, etc.. Here, variety is not a virtue; it does not imply some rich, fecund energy among present-day
artists. The vast menu of modern artistic forms indicates a canonic
vacuum; a confusion and disorientation stemming from an absence
of precept and principle.

These developments may also have serious cultural implications
if indeed beauty possesses the edifying potentials understood by
the Greeks—and their historic achievements would affirm the truth
of the proposition. In order to penetrate the enigma of the beautiful
an art must know itself. Without this clear and steady self-
comprehension, it can never become great; never awaken, elevate,
or inspire. Soup-can aesthetics are incapable of ascending to these
heights. In fact, at its worst, modern art not only fails to ennoble, it
projects a kind of swaggering vanity incompatible with the advancement of culture. In short, a good deal of modern art not only

fails to present culturally serviceable credentials, it may tacitly be contributing to a state of spiritual insolvency.

The solution certainly does not lie in some mindless attempt to replicate the Hellenic aesthetic ideal. On this score, Hegel was clearly correct in attempting to cool the emulative ardor of his fellow Germans who naively persuaded themselves in the 18th and 19th centuries that the only way to become "great" was to "imitate the ancients." The inexorable flow of history is such that we can never retrieve or reconstruct the past—nor should we endeavor to do so. Each era must remain free to explore the world anew and reach its own understanding of value and truth.

On the other hand, it is equally inappropriate to assume that the past has nothing whatsoever to say to the present. The scientific and technological achievements of contemporary civilization have instilled in many a kind of arrogance toward the past. Modernity has anointed itself as the epochal moment; definitive, unprecedented, and without equal. But when it comes to the aesthetic domain there is still much we can learn from the ancient Greeks. In particular, they appreciated the fact that artistic greatness does not lie in some subjective exercise aimed at shocking, amusing, or titillating a given audience. Rather, genuinely great art, the kind of art that nourishes the human spirit and speaks to what is highest and best in humankind, invariably involves an elucidation of the sacred. Which brings us to an obvious and inevasible question: To what extent can it honestly be said that modern art provides spiritual nourishment for contemporary civilization?

Chapter IV

Goat Songs

*"What grievous stroke is spared to a man, what
agony is he without?"*—Sophocles

Introduction

The Greeks were not unique in having developed the art of dramatic performance. We know, for instance, that the Indians and Chinese also had their own highly evolved versions of this art form. There is, however, one dramatic genre that appears to have a uniquely Hellenic provenance—tragedy. The non-Hellenic drama for which we have evidence is typically joyful and festive. Classical Sanskrit drama, for example, has been described as romantic, tender, and humorous (Cornford 186). By contrast, Greek tragedy displays little concern with putting smiles on the faces of its audience. Rather it tends to project nightmares designed to provoke, horrify, and stun those witnessing the tragic events. Yet the intention here was not simply to send shivers down the spines of the spectators. There is in fact a larger purpose behind Greek tragedy, namely, to compel viewers to reflect upon the mystery and terror of human existence and to do so in a fashion that finds no comfort in religious teaching or philosophic precept. Viewed from a cultural perspective, the inquiry encouraged by the Greek stage was part of that irrepressible "intellectual fearlessness" that typified Hellenic civilization in general (Jebb 20); it was another manifestation of Hellas' rationalistic spirit that dauntlessly sought discovery in every domain of human experience.

In retrospect we now know that "tragedy" as an indigenous cultural expression has flourished only four times in history: 5th century Greece, England during the reigns of Elizabeth I and James I; 17th century France; and Europe and America during the late 19th and early 20th centuries. We also know that whatever form of tragedy we examine, be it Roman, Elizabethan, Jacobean, Neoclassical, etc., all are indebted to the Athenian prototypes. But how were these classical paradigms devised? What were the conditions among the ancient Greeks that allowed for the birth of tragedy?

Part of the answer lies in the famous analysis of poetic beginnings advanced by Aristotle. In his Poetics, Aristotle argues that man is the most imitative of all creatures and that his mimetic instinct is stimulated by the fact that such experiences are educative and therefore a source of peculiar delight for this species (1.4). Part of this imitative penchant includes a natural tendency to mimic tune and rhythm; it is from these specific origins that poetry, including dramatic poetry, evolved.

Aristotle's observations are certainly not delimiting; the imitative instinct is not unique to Hellenes but is rather a universal human propensity. In principle then, any people might have developed the poetic form we call "tragedy." The fact that this did not occur suggests that there were other uniquely indigenous elements operating in ancient Greece that facilitated the development of tragedy. One aspect of Hellenic culture that may have lent a specific impetus to tragic drama is the acute suffering the Greeks perceived at the core of the human condition. This perspective seems well attested at least as far back as Homer (late 8th century B.C.). In the Iliad, for example, the gloomy plight of mankind is likened to a "generation of leaves," according to a famous exchange between Glaucus and Diomedes (6.14 6-9). Later in the same work, Achilles offers Priam a powerful meditation on the unhappiness that haunts human existence. Zeus holds two urns, one filled with evil, the other with blessings. Some men receive a mixture of the two and live lives that pendulate between joy and sorrow. Others receive exclusively from the urn of evil and consequently experience lives afflicted by relentless misery and suffering (24.525-33). Significantly, there is no mention of anyone receiving gifts exclusively from the urn of blessings; the most we can hope for are brief interludes of good fortune punctuated by inexorable expanses of torment and calamity.

Similar sentiments are also expressed in the poetry of numerous Greek authors. In the same spirit, Theognis offered the depressing view that the best lot for a man was to never be born, but failing this, he should pass through the gates of Hades as quickly as possible (425-428). Solon, the great Athenian lawgiver, warned that human existence is riddled with insecurity and risk and that no mortal under the sun can be counted as happy (13.65-70, 14; also Plutarch 27.7). Pindar, perhaps the greatest Greek lyricist, observes that man is but a creature of a day, a dream in a shadow (Pythian Odes 8. 95-7). The same bitter logic can also be traced in the writings of Hesiod, Archilochus, Semonides, and others. From the available evidence then, one would have to conclude that while the Greeks may not have developed a systematic philosophy of the "tragic"—we look in vain for a Hellenic Miguel de Unamuno[*]—

---

[*] It should be noted that Unamuno was professor of Greek at the University of Salamanca and was no doubt fully conversant with the abundant sense of the tragic operating among the Hellenes.

the fact remains the Greeks display an extraordinary interest in and sensitivity toward what Schopenhauer would later call "the wail of humanity."

In addition to these sensitivities, which seem unusually pronounced in Hellenic civilization, there is perhaps a sociopolitical explanation for the singular emergence of tragic drama among the Greeks. Tragedy can only evolve in a social environment where the concept of human nature has attained a considerable degree of development and, in particular, where an adequate differentiation has occurred between the divine and human spheres. This delineation is essential for tragedy because the critical opposition of man on the one hand, and the gods, fate, and destiny on the other, is an essential feature of tragic literature (Vernant & Vidal-Naquet 46). In theocentric cultures, where the ubiquity of religious prescription in such that the development of free individuality is either greatly impeded or rendered impossible, there can be no "tragedy" as we understand that term. Here, Hegel was undoubtedly correct when he observed that dramatic poetry was the unique fruit of the Greek genius because it required... "a live conception of individual freedom and independence" (1975, 1205). In this regard, the Greek city-state, and above all Athens, not only provided the venue for dramatic performance it also nourished the preconditions (intellectual, psychological, and spiritual) that made tragedy feasible. The result was the creation of a remarkable literature which along with its capacity to instill fear and trembling, also lends courage and dignity to the trauma of human existence.

Origins

The origins of Greek tragedy, despite the theorizing of historians, anthropologists, archeologists, and philologists, remain obscure. Not even Aristotle's <u>Poetics</u> has provided much assistance—indeed, his cursory remarks on origins are confused, even contradictory (see below). As a result, some scholars are resigned to the fact that the issue of origins will forever remain unresolved (e.g., Burkert 87), while others have gone further, dismissing the entire question as irrelevant (e.g., Taplin 23). The majority of scholars, however, remain undaunted; they refuse to allow an inconvenience such as a lack of concrete evidence to stand in the way of a new hypothesis.[*]

The welter of theories regarding the genesis of tragedy is essentially reducible to three major theses. The first involves a view advanced by Aristotle; viz., that tragedy evolved from the ancient dithyrambic revelries. The term dithyramb refers to a choral ode accompanied by the flute, sung chiefly in honor of the god Dionysus. Some have speculated that the dithyramb originated among the Thraco-Phrygian peoples and appeared in Greece originally as riotous, wine-inspired songs (Pickard-Cambridge 1997, 47). But over time, the dithyramb lost its ribald, frenzied quality[†] and became part of a more formalized civic celebration involving a circular chorus of fifty male singers.

There are several important poetic figures associated with the dithyramb. Simonides was apparently a master dithyrambic poet, having registered fifty-six victories for himself. Dithyrambic elements also influenced the poetry of Pindar and Bacchylides (Lesky

---

[*] There are a few concrete facts. For one thing, most scholars agree on the etymology of the term "tragedy;" viz., that it stems from the words *tragos* (goat) and *aeidein* (to sing). Literally, therefore, tragedy means "goat song." Also, the Parian Marble has provided us with some key chronology. It reports that tragedy was first officially performed at Athens around 534 B.C. The prize awarded was a goat and the first recorded victor was Thespis.

[†] Perhaps as a result of a thematic fusion with epic poetry.

29). But perhaps the most important name, at least with regard to origins, is Arion of Methymna who lived at Corinth[*] during the reign of Periander (625-585 B.C.) and who is identified by Herodotus as the first man to compose and name dithyrambs (1.23). The problem here is that we possess a much earlier fragment from Archilochus of Paros who boasts knowledge of how to "...lead the fair song of Lord Dionysus, the Dithyramb...". Arion, therefore, cannot possibly be the inventor of the dithyramb though he may have been the first to lend formal composition to such poetry.

In any event, Aristotle claims tragedy developed slowly from these dithyrambic foundations. Specifically, at some point the *exarchon*, or leader of the dithyrambic chorus, emerged as a full-fledged actor facilitating thereby the birth of tragedy (Poetics, 4.14).[†] Immediately after having made this statement, however, Aristotle proceeds to announce that tragedy and comedy evolved from a common source—the Satyr play (4.17). Satyr plays, at least those for which we have evidence, were short, burlesque performances in which ancient legends were treated farcically. The costumes, language, and gestures were typically obscene. Little imagination is needed to trace the origins of comedy to these satiric dramas but an obvious question arises: How can tragedy's elegance and solemnity stem from such coarse foundations? Not only has this issue vexed modern scholars, it seems also to have puzzled ancient audiences. In the popular imagination Dionysus and his festivals were inextricably tied to wine-induced merriment, but they

---

[*] Corinth and Sicyon were apparently early centers of dramatic performance, which along with certain etymological evidence mentioned by Aristotle (Poetics, 3.5-6), formed part of a claim in antiquity that tragedy was a Dorian invention. Dorian influence is certainly evident in the choral elements of tragedy, but what we today would describe as genuine tragedy was uniquely Athenian.

[†] Thespis is, of course, the individual credited with this innovation.

saw none of this on the tragic state which prompted them to ask, "*ti tauta pros ton Dionuson?*" (What have these to do with Dionysus?)[*] All of this casts serious doubt on Aristotle's account of the evolution of tragedy. More, it suggests the real possibility that comedy and tragedy underwent autonomous developments, the details of which remain unknown.[†]

From festival celebration we turn next to ritual observance as a possible source of tragedy's origins. Several ritual schemes have been advanced including one suggesting that blood sacrifice stands at the original core of Dionysiac performance (Burkert 102). Advocates of this position argue that animal sacrifice was actually a device aimed at helping humanity confront the awful reality of death while, at the same time, seeking to delimit man's potential to shed human blood—a necessary measure because the hideous possibility of human sacrifice lies behind every animal sacrifice (Burkert 111). Tragedy, it is argued, arose directly from these dark and dreadful foundations, remnants of which are clearly visible in certain plays, perhaps most strikingly in the *Agamemnon* where the King and his Trojan concubine are slaughtered like beasts (see also *Women of Trachis* and *Medea*).

Another ritual-based explanation suggests that tragedy arose from the commemorative worship of deceased heroes (e.g., Ridgeway 1966). Here it is argued that the dramatic chorus, from the

---

[*] Pratinas is the poet most closely associated with Satyr plays. It has been argued by some that he attempted to restore the traditional Dionysian element to the dramatic performances in an attempt to correct the god's neglect. The evidence for such a claim remains scant (Pickard-Cambridge 1997, 95).

[†] Pickard-Cambridge (1997) argues that tragedy evolved from unrecorded rustic dramas that eventually mingled at Athens with various forms of lyric poetry. Eventually, a prologue and set speeches delivered by a separate actor were added to the original song and dance of the chorus, forming thereby "tragedy" as we understand the term (163 & 219).

very outset, had "nothing to do with Dionysus." Indeed, the only genuinely Dionysian element in the Attic performances were the satiric skits. Everything else is traceable to ancient hero-worship which explains the centrality that tombs for the dead play in several of the dramas (e.g, *Persians, Libation Bearers,* and *Suppliant Maidens*). The union of hero-worship with the cult of Dionysus occurred at some distant, unrecorded moment in the past when the latter was simply superimposed over the former. Advocates of this view offer a much quoted section of Herodotus in support of their position. It involves the efforts of Cleisthenes, the tyrant of Sicyon, to transfer the tragic choruses away from the hero Adrastus and reassign them to Dionysus (5.67). This, it is argued, is an illustration of the original heroic substructure of tragedy that lies beneath the Dionysian superstructure.

A third ritual scheme bespeaks a heavy indebtedness to comparative anthropology and, in particular, to the research of Sir James Frazer.[*] Here, Dionysus is identified as a vegetation god and as such is linked to Osiris, Attis, Adonis, and Thammuz and, like these other deities, he represents the eternal cycle of life-death-regeneration (Murray 6). Supporters of this view, specifically a group of scholars known as the "Cambridge Ritualists" (i.e., Jane Harrison, Gilbert Murray, and F.M. Cornford), argue that tragedy evolved from the rituals performed in honor of Dionysus as *Eni-autos-Daimon* (year-spirit). They claim to have identified lingering traces of these ancient rituals in the plot patterns of certain plays, especially in the later works of Euripides.[†] Furthermore, certain members of this group maintain that comedy, too, had its origins

---

[*] See Frazer (1959) Sections 273-282.

[†] The alleged parallels to ancient ritual include contest, pathos, messenger, threnos, and theophany (See Murray in Harrison 1962, Appendix, Chapter 8).

from the same myth-ritual nucleus. The difference between the two dramatic forms lies in the fact that whereas comedy stressed character and subordinated plot, tragedy did the reverse (See Conford 173-74). *

Our final thesis regarding the source of ancient tragedy boldly rejects the cultic ritual hypothesis, and, in particular, the evolution from festival theory popularized by Aristotle. Instead, it argues that tragedy was the product of a series of daring experiments stemming from the poetic genius of two individuals—Thespis and Aeschylus (Else 1965, 2). The formal designation of actors, prologues, set-speeches, in short, all that transforms the original structures of lyric poetry into genuine tragedy, is ascribed to these two men. Tragedy was never part of an organic growth from Dionysian soil; tragedy was Dionysian only as a result of Peisistratus' decision to include the plays in the City Dionysia (Else 1965, 30). Beyond this tenuous link there was no connection whatsoever, as we see clearly from the fact that the extant dramas display none of the ecstatic, frenzied quality associated with Dionysus and are instead sober, rational, and dignified. Here again it was the inventive spirit of Thespis and Aeschylus that lent tragedy its unique flavor because they elected to make epic poetry a thematic mainstay of their works.†

But what of our primary source; what of the "authority" of Aristotle's statements in the Poetics? Advocates of the "innovative genius theory" allege that it is precisely this "authority" that is responsible for perpetuating an absurdity. Had anyone other than Aristotle advanced the dithyramb/Satyricon doctrine, it would have been dismissed out-of-hand long ago (Else 1963, 172). In truth, it is con-

---

* This view, along with much of the Cambridge School's thesis, has been effectively rebutted by Pickard-Cambridge (1997).

† Athenaeus (8.347e) reports that Aeschylus described his works as slices from Homer's banquet.

tended, Aristotle had no special information at his disposal regarding the origins of tragedy—he was speculating in the same sense that we continue to speculate. By the sheer weight of his name, Satyr plays were falsely made the fount of tragedy when in fact they were adventitious satellites.

Production Details

Festival Calendar

The term "Dionysia" does not refer exclusively to the city festival where the timeless works of Aeschylus, Sophocles, and Euripides were first performed. Actually, the term is generic and refers to a series of celebrations honoring the god Dionysus. Each of the four winter months had its own festivity: the rural Dionysia occurred in December; late January saw the Lenaea; February was the month in which the Anthesteria was celebrated; and finally, in late March the Athenians produced their major event the City or Great Dionysia.* Of the four festivals, the City Dionysia was the last to be organized and was done so under the auspices of the tyrant Peisistratus.

Preliminary ceremonies leading to the City Dionysia included a procession in which a *xoanon*, or wooden image of the god, was taken from a site near the Academy and escorted by torchlight to the Theatre of Dionysus. This was in fact a re-enactment of the cult's original transfer to Athens from the town of Eleutherae on the Attic-Boeotian border. Formal activities commenced on the

---

* Comedy was particularly important at the *Lenaea* (the term probably means "wine press"), although tragedies were also performed. The Anthesteria was a celebration of the "new" wine and also included a ceremony to placate the hostile spirits of the underworld.

tenth of Elaphebolion (late March) with a religious *pompe*, which included a procession of phalloi. Individual celebrants, both men and women, carried small versions of the fertility symbols as they marched. These were made of fig wood and were carved new each year. In addition, a large cart-drawn phallus was also part of the procession.[*] On their way to the theatre, the celebrants stopped at the agora to salute the other deities at the altar of the Twelve Gods. The parade concluded with a series of sacrifices and with libations poured by the ten *strategoi* (senior military and political officials) in the precinct of Dionysus' temple near the theatre.

Now the performances could begin. In all, the contests of the Great Dionysia ran for five days. During the 5th century the first day was set aside for dithyrambic contests which included ten boys choruses and ten adult male choruses.[†] These were inter-tribal competitions. The remaining four days were dedicated to dramatic performances: five comedies were presented on the second day with the remaining three days dedicated to tragedy.[‡] Three tragic playwrights were chosen in advance by the eponymous archon (a senior official in charge of the festival) who assigned choruses to those chosen. The exact method by which a poet was selected is not clear—Plato hints that auditions were conducted (Laws 8817d). In any event, each playwright was responsible for composing a to-

---

[*] One of the scholiasts explains the origins of the phallic processions: When Dionysus was first introduced into Attica, he was not well-received. As punishment, the god inflicted a disease upon the genitals of his detractors. The phalloi were a way of honoring the god for curing the affliction.

[†] The number of performers directly involved in the production of the City Dionysia would have been about twelve hundred. The viewing audience during the classical period is estimated at roughly half the total citizen population of Athens or something close to twenty thousand.

[‡] The order and number of performances remain uncertain and almost certainly varied over time.

tal of four plays: three tragedies and a Satyr play. The general term used to describe the group of four plays was *didascalia*, meaning a "teaching," because the author had to teach them to the actors. When the four plays reflected a thematic unity (which was not required), they were called a tetralology (Haigh 13). On the day of their performance, the plays would be presented in succession—there were no intermissions in Greek tragedy.

The Theatre

It is easy for modern readers to lose sight of the fact that the tragedies, as well as the comedies (for all their raucous obscenity), were part of a religious observance. Technically, the theatre itself was a sanctuary and attendance at the dramatic performances constituted an act of religiosity. This explains the fact that serious misconduct within the theatre precinct was treated not simply as a crime but as a sacrilege punishable by death—although, the Athenians seem to have been disinclined to seek capital punishment in such matters.[*]

In early times, the dramatic performances of Athens were apparently held in the agora (market place), but about 500 B.C. a permanent site was designated at the southern base of the Acropolis. The original theatre of Dionysus was constructed of wooden bleachers and was undoubtedly rebuilt many times. Finally, in the late 4th century B.C., the Athenian statesman and orator, Lycurgus, saw to the construction of a stone theatre, the remnants of which survive today. An estimated seventeen thousand spectators were

---

[*] We know of several noted examples of wrongdoing occurring in the theatre such as the fistfight between Alcibiades and Taureas and the assault of Meidias upon Demosthenes. These did not result in capital punishment, but we are told of one Ctesicles who was put to death for attacking a personal enemy in the Dionysian procession (see Demosthenes, Against Meidias 180).

accommodated by the classical era's version of the theatre. The facility was divided into three basic areas: the *theatron* where the audience sat; the orchestra (literally the "dancing place") where the chorus and actors were originally located; and the *skene*, a wooden stage building where actors changed costumes and where various pieces of stage equipment were stored. Eventually, the actors were relocated away from a low wooden stage near the orchestra to a long elevated platform on top of the *proskenion* (a building before the skene) called the *logeion* ("talking place").

Although scenery has become an important aspect of modern dramatic presentation, visual realism was not a priority for the Greeks. Aristotle credits Sophocles with having introduced *skenographia* (scenery painting) in the mid-5th century (Poetics 4.16), which implies the earliest tragedies had no background scenery at all. Later, during the Hellenistic era, scenery became quite elaborate and much more vital to the dramatic productions.

As part of their stage productions, the Greeks also used various devices and props. Perhaps the most famous being the *deus ex machina* or "god from the machine" (a 4th century B.C. term) in which a deity suspended in a crane-like device intervened in the dramatic action. Euripides was famous for his use of the "machine" (nine of his extant plays employ it), but others too resorted to this dramatic expedient (e.g., Sophocles in *Philoctetes*). In addition, the ancients employed the *ekkyklema*, a wooden platform on wheels used to display a corpse; the steps of Charon, a structure used to convey ghostly figures from the underworld to the stage; and the *bronteion*, large metallic sheets onto which stones were thrown to simulate thunder.

Finally, a word on acoustics. The Greeks obviously exercised great care in selecting sites for their theatres. Both the auditory potentials as well as the general aesthetics of a given location were

taken into consideration. But beyond this attention to physical setting, the Greeks also developed certain techniques to further enhance and refine natural sound quality. The Roman architect and
engineer Vitruvius (5.5) describes the Greek habit of placing
bronze "sounding vases" throughout their theatres. Properly located, these vessels would resonate with the actor's voice producing an enhanced auditory effect. The current condition of the theatre of Dionysus (Athens) is ill-suited to forming any opinion on
sound quality in ancient times. However, the theatre at Epidaurus,
the best preserved structure of its kind, continues to fascinate tour-
ists with the quality of its remarkable acoustics.[*]

The Chorus

Tragic poets had to make application to the eponymous archon
in the hope of receiving a chorus. If the chorus was assigned, it was
the poet's responsibility to instruct the *choreutae* (individual chorus members) in the music and choreography of the play.[†] In early
times, the poets would often act as well—Aeschylus and Sophocles
both acted in certain of their own tragedies. The size of a chorus
varied in accordance with the nature of the performance; a dithyrambic chorus contained fifty choreutae; the choruses of old comedy had twenty-four members; and the Aeschylean chorus was
composed of twelve performers which was later increased to fifteen by Sophocles. The various choruses also differed with respect
to formation. Dithyrambic choruses were circular, but a tragic cho-

---

[*] The theatre is still in use today and accommodates an audience of fourteen thousand.
The normal speaking voice of an individual standing in the orchestra can be heard by
someone sitting in the uppermost row of seats 150 feet away.

[†] By the 4th century B.C., professionalism had penetrated almost every facet of Greek
tragedy. There were professional singers, musicians, dancers, actors, and trainers.

rus was rectangular in shape (5 files x 3), a pattern analogous to a hoplite battle line (Csapo & Slater 353). The chorus would enter the theatre from the audience's right, marching to the tones of a flute, eventually assuming its position in the center of the orchestra. Those choreutae closest to the audience were called the *aristerostatae*, i.e., the most handsome and skilled members of the chorus.

In terms of who exactly made up the chorus group, we know the following: All participants were males chosen from the same tribe as the choregos; during the earlier periods of Greek tragedy the choruses were comprised exclusively of amateur performers; and only Athenian citizens were allowed to participate in choruses for the Great Dionysia.[*] There is a question, however, as to what role, if any, the *epheboi* (18 to 20-year-old cadets) played in the choruses. At least one scholar (Winkler in Winkler & Zeitlin, 1992) has argued that these well-conditioned young men comprised the tragic choruses exclusively. The evidence for this view stems in part from the obvious rigors associated with singing and dancing through four consecutively performed plays (see Plato, Laws 665e-8); certain pottery remains, particularly the Pronomos Vase (Naples); and several remarks offered by Aristotle regarding ephebic drills conducted in the Theatre of Dionysus (Ath. Const. 4.2.4). The difficulty with all this lies in the fact that we have no firm evidence for the ephebic institution prior to the late 4th century B.C.

The cost of training, costuming, and feeding a tragic chorus was considerable. In order to be properly prepared for the actual performances in late March, the choruses began training months in advance. The shouldering of these expenses fell to the *choregos*

---

[*] Metics (resident aliens) were allowed to participate to a greater degree in the other Dionysia, but at the city festival any chorus master using a non-Athenian in his group was subject to a fine of one thousand drachmas.

(literally, "chorus driver"), an affluent individual nominated by the archon to perform this liturgy (public burden). Lavish expenditure on the part of a choregos was a critical component of a play's success. Most choregoi were willing to spend freely because a victory brought public acclaim and honor, and in the dithyrambic competition, a tripod prize which the choregos had a right to inscribe and display publicly.[*] When, on occasion, a choregos proved stingy, the archon had an official duty to compel an appropriate level of expenditure. According to an extant speech of Lysias, the cost of subsidizing a tragic chorus in the 4th century B.C. was thirty minae or three thousand drachma (21.1). For the rural festivals the Athenians devised a means of lightening the financial load through a practice known as *synchoregia* in which several sponsors combined to defray the production costs.[†]. Eventually, in the 4th century, Demetrius of Phaleron abolished the choregoi system entirely, replacing it with an elected state official known as the *agonothetes* ("competition administrator") who controlled a state-subsidized budget designed to cover expenses.[‡]

Although in the opinion of many scholars the chorus was the original fount of tragedy, it failed to retain its central significance over time. Eventually, the spoken as opposed to the sung elements came to prevail—in other words, what the chorus lost, the actors gained. We can trace this evolution clearly in the extant plays. In Aeschylus' *Suppliants*, an early play, fifty percent of the drama is dedicated to choral lyrics, but his later works reduce the choral dimension to twenty-five percent or less (Harsh 21). The "new" trag-

---

[*] See "Nicias" in Plutarch, Lives 524d.

[†] It is not clear whether this system was adopted for the City Dionysia.

[‡] Although there is evidence the agonothetes continued to contribute money from his own resources (See Csapo & Slater 143).

edy of Euripides reflects an even more radical transformation. In his *Orestes*, for instance, the chorus figures for only about ten percent of the performance.[*] In addition, Antiphon and Euripides began to experiment with generic choral odes which had no organic relations to the dramatic action. These new songs were called *embolima* ("inserts"), and they further marginalized the chorus by reducing its role to that of mere musical interlude—a trend Aristotle found objectionable (Poetics 18.20).

Meter, Music and Dance

It is easy for a modern audience viewing a play such as *Desire Under the Elms* or *Death of a Salesman* to lose sight of the fact that the ancestors of these, and all other tragedies, were fundamentally poetic works.[†] Well before the classical era Greek poetry had developed a series of remarkably complex and varied metrical systems (see West 1982) which, in the hands of a skillful playwright, would not only fill a theatre with mellifluous song but could also contribute materially to the flow and content of the drama itself. In other words, the poetry of Greek tragedy was substance as well as sound and Greek audiences were acutely sensitive to the metrical cues they received from the stage.[‡] When, for example, they heard the marching beat of the anapestic meter, they knew the chorus would soon be making its entrance (*parados*). When they perceived the stately tones of hexameter verse, they understood that some

---

[*] Although in the *Bacchae*, Euripides' last work, the number increased to twenty-seven percent.

[†] Neither Eben Cabot or Willy Loman deliver their lines in verse, but the actors and choruses of Greek tragedy conveyed every thought and every passion poetically.

[‡] This may help explain the lack of concern the Greeks apparently had with stage direction. The flow of the drama was dictated by elements inherent in the play itself (see Taplin Chapter 2).

heroic or perhaps divinely inspired scene was about to unfold. The trochaic tetrameter, the "running" meter, was the peculiar poetic form of the chorus by which its graceful song and dance were guided, while the iambic was the actor's special meter ideally suited for dialogue and debate. In short, the prosody of Greek tragedy was a highly sophisticated arrangement of sounds, rhythms, and meanings that contributed directly and substantively to the dramatic excellence of the performance.

With regard to ancient music, there is generally little firm evidence for the 5th century. We do know, however, that originally the music of Greek tragedy was entirely subordinate to poetry, i.e., the music was made to fit the words. We know also that the early music was simple; that the chief instrument used was the *aulos*, or double flute, and that only a limited range of musical modes were employed. In particular, the Dorian and Mixolydian modes were, according to Aristoxenos, the dominant forms (West 1992, 352).[*] But by the late 5th century music began to take on a life of its own. Led by the innovations of Melanippides, Cinesias, Philoxenus, and above all Timotheus, the music became complex, florid, and wildly inventive. By the Hellenistic period the music had actually eclipsed the words in terms of artistic priority and the virtuosi of instruments such as the aulos and kithara were now treated as major celebrities (Anderson 143). The impact of these developments can be seen directly in certain of the tragedies, especially the works of Euripides (e.g., *Phoenician Women*, *Orestes*, and *Iphigenia in Aulis*). Not unexpectedly, this passion for exotic music was roundly criticized in some quarters. The comic poets were quick to lampoon this *kainos* ("newfangled") music—a good example being Aristo-

---

[*] The Dorian modes' ethos was described as stately and dignified while the Mixolydian was seen as more emotive and lamentary.

phanes' parody in the *Birds* (227-30). Plato, too, found the changes distasteful, criticizing what he saw as pretension, if not licentiousness, in the novelties of men such as Timotheus (<u>Laws</u> 700d-e and <u>Rep</u>. 397a).

The details of ancient choreography remain, as so much else, something of a mystery, but we are reasonably certain of a few points. First, we know that the poets who wrote the plays were also intimately involved in the choreographic aspects of their works. Phrynichus and Aeschylus, for example, were highly respected dance masters.[*] We also know that the Greek term for "dance," *orchesis*, implied something much broader than our modern word. In Attic tragedy, dance was used to reveal the inner spirit of the play; it was a means of delineating and amplifying the poetic message of the drama. To achieve these ends, Greek dance tended to be highly eurhythmic, i.e., it attempted to interpret the music through bodily movement. The entire body, not just the feet, was employed in a highly expressive series of gestures and postures. The arms and hands,[†] in particular, played a critical role in conveying the ethos of various characters and in denoting the relative significance of various aspects of the plot. In terms of its overall character the dance of ancient tragedy was serious, dignified, and orderly, all qualities that convinced Plato to allow such dance in his Cretan city (<u>Laws</u> 816a-b). This vivid and elegant dance, combined with the music and poetry, created a unique blend of artistic elements that became the theatrical hallmark of ancient drama.

---

[*] As were certain of the performers, such as Telestes, who was noted as the primary dancer for many of Aeschylus' plays.

[†] The Greeks actually had a specific term for the use of hand gesture in dance - *cheironomy*.

Actors

Thespis has traditionally been credited with having "invented" the actor's[*] role which eventually transformed choral performance into genuine drama. This process was greatly advanced by Aeschylus, who added a second actor, a modification which not only continued the shift of dramatic emphasis away from the chorus, but also infused the performance with a new dynamism that allowed for unprecedented levels of character and plot development (Kitto 32). In the end, Sophocles included a third actor which, according to Aristotle, brought tragedy's development to a natural conclusion (Poetics 4.16). As it turns out, the Greeks never transgressed this so-called "third actor rule" which had the effect of imposing certain limits on the dramatic range of their presentations—a restriction that may have been less strictly observed among the comedic playwrights (Csapo & Slater 222).

In the early days, the poets themselves served as actors in their own works. Thespis, Aeschylus, and Sophocles all acted to varying degrees, but after Sophocles the practice was discontinued. The principle actors (protagonists) were eventually chosen by the state and assigned by sortition to the three poets selected to present tragedies. The state did not concern itself with the appointment of the second (deuteragonist) and third (tritagonist) actors who were chosen by the principal actor. In the 4th century the lot was discontinued in favor of a system in which the actors were rotated among all of the competing poets (Haigh 230).

The outfits worn by ancient actors were an important aspect of the tragic production. Although the Greeks did not necessarily

---

[*] The Greek word for actor is *hypocrites*. The original meaning of the word seems to have been "one who answers," referring to the responses given to the chorus by the "actor" during the earliest phases of Greek tragedy.

strive for historical accuracy in their costumes, they did seek to portray the various performers in a grand and impressive fashion. The major characters, therefore, were typically adorned in flowing robes dyed in an unusual variety of brilliant colors. This manner of presentation is attributed to Aeschylus and it seems his innovations set a standard from which ancient tragedy varied little over the centuries. In an effort to enhance the stature and dignity of certain characters, body padding and thick wooden-soled boots known as *kothornoi** were used (height was an indication of status). These latter devices were particularly popular during the Hellenistic period.

Perhaps no aspect of ancient costuming was more emblematic of Attic tragedy than the masks worn by the various performers.[†] As it so happens, it was fully appropriate that a festival celebrating the god Dionysus employ masks. In fact, Dionysus was well known in ancient times as a "mask" god (Csapo & Slater 94), and one of the most common representations of the deity, particularly on Attic vases, was a simple pole with a mask of the god suspended from the top. The connection between mask and god is further illustrated by the 5th century practice of displaying the most recently used masks from the architrave of Dionysus' temple.

In terms of specific origins, the Sudas[‡] tells us that Thespis originally painted his face with white lead during his performances

---

[*] References to this footwear in Aristophanes are used to suggest effeminacy. There was also a political meaning to the term, indicating a person of fluctuating political loyalties (because the boots could fit either foot). It was applied to the 5th century Athenian politician Theramenes whose political loyalties vacillated between democracy and oligarchy.

[†] Both the tragic actors and chorus members wore masks which were entirely distinct from the comedic masks.

[‡] A Greek literary encyclopedia compiled in the 10th century A.D..

and that he eventually used masks made of linen. Later, other mask materials would include cork and wood—all highly perishable, with the result that today we possess only terra cota and marble replicas.

It should be noted that masks were much more than decorative instruments. In fact, they met a variety of practical and dramatic needs. It has been argued by some, for instance, that the masks had a megaphonic effect and therefore aided actors in projecting their voices. This is dubious, but one virtue masks definitely did possess was their ability to allow actors to play multiple roles. Given the limited number of actors assigned to each tragedy, this was an important and necessary asset. Another purpose that masks served was to reinforce the nature of a given character by matching the mask to the role. For example, there were masks to represent the regal monarch,[*] the old slave, the mournful woman, etc. Indeed, Pollux, an author from the 2nd century A.D., describes twenty-eight distinct varieties of masks. Again, the masks were chiefly representations of various character types, although we do know of a celebrated exception to this general rule.[†] Furthermore, masks served as aids in communicating the dramatic flow of the play; a messenger bearing good news enters wearing a mask reflecting joy, but one who delivers word of disaster displays a mask indicative of gloom and grief.

---

[*] Important status differentials were also communicated by the masks. The key mechanism here was the *onkos*, a pronounced elongation of the mask indicating a person of high rank.

[†] But significantly the exception comes in a comedic performance. Aelian tells us that Aristophanes' *Clouds* used a life-like mask of Socrates. Socrates himself was in the audience and allegedly stood to allow those viewing the performance to compare the representation with the original.

As Greek tragedy advanced beyond its Attic boundaries, the status of actors increased greatly—something that Aristotle describes in his <u>Rhetoric</u> as a sure sign of the art's deterioration (3.1).[*] The profession itself seems always to have been highly regarded by the Greeks (it was the Romans who later viewed actors as an unsavory bunch) and the names of some of the "superstars" of ancient tragedy have come down to us, e.g., Kleandros, Saondas, Nikomachos, Kephisophon, etc.. We also know something of the bitter professional rivalries that ensued between luminaries such as Mynniscus and Callippides.[†] In addition, we have an excellent illustration of how seriously these men approached their craft in an account told of the actor Polos of Aegina. Polos was a renowned performer who, among other things, instructed the great Athenian orator, Demosthenes, in public speaking. The story goes that while acting the lead in Sophocles' *Electra*, he appeared on stage carrying an urn containing the actual ashes of his recently deceased son. This was apparently done with the express intent of lending an emotional depth to this performance.

Toward the end of the 4th century, Attic drama became an international art form which had the effect of greatly enhancing the prestige of actors.[‡] In fact, first-rate actors could command a series of handsome dispensations for themselves, including military exemption, safe passage during wartime, and immunities from taxa-

---

[*] Specifically, Aristotle deplores the fact that in his time the actors had become more important than the poets.

[†] Mynniscus acted for Aeschylus and was a member of the "old" school, while Callippides was part of the new, "realist" school. Mynniscus dismissed his younger colleague's work as "ape-like" (<u>Poetics</u> 26.4).

[‡] The status of actors was such that they apparently felt entitled to edit and amend the texts of old plays at will. This necessitated the production of authoritative editions by the Athenian statesman, Lycurgus in 330 B.C..

tion, including liturgies. Moreover, actors were even named to ambassadorial posts and dispatched to conduct negotiations in foreign cities. Particularly prominent Thespians were also in a position to collect multiple citizenships, even from notoriously restrictive cities like Athens, as the cases of Neoptolemus and Aristodemus illustrate. Also in the 4th century, we discover the first evidence of local actors' guilds (*synodos*). From the start, these associations embraced all those involved in the dramatic productions— musicians, dancers, costumers, mask makers, etc.. The expansion of such organizations was greatly stimulated by the patronage extended drama by the Macedonian monarchs and later Hellenistic kings. By Roman times, the local guilds had evolved into what amounts to the world's first international trade union based at Rome (Csapo & Slater 241).

The Audience

The Theatre of Dionysus at Athens accommodated approximately seventeen thousand spectators. The composition of this audience was primarily Athenian citizens, but it also included a fair number of foreign visitors because the weather in late March once again made sea travel possible. We also know that boys were allowed to attend the performances, as did slaves. There is some question, however, regarding female attendance. Aristophanes and Plato mention women at the festival, but not all scholars accept these references. The story that pregnant women spontaneously miscarried upon viewing the monstrous ugliness of Aeschylus' Furies comes from very late sources and is extravagant on its face.

Originally there were no charges for admission, but eventually a ticket (*symbelon*) system was devised. At first, this ticket arrangement may have been controlled by a corporation that temporarily leased the theatre. Eventually, the state itself becomes the direct agent for ticket distribution, at which point a standardized fee of two obols (one-third of a drachma) was established.* This rather modest sum was still prohibitive for the poorer citizens who consequently petitioned for relief. A subsidy ascribed to Pericles known as the Theoric fund ("Spectators" fund) was purportedly established in the late 5th century.† Almost immediately, the more affluent elements began to subvert the system by also seeking the dole.

In terms of seating arrangements, the Athenians followed a certain protocol in distributing the prime, front row seats (*prohedria*). The most important seat, the seat of honor so to speak, was set aside for the priest of Dionysus Eleuthereus. In addition, special reserve seating was extended a variety of visiting dignitaries, public benefactors, the judges, religious officials, generals, members of the *boule* (council), the *epheboi* (cadets), orphans of those killed in battle, and the *nomophylakes* (protectors of the law). Although we possess tickets inscribed with tribal names (suggesting assigned seating), these particular tickets may only have applied to the dithyrambic competitions, which were organized on a tribal basis. In all likelihood, with the exception of the *prohedria*, all seating at the tragic performances were "open."

To describe the Athenian citizenry as "intensely" interested in the Dionysian performances would be to understate their sentiments egregiously. During the festival all political and governmental activities were suspended. Upon posting bail, even prisoners were furloughed so that they might attend the competition. Once in attendance, the Athenians were swept up by the powerful psycho-

---

* Despite the relatively large size of the theatre, ticket supplies were inadequate. In addition, foreigners could not purchase tickets on their own but had to use Athenian middlemen: Scalping is not unique to the modern era.

† In actuality, the fund was probably established by Eubulus in the mid-4th century.

logical and emotional imagery emanating from the stage. Herodotus (6.21) provides us with an excellent illustration of this. It involves Phrynichus, a contemporary of Aeschylus, who in 492 B.C., produced a play entitled *The Capture of Miletus* which portrayed the misery of the Miletians at Persians hands. Upon viewing the work, the Athenians burst into tears and not only forbade the play's reproduction, they also fined its author one thousand drachmas. It was precisely outpourings such as these that Plato found not only repugnant but politically and socially dangerous (<u>Rep</u>. 606).

Audiences also showed little hesitation when it came to expressing their artistic preferences. Booing, hissing, and the kicking of sandals against wooden or stone benches were common expressions of disapproval. We know also that spectators were not above launching various objects at performers unfortunate enough to be involved in an unsuccessful play. The missiles of choice seem to have been chiefly food items such as figs and olives but on occasion even rocks were hurled.* Sometimes audience reaction was so hostile that officials were forced to suspend a given performance and move on to the next play. Unruly conduct such as this necessitated the presence of the *rhabdouchoi* or "rod holders," a kind of theatre police charged with the responsibility of maintaining some semblance of order. On the other hand, these same fierce critics were just as quick to call for an encore when they beheld a truly outstanding work.

Like so many other aspects of their agonistic culture, the Athenians organized the Dionysia on a competitive basis: playwright against playwright, actor against actor, and choregos against chore-

---

* During the performances refreshments in the form of dried fruits and confections were served. In addition, wine was consumed which may have contributed to the "demonstrative" nature of the audience.

gos. An official record of the competitions known as the *didaskalia* has survived in part, and it includes, among other details, the names of presiding archons, the names of the dramatists in order of success, the titles of the plays entered by each poet, the name of the victorious protagonist, plus that of the choregos who sponsored the winning play. Naturally, contests such as these required judges and the Athenians devised a complex mechanism, certain details of which remain obscure, aimed at assuring a fair and reasonable outcome. The process began with the council who drew up a list of names from each of the ten tribes. The names were placed in ten separate jars and sealed. At the beginning of the festival, the eponymous archon drew ten names, one from each urn. These ten individuals then served as the judges and would rank order the tragedies on tablets. The tablets were then placed in an urn from which the archon would select five at random. The victory was assigned based on the rankings reflected on these five tablets (Pickard-Cambridge 1973, 96-97).[*]

Significantly, this balloting process was not kept entirely secret. After the contest had been decided, the names of the five judges who had determined the outcome were made public which no doubt meant the judges were subject to threat and reprisal from the general audience as well as influential individuals. Andocides gives us an example of the latter involving Alcibiades[†] (see <u>Against Alcibiades</u> 20-21) and we know the former existed because the Greeks actually had a term for audience demonstrations designed to influence the judging. It was called *thorubos*, which loosely translates means "ruckus." In addition to these constraints, pressure

---

[*] Anyone found guilty of tampering with any facet of the judging procedure was subject to the death penalty.

[†] The contest at issue here involved a boys' chorus in the dithyrambic competition.

on judges was compounded further by laws that could result in their prosecution and imprisonment if a verdict was determined to be unjust (Haigh 37).

Once a victorious playwright had been identified a herald announced his name along with that of the choregos. Their heads were then crowned with garlands of ivy. The Parian Marble indicates that the original prize for a tragic victor was a goat and for the comedic playwright, a jar of wine and a basket of figs. As the state became more heavily involved in the festival's organization, cash prizes became the norm. Monetary awards were not extended the choregos, but after 449 B.C. the winning protagonist also received money for his efforts.[*] In addition to the public acclaim and the cash, the playwright might also receive a celebratory parade home. It is this jubilant *pompe* and its aftermath, marking the victory of Agathon, that Plato immortalized in this Symposium.

The Holy Trinity—Aeschylus, Sophocles, and Euripides

Only thirty-one tragedies survive from the great poets of the 5th century and of these, seven are the works of Aeschylus.[†] During his lifetime he achieved a remarkable reputation not just at Athens but throughout the Greek world. He was, for instance, an honored guest of Hiero at Syracuse and he spent the final days of his life as a noted celebrity at Gela. Notwithstanding his widely acknowl-

---

[*] The exact amount of these cash awards is unknown but presumably it was substantial given the amount of time and energy one was expected to invest in the play's production.

[†] The ancient sources suggest that Aeschylus wrote between seventy and ninety plays during his lifetime. Thirteen of these plays were awarded first prize. In all, as many as one thousand tragedies may have been produced at Athens during the 5th century (Knox 1968, 8).

edged genius as a playwright, the funeral epigram commemorating
his death (456-455 B.C.) made no mention of his poetic prowess.
Apparently the achievement of which he was most proud, the act
by which he wished to be remembered, was his military service as
one of the *Marathonomachoi*, i.e., the men who had stood at Marathon and repulsed the Persians.[*]

Artistically speaking, Aeschlyus was a "master" in every sense
of the term. Not only is he to be credited with having added the
ingredient (the second actor) that allowed for the art's full flower-
ing, his plays also brought to the stage a spiritual grandeur and
loftiness of tone hitherto unknown. Not even Aristophanes, whose
caustic irreverence seemed to know no limit, could bring himself to
deride the achievements of Aeschylus. Indeed, in the *Frogs* he extends his tragic colleague a respect bordering on homage. Nor was
Aristophanes' praise an isolated sentiment among Athenians. Upon
his death, Aeschylus was accorded the singular distinction of having his plays reproduced at the Great Dionysia.[†] Modern opinion
continues to affirm ancient assessments. Jebb claims that Aeschylus can legitimately be thought of as a second Homer and Swin-
burne declared the *Oresteia* perhaps "the greatest achievement of
the human mind."

In terms of tragic perspective, Aeschylus was the most theological of the three great 5th century playwrights. Among other things,
he presents his audience with an enlarged view of Zeus casting him

---

[*] In translation, the epigram reads as follows:
> "This tomb the dust of Aeschylus doth hide,
> Euphorion's son, and fruitful Gela's pride,
> How tried his valour Marathon may tell
> And long-haired Medes who know it all too
> well."

[†] In 386 B.C. other tragic reproductions were allowed and in 339 B.C. certain comedic
works were extended this honor.

as the ultimate guardian of order and justice and as the author of an experiential dynamic involving the following sequence: Action-Guilt-Suffering-Insight (Lesky 77). What Aeschylus really offers here is a kind of theodicy in which suffering functions as part of god's plan to potentially advance the human condition. In this scheme, suffering is man's guidebook, the map by which he gains a proper grasp of reality. The gods, therefore, are not gratuitously cruel toward humanity. On the contrary, suffering is redemptive to the degree that it restrains human excess and corrects misconception. All of this indicates that Aeschylus does not subscribe to a dismally tragic world-view. Although Aeschylus would readily acknowledge the trauma of human existence, he also insists that suffering brings insight (*pathei mathos*) and that in the end, there is light awaiting us at the end of the tragic tunnel.

Sophocles was born in 496 B.C. and enjoyed an extraordinarily long and successful life. He is said to have written more than one hundred twenty plays of which seven survive, including the one work which many, including Aristotle, consider the quintessential tragedy—*Oedipus the King.*[*] He secured first prize in the tragic competition at least twenty times and is said to have never placed lower than second. It is also reported that he was the first to break with the tradition of trilogies in favor of single, self-contained plays. Like Aeschylus, he too was actively involved in the civic affairs of his city having served as general, along with Pericles, in the suppression of the Samian revolt (441-439 B.C.).

Among Sophocles' most important artistic innovations was the introduction of the third actor, a move quickly adopted by other

---

[*] Despite its well-deserved fame, *Oedipus Rex* placed second in the competition. Sophocles was defeated on this occasion (427 B.C.) by Philocles, a nephew of Aeschylus.

playwrights. The significance of this improvement lay in the fact that a third *hypocrites* helped facilitate character development to an unprecedented degree. While it remained true that Greek tragedy focused primarily on plot, in Sophocles' hands characters came to exhibit a depth and complexity that lent new meaning to the notion of "hero." Dramatic figures such as Oedipus, Ajax, Antigone, and Electra are no longer subordinate instruments designed to simply advance the story line of a given play. Sophoclean characters have personality and substance; they are not feeble pawns driven by malignant destinies but rather through courage, conviction, and a heightened sense of self, they achieve a certain vindication even in the face of unspeakable misery. The impact of these developments allows us, for the first time, to speak in terms of "heroic greatness." The *Oresteia* is a masterpiece of style and spectacle but there is no individual in this work that can compare with the great souls of figures such as Oedipus or Antigone.

What are the component elements of tragic greatness as presented by Sophocles? Generalization in such matters is admittedly a perilous business, but there are certain recurring patterns discernible in Sophocles' plays, one of the most prevalent being loneliness. Ajax, Oedipus, and Antigone are not the sort of individuals who seek remedy or comfort from their compatriots. They are *monos*, alone. Their strength and endurance comes from within. They are *authadeia*, self-willed, independent personalities that remain fiercely committed to paths of their own choosing. And herein lies another prevalent feature of Sophoclean heroes. They are not mere sufferers, they actively battle the fate that envelopes them. Passivity and acceptance are anathema to such figures as is any adjustment that hints at compromise or contrition.[*] Instead, Sophocles' heroes are prepared to offer stubborn, blind, even hopeless resistance because an unbowed, dignified demise is preferable to whimpering concession.

Sophocles was keenly sensitive to the dark forces that hover about human existence and there is nothing in his conception of heroic greatness that suggests immunity from the tears and bitterness such forces bring. Nevertheless, he does seem to suggest that notwithstanding the impermanence and insecurity of all things human, an individual who clings to his essence reaps a certain reward: Ajax does receive his burial; Antigone does extend her brother the honors due the dead; and Philoctetes will rejoin the Greek host and triumph at Troy (Knox 1983, 162). Above all, this rule of "victory" in the face of malignant fate seems to apply to Oedipus, the incestuous parricide who is both sower and seed. No one experiences agonies comparable to those suffered by this accursed man. Yet, even as an aged suppliant, after years of the most appalling degradation, his fiery soul continues to burn. And as if to acknowledge the virtue of an indomitable spirit, the gods not only grant a Teiresian insight to Oedipus, they extend this recalcitrant old man a painless death and a beatification worthy of a god.

I believe it would be a mistake, however, to conclude from *Oedipus at Colonus*, or any other of Sophocles' works, that the playwright had a need for happy endings or that he felt some artistic obligation to solace his audience. If we can indeed speak of "rewards" for those manifesting heroic greatness, we must never

---

[*] It is for precisely this reason that characters such as Jocasta and Creon do not qualify as heroes. Jocasta is an escapist who cannot endure the horror she sees unfolding before her eyes. She chooses the supreme evasion—suicide. Creon, in the end, proves to be one of those trees that yields to winter's floods spoken of by Haemon. His collapse is total and thoroughly unheroic.

lose sight of the fact that these are compensatory triumphs that come only at the end of a long and horrible crucible. Sophocles obviously admires the splendid obstinacy of an Oedipus or an Antigone—a quality that allows man to transcend the miseries that threaten to swallow him whole. But Sophocles also remains forever mindful of the blood and tears that inevitably preceed such exultant moments.

In the year 441 B.C., Euripides registered his first victory in the tragic competition, a feat he would repeat only four more times over the course of his life.[*] In all, he wrote about ninety plays, but while he lived, he never achieved the kind of universal acclaim enjoyed by Aeschylus and Sophocles. In 408 B.C. he withdrew from unappreciative Athens and went to the court of Archelaus of Macedon where he died soon afterwards.

During the 19th century scholars routinely identified Aeschylus as the man who "invented" tragedy, Sophocles as the poet who brought the art to its perfection, and Euripides as the individual who marked its decline. Aristophanes would have endorsed this last assessment with little hesitation as we see from his treatment of Euripides in works such as *Acharnians*, *Thesmophoriazusae*, and *Frogs*. But Euripides was not entirely without his defenders. Aristotle called him "the most tragic of the poets" (Poetics 13.10) and Goethe defended him zealously against Schlegel's reproofs.[†] Moreover, history would eventually vindicate Euripides. Not only would the popularity of his works surpass those of Aeschylus and Sophocles in later centuries, his long-range influence on drama was

---

[*] His last victory was actually scored posthumously.

[†] Goethe wrote, "If a modern man like Schlegel must pick out faults in so great an ancient (Euripides), he ought only to do it upon his knees" (182).

probably greater than either of his more acclaimed colleagues (Jebb 210).

Why then were his works so little appreciated in his own day? In great measure the answer to this question lies in the innovative and experimental nature of Euripides' works. Exactly why certain artists acquiesce readily to conventional standards while others reject traditional norms as unacceptably constraining is a difficult question. One thing is clear however the iconoclasm of Euripides does not stem from an inability to compose plays along customary lines. The *Bacchae*, produced after Euripides' death in 406 B.C., could have been written by either Aeschylus or Sophocles. Perhaps in Euripides' case the answer lies in the spirit of the age, which changed so remarkably in the brief span of years separating the lifetimes of Aeschylus and Euripides. The new era that claimed Euripides loyalties had in particular been shaped by the sophistic revolution. Tradition has it that Euripides not only received the unorthodox scientific teaching of Anaxagoras but had also studied with Protagoras and Prodicus. What he undoubtedly took away from these experiences was a critical, if not subversive, attitude toward received opinion and past practice. We see this clearly in many of his plays: The *Trojan Women* exposes the sham glory of war; in the *Trachiniae*, *Ion*, and *Heracles* prevailing attitudes toward the gods are severely challenged; the *Medea* confronts the status and treatment of women; and Euripides' *Orestes* seems intent upon discrediting the entire heroic tradition. In short, Euripides, a child of his age, was prepared to gore every sacred cow he encountered.

Something must also be said about the stylistic innovations Euripides brought to the stage. The heroic grandeur of Aeschylus and Sophocles is conspicuously absent in the work of Euripides. Instead, we encounter an extraordinary new realism which is what

Sophocles referred to when he said Euripides presented people as they were, while he, Sophocles, presented them as they should be (Poetics 25.11). Gone were the grand heroic figures that awed the audiences in times past. Kings and queens no longer appeared in regal majesty; instead, it seemed as if the common man had risen from his theatre seat and forced his way to the stage (Neitzsche 1967, Section 11). In the eyes of conservatives like Aristophanes, it must have appeared as if tragedy had been reduced to its lowest common denominator; as if a church had been converted into a cinema (Kitto 362).*

In addition to the diluted stature of his characters, Euripides also invested them with a psychological depth and introspective quality absent from earlier dramatic presentation (Snell 11). Perhaps the most obvious example of this tendency is found in *Medea* where Euripides explores the darkness of the human heart in much greater detail and subtlety than ever before. Accordingly, his conception of tragedy has little to do with a violation of some cosmic order or with a divinely contrived didactic scheme. Instead, we are encouraged to peer within and to recognize the fact that uncontrolled passion has the capacity to negate everything rational and decent in life, that *thumos*, not fate, is the mother of our misery.

The spirit of innovation that commands so much of Euripides' energies may also explain some of the most important aspects of his poetic legacy. Works such as *Alcestis* and *Ion* are difficult to categorize as tragedies. They read instead like dramatic hybrids combining tragic elements with various romantic and comedic features. We find in these plays everything from hairbreadth escapes

---

* Another important stylistic change in the works of Euripides is a movement toward melodrama. In such plays as *Alcestis*, *Ion*, *Helen*, and *Iphigenia in Tauris*, the high tone of earlier tragedy is gone, replaced by a new spirit of theatricality aimed more at excitement and pure entertainment than the conveying of some profound message.

to fairytale endings; the sort of material that would become the stock in trade of Middle and, particularly, New Comedy. In fact, it is Euripides, not Aristophanes, who exercises the greatest influence upon such major New Comedy authors as Menander,[*] Diphilus, and Philemon. The latter was so enamored of Euripides that he reportedly declared, "If in truth the dead have consciousness, gentlemen, I would hang myself so as to see Euripides." It seems fair to say then, that despite the lack of critical acclaim he received during his lifetime, Euripides not only ranks among the greatest tragedians who ever lived, he is also the inventor of what was to become the master pattern of Western comedy (Knox 1986, 268).

Conclusion—The Meaning, Function, and Message of Greek Tragedy

For the Athenian, the Great Dionysia was an expression of religious devotion as well as a manifest source of inspiring entertainment, but it may also have served another important purpose. In recent years an extensive body of research has surfaced (Meier 1993, Gregory 1997, Euben 1986, etc.) concerning the sociopolitical significance of the tragic stage. Based on these findings some scholars have concluded the theatre contributed nearly as much to political culture at Athens as the Pnyx.[†] Specifically, it is noted that tragedy developed at a time when an entirely new civic ideology was asserting itself in the city. The old aristocratic values and privileges were under attack, and as a result of the politics of men like Cleisthenes, Ephialtes, and Pericles, they would soon be restricted

---

[*] Menander borrows entire lines from Euripides' works which has made distinguishing fragments from the two authors a significant challenge for scholars.

[†] That the theatre was a political force at Athens seems to be corroborated disparagingly by Plato who condemns what he calls *theatro-kratia* (Laws 701a-b).

to an unprecedented degree. Given the turbulent propensities of Greek society, these moves were unlikely to ensure domestic tranquility. In fact, they constituted a palpable threat of fratricidal violence. Under these volatile conditions, the tragic performances may have provided an important mediating service. By elasticizing the traditional myths and legends to cover the emerging reality of democratic Athens, the playwrights afforded the city a peaceful mechanism for exploring new political options, "debating" pressing social issues, and for easing some of the social stresses that occurred during this transitional period.[*]

In addition to its civic utility, tragedy also furnished important meditative opportunities in which the Greeks probed the major issues and confronted the great mysteries of human existence—suffering, mortality, justice, fate, madness, pride, dignity, etc. In this sense, Gabriel Marcel was correct when he observed that drama was a kind of philosophy "…in its virgin state." What were the conclusions the Greeks drew from their tragic explorations? What were the tacit lessons offered by the master playwrights of the 5th century? Here we run the risk of generalizing in matters that do not lend themselves to neat summation. However, there are certain recurring themes which constitute an essential core of tragic insights and perhaps none is more pervasive than the view that life is a wound that does not heal. Try as we might to attain secure footing, we remain naked and vulnerable, "like flies to wanton boys." Under these precarious conditions we cling desperately to dreams of a life charmed by stability and good fortune, but in the end harsh reality compels us to admit there are no formulas or

---

[*] Perhaps the tragedies also provided a few brief moments whereby the contentious, envy-driven Athenians could set aside their differences and ponder the universality of human suffering against which distinctions of wealth, power, and family lineage seemed small and unimportant.

sanctuaries capable of shielding us from life's travail. When, on occasion, our lives are brightened by moments of happiness the tranquility invariably proves short-lived. We soon experience presentiments of evil, which affirm the brevity of these joyous interludes and alert us to the impending resumption of calamity and pain. In short, the Greek view of the human condition stresses the insecurity and futility that accompany us always—in Greek eyes, we are like sacrificial victims being driven to the altars.

To complicate matters, this gauntlet we call life is utterly defiant of rational explanation with the effect that our suffering is compounded by bewilderment and hopelessness. As rational beings, we naturally desire to dispel contingency from our lives; we strive to make human agency the governing dynamic of existence. But our efforts to live beyond the mercurial grasp of *tyche* (chance) is doomed because the world routinely imposes appalling suffering notwithstanding our plans and preparations. If only there were some rationale for the misery, it might at least help us to come to grips with our plight. Suffering in the form of supernatural punishment, for example, might actually furnish a certain comfort in the sense that we would at least know a heavenly guardian was on duty ready to penalize those who transgressed the natural order of things. But at some point in their tragic assessments the Greeks seem to have arrived at the possibility of something far more disturbing than the prospect of divine retribution viz., the possibility that there is no order whatsoever. What if our lives unfolded in a world that was entirely disordered, incoherent, and unintelligible? What if it was a place where the wicked were not necessarily called to account and where the idea of merited punishment had no meaning? What if our world were a realm where agony radiated outward in purely random vectors afflicting the lives of the innocent as readily as the guilty? What, in other words, if there were an irrational evil embedded in the nature of reality itself; an evil absurd and meaningless?[*] I believe the Greeks did entertain such a possibility and that the "fate" of Oedipus points in this direction (see Appendix III).

In addition to the disquieting idea of irrational evil, the Greeks also took from tragedy something more affirmative, something that broadened and informed their humanistic attitudes, viz., that we are all, Greek and non-Greek alike, children of misfortune. As early as Homer, the Greeks seem to have acknowledged the ecumenical power of suffering, as we see in the common tears shed by Achilles and Priam in the final book of the Iliad. Increasingly, they came to appreciate that the human condition dictates that everyone press his lips to the cup of bitterness and that such experiences not only transcend traditional distinctions of race and culture, they also render them superfluous. The best example of these perspectives from the extant tragedies is Aeschylus' *Persians*. The play was produced just eight years after the battle of Salamis, i.e., while the memories of the Persian sack of Athens and the desecration of her religious shrines were still fresh in Athenian minds. Yet the play portrays the Persians as a good and noble people, as common sufferers whose catastrophic defeat merits condolence and pity. All this sympathetic depiction from a playwright who had personally fought the Persians at Marathon and who had lost his own brother at that same engagement! It has been said that Homer taught the Hellenes to be good Greeks. It might be added that tragedy taught them to be good human beings.

The Greeks derived all of these "benefits" from their plays and more, but there is one thing they did not take from their plays, viz., a curative strategy for delimiting or preventing human suffering.

---

[*] The essential work on this point is Whitman (1966).

As a result, those seeking comfort from the ancient plays are bound to be disappointed because Greek tragedy offers few if any remedies along these lines. In truth, none of the 5th century playwrights attempted to decode, dispel, or resolve the enigma of tragic existence. What their works offered instead was a dramatic inventory of the many thorns life is prepared to bury in our flesh. Accordingly, the aspirations of Greek drama are rather limited: to encourage us to ponder the spectacle of universal suffering and to constrain us to ask the eternal question, "Why?". It is this last point, the "why" of suffering, that continues to link us to the Greeks because it remains just as much our question as it was theirs, despite the passage of 2500 years. To their credit the ancients boldly acknowledged the brute fact that this is a question without answer. Yet, if the Greeks were disinclined to offer us solutions in these matters, they did at least offer us encouragement. As human beings we are *deinon* (*Antigone* 369), i.e., "wondrous," and there is nothing more extraordinary than our capacity for militant resistance in the face of life's malice. During these episodes of inspired resistance, a sufferer transcends his circumstance and lends a spiritual dignity to his life that has no equivalent, even among the gods. So if we can legitimately speak of a message contained in Greek tragedy, it is simply this—stagger on, child of a much tried race, for there is no escape from your wretchedness, but do so with the understanding that your defiance makes you superior to the forces that crush you.

Appendix I: Interpretations

As an artistic category, tragedy has been analyzed and assessed from a wide variety of perspectives—structural, historical, political, religious, psychoanalytic, linguistic, etc. In addition, the roster of interpreters includes an equally diverse assortment of some of the most formidable minds in history, men such as Aristotle, Corneille, Dryden, Lessing, and Nietzsche, to name just a few. The fact that tragedy has received attention of this sort not only suggests its special status in the aesthetic pantheon, it also indicates a continuous capacity to speak to us in a profound and deeply meaningful fashion despite the passage of time.

In what follows, we shall briefly consider a few of the more famous assessments of tragedy. It is worth noting in advance that this muster of opinions presents an instance of great minds not thinking alike. The interpretations put forth vary enormously from thinker to thinker and tend to say more about the spirit of the age in which the commentator lived as well as his personal predilections, than about the universal qualities of Greek tragedy. Consequently, there is no exhaustive theory of tragedy, no all-encompassing conception that has emerged from the many attempts to analyze the poetic achievements of men like Aeschylus and Sophocles. This is not to suggest that Aristotle or Hegel were uninterested in achieving such a transhistorical, all-purpose perspective. All of the individuals examined are to one degree or another, guilty of seeking this universality at the expense of precision and consistency. Typically, we encounter critics who are less concerned with analysis than with superimposing some preconceived notion of the way in which tragedy is supposed to operate. Where the "facts" remain noncompliant, the analyst's response is typically Procrustean; the recalcitrant data is either trimmed, stretched, or ignored entirely. If there is a lesson to be learned from any of this it is simply that although our desire to see orderly patterns and predictable movements in Greek tragedy is difficult to resist, facile schematization must be avoided because Greek tragedy is ultimately nothing less than an expression of the human spirit and as such its richness and complexity may forever defy formulaic reduction.

Aristotle

Aristotle's Poetics is the first treatise on literary theory in history. Unfortunately, the text we possess is incomplete and highly disjointed. Moreover, the language is often obscure and certain of the arguments are not only ambiguous, they also seem contradictory with other premises Aristotle advances. As a canon of the tragic art, the standards set forth in the Poetics appear inconsistent with the actual practices of the great dramatists, but if this work proved less than prescriptive in its own day, its impact on later ages was enormous. Renaissance scholars treated it as the gold standard of literary assessment and generations of later authors—everyone from Milton, Racine, and Fielding to Goethe, Lessing, and Coleridge—were powerfully influenced by the norms presented here in the later 4th century (Rees 23).

From the outset, the Poetics reveals the peculiar mindset of its author: a provocative blend of science and apriorism. At times, the work reads like a biological treatise and proceeds like a dissection in prose (e.g., 6.9, 12.1-3, 15.1-6). At the same time, however, the teleological worldview which tends to color so much of Aristotle's thinking is intrusively evident (e.g., 4.16-18). Taken together, these seemingly disparate elements contribute substantially to Aristotle's famous definition of tragedy, a definition that is certainly not without its difficulties:

> Tragedy is, then, a representation of an action that is heroic and complete and of a certain magnitude—by means of language enriched by all kinds of ornament, each used separately in the different parts of the play: it represents men in action and does not use narrative, and through pity and fear it effects to these and similar emotions (6.2).

Aristotle proceeds to elaborate and in doing so makes plain his conviction that plot, and especially complex plot as opposed to character, is the very soul of tragedy (6.19). This view does not correlate well with modern drama where so much depends on dramatic personality, but Aristotle was correct in asserting that the emphasis in ancient tragedy fell on events not personage. Our modern fascination with character is traceable to the Renaissance, not the Greeks, and in the few cases where the ancient plays do focus on a given character, that figure is typically presented more as a "type" than as an individual (e.g., the suffering king, the raging wife, the vengeful son or daughter).

Still, the hero is nevertheless an important facet of ancient tragedy, if for no other reason that he/she is the instrument by which tragic events are propelled, generating in the process, that sense of *eleos kai phobos* (pity and fear) that Aristotle deems essential to tragedy. In order for the audience to experience these sentiments, the hero must be of a certain sort. He cannot, for instance, be too ordinary because great tragic falls require height. Accordingly, the hero must be a person of some distinction yet not so lofty that the associative bond between character and audience is entirely compromised. And while the hero need not be a preeminently virtuous individual, the disaster suffered by the hero should not result from villainy, but must stem instead from some *hamartia* (flaw or error).[*] Toward such an individual we are capable of feeling pity and fear: pity for a fate largely undeserved and fear from the recognition that the hero's misfortune could be our own (13.4).

But as Aristotle's definition indicates, there is more to tragedy than merely experiencing pity and fear. He also claims that tragedy can effect a beneficial "relief" or catharsis of these and related emotions. There is little debate regarding Aristotle's motivation in taking up this line of argument—he is attempting to refute the austere criticism Plato leveled at the psychological impact of mimetic poetry (Rep. 377a-398b and 595a-608b). Unlike his master, Aristotle believes that the experience of a tragic audience can be both healthy and pleasurable. Serious questions do arise with the precise meaning of the term "catharsis." Traditionally, the term has been seen to refer to a purging of the emotions; an interpretation that corresponds well with certain remarks offered in the Politics (8.4). However, a more detailed examination of the etymological subtleties surrounding the word reveals a much wider and more complex semantic field. Not only are there well established religious and medical applications for the term, there is also evidence Aristotle could be referring to a kind of intellectual clarification experienced by theatre-goers (see Golden 1969 and Nussbaum 1986).

In any event, the Poetics is a remarkable early attempt to understand the many elements comprising one of mankind's most im-

---

[*] The meaning of this term and, more importantly, its relevance to tragedy is open to question. Aristotle seems to assume pride must precede the fall, but this may in fact be part of an apriori moral assumption on his part and not a fixed rule of tragedy. It does not, for instance, fit the details of *Oedipus the King* which Aristotle saw as the quintessential Greek tragedy (see Whitman 36-37 & Else 1965, 385).

pressive artistic achievements. Specifically, it is difficult to read this book without being taken with the author's taxonomic genius, with his ability to logically disassemble a complex structure and analyze each component with intelligence and insight. On another level, however, one is left unimpressed and dissatisfied. Nowhere in the text does Aristotle spread his philosophic wings and discuss the manner in which tragedy speaks to the human condition. Instead, we receive a pallid and rather dull rendition of the mechanics involved in proper tragic composition—as if dramatic poetry were some abstract activity whose meaning lies solely in the details of plot, meter, and characterization. In short, Aristotle extends us a clinical analysis when what we seek instead is insight regarding the great existential question that stands at the center of all tragedy: the meaning (if, indeed, there is meaning) of human suffering.

G.W.F. Hegel

Hegel's understanding of tragedy was heavily conditioned by his philosophy of history where he argued that historical process was not a random collage of unrelated events but rather, the latent embodiment of *Geist* (spirit). The contingency of events by which history seemed to be governed, was for Hegel, more apparent than real. In truth, what seems sporadic and ephemeral is actually part of a teleological order whose end and purpose is the manifestation of universal moral law. It was from within this same context that Hegel sought the essence and meaning of tragedy. His conclusion was that tragic drama is a conflict of right against right, a contention between equally valid but mutually exclusive ethical claims. Significantly, there is no crime here, no *hamartia* that triggers the calamitous chain of events resulting in human misery. There is only an inevitable conspiracy of circumstance resulting in a disastrous "collision" between two legitimate sets of values. The full depth of the conflict, as well as the true nature of the individual combatants, is revealed via this struggle, which eventually results in reconciliation and a restoration of order (Hegel 1975, 1159-60).

According to Hegel, Sophocles' *Antigone* was the ideal illustration of Greek tragedy and a masterpiece beyond all others (1975, 1218). Here we find the classic conflict of filial piety and civic obligation; between duty to loved ones versus duty to the state. Antigone is right to insist upon the burial of her brother; the most ancient traditions mandated such rites. Creon as king is also justified in his belief that the community's very existence depends upon obedience to the laws. The two "rights" generate a series of terrible wrongs. Though the lives of both characters are shattered irrevocably,[*] Hegel believes that a redemptive virtue grows from the wreckage, viz., a higher and more universal spiritual truth.

To his credit, Hegel does not beg the philosophic question of human suffering. Unlike Aristotle who treats tragedy synthetically, as if it were merely the product of certain compositional rules, Hegel sees tragedy as a vital force alive in the world. Where his interpretation falters, however, is in its insistence that the pattern of destructive conflict somehow issues in the restoration of harmony and order. These views correspond much more closely with Hegel's own philosophy of history and with his convictions regarding the progress of the world-spirit, than they do with Greek tragedy (Gellrich 47-8). Where, for instance, is the reconciliation in *Antigone*? The play closes with a spate of calamities: Antigone, Haemon, and Eurydice dead, and Creon condemned to simmer in

---

[*] In Hegel's scheme historical process cares little for the individual. Indeed, he likens history to a "slaughter-bench" where both individuals and entire peoples are sacrificed on behalf of the spirit's unfolding (Hegel 1900, 21).

his own self-recriminatory juices for the rest of his life. Hegel's response to such catastrophe is to encourage us to look beyond our tears implying there is solace to be had in the grand sweep of history. But is this the message of the ancient dramatists? It is not more accurate to conclude that the Greeks believed that human existence was plagued by savage uncertainty; that confusion, instability, and chaos are apt to defile every plan and to dash every dream? Rather than harmony and order, plays such as *Antigone* seem to offer an unvarnished view of the anguish of human existence along with the disturbing possibility that the journey of life may be little more than an ongoing pageant of suffering and tears.

Nietzsche

In 1872 Nietzsche published his <u>Birth of Tragedy</u>. From the outset, this innovative approach to understanding the origins and meaning of Greek tragedy was controversial. Some reviewers, such as Ulrich Wilamowitz-Moellendorff, argued that the work was entirely lacking in merit and that its author had displayed a reckless disregard for the canons of scholarship. Others, such as the noted philologist Erwin Rohde, defended Nietzsche by exposing the misinterpretations and errors of his critics' assaults. In the end, however, even Nietzsche tended to reject his first book as little more than youthful bombast describing it as "...ponderous, embarrassing, image-mad, and image-confused..." (1967, 19). Despite even this disavowal however, <u>Birth of Tragedy</u> is not so easily dismissed. Although it may indeed be characterized as a juvenile musing as compared with Nietzsche's mature thought, it nevertheless contains an undeniably provocative thesis which, despite its generality and lack of annotation, offers a powerfully suggestive view of the spiritual dynamics underlying Greek tragedy.

Unlike Winckelmann, Nietzsche did not perceive Greek aesthetics exclusively in terms of the "serene beauty" mirrored by Apollinarian restraint and measure. For Nietzsche, the art forms associated with Apollo, particularly sculpture, are merely representative. They reflect a desperate attempt to mitigate the suffering of the individual by creating for him a blissful illusion of comforting phenomena (1967, section 16). There is also, according to Nietzsche, a more profound artistic impulse whose peculiar embodiment is music—the Dionysian. Unlike the Apollinarian art, the Dionysian imagery does not operate on a symbolic level. In Nietzsche's view, it conveys something far more fundamental, viz., the very substructure of human existence and as such, transcends image, concept, and word. Music, as the unique medium of the Dionysian, is a voice from the realm of Being that provides us with metaphysical truth, with the "thing in itself" (1967, section 16).[*] Nietzsche also notes a further distinction between the Apollinarian and the Dionysian: Whereas the former contributes to subjectivism and individuation, the latter exhibits an integrative power that transcends subjective ego and unifies us with our fellows and with nature itself (Silk 64).

According to Nietzsche, art is the highest task and true metaphysical activity of life (1967, Preface), and the highest form of art ever devised by man is tragedy. It came into being through a unique synthesis of the Dionysian and Apollinarian instincts resulting in something of inestimable value, viz., an appreciation for the wisdom and necessity of suffering. For Nietzsche, Greek tragedy was an act of courage, an unflinching attempt to take the measure

---

[*] At this stage of his development Nietzsche was still heavily influenced by the thought of Schopenhauer—particularly by the latter's view of music (see v. 2, chapt. 39 of The World As Will and Representation).

of life's horror. The ancient plays fix their gaze firmly upon the misery and absurdity that torment humanity but to their credit, the Greeks did not allow themselves to be overwhelmed; they never lapse into fatalism. Instead, in their hands, Nietzsche believed that tragedy became a kind of aesthetic reprieve through which misery and ugliness were converted into a sublime beauty that transcended the merely phenomenal (see 1967, Sections 3 and 4). And it was this same extraordinary beauty that redeemed man by revealing his place in the indestructible unity of all Being. It is here that Nietzsche parts company with Schopenhauer for whom Greek tragedy merely summoned us to a dismal resignation. Nietzsche, by contrast, saw the ancient plays as revelational and celebratory; as a source of metaphysical comfort and joy (1967, Section 7). Like all important art, Greek drama attempted to answer the great existential question, "What is life?" Nietzsche's response is that life is often unfair, cruel, and predictably scornful of human intentions, but it nevertheless remains worthy of man's fervent affirmation.

Unlike most of the other major commentators, Nietzsche offers not only an analysis of the meaning of tragedy, but he also provides an account of its demise. In his view, the decline of Greek tragedy was not related to the political and social deterioration of the polis but rather to the growth of rational philosophy and science. Advances in these domains helped foster a naïve optimism that promised not only a solution to the riddle of life but a panacea for the agony of existence (1967, Section 15). At the same time, rationalism also proclaimed a new standard of beauty that completely superseded Dionysian aesthetics—the idea that in order for something to be truly beautiful, it had to be intelligible. Nietzsche characterized this orientation as "aesthetic Socratism," an artistic counterpart to the dictum, "Knowledge is virtue" (1967, Section 12). It received its dramatic embodiment in the new realism of Euripides who was the first to inject the rationalist poison into tragedy. The results, according to Nietzsche, were fully predictable: the death of tragedy. By attempting to supplant the somber wisdom of suffering with the cheerful enthusiasm of rationalism; by offering dialectic as an alternative to the goat-song, Socrates and his followers rendered genuine tragedy impossible.

Few works can rival the insight and ingenuity of Nietzsche's Birth of Tragedy, qualities that have rightly ensured its status as one of the subject's standard texts. Still, we are entitled to ask whether this work represents an example of scholarly revelation or an act of philosophic creation. Did Nietzsche's insights flow naturally from a new and profound assessment of Greek drama or were they pre-existing constructs hammered into place to fit the cultural conditions of 5th century Athens? As we have seen in each of our three sketches, great thinkers tend to bring along correspondingly great conceptual baggage. Here, Nietzsche himself furnishes us with a clue and perhaps a confession. He observes that at heart all philosophers, notwithstanding their claims to objectivity and truth, are dogmatists and that their works must ultimately be assigned the status of involuntary memoirs and "personal confessions" (1966, Section 6).

Appendix II: Greek Tragedy And The Bible

The Book of Job and the Passion of Jesus are sometimes offered as biblical parallels to Greek tragedy. While it is true one of the prime features of tragedy, viz., suffering, is powerfully presented in each of these accounts, neither of them can be properly categorized as "tragedy" in the Greek sense. The story of Job's torment is actually a kind of theodicy designed to justify the perplexing ways of God to Man. There is little along these lines to be found in Greek drama, where, if anything, the message seems to be that there is ultimately no logic or justification for the chaos that disrupts our lives. For the Hebrew, the agonies of Job may appear baffling and cruel but they are nevertheless part of the Almighty's design and are therefore not to be challenged, must less defied. By contrast, Greek tragedy seems peculiarly dedicated to applauding human resistance to the gods and to fate. Indeed, it is precisely this recalcitrance that constitutes the core of heroic personality and here, too, we detect another major point of demarcation between Job and the likes of Oedipus or Antigone. Job can in no way qualify as a heroic figure. Not only is his resistance to the suffering imposed upon him momentary and irresolute (e.g., 40:4 and 42:6), the entire depiction of Job's fate has been conceived in a manner that denies grandeur and dignity to the victim. Job's status has been deliberately diminished in order to heighten the supreme and imponderable authority of God. In short, the Book of Job tells us that human worth is registered through humility and obedience. This is the key to Job's restoration[*]—the plentiful flocks, the large new family, and a life "old and full of years." In the classic works of Greek tragedy there are no bent knees and no happy endings. There are only inspired examples of men (and women) who nobly contest the forces that will inevitably procure their annihilation.

For Christians, the spiritual agony of Jesus at Gethsemane and his physical torture at Golgotha may appear to be the most sublime examples of heroic suffering in history. However, when these events are viewed from the larger context of Christian theology, the

---

[*] Much of my thinking on this subject has been influenced by Raphael (1961) and Jaspers (1969).

nature of the sacrifice, as well as the heroic quality of Jesus,[*] are readily seen to be non-tragic. One of the fundamental questions raised by Greek tragedy is whether the forces governing the world and shaping human existence are just and good. In the Judaeo-Christian tradition, the posing of such a question is tantamount to blasphemy. This is necessarily the case for a religious tradition that posits the existence of a beneficent, omniscient, and omnipotent deity. If God is indeed, as the faithful describe Him, the conditions requisite for tragedy are largely precluded because with such a benevolent Being guiding the world there can neither be undeserved suffering nor irrational evil (the former would suggest malevolence on God's part, while the latter would indicate impotence). Moreover, the doctrine of grace, with its salvific implication, restricts further the possibility of real tragedy for Christianity. In fact, there is perhaps no single idea more thoroughly at odds with the Greek conception of tragedy than the notion of "grace" because implicitly grace is a promise of ultimate deliverance from tragic predicament. This does not mean, of course, that Christians are immunized from the calamities afflicting the general rank of humanity—they bleed and suffer just as readily as anyone else. But in the final analysis the atmosphere of inescapable doom that pervades the Greek sense of the tragic has no counterpart in Christianity. Life, notwithstanding its many tribulations, is a kind of proving ground for the Christian where suffering has purpose and value as a gauge of spiritual worthiness. Accordingly, the tears shed by a Christian are neither as bitter nor as desperate as those offered by an Oedipus or an Electra because behind Christian suffering there is an ultimate as-

---

[*] The indispensable precondition of heroism is mortality. Jesus may suffer death but as the man-God, he is ultimately victorious, and it is specifically this triumph over death which precludes his status as a hero.

surance that a good and loving God is prepared to heal the wounds and bestow an ultimate bliss. This is not the stuff of tragedy and the Greeks would have none of it.

Appendix III: Was Oedipus Deserving Of His Fate?

Many respectable modern scholars argue that the logic of Greek drama includes the necessity of "sin preceding the fall," i.e., that a tragic hero's "crimes" of character make his suffering appropriate. This view can boast an impressive pedigree in the sense that its origins are clearly traceable to Aristotle's *hamartia* doctrine. But when we attempt to apply these ideas to Oedipus, the greatest exemplar of human suffering in Greek tragedy, the precipitating sins are hard to identify. One of the more popular claims is that Oedipus' zealous demand for information, his unrelenting search for truth, constitutes a kind of Faustian obsession that legitimately brings disaster in its wake (see Knox 1957 and Krook 1969). But nothing in Oedipus' manner or conduct was inconsistent with a king's legitimate efforts to identify a murderer whose presence constituted a mortal threat to his entire realm. And even if his inquisitiveness was excessive, the misery he suffers is so disproportional to the offense, it is impossible to view this suffering as in any way correlate with the crime. Moreover, there is no flaw of character that leads Oedipus to kill his father and bed his mother. These are "fated" disasters over which Oedipus has no control. If there is a character flaw anywhere in this horrendous chain of events it lies with Laius who was specifically admonished by Apollo not to have children, but who sires Oedipus nevertheless. According to the logic of *hamartia*, Laius deserves what he gets on the road to Delphi but Oedipus is a sinless pawn in all this; a victim of blind, remorseless forces that gratuitously destroy his life.

For Sophocles then, "luckless Oedipus" exemplifies man's fate in a world rife with random afflictions, a world where unprovoked misery insinuates itself in many ways that make cure or rescue impossible. His is a fate that bears witness to the fact that all things mortal teeter in uncertain scales and that innocence does not always guarantee a just balance.

Chapter V

Thucydides and the Great War

*"The first page of Thucydides is the beginning of
all true history."*—D. Hume

Introduction – What is History?

There are many strains in Clio's song with the result that "history" can mean many things. If, for example, one were to define history as simply any effort to record events for the sake of future reference, then the work of the cave dwellers of Altamira and Lascaux might qualify as a kind of inaugural historiography. Similarly, the mantle of history might be extended to cover various annalistic compilations such as the Palermo Stele or the Gadd Chronicle. It might also be argued that certain portions of the Old Testament (e.g., the First Book of Kings and both Books of Samuel) are legitimately "historical" (see Mamigliano 115, Hornblower 13, and Barnes 22). But are these extended notions of history genuinely compatible with our modern understanding?

The answer to this question is generally "No," for the reason that the modern view of history is heavily indebted to Hellenism. Our term "history" comes from the Greek word, *historia* meaning "inquiry" or "investigation." This definition implies that by its very nature, "history," as conceived by the Greeks, involved activities of critical inquiry and analysis.[*] It did not seek to simply chronicle events but rather attempted to dissect and assay information in a manner unprecedented in the ancient world. Indeed, it can be said of the Greek historians, and in particular of Thucydides, that they comprise an entirely new genus of historical consciousness, the specific hallmarks of which include a strenuous commitment to factual accuracy, a secular/profane view of events in which supernatural interventions are minimized or denied, and an analytical spirit insistent upon exacting appraisal of relevant data. If these standards of Hellenic historiography sound strangely contemporary, it is because they continue to function canonically as modernity's idea of authentic history (see Collingwood 18). At the same time, these standards are also exclusionary of almost all of that which came before. The mere recording of events, no matter how extensive or detailed, does not constitute historiography.[†] Nor are the various theocratic narratives, common to the ancient oriental civilizations, compliant with the criteria established by Greek historical presentation—this, for the simple reason that faith often obscures fact and devotion tends to preclude analysis.[‡]

If then, we were to summarize the spirit of Greek historiography we might best describe it as fundamentally consistent with the scientific outlook of the Miletians (see Chapter 2). Saying this, however, we must also note that the fervent commitment to historical

---

[*] Castoriadis (114) observes that, "It is a striking fact that historiography properly speaking has existed only during two periods of human history: in ancient Greece and in modern Europe—that is, in the cases of the two societies where questioning of the existing institutions has occurred."

[†] The Egyptians were remarkably diligent analysts, but they were not historians. In fact, true history does not appear among the Egyptians before the priest Manetho in the 3rd century B.C. Significantly his work was written in Greek (Wilcken 309).

[‡] As Collingwood observes, many of those who preceded the Greeks were actually writing religion, not history (12).

truth probably came about as a result of a slow and by no means uncontested development. As is well-known, there are certain powerful anti-historical prejudices operating in the Greek mind. These tendencies, which function on both an ontological and epistemological level, must have significantly impeded the development of Greek historical consciousness. Specifically, there is a strong assumption among the Greeks that permanence is constitutive of reality, or conversely, that the transitory is less real than the immutable (see Armstrong and Markus 116). Historical events unfold in an ever-flowing temporal stream—a chronological variant of Heraclitus' flux—they are therefore less genuine than the enduring aspects of reality. In addition, the Greeks also believed that the ever-changing was fundamentally defiant of human comprehension. Men cannot know that which is continuously involved in transformation; knowledge implies permanence of subject matter. In great measure, this perspective underlies the theories of both the Eleatics and Plato and in a general sense, it also explains the Greek fondness for the enduring truths of the mathematical sciences.

The implications of all this for our analysis is clear—the Greek idea of history is the result of a conceptual evolution. Thucydides, who is without question the greatest figure in ancient historiography, had predecessors who helped refine and advance the techniques of historical reporting which ultimately receive their consummate expression in his <u>History of the Peloponnesian War</u>.[*] These precursive attempts at history tended to center around three distinct subject areas: geography, genealogy, and local history. The individuals associated with these early efforts, men such as Charon, Xanthus, Acusilaus, Hellanicus, etc., are for modern scholars, little

---

[*] Those unfamiliar with certain key details of this conflict are directed to the appendix at the end of this chapter.

more than names, given the loss of their works to time. There are however, two historians about whom we have more information. One is Herodotus, whom Cicero dubiously designated, the "father of history." But before we examine his achievements, a few words about a man who no doubt influenced him, Hecateus of Miletus.

Hecataeus (550-490 B.C.) merits our attention for several reasons. For one thing, he was the earliest *logographer*, i.e., the first to write of past events in prose style. More importantly, his work, although extant only in fragments, nevertheless reveals a critical spirit that would become a prime attribute of Greek historiography. In his <u>Genealogies</u>, for example, he says: "What I write here is the account which I consider to be true: for the stories of the Greeks are numerous, and in my opinion, ridiculous." Hecataeus was fully prepared to reject and/or reinterpret ancient tales that strained belief. Accordingly, he denies the possibility that Aegyptus could have had fifty sons and argues that Cerberus, the hound of Hades, was more likely reptilian than canine. These assessments do not begin to approximate the austere rationalism we will eventually encounter in the pages of Thucydides, but they do mark a nascent movement toward a standard of truth without parallel in antiquity.[*]

In turning next to Herodotus, we enter a new phase in the development of historical method and insight. Happily, Herodotus has left us a fully extant and detailed account of the Persian Wars. What this work reveals is a historian who is part raconteur, anxious to entertain his reader with dazzling tales of "…the great and amazing deeds displayed by both Greeks and barbarians," yet at the same time, a skeptic willing to challenge, evaluate, and reject what

---

[*] For all his skepticism, Hecataeus still did not escape the ridicule of Heraclitus who observed in referring to the historian that much learning does not guarantee intelligence (Diels Fr. 40).

the mass of men find convincing. It is precisely this eccentric blend of the fantastic and the scientific that led Gibbon to observe that Herodotus sometimes writes for children and sometimes for philosophers (see also Cicero De Legibus 1.5).

With regard to the fabulous, Herodotus, the storyteller, can rival almost anything found in the Homeric poems and for this reason he has been described as the "Homer" of the Persian Wars by at least one commentator (Bury 1958, 73-4). Among other things, his penchant for the fantastic includes: Arabian flying snakes (2.75), a fountain of youth among the Ethiopians (3.23), gold digging ants the size of foxes (3.102), cattle that walk backwards as they graze (4.183), and a Persian army so enormous that it drinks entire rivers dry (7.21). In addition, Herodotus continues to subscribe to many of the traditional religious beliefs. He is convinced, for example, that the gods do play a role in directing the affairs of men and specifically that the hubris-nemesis dynamic is a powerful force underlying the vicissitudes of history. Moreover, Herodotus also states, in a most unequivocal manner, that he has full faith in the veracity of oracles and that he is disinclined to question them when they are expressed in unambiguous language (8.77).

For all his credulity, there are nevertheless some important and genuinely critical dimensions to Herodotus' history. In Book VII, for example, he alerts his reader to the fact that although he feels bound to report the stories that have been presented to him, he feels no obligation to believe them (7.152). Applying this principle, Herodotus is prepared to question the substance of the ancient tale regarding Minos' naval hegemony (3.122)—something which not even Thucydides was prepared to do. In addition, Herodotus also merits praise for the principled objectivity with which he portrays the non-Hellenic peoples—especially the Persians. To his credit, Herodotus does not write a chauvinist history; he admires both the culture and the courage of the Persian foe. Detachment such as this is certainly an admirable and necessary quality in a historian. As it turns out, however, these unbigoted sentiments actually earned him the enmity of certain Greek commentators. In particular, Plutarch is quick to label him a *philobarbaros*, or "lover of barbarians," while simultaneously deploring what he saw as a pro-Athenian bias in the History.[*]

Thucydides and the Birth of History

Despite having composed a kind of prose epic, the fact remains Herodotus and his History were a necessary pre-condition for the critical/scientific achievements of Thucydides. Yet this is a point difficult to grasp as one begins to read the latter, because his manner is so advanced, so discerning, so entirely dedicated to the presentation of corroborated fact, that one has the impression of reading a modern historian, not a man born a mere two decades or so after Herodotus. Above all, in Thucydides we encounter a historian who has completely abandoned any aspiration to simply please the ear of his reader (1.21.1). His purpose instead, is didactic and toward this end, as we shall see, Thucydides makes a diligent and unremitting search for truth, the essence of his enterprise.

There are so many noteworthy dimensions to Thucydides' achievement; so much that merits detailed examination that narrowing the range of treatment becomes a considerable challenge. One area that cannot go unassessed, however, are the stylistic features of the History. The prose works of Thucydides are the most

---

[*] It may be that Plutarch's assaults were motivated by Boeotian pride. Herodotus notes that with few exceptions the Boeotians had "Medized" during the Persian Wars; i.e., they had supported Persia against the Greek cause. Plutarch may be out to discredit Herodotus, making him the "father of lies," not history, in an effort to exculpate his people (see "The Malice of Herodotus" in Moralia, esp. 847b-c).

complex in all of Greek literature (Hadas 123). In them we encounter elaborate parallelism, dramatic shifts in tense, and exotic new uses of words that are simply without parallel in any Greek author. These innovations, though certainly noteworthy, are not without their difficulties. On occasion they result in wordy muddles that not only torment modern translators, but even vexed and confounded the ancient commentators.[*] The origins of these bold linguistic experiments are no doubt related to the rarefied intellectual atmosphere in which Thucydides was operating. In his day, Athens had become a haven for experiment and heterodoxy—a city whose spirit was increasingly influenced by the innovative likes of Pericles, Anaxagoras, Phidias, Protagoras, and Euripides.[†] Traditional modes and orders could no longer restrain the provocative energies that began to transform Athens into "the school of Hellas." Thucydides was very much part of the great experimentalism of the late 5th century B.C., but at the same time his innovations were advanced in a literary style that remains, for all its complexity, subtle and decorous. Rarely, for example, do we find Thucydides attempting to bludgeon his reader with imperious, prescriptive statements. In fact, authorial intrusions of any kind are exceedingly rare in the History. What we discover instead, is an unobtrusive instruction quietly embedded in the narrative itself which gently leads the

---

[*] While acknowledging him to be the greatest historian, Dionysius of Halicarnassus nevertheless criticizes Thucydides for the obscurities created by his stylistic novelties (see Critical Essays, sections 13, 24, 35, 46, & 52). For a similar modern assessment see Gomme 2:131 and Abbott 227.

[†] No doubt the intellectual pluralism of 5th century Athens stimulated many exchanges across "disciplinary" lines. Scholars have long noted, for instance, the affinities between certain aspects of the History and Greek drama (see Ehrenberg 53; Cornford, Chapt. 8; and J.H. Finley 1967, Chapt. 1). There is also evidence to suggest that Thucydides was influenced by several treatises of the Hippocratic Corpus, such as *Prognostics*, *Epidemics*, and *Acute Diseases* (see Cochrane, esp. Chapt. 3).

reader to certain "necessary" conclusions.[*] It was precisely this tacit tutelage that earned Thucydides the high praise of Thomas Hobbes who observed, "...the narrative itself doth secretly instruct the reader, and more effectively than can be done by precept" (1843, xxii).

Beyond matters of style, Thucydides also merits praise for the consistent integrity of his presentation. Ancient Greece was an exceptionally contentious culture, even by modern standards. Had Thucydides used his History to promote a political cause, or to further some personal viewpoint, he would have been operating in a manner fully consistent with the polemical spirit of the Greeks. Instead, what we find is a remarkable neutrality and fairness of which there are numerous examples. As an Athenian, for instance, Thucydides might have engaged in partisan presentation as he drew the battle lines between Sparta and Athens. But, in fact, he never allows his evaluative scales to tilt one way or the other. The misdeeds of both people are presented fairly and accurately—the Spartan outrage against the Plataeans (3.68) is balanced by the outrageous brutality of the Athenians at Melos (5.85-116).

Again, as a member of the Athenian aristocracy, Thucydides might naturally have evidenced an oligarchic bias in the political assessments proffered in the History. But here, too, Thucydides remains not only non-prejudicial in his views, he actually registers strong disapproval of the oligarchs whenever the facts demanded such criticism (e.g., 6.39, 8.48, 8.65).

A further example of Thucydides' penchant for fairness is evident in his treatment of the Athenian statesman, Pericles. Thucy-

---

[*] The more than forty speeches presented in the History are also part of this instructional scheme. Their function is to indicate points of preeminent importance and to provide the reader with an opportunity for reflective pause.

dides was apparently related to the Philaidae, a powerful oligarchic family, which claimed such famous members as Miltiades, the hero of Marathon, and his son, Cimon. In the political struggles of Athens, a fierce rivalry arose between the Philaidae and the Alcmaeonidae, a clan which backed the demos against the city's oligarchic elements. Pericles was a member of this rival household but Thucydides' admiration for him is nevertheless extensive and unqualified. In fact, the portrait offered by the historian makes clear Thucydides' belief that Pericles was the greatest statesman in Greece.

A final, and perhaps more telling illustration of the qualities of fairness and objectivity to be found in the pages of Thucydides, stems from a pivotal moment in the historian's own life. In 424 B.C. Thucydides had been chosen *strategos* (general) and assigned the task of protecting Athenian interests on the coastline of Thrace—in particular, the Athenian colony of Amphipolis.[*] Unfortunately for our historian the city fell to the Spartan general Brasidas which resulted in Thucydides' banishment for twenty years. Now the incredible aspect of all this lies in the manner with which Thucydides reports the unhappy details of this episode (4.l04-107). One might expect that Thucydides would use this opportunity to engage in some form of exculpatory rhetoric; to shift responsibility to others, or at least to denounce the harsh penalty leveled at him by the Athenian people. In fact, we find none of this—no excuses, no pleading, and no protests. The methodical, dispassionate presentation of the facts is never for a moment disrupted by attempts at exoneration. This relentless commitment to impartiality remains

---

[*] The significance of Amphipolis for Athens was both strategic and material. As long as it remained in Athenian hands it barred further Lacedaemonian expansion in the region. In addition, Amphipolis was a key source of mineral wealth for Athens as well as of the timber needed for ship-building (see History 4.108.1).

one of the most remarkable features of the work and a clear demonstration that the idea of "history" has ascended to a new and unprecedented height (see Gomme 3:584).

A sweeping disregard for supernatural explanation is another noteworthy feature of the <u>History</u>. Thucydides' historiographical standards are strongly secular and as a result extra-human elements all but disappear as casual factors in the pages of his work (M.I. Finley 1959, 3)—as distinct from Herodotus for whom oracles, divine jealousy, and god-inspired delusion play a powerful role in explaining the vicissitudes of the Persian Wars.[*] In effect, Thucydides displays a thoroughly "godless grasp of war and politics" (Hornblower 43). Indeed, it has been observed correctly, that there is less metaphysical preoccupation in Thucydides than there is in the 16th century thought of Descartes (Cornford 74).[†]

Illustrations of Thucydides' commitment to a de-mystified view of the human condition are numerous and telling. During the *Epitaphios* (Funeral Oration), for instance, where one might reasonably anticipate some mention of supernatural forces, there is a conspicuous silence with regard to heaven, the gods, and religion. Similarly, the plague that devastated Athens at the war's outset is not the result of providential displeasure; Thucydides notes that the same scourge had affected Ethiopia, Egypt, and Libya (How might an Egyptian or Hebrew have explained this pestilence?). Moreover, the historian pointedly observes that the plague was non-discriminating in selecting its victims. Religious scruple provided

---

[*] For an alternative view regarding Thucydides' attitudes toward oracles, see Marinatos 1981.

[†] It should be noted that Thucydides does consider the role fortune (*tyche*) plays in human affairs, but he never associates fortune with the will of the gods. For him, chance or luck is a brute force that randomly imposes itself upon the affairs of men; *tyche* never equals nemesis.

no immunity; the pious died just as readily as the wicked, an observation repeated later in Thucydides' assessment of the fate of Nicias (7.86.5). In addition, Thucydides displays little patience with the childish fears associated with certain natural phenomena such as eclipses or thunderstorms. These are either explained away in terms of natural causation—the tidal wave at Euboea was the result of an earthquake (3.89.5)—or simply dismissed out of hand.

There is one event in the History, which, above all, might have lent itself to supernatural explanation, viz., the Athenian debacle at Syracuse. I suspect even some modern readers find it difficult not to ascribe this climactic episode to preternatural causes. Thucydides, however, has no trouble whatsoever in severing any causal link between the butchery at Melos, where the Athenians are guilty of a deplorable act of violence, and their disastrous defeat on Sicily. In fact, he makes clear his belief that Athenian ambitions as unbridled as they became, still might have been achieved were it not for a series of debilitating domestic intrigues (2.65.11 and 8.89.3). All of which indicates that divine retribution had, in Thucydides' view, nothing to do with the catastrophe; Melian blood does not haunt the Athenian expedition at Syracuse. For Thucydides, the weal and woe of life is determined by men, not gods.

There is no feature of Thucydides' work more admirable, more thoroughly consistent with the tenets of modern historiography, than his vehement commitment to *ekrebeia* (factual accuracy). Not only does this dedication distinguish Thucydides from all previous "historians," in great measure it also helps establish "truth" as the standard by which all genuine history would be judged.[*] The extent

---

[*] This point is well summarized by Dionysius of Halicanassus who states, "History is the High Priestess of Truth in our view, and Thucydides concerned himself above all with recording the truth, neither adding to nor subtracting from the facts unjustifiably..." (8). See also Lucian, How to Write History 41 and on the idea of truth as the

of Thucydides' resolve in these matters is made plain from the very outset of the History. He will not invent, nor will he rely upon those who have invented. Instead he will earnestly attempt to discover. His investigative energies are entirely committed to testing contemporary events not only because the current conflict is the "greatest motion" to ever stir the Hellenic world, but because by making contemporary events paramount he will have at his disposal a significant fund of concrete information which he could never hope to acquire for any earlier war (1.2). Only in this fashion will he be able to compose a proper history, i.e., one that does not rely upon poets and storytellers.[*]

Even with this approach however, the task of recording a historically credible account of the Peloponnesian War remains challenging. This is because the majority of men are not only slow to exert themselves in ascertaining the truth, they are at the same time incurably credulous (1.20). Even in matters of great national significance most people are content to rely upon unfounded reports and hearsay.[†]

As a corrective for these deficiencies, Thucydides informs his reader of the extraordinary measures he has taken to guarantee accuracy. In chapter twenty-two of the first book, Thucydides presents his reader with a methodological manifesto, which is without precedent in antiquity. It states that he considers it his "duty" to

---

standard of real history, see Cicero De Oratore 2.15 and Polybius, The Histories 12.12, 12.27, and 38.4)

[*] Thucydides questions the worth of Homer (1.10.3), corrects the History of Herodotus (1.20 and 1.21), and chastises the work of Hellanicus (1.97.2).

[†] The great example of this credulity involves the so-called Tyrannicides, Hermodius and Aristogeiton, who, according to Athenian lore, struck a blow for democracy by killing the tyrant Hipparchus. As it turns out, not only did their motives have more to do with erotic jealousy than political principle, but Hipparchus was not even tryant at the time of his death (1.20.2).

offer as factual only that material which has been rigorously researched and certified. He acknowledges the difficulty of relying upon eye- witness testimony, specifically noting the frequency of conflicting accounts and the possibility of prejudicial reporting. All of these factors are taken into account and laboriously weighed and balanced in an effort to arrive at the truth. With regard to his use of speeches, Thucydides readily admits these are reconstructions, but he also assures us that they adhere as closely as possible to what was actually said (1.22.1).

Declarations such as these have led certain modern commentators to credit Thucydides with having written the first true *Wissenschaft*, or "scientific" history. Along these same lines, some have attempted to make Thucydides the spiritual ancestor of the 19th century scientific historians—men like Niebuhr, Humbolt, Boeckh, Droysen, and above all, Leopold von Ranke.[*] While there is much that is suggestive of modernity in Thucydides, it would be wrong to conclude that he was a Ranke before his time (Schrimpton 46). A strictly empirical-scientific method in a form employed by modern historians is simply beyond the capacity of any 5th century thinker, even Thucydides, and while there is evidence that our historian did consult certain documents in a fashion analogous to modern researchers (such as the decree regulating the Melian expedition in 416 B.C.—see Tod 192), documentary analysis was at best a minor and sporadic aspect of his investigative technique. More than anything else, we must bear in mind Hobbes' keen observation regarding the subtle instruction Thucydides has woven into his narrative. There is, in other words, a normative agenda in Thucydides which

---

[*] H.E. Barnes states, "Leopold von Ranke, at the opening of the nineteenth century, did not expound more earnestly than Thucydides had at the close of the fifth century BC the basic tenet of scientific history, namely, the accuracy of data must be the foundation of true historical writing" (30).

means he was not content *"wie es eigentlich gewesen"* (simply to show how it really was), to use Ranke's famous definition of the historian's task.[*] We are entitled therefore, to laud Thucydides on many counts—his deft and elegant literary skills, his commitment to truth, his unwillingness to be bound by the standards and methods of the quasi-historians who came before—but it is best that our enthusiasm be tempered by an equally forthright acknowledgement of the discontinuities between "history" ancient and modern.

History as Pedagogy

It is no longer fashionable to expect history to yield up "lessons" by which current affairs can be gauged and future events anticipated.[†] Santayana warned that those who did not understand history were doomed to repeat past errors but modern man seems quite willing to take his chances. As a result, where history is studied at all today, the purpose is chiefly informational—dates, places, personalities. We no longer seek the grand designs and transcending principles because efforts in these directions tend to not only violate the rules of modern empiricism, they also imply a certain willingness to tolerate mystagogy; "history" in the sense of Spengler and Toynbee, is no longer permissible.

But what of the ancient Greeks? How did they approach historical fact versus historical principle? History viewed as a matter of

---

[*] G.G. Iggers has argued that our notions of scientific history as practiced by Ranke are false and that he was not the "soul-less positivist" he has been made out to be. In fact, Ranke agreed fundamentally with Hegel that true history and true philosophy are basically identical. If this assessment is correct then, Thucydides and Ranke, as we shall see, are indeed closely related but not in the manner ordinarily assumed (63-65).

[†] Hegel's observation that history teaches one lesson, viz., that men do not learn lessons from history is consistent with modern assessment. But Thucydides seems more inclined to argue that, "History is philosophy teaching by example," a view attributed to Dionysius of Halicarnassus by Bolingbroke.

factual curiosity, as simply the amassing of data, had little or no meaning for the Hellene. Facticity per se could not command the attention, much less the enthusiasm, of the Greek mind. In and of themselves, the facts were inert and relatively useless unless some larger pattern of meaning could be extracted from the details. The instinct for such meaning is not only a feature of Greek historiography. It is, in more general terms, a deeply ingrained feature of all Greek intellection. It bespeaks a native impulse for the generic, a longing to grasp the one within the many (Finley 1942, 50 and Starr 127).

Thucydides is certainly no exception to this rule; in fact, he is paradigmatically representative of the Greek demand for *to saphes* (principles). As we have seen, the factual integrity of Thucydides' narrative presentation is beyond serious question, but in the final analysis even these diligently validated facts are relegated to the status of ephemeral detail because the ultimate aspiration of the History is to arrive at the governing patterns that underlie the flow of events. In other words, Thucydides uses particular data as a means of passing beyond them, all in the hope of arriving at what is universal and permanent (deRomilly 1977, 16; Palmer 8; Jaeger 1:389; Grene 26; Finley 1942, 50). It is the desire to arrive at these larger, more lasting postulates that not only determines certain stylistic features of the work[*] but also lends The History a conceptual, philosophical quality that makes Thucydides something more than merely a gatherer of facts (Kagan 1994, 373; Strauss 236). In some sense then, Thucydides defies Aristotles' classic distinction between history and poetry in the Poetics (9.2-3), where he argues

---

[*] This explains, for instance, why Thucydides tends to de-emphasize biographical detail in his History. Unlike Herodotus, he displays a considerable impatience with the local, the personal, and the isolated episode (Abbott 166; Westlake 1968, 39; Cogan 242).

that poetry is more scientific and serious than history because the former presents what may occur in the future, while the latter merely records what has already been. Our historian was not content to simply relay, "what Alcibiades did and what he suffered." He was specifically committed to discovering the recurring patterns of history with an eye toward their prognostic value.

Now at this point it is necessary to define precisely what is meant by terms such as "principles," "patterns," "universals," etc. as applied by Thucydides. Experts have long noted that the ancient Greek view of history tended to be cyclical, as opposed to the modern conception which is rectilinear and therefore at least implicitly suggestive of some form of progress.[*] But the notion of "recurring cycles" as applied to the Greeks can be highly misleading if it is taken to indicate some scheme of lockstep determinism. The Greeks certainly preferred to take a broad view of life and they may also have been disinclined to allow "details" to discredit some neatly conceived theory but this does not mean they employed facile formulas to deny the complexities of a given subject matter. This is particularly true of Thucydides who, while entirely committed to revealing the inner logic of the Peloponnesian War, is nevertheless deeply sensitive to the specific conditions that shaped the conflict. As a result, Thucydides never claims to have discovered any "iron laws" of history. He never proffers any ready recipes to make sense of the politics, personalities, or military dynamics of the struggle. Nothing is ultimately fixed or final in the assessments he makes because Thucydides' greatness as a thinker includes a full grasp of and a deep appreciation for, the contingencies that

---

[*] The concept of historical progress is a uniquely modern idea which does not emerge until the Enlightenment era and is specifically associated with thinkers such as Locke, Montesquieu, Condorcet, Diderot, Voltaire, etc. (see Bury 1960 and deRomilly 1977, 1).

shape the human drama. More precisely, he understands that the recurring patterns of history are not ordained as part of some inexorable, metaphysical drama but are instead always subject to alteration by the vagaries of circumstance (deRomilly 1988, 103-4). What we are therefore entitled to describe in Thucydides is an explanatory method in which a limited lawfulness operates without ultimate guarantee. It is in this modest sense alone, that Thucydides hopes to aid us in understanding the past and in acquiring insight about the future.

Human Nature – The Bedrock of History

In the modern era, historians typically tend to frame their explanations for historical events in sociological or economic terms: America's political stability is a result of our nation's enormous middle class, while the collapse of the Soviet Union resulted from a socialist economic system incapable of competing against Western capitalism. While the Greeks were not entirely insensitive to these sorts of considerations, they were clearly not seen as the primary causes of historical phenomena. Instead, poets, dramatists, philosophers, and historians all accepted *anthropeia physis* (human nature) as the basic foundation of history. This essentially psychological perspective included the complete roster of human pathologies— fear, jealously, cruelty, delusion, stupidity. For the Greeks, these were the true engines of historical process constituting a core etiology that would forever shape the course of human events. This explains why Thucydides' brilliant diagnosis of the war's causes is unattended by any preventative formula. In the final analysis, Athenian ambitions, and the terrible destruction they engender for Athens and the rest of Greece, are essentially resistant to permanent remedy. Their excesses are simply reflective of what all men would do under similar circumstances and again, the reason is not foreign, it doesn't lie in the stars, but rather in the very nature of man himself. Human nature then, is the immutable foundation of history and by focusing on this root cause Thucydides can legitimately claim to have written a work of abiding significance (1.22.4; see Woodhead 168 and Pouncy 20).

Although *anthropeia physis* is a thematic constant that resonates throughout the entire History, Thucydides offers one particularly compelling summary of this motif in a speech presented by an Athenian delegation appearing in Sparta immediately prior to the war's outbreak. Their remarks, which include a series of adroit observations concerning the impulses that propel human affairs, have collectively come to be called the "Athenian thesis" (see esp. 1.75-77). The presentation begins by tracing the manner in which Athens has acquired her empire starting with the conspicuous heroism she displayed during the Persian Wars. At war's end the Hellenes were anxious for leadership against the possibility of future barbarian incursion but Sparta shrank from her responsibilities and the allies turned instead to Athens. The Delian League was established under these conditions, but the Athenians soon found themselves "compelled" by circumstances to convert the alliance into an empire, to move from *hegemonia* to *arche*. One of the terms used by Thucydides to convey the notion of compulsion is *nikethentes* which literally suggests being "overwhelmed," i.e., helpless to do otherwise. In particular, the Athenians cite three factors that "drove" them to become a tyrant city—fear, honor, and self-interest (1.75.3 and 1.76.2).* There is nothing particularly remark-

---

* This statement bears a striking resemblance to several key passages in Hobbes' Leviathan. In particular, see 1.13 where Hobbes identifies competition, diffidence, and glory as the three factors that produce conflict between men (cf. Johnson 1993, who argues against these sorts of comparisons).

able about any of this according to the Athenians. They have simply complied with the dictates of human nature and have done what anyone else, under similar circumstances, would have done because any state enjoying power will naturally press its advantage to the limit.

And what of the matter of justice? How do considerations of right and fairness figure in the Athenian thesis? Pleas of justice are always disregarded by those possessing might. No one in a position to secure his aims by strength will ever be deterred from doing so by moral scruple. In this respect, Thucydides directly anticipates the views put forth later by Thrasymachus and Callicles in the Platonic dialogues. In addition, the Athenians present what they see as an eternal logic that will forever govern relations between the weak and the strong: the former, irrespective of right, must submit to the latter. In addressing this point, Thucydides raises an issue that is not only key to his work but was also apparently an object of ongoing debate and analysis among the Greeks from earliest times. In Hesiod, for example, we are told of an exchange between a hawk and a nightingale that reads like a poetic equivalent of the Melian dialogue. The latter, having been seized by the Hawk, cries out pitifully. The Hawk responds:

> "Miserable thing, why do you cry out? One far stronger than you now holds you fast, and you must go wherever I take you, songstress as you are. And if I please I will make my meal of you, or let you go. He is a fool who tries to withstand the stronger, for he does not get the mastery and suffers pain besides his shame" (Works and Days 205-210).

A similar parable is contained in Aristotle's <u>Politics</u> where a fable ascribed to the Cynic Anthisthenes is mentioned in which lions and hares discourse on the merits of equality. The lions debunk claims of equity on the part of weaker species by asking, "Where are your claws and teeth?" (3.8.2.).[*] The message is clear, and it is one that appears again and again in the <u>History</u>: the issue of justice and right can only arise where the power to compel is held equally by both sides. In the real world, one either controls or serves, dominates or is dominated, because human nature will always enfranchise advantage at the expense of justice.[†]

What we discover then is that "All roads lead back to the Athenian thesis" (Orwin 86).[‡] During the Mytilenian debate for instance, Diodotus notes that the rebellious islanders cannot be faulted for their actions because all men are prone to transgression when they see opportunity for advantage, and no system of penalties is powerful enough to deter such impulses (3.45-46). Again, at a conference at Gela, the Syracusan patriot Hermocrates is prepared to excuse Athens' imperial ambitions toward Sicily because these aspirations are simply "an instinct of man's nature" (4.61.5). And finally, the *locus classicus* of the Athenian thesis, the Melian debate, where we are told that both gods and men always, by a necessity of nature, rule when they have the power to do so, with the

---

[*] Hesiod notes that "justice" is a special gift conferred upon humanity by Zeus designed to prevent men from devouring one another like wild animals (<u>Works and Days</u> 275-280). The Realpolitik of Thucydides' History indicates how impotent this gift is in fact.

[†] Even prior to its formal annunciation in the speech at Sparta, there are imitations of the Athenian thesis as early as the "Archeology," i.e., the introductory sections of the <u>History</u> (see 1.8.3).

[‡] These same ideas are also found in the one surviving satyr play of Euripides, *Cyclops*.

result that "the powerful exact what they can, while the weak yield what they must" (5.89.1).

These then are the chief characteristics of the Athenian thesis, a unifying thread that lends texture and substance to the entire <u>History</u> but there is something more. In addition to man's rapacious urge to maximize his own advantage and the corresponding tendency to ignore the dictates of justice, piety, and moderation, men are also according to Thucydides, highly susceptible to the seductions of *elpis* (hope). The modern reader soon realizes that the <u>History</u> employs this term in a fashion significantly different from most contemporary usages. Where we tend to see "hope" as a sustainer of the human spirit in the face of adversity, Thucydides sees *elpis* as a whore. She is the great deceiver, the rotter of minds and the thief of good sense and rational calculation who fraudulently converts gray reality into rose-colored "truth." As a conjurer of illusive wish she blinds us, making the impetuous and reckless seem reasonable and safe with the result that men seek that which can only result in disaster and ruin.[*] Once inspired by this treacherous beguiler, not even the threat of death is capable of restoring an accurate grasp of reality (3.45 and 5.103).[†]

The significance of *elpis* in human affairs is established definitively by Thucydides in his treatment of Athenian designs toward Sicily. Earlier, during the negotiations between Sparta and Athens involving those captured at Sphacteria, the Spartans had warned the

---

[*] Thucydides' views of *elpis* cast the story of Pandora's box in a new light. Humanity should be comforted not because hope remains available, but rather because hope, the heaviest ill the gods could array against mankind, did not escape with the other evils. Greek tragedy presents hope in both a positive (*Prometheus Bound* 250-253) and a Thucydidean fashion (*Antigone* 668-670).

[†] Here Thucydides and Hobbes seem to part company. The latter saw the fear of death as the most powerful of human passions, but Thucydides presents *elpis* as even more compelling than *phobos*.

triumphant Athenians not to allow their unexpected good fortune to fuel their hopes for the future (4.17.4-5). This advice is ignored and instead of enjoying their largesse, the Athenians begin to recklessly calculate future blessings. Flushed by their position of relative advantage, the Athenians manifest a mad dream of western expansion that includes not only Sicily but perhaps even Italy and Carthage (see 6.15.2; 6.90.2-3; also Aristophanes' Knights 174 and 1303)—and all this before having properly subdued the still formidable roster of foes in Greece.

False hope nourished by momentary advantage also stands at the center of the Sicilian debate immediately preceding the expedition. Nicias is cast as the voice of reason. He warns the Athenians not to reach out for another empire before the one they have has been properly secured.[*] He also notes that the Spartans, despite their recent humiliation, are far from finished and that Athens must resist its "morbid craving for what is out of reach" (6.13.1). For his part, Alcibiades sees the expedition as a priceless opportunity for gain and glory and warns that a state like Athens must forever remain active and enterprising; for a tyrant city, peace is inimical to survival—Athens must either expand or perish (6.18.6-7).[†] The assembly finds this logic irresistibly intoxicating and despite a last ditch effort by Nicias to sober Athenian ambition by demanding an armament of unprecedented magnitude, the people endorse the folly proposed by Alcibiades. Indeed, the mental state at Athens is so delusional at this point that Nicias' attempt to dissuade the Athenians actually titillates them further; the more immense the

---

[*] On this point, Nicias echoes the sage advice of Pericles (2.65.7).

[†] Here Alcibiades anticipates directly the view of Machiavelli (see Prince, Chapt. 3; Discourses 1.1; cf. Aristotle, Politics 7.13.15).

undertaking, the more urgently Athens desires it (6.24.3).[*] I have argued above that Sicily and Melos are not linked by any divinely inspired compensatory scheme, but this should not suggest there is no relation whatsoever. Both Athenians and Melians have been lured to the rocks by the siren song of hope: one risked everything on the misguided view that the gods and allies rescue those with just cause, while the others had their wits stolen by the specter of grand enterprise compounded by immoderate desires.

Thucydides does not present human nature as a decorative detail. It is offered instead as the stubborn and irreducible substructure of history. In a sense, he sees the tendencies contained in the Athenian thesis as forces of nature in comparison to which the restraints of reason and justice are paltry and impotent. This is so because men rarely chart the course of their lives by appealing to neutral and dispassionate logic. Desire, typically violent and self-serving, is what too often determines human option. Thucydides does accept, however, the possibility of exceptions to this rule. The luster with which Pericles shines forth from the pages of the <u>History</u> makes this clear. Nevertheless, Pericles and his like are extraordinary exceptions, because rational and moderate voices rarely register with humankind.

These observations, as brilliantly developed and presented as they are, do not constitute the limit of Thucydides' insights regarding human nature. He is also thoroughly conversant with what these points imply for the sociopolitical domain. In particular, Thucydides is acutely aware of the fundamental fragility of society, of the ease with which the bonds uniting human beings in civilized

---

[*] Thucydides stresses this point by his choice of words. When describing Athenian eagerness, instead of using *pothos*, meaning "longing" or "yearning," he uses *eros* to emphasize the passionate, if not irrational quality of the Athenians at this moment.

existence can be tattered and frayed. The catalyst for this sort of disintegration is above all war, the "rough schoolmaster" that empowers cruelty and depravity to the point where man becomes wolf to man. The Corcyrean stasis is perhaps Thucydides' most famous illustration of the resulting horrors; a situation in which even human communication is perverted by violence and treachery (3.82).[*] Add to this the savage episodes of Plataea, Thyrea, Scione, Melos, and most of all the mindless blood-lust of Mycalessus[†] and Thucydides' point is only too clear. The human condition includes moments of moral anesthetization in which madness can flow like a river sweeping before it all that is seemly, honorable, and right.

Conclusion

Early in the <u>History</u>, Thucydides informs his reader that the events which have taken place will, in all likelihood, occur again in the same or similar fashion (1.22.4). This bodeful observation could only be made by a historian who believed he was something more than a mere compiler of facts; a man confident he had pierced the veil of history and consequently possessed genuine insight regarding the march of human events. This does not mean that Thucydides claimed to have discovered Hegel's "cunning of history" or that he subscribed to some Stoic-like scheme of ordained recurrence. The prediction stems instead from the belief that all history is contingent upon human nature and that this foundation is essen-

---

[*] This is a particularly significant observation because the Greeks saw language as a major source of demarcation between man and beast; debasement of language is a debasement of humanity itself (see Isocrates, <u>Panegyricus</u> 48 and <u>Nicocles</u> 5; also Aristotle, <u>Politics</u> 1.1.10).

[†] In describing this massacre by Thracian mercenaries, Thucydides departs momentarily from his role as icy analyst and expresses indignation over the gratuitous slaughter (7.29; see Gomme 4.410).

tial and everlasting. Of course, specific circumstances will alter with time; Thucydides would have been the first to acknowledge that the discontinuities between classical antiquity and the modern world were massive and preclude the possibility of uncomplicated analogizing. But the broad outlines of history, the basic rhythm and cadence, remain timeless according to Thucydides because they are eternally linked to the persistent and irremediable urgings of the human spirit.

Thucydides is also convinced these unrelenting propensities typically incline humanity toward the pathological. In particular, he believed the majority of men, by their very nature, seek to maximize power and advantage and in so doing routinely bring themselves to grief. For Thucydides this failing is the crux of the human condition, or better, the human dilemma, because the quest for power entails a kind of Faustian bargain in which the hunter becomes the quarry.[*] The goal of human agency, the desire to realize one's potentials in life, makes power an indispensable ingredient in a rich and fulfilled existence. Having acquired power however, most will misapply it, defiling in the process not only the rule of law, but even the most rudimentary norms of human decency. There are occasional exceptions—the majestic restraint of Pericles is Thucydides' prime illustration of how power should be managed. The difficulty is that Cleon, not Pericles, is the generic type, the "all too human" representative of the race. Among such men as these the constructive potentials of power are disastrously subverted and in the end become a source of injustice and misery for all concerned.

---

[*] Thucydides believes that all men by nature seek to possess power, but in the end it is often the case that power comes to possess them. This seems to be the implication of Pericles' remarks at 2.63.2.

In presenting these and all other points, Thucydides maintains a sobriety bordering on resignation. Nowhere are we offered any techniques to make gentle the human heart, nor are we ever encouraged to plead the will of heaven for relief in these matters. Indeed, for contemporary readers, fond as we are of our notions of "progress," the pages of Thucydides appear more than a bit gloomy. Here we need to remember that our conception of human advancement is very different than that of the ancient Greeks. Modernity tends to measure progress in terms of technological breakthroughs and material prosperity. But the Hellenes would have scoffed at any idea of progress that failed to address the brutalities that continue to plague humankind. Were he here today, Thucydides would surely remind us that man is at best a semi-domesticated creature, that civilization is skin deep, and that men are by nature strongly disinclined to convert swords into plowshares. Moreover, he would undoubtedly point to the fact that while we may have split the atom and are now capable of littering the modern landscape with all manner of gadgets and contraptions, we are still not one jot closer to having lions lie down with lambs. For Thucydides, human nature is a recalcitrant malady that will ceaselessly register its appalling edicts—a point to which the unprecedented horrors of the 20th century bear grim testimony. Viewed from these perspectives, Thucydides' message is clear: the History of the Peloponnesian War is not an isolated record of human conflict, not some period piece unique to the 5th century B.C.. It is instead, as Thucydides himself argued, "a possession for all time" and as is the case in all histories of profound and lasting significance, Clio's song invariably includes the melancholy strains of her sister, Melpomene, the muse of tragedy.

Appendix*

Causation

In reading Thucydides it is difficult not to arrive at the conclusion that the Greeks were a people bent on self-destruction. Indeed, one could argue that no other people in history has been more ready to measure arms against themselves than the ancient Greeks. In this light, the Peloponnesian War is simply the most spectacular example of a fierce internecine instinct that plagued Hellas throughout most of its history. Exactly why a people united by language, cultural tradition, and historical experience would engage so consistently in fratricidal strife is an intriguing question, but it is not one that specifically concerns Thucydides who instead focuses the bulk of his effort upon diagnosing the precise origins of the great war.

As we might expect from a man of his genius, Thucydides looks beyond the obvious and prosaic range of possible explanations. This war is not, for example, the product of inter-tribal animosity (i.e., Ionian Greek v. Dorian Greek). Nor is the conflict attributable to ideological antagonisms such as those that might occur between democratic and oligarchic regimes. Not even an economic interpretation can furnish the genuine cause of this conflict according to Thucydides for whom the *alethestate prophasis* (the true cause) is related to a long and complex series of events which in turn have their origin in the nature of man himself.

---

* What follows is by no means a comprehensive summary of the Peloponnesian War. It is rather an overview of certain key events and themes essential to a proper comprehension of the war as seen by Thucydides.

Almost immediately after the conclusion of the Persian Wars, relations between Athens and Sparta began to deteriorate. Minus the threat of the Great King's army, the cooperative impulse waned rapidly among the Greeks who soon gave vent to their traditional jealousies and suspicions. In no small measure, this reversion was advanced by Athens' penchant for provocative enterprise—the very sort of restless dynamism Corinth would later decry in her demands for full-scale military action against the Athenians (1.70). On the domestic scene, for example, Athens aggressively sought to expand her influence in central Greece; to gain control of the strategically significant Megarid; and to establish a series of treaty relations that Sparta and her allies could only see as inimical to their interests. In addition, as if this were not enough, Athenian audacity included a number of daring foreign campaigns in places as far afield as Cyprus and Egypt. In the end, most of this adventurism failed to yield Athens any lasting fruit. What it did succeed in producing was an atmosphere thick with tension and ill-will in which many Greek states, including Corinth, Thebes, Megara, Aegina, as well as Sparta became convinced that Athens was a menace whose ambitions knew no limit.

The mounting frictions of this pre-war period were contained temporarily by the "Thirty Year Peace," a feebly palliative measure that did nothing more than delay the impending cataclysm. Tensions remained high throughout the truce but were eventually brought to a boil by three specific incidents: The Corcyrean affair, the Megarian Decree, and the Athenian ultimatum and subsequent siege of Potidaea. Unlike many of his contemporaries, Thucydides did not believe that these situations were the ultimate basis for the war and he is quick to make a distinction between these *aitiai*, or immediate factors, versus the *prophasis*, that is, the genuine, deep-seated cause. In other words, there were inciting or contributory events and there was an authentic determinant which had, by implication, escaped the understanding of popular opinion. Athenian support for Corcyra[*] which resulted in direct conflict between Athens and Corinth was certainly a serious source of the latter's implacable hatred of Athens but this in itself did not "cause" the war. Nor did the Megarian Decree, which apparently barred Megara from the Athenian market[†] and all of the ports of the empire.[‡] Even the Athenian response to Corinthian and Spartan machinations at Potidaea cannot be taken, according to Thucydides, as anything more than a symptom of the foundational cause that subsequently plunged the Greek world into blood.

The true *causus belli*, according to Thucydides, had to do with the disruption of Greece's strategic balance of power. The Spartans and their allies were increasingly dismayed by the relentless attempts of Athens to expand her domain and influence; it did indeed appear that they were "born neither to have peace themselves nor to let other men have it." In essence then, it was not the naval engagement at Sybota or the investment of Potidaea that propelled the Greeks along their disastrous path. In Thucydides' opinion, it was something far more elemental, far more human, that made this conflict inevitable.[§] It was fear (1.23.6 and 1.88). Sparta, intimidated

---

[*] Athens could not allow the second largest fleet in Greece (Corcyra's) to fall into the hands of her Corinthian opponents. Thus, she supports Corcyra in the form of an *epimachia*, a defensive alliance, against her metropolis, Corinth.

[†] For a detailed and insightful analysis of the decree's meaning see de Ste. Croix 1989, chapt. 7, and Appendix XXXV.

[‡] Thucydides does not view the Megarian Decree as terribly significant but common opinion apparently held the interdict as the chief cause of the war. This impression may stem from the comedic stage, specifically Aristophanes (see Acharnians 525-535 and Peace 609-610).

[§] Kagan disagrees with Thucydides and the bulk of historians regarding the war's inevitability (see Kagan 1994, Chapt. 20).

by the scope of Athenian ambition, had concluded that her enemy's expansive lusts could be curbed only by force of arms and that action must be taken now before Athens grew any stronger. True to this outlook and method, Thucydides refuses to identify the cause of the war with what he sees as mere contingencies. Instead, he focuses upon that perennial substratum from which all historical explanation is ultimately derived—human nature, the chief impulses of which are fear, honor, and self-interest (1.76.2).

A Tale of Two Cities

Although the Peloponnesian War was a pan-Hellenic struggle, there were two "great powers" in particular that dominated the political, military, and diplomatic affairs of the period: Athens and Sparta. Despite their fundamental "Greekness," these two people could not be more different in terms of customs, outlook, and ethos and it is these divergencies that explain many of the peculiar rhythms of the conflict. For Thucydides, the vast gap separating the Athenian and Spartan ways of life was reducible to a single image, that between rest and motion. The natural inclination of the Spartans, notwithstanding their well-earned reputation as fighters, was to shrink from the adventurism to which the Athenians were prone. By comparison, they seemed slow, dilatory, and cautious almost to the point of paralysis. This predilection for unruffled inactivity causes considerable frustration among Sparta's allies, particularly the Corinthians, who draw some highly invidious comparisons between their Peloponnesian ally and Athens (1.70)—at one point chiding them as "old fashioned" (1.70.2). In fairness to Sparta, however, one must note that a good deal of this hesitancy was related to the omnipresent threat of Helot insurgency and the equally intractable animosities of Argos. Any major, long-term military commitment on Sparta's part had to be carefully weighed against the prospect of unleashing hostile elements at home.

By comparison, the Athenians were vital, impetuous, and opportunistic (1.70, 7.21, 8.96).[*] Thucydides accents these points when he uses the term *polypragmosyne* to describe the Athenian character, meaning "mettlesomeness" or "busybodiness" (6.87.3; see Ehrenberg 1957). To be Athenian meant being inclined to intrude and disrupt; by their very nature Athenians were the irrepressible assailants of the *status quo*.[†] Unfortunately for Sparta, her phlegmatic manner proved to be an apt foil for Athenian audacity and Thucydides clearly believes that in this matching of Spartan torpidity with Athenian energy lies the explanation for much of the latter's success in the war (8.96.5).[‡] Only when Athens confronts another large, vigorous democracy (Syracuse) does she encounter a force capable of thwarting her dynamism.

The Double Plague

There are two plagues described by Thucydides. The first, and more readily acknowledged pestilence, despoils the flesh of men, while the second devastates the spirit. As the war began, the Athenians implemented Pericles' attritional strategy; the customary clash of hoplite formations would be waived. Rather than take the

---

[*] Although not all Athenians can be so described. There is an interesting role-reversal in the case of two key figures in the History; the Athenian general Nicias displays a timidity characteristic of the Spartans, while the Spartan general, Brasidas, distinguishes himself in a brash Athenian fashion.

[†] As Clifford Orwin puts it, "Owls hoot, olives ripen, Athenians harry their neighbors" (44).

[‡] The key advantage the Spartans enjoy is domestic tranquility. Unlike the rest of Greece, Sparta is spared the nightmare of *stasis*, which proves to be her greatest asset in the war.

field against the Peloponnesians, the Athenians elected to remain safe behind their walls,[*] linked to the outside world by the unimpeded activities of her fleet. As a defensive "island," with vast financial resources,[†] Athens sought to protract the war and slowly erode the military resolve of her enemies. Pericles, ever loyal to his moderate nature, did not seek a smashing victory against Sparta—stalemate would be triumph enough.

In principle, this approach should have produced the results anticipated by Pericles, viz., an opponent frustrated, exhausted, and drained of resources. The actual results were quite different however, particularly for Athens. Not even Pericles, whose prescience is specifically noted by Thucydides (2.65.5), could foresee the dire health consequences inherent in massing the majority of Athenians behind the city's walls. Scholars have long debated the exact nature of the pestilence, everything from measles to ergotism has been proposed (see Gomme 2:150-2). In all probability however, it was typhus that ravaged Athens, the transmission of which was no doubt facilitated by the overcrowding.

The clinical precision with which the epidemic's pathology is described (2.49) remains one of the most vivid illustrations of Thucydides' keen powers of observation, as well as his fierce commitment to detailed accuracy. The same can be said for his analysis of the social consequences wrought by the plague. Not only did the

---

[*] This strategy was not only a major departure from traditional Greek military tactics, it was also inconsistent with the nature of Athens itself—the city of "motion" pent-up behind its own walls.

[†] The fiscal advantage enjoyed by Athens is made clear by Thucydides (1.83.2; 1.52.1; 2.13.3). As a naval power, however, her expenses were far greater than those of the infantry-based Peloponnesian forces. Kagan (1991, 236-7) estimates Athenian war expenses as at least two thousand talents per year. One thing is absolutely clear from this data; no one, including the Athenians, anticipated a war lasting ten years, much less twenty-seven.

disease kill a large portion of the city's population (perhaps one third), it also engendered a lawlessness among the Athenians, a kind of "state of nature," in which the restraints of custom and propriety were abandoned (2.52-2.53). The uncertainties of tomorrow led men to live for today; the pleasures of the moment were indulged wrecklessly and without limit. Fear of the laws, even fear of the gods, could not dispose men to civilized conduct. The lesson proffered here by Thucydides is clear, and it is a point he makes often: There is an alarming degenerative tendency in the human spirit—beneath the surface of our noble institutions and fine words, there lurks something sinister and wanton.

The other plague analyzed by Thucydides is not microbial in nature; it doesn't manifest itself with ulcerations or raging fevers. Rather, this disease discloses its fatal specter by way of social divisions and murderous hatreds. In short, the second plague is *stasis*, i.e., factional strife within the polis. The animosities engendered by this civic malady dissolve the unitive sinews of society, including those hallowed ties (family, friends, and community) that make civilized existence possible (3.82).[*] Thucydides' classical illustration of these tendencies is found at Corcyra where every depravity of human nature is given vent; where neither law nor religion could restrain the bloody atrocities men visited upon one another in an effort to advance the cause of partisan rivalry. The depths of this deterioration became so profound, according to Thucydides, that

---

[*] The ferocity of these internecine struggles is well summarized by G.M. Calhoun who notes the frequency with which *prodasia* or treasonous betrayal figured in Greek politics: "To the Greek, to be ruled by his political opponent was an intolerable humiliation, to be averted at any cost, even if it became necessary to deliver his state into the hands of its foemen... In nearly every instance in which an attack upon a city is described, there is some allusion to parties within the city walls who are making preparations to betray the city into the hands of the enemy..." (141).

even language, that most uniquely human attribute, was subverted by the violence and extremism of the moment (3.82.4).

During the early phases of the war, Athens had shown itself largely immune to the effects of this factional plague. In great measure, her resistance stemmed from the quality of leadership the city enjoyed under Pericles who, by dint of political genius and personal conduct, was able to keep the Athenians focused on the common good. After his death, however, the quality of leadership declined conspicuously (see below); public service was increasingly displaced by private ambition and in Thucydides' opinion, it is this self-centeredness that produced the civil discord that cost Athens the war (2.65.6-ll).

Leadership

There are two individuals in particular upon whom Thucydides heaps unstinting praise in the History—Themistocles and Pericles.[*] Although the former died nearly thirty years before the outbreak of the war, his vision of Athenian greatness continued to inspire and animate Athenian policy throughout our period and beyond.[†] For Thucydides, Themistocles possessed an Odyssean cunning; an uncanny ability to lift the veil from future events and devise plans that would advance Athenian interests. It was specifically this prognostic capacity that led Themistocles to insist upon the fortification of the Piraeus and ultimately to formulate the thalossocratic strategy that resulted in the Athenian empire (1.93.4).

---

[*] Antiphon also receives high marks from Thucydides (8.68.1).

[†] Themistocles was the genius behind Athenian naval strategy, which became an ongoing obsession at Athens. Long after her defeat in the Peloponnesian War, she continued to manifest a thalossocratic madness as we read in the plaintive pages of Isocrates (see Peace esp. 101-105).

If then, Themistocles can be seen as the architect of Athenian imperialism, a view clearly held by Thucydides, it was Pericles who applied the blueprint. No other man in Athenian history so thoroughly dominated the civic affairs of the city—a particularly remarkable achievement given the political volatility to which Athens was prone. For more than thirty years (461-429 B.C.), Pericles was the fundamental force behind every major policy decision of the Athenians. His ascendancy in these matters was so complete that Thucydides refers to him as *protos aner*, the "first man," suggesting by this phrase that Athens was actually a democracy in name only (2.65.9). What the state had in fact become, as a result of the extraordinary leadership of this individual, was a kind of annually reestablished kingship.* Thucydides is deeply impressed by this achievement and as a result he admiringly presents the special qualities that enable Pericles to attain his unique status. Some of these talents are revealed in a speech in which Pericles defends himself against a disgruntled citizenry intent upon holding him accountable for their war-related miseries. Here we are told of four attributes of effective leadership: 1) an ability to determine a correct course of action, 2) a capacity to articulate these measures effectively to the people, 3) an abiding loyalty to the state, and 4) incorruptibility (2.60.5-6). Not only did Pericles possess these virtues "more than other men," he also projected a consistent air of decency and high-mindedness, so much so that he received the nickname "Olympian" among the Athenians. Furthermore, he was the only political figure in Athens with the courage and the capacity to remonstrate the people when necessary. Unlike the other leaders, particularly his immediate successors who routinely pandered to

---

* Starting in the year 443 B.C., Pericles was elected to fifteen consecutive generalships.

the demos, Pericles alone successfully instructed and restrained the people; where the others flattered, he alone dared to speak the truth (2.65.8).[*]

Beyond the considerable gifts he put at the disposal of Athens, there was one thing above all else that Pericles offered his people—a vision of "great politics." In a spirit reminiscent of Homer, Pericles challenged the Athenians to eschew the insipid and transitory objectives prized by others. Instead, he counseled them to set their sights on a fuller region where inspired achievements live on forever. Pericles acknowledges that there are some serious risks associated with his ideal but he reminds Athens that the greatest honors accrue only to those willing to run the greatest risks (1.144.3).[†] By encouraging the Athenians to seek the glow of imperishable glory, Pericles not only registers the measure of his own greatness, he simultaneously illustrates the difference between a statesman and a mere politician.

If Pericles was indeed the "Olympian," then the majority of his successors are perhaps best described as "chthonic." In particular men like Cleophon, Hyperbolus, and Cleon[‡] not only abandon the Periclean paradigm, they positively disfigure it on behalf of selfish advancement and personal gain. In comparison to the likes of Themistocles, Cimon, and Pericles these men are little more than civic opportunists whose methods and purposes indicate a near to-

---

[*] See also Plutarch, Pericles 15.2-3, and for a very different assessment of Pericles, see Plato's Gorgias 518e-519a.

[†] A point unappreciated by Nicias whose dilatory manner costs Athens dearly, particularly at Syracuse. In essence, he is a Spartan in Athenian clothing.

[‡] Thucydides presents Cleon as an archetype for the political deterioration of Athenian politics. He is one of the few figures in our text who is directly censured by the historian (3.36.6; 4.27.4; 5.16.1). This has prompted some to speculate that Cleon may have played a key role in Thucydides' banishment.

tal disregard for the commonweal. Predictably, these developments had an immediate impact upon the tenor of Athenian politics. The moderate strategies and lofty idealism of Pericles were rapidly displaced by depraved appeals to violence and cruelty; justice became the will of the stronger. What in effect Thucydides presents here in the <u>History</u> is a political equivalent of Gresham's Law: the precious currency minted by Pericles is debased and driven out by mountebanks and demagogues.

All of this leads to one rather obvious bit of speculation, viz., what would have happened had Pericles lived beyond the first two and one half years of the war? We can only guess of course, but it is difficult to imagine Pericles endorsing the horrid mistreatment of the Melians or the intemperate folly of the Sicilian campaign. In addition, knowing what we do of his character and policies, it is inconceivable that Pericles would have spurned the Spartan peace offer made during the winter of 425-424 B.C..

The Athenian Experiment

The ancient world had a surprisingly large number of impressive cities, many of which were far older, larger, and vastly more affluent than Athens. Yet Athens' place in history is secure, every bit as secure as that of Ur, Babylon, or Nineveh. The reason for this rests in large part upon an experiment, which began at Athens in the early 6th century B.C. and reached its zenith during the Periclean era. Much of this venture was directly related to a series of political reforms that eventually resulted in "democracy." But the experiment to which I refer involved something far larger than a refashioning of government—democracy was a necessary precondition but it did not encompass the full range of Athenian aspirations in this regard. What in fact Athens sought was the creation of an entirely new environment dedicated to releasing the immense and hitherto untapped energies of the individual. The Athenian experiment, in short, was nothing less than an attempt at spiritual manumission premised upon the belief that when men[*] were fully and truly liberated, they were not only capable of forging their own destinies, they could also achieve greatness. It was the formulation of this ideal and the degree to which the Athenians realized it, that explains Athens' place on the roster of fabled cities.

But what has this to do with Thucydides and the Peloponnesian War? The answer lies in a speech, the *Epitaphios* or funeral oration, composed by the historian and attributed to Pericles.[†] It is in the opinion of many, a masterpiece, perhaps the greatest speech ever composed in Western literature. But the key to this work lies not in its stylistic perfections, which are considerable, but rather in its message which exuberantly declares the virtues of the "open society" and the infinite potentials of liberated humanity. In the speech Pericles draws a series of comparisons between the Athenian and Spartan ways of life. Unlike their opponents, who have secured the loyalties of the people through a mind-dulling and brutal discipline, Athens enlisted the commitment of its citizenry by creating a city worthy of fidelity and sacrifice; a city in which the potentials of individual personality are given opportunity to flower in ways entirely disparate with the harsh and dehumanizing rigors of the Spartan *agoge*. Moreover, Athens provided its people with a

---

[*] Greek prejudice against women is clearly seen in the funeral oration. The only formula for glory Pericles offers the widows of those recently slain is to remain decorously invisible within Athenian society (2.45.2).

[†] The various speeches, of which there are more than forty in the History, are not offered by Thucydides as literal reconstructions. They are acknowledged as his own creations but composed in fundamental compliance with the facts (1.22.1-2).

chance to attain the most precious of all gifts—an opportunity to challenge the limits of human finitude. By working on behalf of the city's eternal renown, the individual too will share in the rays of an immortalizing glory (2.43.2). What in essence Pericles claims here is that Athens has solved the perennial challenge of social organization. It has successfully reconciled the legitimate demands of personal self-expression with the equally legitimate demands for selfless contribution on behalf of the state. Athens is a place where love of self and love of city are coterminous and by successfully harmonizing these potentially contrary demands she has made herself the "school of Hellas;" a source of wonder for the men of today, and for men of all time (2.41.4). Accordingly, Athens can dispense with the services of a Homer because the deeds of free men speak far more eloquently than the words of a poet.[*]

Flower and Weed – The Case of Alcibiades

What I have termed the "Athenian experiment" is of great moment to the history of Western culture because it helped confer two of our civilization's most cherished values: A conception of freedom that not only embraced political liberty but also promoted the ideal of spiritual emancipation; plus a related view of the ripened individual that bears a striking resemblance to modern notions of the actualized self. It is this second endowment in particular that

---

[*] The remarkable achievements of the "Athenian freedom" were fully recognized by Herodotus who describes the sons of Athens as the greatest fighters in the world (5.78). Thucydides also suggests that the amazing staying power of the Athenians even after the Sicilian disaster is to be attributed to the caliber of men the city had succeeded in producing (2.65.12-13).

continues to lend the *Epitaphios* its peculiar relevance despite the passage of twenty-four hundred years.[*]

  But this grand undertaking, for all its historic significance, was not without its difficulties. As noted above, much of this project's viability rested upon the maintenance of a precarious and complex balance between devotion to the common good and devotion to self. In other words, moderation was imperative, yet the record of their history clearly suggests that restraint and forbearance were hardly native instincts for the Greeks. Religious sanctions (Delphi) in this regard were necessary precisely because the Hellenes were temperamentally disinclined to embrace such values. Certainly the portrait of the Athenians offered by Thucydides indicates an inherent tendency for extravagant impulse and excess.[†] There are good grounds for assuming therefore that the Athenian experiment was, from the beginning, beset by a powerful tension; the individual born of the experiment might not only be the source of Athenian greatness, he might through unrestrained ambition, also be the source of her demise. Accordingly, the attempt to liberate the power of personality was risky business because improperly constrained, these energies could prove corrosive to the very balance necessary for the achievement of things great and lasting. The rigors of war made such containment impossible chiefly because Athenian imperialism itself presented object lessons that could only distort and corrupt the individual's civic consciousness. Just as Athens, the tyrant city, loved itself above all other cities, so too the

---

[*] During the First World War the British viewed the Oration as sufficiently germane to justiy its distribution to troops serving at the front—a reminder of the principles for which they were fighting.

[†] The Athenian activities of the First Peloponnesian War, the Melian atrocity, and the Sicilian campaign all illustrate this penchant for inordinancy.

Athenian citizen came to love himself above all his compatriots (see Palmer 27).

These tendencies are given a face by Thucydides, a living incarnation in the person of Alcibiades, son of Cleinias. He is easily one of the most interesting figures in the <u>History</u> and though he is typically branded one of the great scoundrels of all time, he is by no means a pure miscreant. We cannot, for example, place him in the same category with Cleon. In fact, despite being a veritable fount of subterfuge and machination, there is an almost tragic quality about him, albeit not in the classic Aristotelian sense.[*] In truth, he was a composite of extraordinary capacity matched by equally extraordinary faults and deficiencies. With regard to gifts, Thucydides leaves his reader in no doubt, Alcibiades is a man of unusual ability, so much so that even a venture as fatuous as the Sicilian campaign might have succeeded had it remained under his command (6.15.4).[†] Yet his abundant gifts which include beauty, intelligence, and persuasiveness only serve to highlight the ethical amnesia to which he was subject. At base, Alcibiades is a solipsistic blend of peacock and lion;[‡] combining the self-centered vanities of

---

[*] It would be difficult, for instance, to muster much "pity" for Alcibiades in tracing the serpentine details of his career. However, Aristotle's observation that the protagonist's misfortune should stem from some flaw in his character (*hamartia*) might apply to Alcibiades if one were willing to view his egotistical sense of self as a tragic shortcoming (see <u>Poetics</u> 13.4-5).

[†] In considering the career of Alcibiades one is reminded of an observation offered by Erasmus in his work, <u>The Education of a Christian Prince</u>: "For the richer the soil is by nature, the more readily the ground is invaded and taken over by useless grasses and weeds unless the farmer is on the alert" (11). So it is with a man's character: the more promising, the more noble, the more upright it is, the more it is at the mercy of shameful vices unless it is nourished by wholesome teachings.

[‡] The lion image as applied to Alcibiades can be found in Aristophanes' *Frogs* (1431) and may also stand behind similar imagery presented by Plato (<u>Gorgias</u> 484a). The ultimate source for both is probably Aeschylus' *Agamemnon* (717-732).

the former with the ruthless dedication of the latter. The problem from the perspective of the Athenian community is that neither of these dispositions is particularly conducive to civic harmony. Even the minimal fidelities demanded by law and custom are more than Athens could hope to receive from Alcibiades because in men such as he, the dictates of personal advancement negate every duty, every faith, and every allegiance.

The full implication of the phenomenon of Alcibiades is perhaps best seen in a comparison between the winged words of the Periclean oration (2.37-46) and the remarkably self-sanctifying rhetoric offered by Alcibiades during the Sicilian debate (6.16-18). Though separated in time by roughly fifteen years, Thucydides nevertheless presents these speeches comparatively, thereby inviting his reader to gauge the devolution of moral and political affairs at Athens. The elder statesman had encouraged the citizenry to secure their glory by investing in Athenian greatness. He assured them that their sacrifices would generate an everlasting radiance for the city which would illuminate their lives as well. Above all, he urged a passionate and unqualified devotion to civic enterprise, at one point actually advising the Athenians to fall in love with the city (2.43.1).

The remarks of Alcibiades represent a complete inversion of the civic recipe proposed by Pericles. There are no references here to advancing the cause of mother Athens; no advocacy of disciplined sacrifice or for a vicarious glory attained through the advancement of national interest. Instead, Alcibiades immodestly suggests that his uncommon abilities justify dereliction of the societal restraints normally imposed upon individuals. The banalities that guide the lives of ordinary men must not restrain an exceptional individual. In effect, Alcibiades declares that he has outgrown the polis. The city can no longer command his loyalties and is simply a means to his ends; Athens must be satisfied to bask in the glory of Alcibiades. Moreover, the ardent dedication proposed by Pericles is impossible for a self-centered free agent like Alcibiades. He cannot fall in love with the city because he is too much in love with himself. It is this narcissistic absorption in particular, this subordination of public good to private interest, that doomed the Athenian experiment and spelled catastrophe for the most radiant city in ancient Greece.

Chapter VI

Government by the Bean[*]

"The city teaches the man"—Simonides

Introduction – The Polis

At some point during the late 9th century B.C., a new social and political configuration known as the polis or city-state began to emerge among the Greeks. The exact conditions leading up to the formation of the polis remain obscure but they no doubt involved the gradual amalgamation of scattered villages into increasingly larger political units. The Attic *synoecism*, the social and political unification attributed to Theseus, is no doubt a mythic rendering of an actual historical process. The end result was an institutional setting that would not only define the subsequent course of Greek civilization, it would also put Western posterity forever in its debt, and accordingly, the polis has been hailed as the single most important creation of the ancient world (Glotz 1 and Harris 17).[†]

---

[*] This is a reference to the random selection of magistrates at democratic Athens. The process's lack of concern with qualified expertise was denounced by Socrates (Xenophon Mem. 1.2.9).

[†] Although the thousand or more Greek city-states were an undeniable source of cultural vitality, they were also the origin of a divisive parochialism that plagued Hellas throughout its history. Despite common bonds of language, culture, and faith, the idea of "nation" remained elusive for the Greeks. In this regard we should not be misled by

What then were the characteristic features of the city-state and how did the Greeks perceive this fountainhead from which so much of their achievement flowed? To begin with we should recognize that the term "polis" denotes both more and less than the modern idea of "state." Less in the sense of geography, population, and resource base and more with regard to social unity and expanse of public sector. Athens, the one city-state for which we have a reasonable amount of data,[*] well illustrates these points. At its zenith for instance in 431 B.C., Attica was only one-half the size of Delaware (approximately 1,000 square miles) and contained a citizen[†] population estimated at a mere 40-60,000 (see Gomme 47; Munn 62; Finley 1962, 10; Thorley 1 and Stockton 17). Regarding economic assets, the observation attributed to Demaratus by Herodotus (7.102), that poverty was a way of life among the Greeks, was essentially accurate even for a city like Athens which, though wealthier than most Greek states, remained humble in comparison to the material splendor of Egypt or Persia.

---

occasional and limited affiliations such as *amphictyonies* (religious associations), *isopoliteia* (extension of citizen status to outsiders), and *symmachy* (military alliance). The polis lent a narrowness to Greek political experience which, with rare exception, resulted in a continuous cycle of disunity, violence, and vulnerability to external threat. Toynbee (xxiii) was correct when he observed that the Greeks were not a nation, but a society of nations.

[*] And as a result, the majority of statements regarding Greek democracy will be drawn from Athenian examples unless specifically stated otherwise.

[†] For the ancient Greeks, the term "citizen" was a jealously guarded, exclusive designation (the Romans were far more liberal in extending the privilege of citizen status). Women, metics (resident aliens), and slaves were all excluded from the political system with the result that during the classical era at Athens only 14-17% of a total population of 300,000 enjoyed full citizen rights (Sinclair 200). Opportunities for women to engage in politics existed only in the gynocratic fantasies of Aristophanes and were exceedingly rare for metics and slaves as well. When they did occur for the latter two categories, they came as a result of some extraordinary public service, which was then formally acknowledged by the people's assembly (see Garlan 80-84).

In terms of social climate, the ancient city consciously sought a degree of citizen involvement and integration that appears almost authoritarian by contemporary standards. In particular, the Lockean separation of society and state was fundamentally unknown among the ancient Greeks (Ehrenberg 1964, 89). Unlike the modern state, which is chiefly dedicated to the protection of individual rights and property and therefore functions primarily as a juridical entity, the polis was not only a court, it was also a school and a church that aggressively attempted to forge deep psychological and spiritual bonds among its members. This no doubt explains the remarkable frequency with which public festivals were celebrated throughout the Greek world and may also shed light on the peculiar opprobrium assigned the "private" man in the Periclean Funeral Oration (2.40.2). By modern liberal standards, these efforts to engender a homogeneous system of practice and belief appear disturbingly intrusive and have led some to speak of the "omnipotence" of the ancient city and to argue that the Greeks knew nothing of personal liberties (e.g., DeCoulanges 293). While it is certainly true that the Greeks had no metaphysically conceived idea of unalienable rights, and it is true as well that they lacked any constitutional system aimed at delimiting the activities of government, caution must nevertheless be used when attempting to compare ancient and modern notions of liberty.[*] For one thing, much of the conceptual framework underlying such a comparative effort is historically conditioned, which means even the basic terminology ("freedom,"

---

[*] One of the fundamental differences between ancient and modern political perspectives concerns the issue of rights versus duties. Modern political doctrine argues for the existence of certain irrevocable, transcendent human rights against which no government can legitimately intrude. The ancient Greeks, however, viewed duties as logically prior to rights and never viewed personal liberties as a birthright. Before a citizen could make claim to social or political privilege, the Greeks believed he must first discharge his obligations to the state and the community.

"rights," "liberty," etc.) lacks the kind of trans-historical status requisite for legitimate comparison. The only way to avoid false analogy and distortive anachronism is to assess the city-state within its own historical context, i.e., by comparing it with other ancient civic arrangements, not by superimposing modern libertarian standards. Viewed from this angle, the Greek city-state was in fact remarkably progressive in its provisions for personal liberties and rarely subjected its citizenry to the sort of religious, political "slavery" typical of the rest of the ancient world. From the modern perspective, then, it may appear that the ancient city violated the canons of personal liberty by radically narrowing the discretionary domain of the individual. For their part, however, the Greeks would have viewed the contemporary civil order as a vast, disjointed assembly of strangers, a series of isolated islands each with its own castaway.

To say that the Greeks felt a certain satisfaction in having developed the network of social and political bonds we call the city-state would be to greatly understate their sense of accomplishment. The Greeks were convinced that in the polis, they had achieved an institution, which not only addressed all of the fundamental needs of man as *zoon politikon* (man as political animal) but also established the conditions by which the unique characteristics of *to Hellenikon*, "Greekness" itself, were realized. Indeed, it was the polis, more than any other ingredient of Hellenic life, that endowed the Greeks with that cultural chauvinism by which they invidiously compared themselves to the rest of the world[*] —a tendency that received some of its clearest formulation in the works of Aristotle (e.g., <u>Pol</u>. 1.2.18). In particular, there were two gifts granted by the polis which fueled the Greek sense of superiority. First, the oppor-

---

[*] In this regard, Phocylides, a 6th century poet, wrote, "The law-abiding polis, though small and set upon a rock, outranks mad Nineveh."

tunity to live a life secured by the rule of law (*nomos*)[*] and second, the freedom to cultivate and display individual talents.

The high regard with which the Greeks viewed *nomos* is reflected in the renown accorded their great lawgivers. Men like Lycurgus, Charondas, Solon, and Zaleukus were acknowledged as national heroes by their native cities because well-conceived laws were understood as the foundation of every blessing civilization had to offer. This is why Heraclitus advised that a people should fight for its laws as if for their city's walls; why Gorgias argued that the laws were the guardians of justice; why Pindar declared that law was king of all, mortals as well as immortals; why the Spartans saw no shame in describing themselves as the "slaves" of law; and why Solon praised law as the key to order and harmony and as the chief restraint against the unrighteous.

Despite possessing a lofty assessment of human potential, the Greeks were under no illusions concerning the depths to which men were prone to sink when unrestrained by law (see Plato, <u>Laws</u> 766a and Aristotle, <u>Politics</u> 1.1.32-36). They understood fully that when human affairs were detached from law and justice, i.e., when power came to be exercised on an unchecked basis, the city was invariably plunged into a nightmare of chaotic violence. But when law, as opposed to personality, was firmly seated on the throne, men were afforded the gifts of justice and peace because, as Aristotle observed, law is reason without passion (<u>Politics</u> 3.11.4).[†]

---

[*] The term *nomos*, meaning a legal statute stemming from the community, is comparatively new and may be directly related to the reforms of Cleisthenes in the late 6th century. It supplanted the term *thesmos*, which implied a law handed down from some higher authority (MacDowell 44 and Ostwald 173).

[†] The Greeks tended to make little if any distinction between law and morality. Citizens in modern democracies might object to laws that seek to "moralize," but the ancients saw the cultivation of virtue as a prime objective of the legislative enterprise. In their view, any constitutional system, no matter how elaborate or well-conceived,

In a real sense, then, the Greeks viewed law as a kind of salvation, a source of protection, dignity and independence that would restrict the despotic abuses inherent in systems such as the great Asian monarchies. But the city-state did much more than merely immunize against the madness of a ruler like the Persian king, Cambyses. By furnishing the securities of legal due process, the polis also provided a rationally regulated environment where a man could develop and display his capacities freely. The importance of these self-actualizing opportunities cannot be overstated for a culture in which the heroic ideal of personal *arete* remained a powerful force.* But in the process of seeking their personal fulfillment, a quest that typically relied upon the mechanisms of contest (*agon*), the Greeks and their city-states simultaneously accomplished something of immensely greater significance. They discovered, or better, they presided at the birth of the "individual" in a uniquely Western sense of that term (Burkert 278; Hiebel 24-26). For the first time in human history the individual was afforded an opportunity to emerge from the shadows of communal identity and stand tall in the radiance of an unprecedented selfhood. We can trace these developments in a variety of ways. They are seen in a new authorial voice of poets such as Hesiod and Archilochus who present their verse in the first person.† They are evident in the asser-

---

was worthless unless the moral disposition of the citizenry was sound (see von Fritz 334 and Jones 14).

* Hannah Arendt (41) notes that it was precisely these opportunities to cultivate and display individual talents that made the Greeks willing to shoulder the burdens of public life.

† G.E.R. Lloyd (1989, 57) offers the following observation on the uniqueness of Hellenic selfhood, "The extant remains of Egyptian and Babylonian medicine, mathematics and astronomy can be combed in vain for a single example of a text where an individual author distances himself from, and criticizes the received tradition in order to claim originality for himself; whereas our Greek sources repeatedly do just that."

tions of generals such as Miltiades and Pausanias who seek to have their names prominently indicated on the dedicatory offerings commemorating their victories.* The new individualism also explains why Pericles could exercise the kind of personal authority he had over the Athenians as it does the unparalleled spiritual autonomy of Socrates. It is even evident among the ranks of humble craftsmen such as the potters who now insist upon autographing their vases.†

It should come as no real surprise then, that the same culture which set Western man on the path of ripened selfhood would also initiate democracy's maiden voyage. Empowered by his new sense of self and armed with the belief that his voice should matter in the affairs of state, the polis-dweller increasingly came to assert his claim as civic participant. Of course, this process must be understood developmentally; democracy appears only at the end of a long and difficult gestation. In addition, it must be acknowledged that democracy was by no means a universal feature of Hellenic political culture—the dead hand of Spartan oligarchy, for example, remained unresponsive to political transformation. Moreover, even where and when democracy did become firmly entrenched, elitist sub-cultures continued to flourish because democracy, in its ancient Greek form, stressed political equality while simultaneously acknowledging distinctions of social eminence. With these caveats in mind, we may now proceed to examine the historical background of the most daring political experiment in human history— the attempt to exchange scepter and crown for speaker's platform

---

* The conduct of these generals and of other men such as Themistocles and Alcibiades put the lie to DeCoulange's thesis of the city-state's omnipotence. Quite the contrary, as C.H. Whitman notes, in the heart of every Greek we find an anarchist (43).

† Even the underground water pipes were signed by their makers (Phoca and Valavanis 59).

and voting urn. The attempt, in other words, to make citizens out of subjects.

The Evolution of Greek Democracy*

Any consideration of ancient democracy requires that several adjustments first be made to conventional wisdom. For one thing, when most people consider democratic origins, they reflexively turn their attention to Athens during the $6^{th} - 5^{th}$ centuries B.C. and to the innovations attributed to Solon, Cleisthenes, and Ephialtes. While these associations are not wrong, they nevertheless distort certain chronological and distributive truths regarding the historical evolution of popular sovereignty in Greece. With regard to time-frame, the nascent elements of democracy actually lie much further back in Greek history than Solonian Athens. Indeed, the necessary preconditions for the democratizing events of the 6th century were already evident in the epic poetry of Homer. The men who fight at Troy, for example, do not offer their blood as indentured warriors, but rather as free companions who willingly accept the lead of their chieftains. Homeric poetry also suggests that policy formation did not occur in an aristocratic vacuum but included the *vox populi* (e.g., Iliad 2.210 and 18.497, Odyssey 2.25). In fact, there is much in Homer to indicate that key decisions were not the unilateral pre-rogative of any class or group and that kings and elders enjoyed only a limited and contingent sovereignty. The implication of

---

* It has been argued by some that the true origins of democracy are not Hellenic at all but actually occur first among the Sumerians, Hittites, Phoenicians, or various Indian states. The supporting evidence for such assertions is scant to say the least and per-haps the issue was best addressed by M.I. Finley (1973, 14): "Whatever the facts may be about (democracies in early Mesopotamia), their impact on history, or later socie-ties, was null. The Greeks, and only the Greeks, discovered democracy in that sense, precisely as Christopher Columbus, not some Viking seaman, discovered America."

scenes such as those depicted on the shield of Achilles suggests that "the people" were already a force to be reckoned with; that public consent was an accepted aspect of political deliberation. Thus, the evidence from Homer reveals a strong sentiment on behalf of participatory decision-making, a sentiment requisite for any true democracy and one which became peculiarly embedded in Hellenic political consciousness.[*]

As to democracy's point of origin, again we must dispense with certain Athenocentric presumptions. It is commonly assumed that the Athenian democracy was a unique and isolated experiment that eventually became the political paradigm for much of Hellas. None of our ancient sources, however, identify Athens as the inventor of democracy and there is even some evidence that Chios, not Athens, may have been the first genuinely democratic state in the Greek world (Bowra 70; Finley 1982, 114; Robinson 90). It also seems the other Greeks did not sit by idly waiting for democratic institutions to evolve at Athens. In fact, there is much in the ancient record to indicate that by the early 5th century B.C. there were at least eighteen Greek states with popular governments including Achaea, Croton, Acragas, Ambracia, Argos, Cyrene, Megara, Naxos, and Syracuse among others.

But, as indicated above, these democracies, as well as the more noted system at Athens, were not an instantaneous expression of Greek political genius. They were rather the result of an extensive

---

[*] Xenophon's <u>Anabasis</u> provides a good illustration of the degree to which deliberation and democratic process became part of Greek national character. The Greek mercenaries, most of whom hailed from city-states without democratic traditions, demanded to be involved in decision making with the result that the army spent nearly as much time discussing and voting as it did fighting. When the Spartan general, Clearchus, attempted to force his men to march against their will, he narrowly escaped being stoned to death by his own troops (1.3.1-2). For these reasons, the Greek force described by Xenophon has legitimately been called a "marching democracy."

development beginning with traditional kingships. These early monarchies were inclusive posts combining military, legal, and sacerdotal authority in the person of the ruler. Over time, however, kingly hegemony increasingly gave way to the political claims of powerful landed aristocracies. At Athens this group was referred to collectively as the *eupatridae* (literally, "men of noble fathers") and was comprised of approximately sixty dominant *gene* (families) such as the Eumolpidae, Kerykes, Eteoboutadae, Bouzyges, and the Lycomidae. By 700 B.C. the aristocratic encroachment upon kingly discretion was complete. Various archonships (executive administrators), in combination with aristocratic councils, were created which systematically stripped the monarchy of its traditional powers. Between 700-600 B.C. virtually all of the major cities in Greece came under the control of the great families.

The next important phase in the evolution of democracy in ancient Greece involved the formal codification and public display of the previously "unpublished" oral law. This process began in the late 7th century and became more common in the 6th century. At Athens, the first legal code was attributed to Draco in the year 621 B.C.[*] We know very little about Draco and the circumstances leading up to his codification, but it has been suggested that these moves were motivated by an attempt to delimit private blood feuds associated with the Cylonian conspiracy.[†] Prior to the Draconian

---

[*] The name Draco has become synonymous with legalistic severity and with good reason as indicated by the alacrity with which his system invoked the death penalty (e.g., idleness). The austerity of these laws should not, however, obscure their sophistication. The homicide code, for example, makes a clear distinction between premeditated and non-premeditated killing. The later reforms of Solon would maintain this aspect of Draco's system.

[†] Cylon attempted to establish a tyranny at Athens with the assistance of his father-in-law, Theagenes of Megara (c. 630 B.C.). His coup failed however and he and his forces were besieged on the Acropolis by Megacles, the Alcmaeonid. Cylon escaped,

reform, family vengeance, with its enormous potential for public turmoil, was the order of the day in all cases of homicide. One of the more important effects of Draco's code was to assert the state's right to intervene in such cases and to compel the warring parties to accept resolution via state-sponsored mechanisms.

In addition to affirming the state's prerogatives in matters such as homicide, Draco's code also ended the political and judicial monopoly enjoyed by the aristocracy. Previous to these formally inscribed declarations, the law had been a matter of noble whim. The community as a whole was largely reliant upon the legal interpretations set forth by the great households; law and legality were whatever the aristocracy said they were. Draco made law a "public" institution and in so doing greatly diminished the aristocracy's ability to subjectively define and determine the meaning of *nomos*.[*] By fostering this more equitable notion of law, while simultaneously reducing aristocratic prerogative, the Draconian reforms played an important role in establishing the essential pre-conditions necessary for popular sovereignty.

Another key ingredient in the evolution of democracy in ancient Greece ironically involved the tyrannies that arose throughout Hellas during the 7th and 6th centuries B.C.—ironic in light of the inherent contradictions between tyranny and democracy. But given the unique social and political setting of that period, a case can indeed be made for tyranny's contribution in the development of democratic Greece. As originally employed by the Greeks, the term

---

but his followers were dragged from the altar where they had sought sanctuary and executed. This impiety was thought to have brought down a curse upon the Alcmaeonids, which became a rich source of politically inspired accusation against the family.

[*] The publication of the Twelve Tables at Rome had a similar effect upon Patrician authority (see von Fritz 202).

tyrannos did not suggest the patent evil assumed by contemporary usage. The word is probably a Lydian borrowing and when initially employed by the Greeks simply meant "king" (Bowra 77).[*] By the 4th century B.C. the term had taken on a decidedly pejorative connotation, but the record from the 7th and 6th centuries B.C., when tyrannies flourished[†] in many of the major city-states (e.g., Ephesus, Miletus, Megara, Corinth, Samos, Sicyon, Epidarus, etc.), indicates that the brutal abuses associated with a despot like Phalaris were not at all typical.[‡]. Indeed, there are a variety of examples of benevolent dictators, men who generally respected the laws and dedicated their energies to the economic and cultural advancement of their states. The Athenian tyrant Peisistratus is perhaps the best illustration of these benign tendencies.[§]

Who were these tyrants and how did their regimes contribute to the birth of democracy? In virtually every case the individuals who succeeded in establishing tyrannies were members of the upper classes who seized the opportunity to crush their aristocratic rivals by securing the support of the multitude. That the tyrants perceived the greatest risk to their authority from members of this own class is illustrated by the famous advice given by Thrasybulus, the veteran tyrant of Miletus, to Periander, the new ruler of Corinth (Herod. 5.92). Periander sought the advice of his more senior counterpart and dispatched a hearld to Miletus. Thrasybulus took Peri-

---

[*] The earliest usage of the term appears in the poetry of Archilochus (c. 650 B.C.) specifically in reference to Gyges, the Lydian usurper.

[†] Most of the tyrannies lasted for no more than a generation or two. One exception was the Orthagoridae at Sicyon whose tyranny lasted for about one hundred years (Aristotle Politics 5.12).

[‡] Phalaris (c. 550 B.C.) was the tyrant of Acragas who allegedly roasted his enemies alive in a bronze bull.

[§] Aristotle (Ath. Const. 16.7) claims the Athenians thought so highly of Peisistratus' reign, they likened it to the golden age of Cronus.

ander's representative on a brief tour through a cornfield where he proceeded to lop off the heads of the tallest stalks—at no time was there any explicit advice offered regarding political affairs. Perplexed, the herald returned to Corinth thinking his mission a failure. But upon learning of Thrasybulus' actions in the cornfield, Periander immediately grasped the symbolism: the key to autocratic power lay in the reduction of the mighty.

The novel means Thrasybulus chose to communicate his counsel should not lead us to conclude that the message itself was in any way unique. In fact, neutralizing the nobility, particularly by strengthening state mechanisms and by compromising the aristocracy's hold over the small freeholders, were common features of tyrant strategy. The activities of Peisistratus, who ruled Athens intermittently between 560 and 527 B.C., is the definitive example of these tactics.

The available evidence suggests that Peisistratus was a particularly enterprising ruler. Among other things, he initiated a series of ambitious public works including many new roads, an aqueduct system, and the enormous temple known as the Olympieum.[*] He also expanded overseas trade activities and established settlements in the Chersonese which would later prove critically important for Athenian grain supplies. In addition, Peisistratus and his heirs made Athens a major cultural center by promoting numerous festivals and by attracting renowned poets such as Simonides and Anacreon to the city. But from our perspective the most important accomplishment of Peisistratus was the systematic undermining of aristocratic influence in Attica. This was accomplished in a variety

---

[*] The temple was dedicated to Zeus and remained unfinished at the time of Peisistratus' death. Construction was resumed much later by Antiochus IV and was not completed until the time of the Emperor Hadrian.

of ways, all of which involved a shift away from local institutions controlled by the great families to the centralized state machinery based at Athens. By the sponsorship of new religious cults, for example, and by the establishment of pan-Athenian festivals, Peisistratus was able to disrupt the cultic monopoly enjoyed by the landed aristocracy. Peisistratus also moved against one of the chief sources of patrician power by addressing the matter of rural poverty, which had for generations been a breeding ground of aristocratic patronage (Finley 1991, 46-7). He attacked this problem by exempting the poor entirely from certain taxes and by setting up a revolving loan fund that obviated the need for small freeholders to seek support from the nobility. In addition, Peisistratus designated a board of itinerant *deme* (village) judges who went on circuit to distribute justice on behalf of the "national government"—in direct opposition to the juridical authority traditionally enjoyed by the local barons. Peisistratus also expanded the citizen franchise as part of his campaign against the nobles, creating thereby a solid block of supporters whose interests and loyalties were unequivocally aligned with the tyrant.* Collectively these initiatives had the effect of substantially reducing the power of the aristocratic elite, of elevating and ensuring the status of the common man, and of advancing the instruments of centralized state authority, all of which helped clear a path for the democratic revolution that awaited Athens at the close of the century.

No discussion of the evolution of Greek democracy can neglect the contributions made by the Athenian lawgiver, Solon. Unlike

---

* Peisistratus' final installation as tyrant of Athens came in 546 B.C. after the battle of Pallene. His victory was in part secured by the aid of Argive mercenaries who were rewarded with citizen status. Apparently this was a fairly common feature of tyrant strategy and was sometimes practiced on a massive scale. Gelon of Syracuse reportedly extended citizenship to 10,000 of his mercenary troops (Diodorus 11.72.3).

Peisistratus, whose reign came shortly after the implementation of Solon's reforms, Solon did not seek autocratic authority, although tyrannical power was clearly his for the asking. This in itself marks Solon as an extraordinary figure, because while the thought of living under the absolute authority of another man was anathema to a Greek, the lust for such power was the secret longing of every Hellenic heart.[*] In addition to abstaining from despotism, Solon also rendered great service to his native city by steering Athens clear of the violent factionalism that swept much of the Greek world (e.g., Megara, Samos, Miletus, Syracuse), in the 7th and 6th centuries B.C.. During this period, the social tapestry of ancient Greece revealed the presence of the various "dependent" subgroups: the *penestai* of Thessaly; the *gymnetes* of Argos, and the *helots* of Sparta. At Athens, too, the *eupatridae* seem to have been well on their way to reducing the lower classes to a formally indentured status. This was accomplished by a system of loans extended the poor by the rich landholders who then laid claim to the small freeholder's property if the subsidy went unrepaid. Over time, this arrangement created a kind of Attic sharecropper known as the *hektemoroi* ("sixth-parters"), who were continuously obliged to surrender a sixth of their annual crop to the overlord. Default of this obligation could result in the debtor being sold into slavery. Needless to say, the animosities between rich and poor generated by such a system were highly incendiary and no doubt would have

---

[*] By refusing the tyranny Solon made himself an object of ridicule. His critics reportedly assailed him for missing a golden opportunity, one of whom observed, "Now had I the power, I had been only too glad to be flayed for a wineskin and my posterity wiped out, if only I might first have wealth abundant and rule Athens for a single day" (Solon fr. 33, also Plutarch <u>Solon</u> 14.6).

resulted in the same bloody *stasis** that typified many other city-states were it not for the mediatory efforts of Solon.

The first provision of Solon's reforms called for a general cancellation of debt known as the *seisachtheia* ("shaking off of debt"), which effectively ended the indenturing of the peasantry and also arranged for the restoration of their farms. In addition, all debt-based enslavement was nullified and those who had fled Attica or had been sold abroad were recalled. Further assistance was rendered the poor by limiting the export of foodstuffs, which had created shortages at home while simultaneously inflating domestic prices. Additionally, Solon was responsible for a highly significant restructuring of the citizen orders based on agrarian productivity, as opposed to aristocratic ancestry. Now political status and the right of participation in the affairs of state would be determined by agricultural wealth as measured by a unit known as the *medimnos*:[†] the greater the number of *medimnoi* generated by a man's properties, the higher his political status.[‡]

In terms of governmental apparatus, Solon is generally credited with having established a *boule* (council) of 400 members (100 representatives from each of the four Ionic tribes) which enjoyed probouleutic authority (the right to set the assembly's agenda). He also initiated the *eliaia*, a judicial session of the assembly where all citizens were allowed to appeal the verdicts of the magistrates.

---

[*] Stasis refers to violent civic disorder within the city-state.

[†] A medimnos was a wet/dry measure of agricultural produce corresponding to 50 litres of liquid (oil or wine) and 1 ½ bushels of grain or fruit, i.e., about 85 lbs.

[‡] There were four classes established by this assessment. The highest group were called the *pentakosiomedimnoi* whose properties produced 500 medimnoi or more per year. The next group was the *hippeis* who produced 300-500 medimnoi, followed by the *zeugetai* (200-300 medimnoi), and the *thetes* (less than 200 medimnoi). Only members of the first two classes could seek the archonships, and thetic participation was restricted to the popular assembly and the court.

Over time, this privilege would greatly weaken the authority of the traditionally aristocratic archonships. Perhaps most importantly of all, Solon allowed the *thetes* to participate in the assembly and the *eliaia*. The latter allowance was, according to Aristotle (<u>Pol</u>. 2.9 and <u>Ath. Const</u>. 9.1), pivotal for the subsequent development of democracy because in his view, the class that dominated the voting pebble would inevitably come to dominate the constitution.

The Solonian system, for all its progressive and ameliorative insight, was not a democracy. Nor is there anything in the record, including the lawgiver's own poetry,[*] to indicate that Solon was in any way guided by what we might today term "democratic ideology."[†] Had he been so motivated he almost certainly would have acceded to the traditional demand of the poor—namely, a sweeping redistribution of land. Instead, he limited access to senior administrative positions, preserved the authority of the ancient aristocratic council (Areopagus), denied thetic access to the *boule*, and generally maintained the system of privilege historically enjoyed by those of gentle birth. In light of all this, perhaps the best way to describe Solon is to employ the term chosen by Aristotle and Plutarch, *diallaktes* (mediator); one who stood with his shield protecting both sides, suffering neither to prevail unjustly (Solon fr. 5).

But while we are not entitled to portray Solon as a "democrat," it is nevertheless true that the measures he instituted and the civic climate he helped generate were vital to the subsequent develop-

---

[*] "For to the common people, I gave so much power as is sufficient. Neither robbing them of dignity, nor giving them too much" (Solon fr. 5; Plutarch, <u>Solon</u> 18.4; Aristotle, <u>Ath. Const</u>. 12.1).

[†] Those who interpret the Solonian reforms as a "bourgeois revolution" are making too much of the class revisions and are also guilty of anachronism (e.g., Sagan 1991). In fact, the system is more accurately described as a timocracy, i.e., a political arrangement based on honor or wealth.

ment of popular sovereignty. Not only did he liberate the people as Aristotle noted (Ath. Const. 6.1), he also expanded the civic opportunities of the lower classes to an unprecedented degree. In so doing, Solon contributed to a fundamental change in the consciousness of the common man; no longer would he perceive himself as merely the passive client of a ruling aristocracy. From this point on he would increasingly display a sense of collective empowerment that would become the very essence of Athenian democracy.

The next significant figure in the evolution of popular government at Athens, and perhaps the most important of all, is Cleisthenes, the individual typically cited as the founder of Athenian democracy. Building upon foundations established earlier by Solon and Peisistratus, Cleisthenes, a leading member of the Alcmaeonid family, succeeded in initiating a series of wide-ranging constitutional reforms in his native city.* But before he could accomplish these changes, two preconditions had to be met. First, the Athenian tyranny had to be eliminated and second, Cleisthenes had to survive a power struggle against a key aristocratic rival, Isagoras.

The first condition was satisfied as a result of Spartan military intervention, as encouraged by the Oracle of Delphi. The reason for Apollo's interest in this affair had more to do with money and politics than matters of piety. The god's temple had been destroyed by fire and the Alcmaeonids (now exiled from Athens) had contracted with the Amphictyonic council to restore the facility. In doing so, the Alcmaeonids spent lavishly, far exceeding their obligations under the agreement which prompted the Oracle to instruct King Cleomenes of Sparta to "set Athens free," which would also presuma-

---

* Cleisthenes' innovations, impressive as they were, may not have been very original. Herodotus (5.67) claims he was merely imitating prior reforms initiated at Sicyon by his maternal grandfather, the tyrant Cleisthenes. Similar reforms seem to have also been implemented earlier at Corinth and Miletus.

bly result in a restoration of all exiles. For his part, Cleomenes was more than willing to oblige the Oracle, given the fact that the Athenian tyrants had often aligned themselves with Argos, Sparta's chief rival. Accordingly, in the year 510 B.C., Hippias, the eldest son of Peisistratus, was driven from the city, creating a power vacuum that two aristocratic factions, one led by Isagoras and the other by Cleisthenes, were most eager to fill.

In the ensuing struggle, Isagoras enjoyed two important advantages—he had been elected archon for the period 508-507 B.C. and, as subsequent events would soon reveal, he also enjoyed Spartan backing. In an attempt to counter these assets, Cleisthenes made a daring move. He initiated a partnership with the *demos* (Herod. 5.66) by advancing a program of popular reform. The success of this strategy prompted Isagoras to appeal to Cleomenes who justified intervention by invoking the hereditary curse of the Alcmaeonids. Cleisthenes was compelled to flee the city along with 700 other families allegedly involved in the impious slaughter of Cylon's followers. Emboldened by the presence of his Spartan allies, Isagoras sought to consolidate his authority by dissolving the council. This, however, provoked spirited resistance from the people who besieged Isagoras and the Spartan forces on the acropolis. The would-be usurpers were eventually allowed to withdraw, but two years later (506 B.C.) Cleomenes and his co-regent returned with a larger allied force. In the end, however, opposition from Demaratus, the other Spartan monarch, plus objections from the Corinthian contingent, prevented any further intervention at Athens. Cleisthenes was now free to conduct his experiments.

He began by abandoning the old Ionic tribal scheme as a basis for political activity, replacing it with a more complex structure involving ten new tribes (phylai) consisting of one section from each of the three major geographic regions (city, interior, and

217

coast) into which Attica had been divided. Each of these geographic units was made up of ten districts known as *trittyes* (thirds). From each of the three geographic subdivisions, one of the ten constituent trittyes was selected and assigned to one of the ten new tribes so that each consisted of three trittyes drawn from different areas of Attica. The trittyes were themselves comprised of *demes* (villages) which formed the basic unit of Cleisthenes' political reorganization. There were something on the order of 139-150 demes in Attica which meant that on average each trittyes was made up of 4-5 demes (see Thorley 23-24, Sinclair 3-4, and Stockton 59).

Under Cleisthenes, the demes became the new centers of citizen certification, in direct opposition to the customary system dominated by the *eupatridae* where citizen status was contingent upon kinship affiliation to powerful families (gene) and brotherhoods (phratries).[*] Now, when a young man came of age, his name was entered upon a deme registry which became the authoritative test of his citizen status, as well as the official instrument of personal identity. Henceforth, citizens were expected to identify themselves by citing the deme where they had been enrolled as opposed to their father's name or clan affiliation.[†] These new arrangements must have been enthusiastically endorsed by the marginalized elements of Athenian society (the landless poor, resident aliens, and freedmen) because in rejecting clan and tribal association as the measure of citizenship, Cleisthenes was able to greatly expand

---

[*] The gene and phratries continued to operate after the Cleisthenic reforms, but only in a social and religious context. Their political significance had been fundamentally neutralized.

[†] Cleisthenes' efforts to replace patronymic reference with demotic citation was not entirely successful. By the 4th century the demotic had still not entirely supplanted the patronymic.

civic privilege at Athens (Arist., Politics 3.1.10). In addition, his reforms must have been popular because they functioned as an indemnity against another aristocratically inspired *diapsephismos*, an invidious public scrutiny of family background such as the one in 510 B.C. which sought to disenfranchise those of questionable lineage. Finally, the Cleisthenic reforms received support because they granted something traditionally prized by every Greek community—local autonomy. Each deme was in essence a polis in miniature with its own *demarch* (mayor), assembly, and court. These institutions not only allowed locals a chance to manage their own affairs, they also provided an opportunity for citizens to hone their skills as members of a participatory democracy.

Reorganization of the citizen body was not Cleisthenes' only innovation. He also expanded the Solonian *boule* to five hundred members (fifty *bouleutai* from each of the ten tribes) and he is additionally credited with having introduced the institution of ostracism (see below). Nevertheless, it was the "mixing" of the Athenian population, to use Aristotle's term (Ath. Const. 21.2), in conjunction with the deme system, that constituted the most significant alterations.

What exactly were the implications of these innovations and how did they contribute to the expansion of democracy? Under the old system, powerful clan groups employed their wealth and status to maintain a network of local retainers. As a result of the insertion of fresh populations with whom the ruling gene had no prior history, aristocratic influence over the common man was significantly reduced.[*] Moreover, the new system also ended the monopoly en-

---

[*] Hignett (1962, 14) argues that the Cleisthenic reforms were not an attempt to weaken the great households but instead aimed at nullifying regional interests on behalf of larger national unity.

joyed by the gentry in designating citizen status. Prior to Cleisthenes' revisions, membership in a *phratria* was the exclusive criterion for citizenship and only the sons of members were eligible for installation. This meant that civic privilege was determined by a closed corporation where proper birth constituted the price of admission. With the advent of the deme system however, locality replaced kinship as the basis of citizenship, which simultaneously allowed for a more incorporative understanding of the term *polites* (citizen).

What, in effect, Cleisthenes succeeded in doing was to bring to fruition a process begun earlier by the tyrants, viz., the abasement of patrician power and influence, without which the mature democracy of 5th century Athens could never have evolved. Clearly, this achievement distinguishes Cleisthenes as a pivotal figure in democracy's progress. What is far less clear however, is the motivation that guided Cleisthenes' actions. Herodotus' assessment (5.66) strongly suggests that Cleisthenes was not inspired by exalted democratic purpose, that he became a *philodemos* of necessity having been bested in the infighting against Isagoras. Some scholars have even suggested that the reforms were actually part of a scheme to enhance the power of Cleisthenes' own clan which stood to benefit from a gerrymandering of the demes in the vicinity of the city (Forrest 1966, Seley 1976, Thorley 1996). In the final analysis, however, Cleisthenes' intentions, whether they be pure or opportunistic, are not as significant as the results—a constitutional framework that served Athens well for centuries to come and marked one of the high points in the development of popular sovereignty in the ancient world.

Guided by the egalitarian logic implicit in much of the Cleisthenic reforms, it was inevitable that the *demos* would mobilize against any and all vestiges of aristocratic privilege. One of the first moves along these lines came in 487-486 B.C., shortly after the victory at Marathon. The target was the archonships, which had traditionally been an administrative monopoly of the wellborn. These officials would now no longer be elected but were instead chosen by lot from a list of five hundred candidates put forth by the tribes. After 457 B.C. eligibility for these posts was expanded to include members of the *zeugitai* class and by the 4th century, even the prohibition against *thetic* involvement was ignored.

The next target of democratic reduction was the venerable aristocratic council known as the Areopagus. Since the days of the Athenian monarchy, the Areopagus had served as a living embodiment of the political and social chasm separating the common man from the patriciate. The scope of the council's authorities was extensive in all judicial matters including homicide, arson, and personal injury cases. Moreover, the Areopagus enjoyed a general mandate to serve as the guardian of the laws (*nomophylakia*).[*] In essence, the council ran the state for much of the period preceding the democratic developments being traced here.

By the late 6th and early 5th centuries B.C., the Areopagus must have been seen by the majority as a vestigial organism utterly at odds with recent democratic advancements.[†] Antiquated or not however, the Areopagus still had its supporters. In particular, Cimon, the son of Miltiades, was the champion of conservative causes at Athens, both foreign and domestic, as demonstrated by his support for the Areopagus and his advocacy of closer ties with Sparta. Cimon's pro-Spartan sentiments were tested in 464 B.C. as a result of a large-scale helot revolt centered at Mt. Ithome. The

---

[*] Its original powers included supervisory authority over the archons as well as a right to quash decrees from the assembly.

[†] In particular, the lifetime appointments to the Areopagus must have been particularly offensive to democratic sensitivities.

Athenian statesmen gathered a force of four thousand hoplites and marched to the assistance of Athen's ancient "yoke-mate" (Sparta). But while Cimon and his forces were away, opponents of the Areopagus, led by Ephialtes and a young protégé named Pericles, moved against the council. The assault came in the form of a series of strategic prosecutions against key council members followed by a systematic denuding of the council's powers, which were redistributed to the council of five hundred, the assembly, and the courts. After 402 B.C., the Areopagus retained its right to try homicide cases and also remained involved in certain categories of religious litigation, but the council's traditional role as the voice of *eupatrid* preeminence had been silenced forever. For his trouble, Ephialtes was assassinated in 461 B.C., but his death could not alter the impact of removing the last vestige of institutionalized privilege enjoyed by the lords of Attica. The aristocracy would continue to participate in the civic affairs of the polis, but it would now do so at the pleasure of the *demos*.

All that remained now was for the people to consolidate its position as *kyrios* of the city. This process was advanced in no small measure by the social and political transformations engendered by Athenian naval strategy. During the second Persian War (480-479 B.C.) Themistocles had opted for "wooden walls" as opposed to a traditional hoplite defense against Xerxes' hordes. As a result, the *nautikos ochlos*, who were at best a peripheral element within the political community, became critically important in the war effort. Although too poor to purchase armor, this mass of unwashed commoners deftly manned the fleet at Artemisium and Salamis, establishing what Pindar would later describe as "Liberty's cornerstone" (Plutarch Them. 8.2). These thetic contributions, in conjunction with the all-important role the navy would subsequently play in advancing Athen's imperial ambitions and in defending the city during the Peloponnesian War, made the political demands of the lowly oarsmen impossible to deny.

These shifts in the political center of gravity resulted in the mature democracy of the mid and late 5th century B.C. The chief characteristics of this system included little or no limitation on popular participation, a heavy reliance upon sortition, pay for public service, aggressive restraint of magistrate authority, dominance of key political institutions by the demos (e.g., assembly and courts), and a significant reliance upon popular decree as the final word in all affairs of state (see Aristotle, Politics 4.4-7). In addition, the ripened democracy of this period spawned a new species of politician. Unlike traditional leaders drawn from the landed-aristocracy, these new *prostatai tou demou* (champions of the people) came from the industrial and commercial classes.[*] According to Aristotle, whose assessment in these matters must be deemed highly tendentious, the combination of these factors resulted in a regime that was corrupt, unstable, and misguided. At least some portion of the population must have agreed with the philosopher because the Athenian democracy was deposed twice toward the end of the 5th century: once in 411 and again, under Spartan instigation, in 403. But the larger Athenian commitment to popular sovereignty was not to be undone by the likes of a Periander or a Critias. Accordingly, these oligarchic coups failed in short order and democracy, with some moderating adjustments, was firmly re-established.

Throughout most of the 4th century Athenian democracy not only held its own, it flourished. In fact, the available data suggests attendance rates at the assembly increased during the period despite a decline in population (Hansen 1976, 132). But circumstances at a

---

[*] Cleon's money had been made from a tannery, Cleophon's wealth stemmed from a lyre-making enterprise and Hyperbulus owned a lamp factory.

small Boeotian town named Chaeronea soon set in motion a series of events that dramatically altered the history of democratic Athens. There, in the year 338 B.C., Philip and his son, Alexander, crushed a combined Athenian-Theban force, establishing thereby a Macedonian hegemony over much of Greece. Upon learning of Alexander's death in 323 B.C., Athens, along with several other Greek states, rebelled against Antipater, the Macedonian regent, in the so-called Lamian War. In 322-21 Antipater defeated the coalition and imposed an oligarchy upon Athens, which effectively ended that city's historic experiment with government, by, for, and of the people.

The Government of Democratic Athens

The Assembly

The term *demos* (people) is often used as a kind of shorthand when referring to ancient Greek democracy, and at Athens there was one unit of government in particular that specifically embodied the notion of *demos*, that symbolized the essence of popular sovereignty as the Greeks understood that concept. This institution was the *ecclesia*, or people's assembly. No other institution, not even the unusually large courts (*dicasteria*), enjoyed the same populist connotations as the *ecclesia*. By comparison, these judicial structures were merely fractions of the *demos* acting as designated agents on behalf of the ultimate authority constituted by the assembly (Hansen 1978, 135). For the Athenians, then, to speak of democracy was first and foremost to think of the large, open sessions of the *ecclesia* where any and all citizens were free to attend, speak, and vote on virtually any issue the people deemed worthy of its consideration.[*]

As a deliberative body, the *ecclesia* was quite active with at least forty regularly scheduled meetings per year plus any number of additional sessions as needed. Once each *prytany*,[†] a special meeting was held to consider particularly important state business such as the review of public officials, food supply, national defense, etc. This session was known as the *kyria ecclesia* and those attending received extra pay—1 ½ drachma as opposed to the normal compensation of 1 drachma (late 4th century). The expenses associated with seating the assembly for a year were significant, perhaps 45-50 talents, which may cast some doubt on the quality of civic motivation among the Athenian citizenry. Specifically, the fees Athenians came to expect for their civic service may appear to be an ancient equivalent of the modern pork barrel, but what we need to consider here is the fact that the ancient city-state was actually a sort of joint stock company in which accrued value was appropriately distributed to the citizen share-holders (Greenidge 166).

When the *ecclesia* was in session, it met in a variety of locations within the city district. In archaic times meetings were held in the *agora* and later, during the classical period, we learn of assemblies at the Piraeus and the theatre. But the most frequently utilized site was the *Pnyx*, located immediately west of the acropolis. The original area was approximately 2,400 square meters but was subsequently enlarged at the end of the 4th century by Lycurgus. Mod-

---

[*] On some occasions the *ecclesia* could also function as a court, hearing important public cases such as *eisangeliai* (impeachment for crimes against the state). After 362 B.C., cases such as these seem to have been referred to courts possibly because it was less expensive to seat a *dicasterion* than it was to seat and pay the assembly.

[†] A *prytany* was a unit of time corresponding to 1/10th of the year during which 50 members of the *boule* were empowered to serve as the council's executive committee.

ern estimates (Hansen 1976) suggest that a typical session involved about 6,000 citizens. Attendance was presumably higher at the principal meetings, given the enhanced pay rates. Under normal circumstances there was no mandatory quorum, but if the assembly was considering extraordinary business such as ostracism, the granting of citizenship, or special financial exemptions, a minimum of 6,000 citizens had to attend. There seems to have been no formal seating arrangement for the rank and file, although we are told of unofficial attempts to organize groups of partisans in an effort to create politically motivated claques (Plutarch, Pericles 11).

With regard to authority, the *ecclesia*, particularly in the second half of the 5th century, exercised enormous power given its right to issue administrative decrees known as *psephismata*. During this period there was little meaningful distinction between a permanent rule (nomos) and a popular decree tied to specific circumstances. After the restoration of the democracy in 410 B.C., efforts were made to more clearly delineate and prioritize the two categories; existing laws were revised to eliminate obscurities and eventually decrees were no longer permitted to overturn standing laws[*] (Hornblower and Spawforth 825). These were conservative moves aimed at forestalling undisciplined and impulsive policy-making by the *ecclesia*.[†] After the removal of the Thirty Tyrants in 403, addi-

---

[*] An earlier move along these same lines involved a special prosecution aimed at thwarting hastily conceived *psephismata*. It was called the *graphe paranomon* and it was designed to protect long established law at Athens. Our earliest reference to this *graphe* occurs in a speech by Andocides (On the Mysteries 17) in 415 B.C., but the establishment of this mechanism may actually date from the time of Ephialtes. If convicted, the guilty party was typically fined, but Demosthenes (Against Timarchus 138) also mentions an instance of capital punishment.

[†] The need for these restrictions is well illustrated by the dreadful abuses associated with the treatment of the generals after the battle of Arginusae (406 B.C.). Here, popular decree was allowed to overwhelm existing law and when the assembly was reminded of the illegality of its actions, the majority protested, "…it was monstrous if

tional restraints were imposed with the establishment of large legislative review boards known as the *nomothetai* (see Demosthenes, Against Timarchus 20-23). The purpose here was to decelerate the law-making process, allowing the demos full opportunity to carefully review intended additions or alterations to the law. Moreover, the new procedure provided for a shift of legislative discretion away from the *ecclesia*. Now when the assembly voted a change to the legal system, the proposal was forwarded to the *nomothetai* where the final determination was made.

In terms of the assembly's manner and bearing, many of the same concerns scholars have expressed about the courts apply as well to the *ecclesia*. In particular, theatricality was, no doubt, a prominent aspect of the deliberative process and one can easily envision episodes of mass agitation triggered by dazzling displays of rhetoric. But for all the hoarse tones and bombast, the Athenian assembly nevertheless bore important fruit for the history of democracy to the extent it demonstrated the capacity of free men to gather, discuss, and chart their political fate in an atmosphere fundamentally unencumbered by the inequities of birth and rank.

The Council

The council or *boule*[*] served in a probouleutic capacity for the assembly, i.e., it enjoyed pre-deliberative authorities in advance of the *ecclesia's* formulation of policy. Specifically, the council was

---

the people were to be prevented from doing whatever they wished" (Xen Hell. 1.7.12-13). The dilemma lay precisely in the people "doing whatever they wished."

[*] The history of the council's formation is open to question. Most scholars credit Solon with its invention, but some have argued that the only Council of Athens in the early 6th century was the Areopagus (e.g., Hignett 96). Cleisthenes established the Council of 500 at the close of the century and it is this institution that operated throughout the classical period.

responsible for constructing the agenda utilized by the assembly and at least initially the *boule's* prerogatives had the effect of limiting the *ecclesia's* discretion. This arrangement was probably an attempt at checks and balances against the popular assembly, but as democracy progressed, the ultimate sovereignty of the *ecclesia* became definitive and irresistible. The assembly began to freely amend the *boule's* protocols and even "suggested" in advance items that should appear on the agenda.

In classical times the *boule* was composed of 500 members (50 councilmen from each of the 10 tribes) chosen by lot. Candidates were required to be at least 30 years of age and could serve for a maximum of two, non-consecutive one-year terms. Of the 3,000 *bouleutai* (councilmen) whose names have survived, only 3% held the position twice (Stockton 86 n.36). Council members were compensated for their services, a practice that may have begun as early as the 460's. By the 4th century, the membership received 5 obols per day and could meet as many as 260 days per year. Allegations of financial impropriety against the *boule* were not uncommon (see Pseudo-Xenophon <u>Const</u>. <u>Of Athens</u> 3.3 and Aristophanes <u>Wasps</u> 655 and <u>Thesmo</u>. 936-9) but remain difficult to assess.

The most important function of the *boule* was its agenda-setting responsibilities vis-à-vis the assembly, but, in addition, the *boule* played a key role in the state's administration. The council was divided into ten groups called *prytaneis* (presidents), again representing each of the 10 tribes. These groups served on a rotating basis for 1/10th of the year as the *boule's* standing committee—the order of rotation being determined by lot. The *prytaneis* had their own office building in the agora known as the *tholos*, so named for its circular shape. It was located near the *bouleuterium* where plenary council sessions were normally convened. Each day the *prytaneis* chose one of its members to serve as *epistates* (foreman). He and one-third of the *prytaneis* were required to remain on duty in the *tholos* for a period of 24 consecutive hours. During this brief tenure, the *epistates* was in essence the head of state. He was responsible for chairing any meeting of the council or assembly and, in addition, he controlled the state seal and the keys to the treasury.[*]

Beyond these special administrative duties, the *boule* also supervised magistrate activities, participated in various financial audits, oversaw public works and festivals, received foreign emissaries, ensured military preparedness for the mounted and naval forces, and acted upon directives received from the people's assembly. This last activity is important because it highlights the working relationship between the *boule* and the *ecclesia* during the democratic era. In particular, it reveals a dramatic shift of fortunes between the two institutions; where the *boule* had once been the aristocratic advisor to kings, it increasingly became the servant of lord *demos*.

The Courts

In Aristophanes' *Clouds* (207-8), Strepsiades, one of the leading characters, examines a map and cannot believe the area marked "Athens" is indeed the famous city because he sees no jurors sitting! The litigiousness of the Athenians is well known and well documented. Indeed, their enthusiasm for judicial contest has prompted one scholar to observe that the Athenians probably spent more man hours judging than any other people in history (MacDowell 40). What was the nature of their system, and how did the ancient *dicasteria* (courts) correlate with modern courtrooms?

---

[*] The procedures employed by the *boule* and its sub-committees must have been fairly complex, so much so that even Socrates found them perplexing (Plato, Gorgias 473e).

In the early 6th century, during the archonship of Solon, trials conducted by the people were instituted for the first time. In all probability the original popular court (*eliaia*) was simply a judicial session of the *ecclesia*. Eventually, as the volume of litigation increased, it became necessary to divide the *eliaia* into specific *dicasteria*. The exact moment of this division remains unclear; some have argued it took place in the 6th century; others believe the formation of discrete judicial units did not occur until after the major democratic reforms. In any event, by the mid 5th century, a jury pool of 6,000 qualified (30 years of age or older) volunteers was established each year. To encourage participation, pay was introduced by Pericles,[*] which had the important effect, despite the modest nature of the stipend, of involving more citizens from the lower classes in the judicial process. We are not sure of the procedure used in the 5th century to assign jurors to specific courts, but our information regarding the 4th century reveals an increasingly complex lottery arrangement outlined in detail by Aristotle (see Ath. Const. 63-6). Eventually, the Athenians even invented a machine called the *cleroterion* designed to randomly assign jurors to courts. Apparently, these elaborate measures were necessary in order to protect against the subornation of dicasts. We are told, for example, that Anytus, one of the three indictors of Socrates, successfully bribed a jury after his failure to prevent the loss of Pylos in 409 B.C. (Ath. Const. 27.5). Lysias reports that even after the changes in jury selection techniques, Ergocles and his colleagues managed to bribe 2,100 jurors (Against Philocrates 12);[†] and Isocrates, writing in the mid 4th century, assures us that bribery in

---

[*] Pericles' motives for the introduction of juror pay may not have had much to do with enhancing public participation. According to Aristotle (Ath. Const. 27.3-4), the real motive was to counteract his rival Cimon's generosity toward the common man.

[†] Doubtless this figure reflects the hyperbole of the speech writer.

general, despite the threat of harsh penalty, was common at Athens (On the Peace 50).

Perhaps the problem of corruption explains in part one aspect of the ancient judiciary that never ceases to astonish the modern reader, viz., the magnitude of the juries that sat at Athens. The size varied according to the nature and public significance of the case. Private disputes might typically impanel 200 jurors, but a high profile public case might involve 2500 dicasts or more.[*] Bribing massive panels such as these would not only present an immense financial challenge, it would also entail activities that would have been virtually impossible to conceal.

It seems that money also had an unfortunate tendency to intrude itself upon the substantive aspects of courtroom activities. We know that part of the state's financial strategy included incomes derived from court-inflicted penalties with the result that, when the public coffers were low, there must have been a strong temptation to seek solvency at the expense of justice (Harrison 2:212). Indeed, it seems some prosecutors were not above reminding the jury that their juror fees were in jeopardy unless the state's treasury secured fresh funds via a conviction (see Lysias, On the Property of Aristophanes). In addition, the rich must have been particularly vulnerable to vexatious lawsuits during times of financial exigency. Sycophants, the judicial locusts of ancient Athens, undoubtedly became particularly emboldened under such conditions (see below).

With regard to courtroom procedure, the Athenian *dicasteria* present a very different setting than anything to which we can point

---

[*] Given the fact that these large juries were paid for their services, the annual cost of operating the judicial system must have been significant—although Aristophanes' figure (Wasps 661) of 150 talents per year is an obvious exaggeration.

in the modern world. Most significantly, this was a system run entirely by amateurs; there was no professional administration of justice at ancient Athens—no judges, public prosecutors, or public defenders.* Magistrates did preside at these sessions, but they constituted a mere procedural presence. In no sense did they function in a capacity equivalent to that of a modern judge; specifically, they did not fact-find, define the law, or instruct the jury. These critical functions were in the hands of the dicasts themselves who were selected without regard to legal expertise or experience. The explanation for the absence of legal specialists† in Athens may lie in a democratic bias that saw the expert as incompatible with egalitarian principle and as a potential threat to the *demos'* authority (see Calhoun Chapter 5).

The absence of legal professionals formally assigned the task of discharging the state's judicial business resulted in a variety of unwelcome consequences. Absent a public prosecutor, for example, litigation was typically initiated by private citizens.‡ This provided opportunity for prosecutions based on motives completely unrelated to public spiritedness, including financial gain (sycophants) and personal enmity. As a result, the courtroom atmosphere was often reduced to a level where calumny and defamation, not the

---

* On some occasions the assembly did appoint individual citizens to serve as prosecutors.

† There were, however, a few private citizens with specialized legal knowledge. Isaeus was apparently an expert in property law and Antiphon was an authority on statutes dealing with homicide.

‡ There were two basic categories of prosecution at Athens—*dike* and *graphe*. The former was a suit of private action and could only be brought by the wronged party (e.g., the family of a murdered man). The second form of prosecution was initiated by Solon and was a public suit that could be lodged *ho boulomenos*, i.e., by anyone. It was this *graphe* that became the weapon of choice in the hands of politically motivated citizens.

merits of the case, became the central focus of the proceeding. In addition, by investing prosecutorial authority in private hands, the Athenians also allowed for a dangerous infusion of "politics" into their judicial system.[*] Over time, the court sessions became de facto testing grounds for the policies and proposals of high-profile public figures (Miltiades, Cimon, Pericles, Alcibiades, et al.) and their circle of friends. As a result, instead of distributing justice, the courts became involved in dispensing politically inspired retributions including fines and banishments. In the murderous hands of The Thirty, this retributive mentality resulted in nothing less than judicial murder. For Critias and his colleagues the courts became an oligarchic gallows where political opponents such as Cleophon, Strombichides, Dionysodorous, and Eucrates were extended "ultimate justice."

Another malady of the Athenian judiciary that resulted in instability and confusion was a near complete lack of reliance upon legal precedents. Modern judicial experience has demonstrated the wisdom of *stare decisis* as a means of protecting against judicial impulse and the dangers of ungrounded legal interpretation. At Athens, however, any suggestion that a seated jury should be limited by the actions of earlier dicasts would have produced considerable indignation. Each case was essentially treated *de novo*, leaving jurors free to determine a given question independently of previous judgments. This meant that demonstrably similar cases could result in remarkably different verdicts. The failure to acknowledge precedents also tended to create a kind of substantive vacuum that was

---

[*] Aeschines (Against Timarchus 2) attempts to justify politically-inspired prosecution by arguing that, "private enmities correct public abuses," but the improprieties to which this logic led cannot be denied. The fact that Aristophon was charged 75 times with attempting to subvert the laws of the state without a conviction illustrates the point (see also Demosthenes, De Corona 249).

233

often filled by legally immaterial considerations such as the quality of the speech making or the effectiveness of some histrionic display.

Although in principle, missteps taken by the *dicasteria* could be corrected by the people's assembly, in truth the boast made by Philocleon in <u>Wasps</u> (587) that jurors enjoyed an unchecked potency, was fundamentally correct. The courts did indeed wield enormous power, and their verdicts were essentially final. In itself, this concentration of judicial authority might not have been a problem had the Athenians been able to address two crucial shortcomings. First, the considerable fluidity of their legal codes which invited haphazard and uneven juror interpretation. Second, an unrelenting and apparently irresistible tendency to convert the courts into political battlegrounds.* This last point is arguably the most manifest shortcoming of the entire democratic regime at Athens. The idea of an independent judiciary systematically and dispassionately distributing justice is an ideal seldom realized among the Greeks. At Athens, Lady Justice needed more than a sword and scales. She needed full-body armor and eyes in the back of her head.

Administration

Democracy at Athens was a remarkably labor intensive enterprise. In his <u>Athenian Constitution</u> (24.3) Aristotle claims there were 700 *archai*, or public officials, operating throughout the city-state during the 5th century. Given the limited size of the citizen population, this figure has prompted skepticism among certain scholars. However, others have argued that Aristotle's claim, al-

---

* Unlike the Romans, the Greeks never developed blood sports like gladiatorial games. They didn't need to—they had politics.

though large, is correct and that, in fact, the list presented by the philosopher is not exhaustive, that hundreds of additional administrative positions can legitimately be added (Hansen 1980, 163). If this latter assessment is accurate, it means that roughly five percent of the total citizen population in the late 4th century served as magistrates each year.* When we add this administrative total to the 6,000 jurors impaneled annually, plus the 6,000 assemblymen who routinely attended the meetings of the *ecclesia*, and the 500 *bouleutai* assigned the council, we begin to appreciate the highly participatory nature of Greek democracy—one of the key distinctions between the ancient and modern systems.

Among the many officials serving at Athens, none were more important initially than the nine archons. The three senior members of this group were the *archon basileus* (king archon), the *eponymous archon* who gave his name to the official year, and the *polemarchus*, or war archon. The remaining six members were the *thesmothetai* (law setters). Eventually a tenth archon, a kind of secretary, was added. Originally, the archons were the most powerful figures in the state. They were chosen exclusively from the aristocracy and upon vacating their administrative positions they became permanent members of the Areopagus. With the advent of democracy however, eligibility expanded and in 487, archons began to be selected for their one-year terms by lot. In addition, as the democracy evolved, the archons increasingly forfeited power in favor of newer administrative positions and mass institutions such as the courts.

---

* For the 5th century, Hammond (85-6) estimates that 10,000 citizens out of a population of 30,000 may have been receiving some form of compensation for public service and that after the Peloponnesian War public service expenditures may have been 200 talents annually.

Another important group of public servants were the *strategoi*, a board of ten generals who by the 5th century had not only absorbed the military responsibilities of the ancient *polemarchus*, but had also become the leading political figures in the city.[*] The general-ships were unlike most other *archai* in the sense that they were elected posts renewable on an open-ended basis, as the remarkable career of Pericles illustrates with its fifteen consecutive re-elections starting in 443 B.C. In addition to commanding the land and naval forces, the strategoi presided at trials involving all matters associated with the military. They also had the exclusive right to attend sessions of the *boule* and to submit proposals directly to that body. In addition, their duties included the enrollment of soldiers, the designation of triarchs (naval sponsors) and control of the schedules for certain extraordinary taxes relating to military needs (Harrison 2:32).

Athens also had a variety of public officials dedicated to managing the state's financial affairs. Key among these were the *logistai*, a board of 30 men (5th century) appointed by lot who served as public accountants overseeing all payments to and from the sacred treasuries. In addition, there were two other boards of financial managers with the same title involved in the auditing of magistrates' accounts and with the *euthyna* ("straightening"), the end-of-term scrutiny required of public officials (see below). There was also a group of officers called the *poletai* who dealt with the revenues generated by the sale of confiscated property and who arranged financial details with the tax farmers. And we know, too, of

---

[*] Virtually all those identified by modern historians as the "great" statesmen of ancient Athens established their reputations through the opportunities presented by the *strategos* post—e.g., Miltades, Themistocles, Aristides, and Pericles. It should also be noted that with very few exceptions, the *strategoi* came from the powerful aristocratic families.

the *practores* who collected the fines assigned by the various Athenian courts.

Our sources speak as well of a large number of public officials involved in the day-to-day management of the city's affairs. There was, for example, a board of public safety known as the "Eleven" who supervised the 300 Scythian archers (the police), managed the city prison system, and carried out sentences of death imposed by the state. Additionally, we know of officials assigned the task of doing everything from ensuring the cleanliness of Athens' streets to safeguarding the integrity of the weights and measures used in the marketplace. There were even ministers of corn (*sitophylakes*) who oversaw the sale of various grains at Athens and Piraeus with an eye toward guaranteeing adequate supply.

What we discover then, in examining the "bureaucracy" of the Athenian state, is an unusually high rate of citizen participation, a civil service largely comprised of amateur officials, and an appointment technique driven almost entirely by the luck of the draw. The modern reliance upon professional administrators, upon career bureaucrats with extensive tenures, would never have been tolerated at Athens. Any system that failed to provide the average citizen with a continuous opportunity for administrative assignment would have been viewed as inherently disfranchising and therefore incongruent with populist precept. Moreover, the Athenians were highly suspicious of any civic arrangement that might lead to entrenched power—better a learning curve than a tyranny of the bureaucracy.

Public Accountability

Democracy assumes implicitly that a responsible political order can result from the collaborative efforts of free citizens. The democrat believes that people can be trusted to minister to their own political affairs; that the citizenry is capable of the kind of balanced and reasonable conduct upon which democracy must, by its very nature, rely. As votaries of popular sovereignty one might expect the Athenians to reflect some, if not all, of these ideals. Yet when we examine the standards of accountability leveled by the Athenians at their public servants, we discover a paradox: a democracy that formally and extensively views its citizens with grave distrust.[*]

The suspicions referred to here are reflected in a variety of procedural and institutional arrangements. One of the reasons, for instance, that public officials typically served on "boards," as opposed to being allowed to discharge their responsibilities separately, was to circumscribe the ambitions and corrupt intentions of any individual member.[†] In addition, the Athenians established a veritable gauntlet of public examinations before, during, and after the assumption of a magistrate's official position. Prior to the appointment, an individual was subject to a public scrutiny known as *dokimasia* conducted by either court or council. The interrogations of this session were not intended as a talent search; *dokimasia* was more of a discovery exercise aimed at determining the civic and moral suitability of the candidate. In the process, a man's entire life went on review; what was his ancestry, where were his family's tombs, were his taxes paid, had he honorably discharged his military obligations, did he extend proper care to his parents? (Aristotle, Ath. Const. 55.3). Witnesses had to be produced to verify the responses, after which the presiding examiner asked if anyone wished to bring a charge against the candidate.

---

[*] We anticipate finding the logic of Thomas Jefferson and instead we discover the cynicism of Thomas Hobbes.

[†] Typically, these boards were composed of ten members.

Unlike Roman officials who were virtually immune from attack during their terms in office, the Athenian public servant was continuously scrutinized even while on active duty. During the *kyria* session of the *ecclesia* once each prytany, a special vote was taken called the *apokheirotonia* to determine whether office holders were performing their duties appropriately. In other words, approximately every 36 days, an official was reviewed and voted upon. If the vote went against him, the accused individual was deposed and subsequently tried in court. This was the method by which Pericles was removed from office in 430 B.C. (see MacDowell 169).

Again, at the close of a magistrate's term he was required to submit to the *euthyna*. This examination was required of all appointed officials, including members of the *boule*. It involved several phases, chief of which was a financial audit where anyone found guilty of *klope* (embezzlement) had to repay ten times the original sum or merely the principal itself in a case of simple fiscal ineptitude (*adikion*). Failure to pay resulted in disfranchisement for the official and his descendants. Beyond the audit aspect, the *euthyna* also involved an open session where any citizen could accuse a public servant of neglect of duty or misuse of authority. During the 4th century if the charges were deemed valid, they resulted in a trial conducted in a court determined by the specific nature of the alleged crime.

The Athenians also established a variety of prosecutive options that might be employed against public officials, perhaps the most notorious being *eisangelia* (impeachment). This proceeding could be initiated at any time by any citizen against any other member of the community. The Areopagus probably heard these cases originally, but after the reforms of Ephialtes the council and courts assumed the right, and from 360 B.C. on, it seems the *dicasteria* alone dealt with these matters. *Eisangelia* typically involved the most serious criminal allegations, such as treason and deception of the people. The motivations for bringing such suits were "complex" to say the least, and provided a perfect opportunity to vent personal hatreds and level political scores.

There was one category of public servant in particular for whom *eisangelia* was a virtual sword of Damocles—the *strategoi*. As is well known, the Athenian democracy took a less than charitable view toward those who failed the city militarily. The non-victorious general, irrespective of circumstances that may have made success impossible, was routinely brought up on charges, often being accused of *dorodakia* (bribe-taking) or *prodosia* (betrayal). In a speech delivered by Demosthenes in 351 B.C., the orator claimed that a general stood a greater chance of being killed as a result of *eisangelia* than of dying in combat (First Philippic 47). As preposterous as this may sound, the evidence indicates that Demosthenes was not exaggerating.[*] Typically, it seems that two generals from each board of ten *strategoi* were subjected to the impeachment with the result that while we know of three generals who died in battle during the 4th century, we know of six, possibly eight, *strategoi* who were sentenced to death via *eisangelia* (see Hansen 1975).[†] If a general were fortunate enough to escape capital punishment, the alternative was often a crippling financial penalty; Miltiades' failure at Paros resulted in a fine of 50 talents, and Timotheus is said to have been assessed a staggering 100 talents—later reduced to 10 talents after his death (Roberts 28).

---

[*] This begins to explain some of the catastrophic decision-making of Nicias during the Battle of Syracuse (Thucydides 7.48).

[†] Not even death could spare the accused in some cases. Phrynichus, a 5th century Athenian politician, was impeached posthumously. His corpse was disinterred, his property confiscated, and his house razed.

It seems then that Athens, for all its democratic fervor, was very much committed to the logic of Lord Acton—"power tends to corrupt"—and as a result, the Athenians rigorously circumscribed administrative authority. Above all, they seemed intensely interested in hindering the growth of executive authority—particularly as it pertained to the board of generals. No other officials in the state's administration were more tightly tethered, none more powerfully reminded of the fact that they were public servants—emphasis on the word "servant." In the end, this restrictive mentality paid Athens an important dividend, one that was critical for the long-term preservation of the democracy, it prevented the advent of personality cults and the development of private armies. Unlike Rome, Athens never saw the likes of Marius, Sulla, Pompey, or Caesar, men whose stellar careers progressed at the expense of democratic institutions.[*] At Athens, the aspiring egos of such men were crushed by a jealous god called the *ecclesia*, an institution fundamentally intolerant of the ambitions of would-be deities.

Financing The State

Financing the Athenian democracy was a complex and costly matter for at least two reasons. First, there was the expectation of *misthophoria*, i.e., the public financing of civic participation.[†] Pericles established this precedent by extending pay to the dicasts in 451-450 B.C. Shortly thereafter, magistrates and *boule* members received compensation and in the early 4th century those attending

---

[*] Not that the Roman Republic was genuinely democratic in an Athenian sense. In truth, Rome before the Principate was an oligarchy with democratic veneer.

[†] Pay for civic involvement is typically associated with the Athenian democracy, but there is evidence it was also used by other city-states such as those involved in the Boeotian federation and on Rhodes.

the assembly were also remunerated.[*] Accurate estimates of what these pay arrangements cost the state annually are impossible to calculate, but they must have been significant. Secondly, the Athenian democracy was a maritime nation whose fortunes, militarily and commercially, were tied to the navy. The yearly expense of maintaining a single trireme (a military vessel) may have been as much as one talent,[†] and with a fleet the size of Athens,[‡] the fiscal burden associated with naval operations was undoubtedly immense. How did the Athenians finance these and the myriad other expenses associated with running a state?

Surprisingly, the Athenians had nothing analogous to the modern system of personal income tax. Direct taxation upon the person was in general rarely employed by the Greeks as a matter of social ideology. Levies such as these were seen as servile and degrading, the mark of a slave (see Demosthenes, Against Androtion 54-5). At Athens the only group routinely subject to a direct tax were the resident aliens who were required to pay the *metoikion* (twelve drachma per year). A rare exception to these assessment strategies was a special tax, typically a war tax, called the *eisphora*. This was an extraordinary, short-term measure first used at Athens during the Peloponnesian War in 428 B.C. (see Thucydides 3.19). It was

---

[*] Aristotle condemned the entire concept of *misthophoria* because he believed it nourished the citizenry's baser instincts (Politics 2.4.11).

[†] The term "talent" is both a designation of weight, approximately 57 lbs., and a monetary unit. In ancient Athens a talent corresponded to 6,000 silver drachma. At the close of the 5th century, a common worker's wage was one drachma per day for an annual income of roughly 300 drachmas.

[‡] The size of Athens' fleet varied over time, but during the debate that preceded the Sicilian expedition, Nicias called for a force of not less than 100 triremes and an equal number of transports. The people authorized his request (Thucyd. 6.25-26). During the Persian War (480 B.C.) the Athenian fleet created by Themistocles is said to have contained nearly 200 vessels (Herod. 7.144).

not a progressive tax and therefore only applied to members of the hoplite class or higher, making it applicable to approximately one-third or less of the total citizen population (Jones 35).

The more routine methods of securing the essential state funds were a series of indirect taxes, such as the 2% import and export levy on all goods passing through the port of Piraeus. Athens also generated significant revenues by selling private leases for the operation of the state-owned mines at Larium. In addition, there were court-ordered liquidations, market fees, and various state-imposed fines. Perhaps the most unusual source of revenues at Athens was the mandated philanthropy known as *leitourgia* ("work for the people"). These were obligatory acts of public service required of the wealthiest members of the society,[*] a practice that may have begun at the time of the Cleisthenic reforms and continued at Athens until their abolition in the late 4th century. At Athens during the classical era, there were both state-wide and deme liturgies, the former being divided into two broad categories—military and festival. The chief military liturgy was the trierarchy, the most costly of all public services, which required funds not only to operate a ship for a year but to command it as well.[†] The festival category included the major expenses associated with preparing a chorus for the musical or dramatic celebrations plus a variety of minor liturgies, including sponsorship for teams competing at various athletic contests (gymnasiarchy), and the subsidy of public banquets (hes-

---

[*] Other cities such as Mytilene and Siphnos also seem to have required these civic contributions and although Demetrius of Phalerum ended the system at Athens, an analogous arrangement known as "euergetism" was common during the Hellenistic period.

[†] During the 4th century the extraordinary costs of the trierarchy was made somewhat more tolerable by distributing the expense among companies (*symmoriai*) composed of the 1,200 richest citizens.

tiasis). Later, the rich were also periodically expected to assist the state's cash flow by advancing funds against anticipated tax revenues.

The estimated wealth of a typical liturgist was probably in the 3-4 talent range. If a citizen believed he had been unfairly designated to perform "the people's work" in the sense that there were others more affluent and therefore better able to assume the burden, he had the option of lodging a formal challenge known as an *antidosis*. Here, the individual challenged was expected to either exchange property with the challenger, as a demonstration that he was not wealthier, or perform the liturgy originally assigned the man proposing the exchange. Actual exchanges did occur but were probably quite rare. In the majority of cases the rich seem to have "graciously" accepted their role as public benefactors.* The reason for this is not difficult to understand given the cultural norms of ancient Greece. The key incentive to contribution was the public notoriety that accrued to donors; affluent citizens were not opposed to expending their personal resources as long as it provided that which was sought by every Greek irrespective of economic status—honor, glory, acknowledgement.

Sortition

As a method of allocating political office, the lot rapidly became a signature feature of Athenian democracy. In truth, however, selection "by the bean" was a very ancient decision-making technique, probably of religious origins, and was in no way unique to Athens (Headlam 11). Priests and other sacral officials were often

---

* However, Aristotle suggests (Politics 5.4.1) that a prime cause of revolutions was demagogue-inspired excesses against people of property which caused the rich to band together in opposition to the *demos*.

chosen by lot and at Delphi the god himself frequently revealed his will through its use. The precise moment of its first employment at Athens is not known. Aristotle (Ath. Const. 4) claims that the lottery system was already in use at Athens during pre-democratic times, a point echoed by Plutarch (Pericles 9). Others have argued that sortition at Athens only began with Solon or perhaps with Cleisthenes. In any event, what we know with certainty is that the lot became, with a few significant exceptions, the primary means of civic selection after 487 B.C. Only the generals and a number of senior financial officers continued to be chosen by election beyond that point.

The reasons why sortition became an integral aspect of Athenian democracy are related to both practical and ideological factors. Ideologically speaking, the lot was an affirmation of the egalitarian principles that figured so prominently at Athens. Its use was a clear statement of democratic conviction that the average citizen was not only entitled but also capable of effectively participating in the affairs of state. In addition, the lot also spoke to a variety of practical concerns dear to the Athenian *demos* such as the perennial anxiety over entrenched power. Sortition ensured a random supply of freshly chosen public servants, none of whom had any realistic prospect of securing tenure for themselves. This meant that power would remain where the democracy intended, in the popular assembly, and not in the hands of an over-enfranchised administration.

The Athenians also embraced the lot because of certain suspicions they held regarding elections. Interestingly, elections at Athens were not seen as examples of democracy in action but as procedures favorable to oligarchic interests. The reason for this lay in the Athenian's keen appreciation of wealth's ability to influence the outcome of an election. To their way of thinking, sortition alone was genuinely democratic in the sense that it assigned citizens to office irrespective of financial status. In principle, sortition also precluded certain potential corruptions affiliated with elections such as voter intimidation and bribery. Moreover, selection of public officials by lot prevented the development of "party government" at Athens, which undoubtedly would have greatly inflamed a pre-existing and abundant instinct for faction. And finally, sortition, as opposed to election, spared Athens the effects of having significant numbers of malcontents, men who had been publicly humiliated by electoral defeat, intriguing and plotting in an effort to restore their public images. It is very possible then that the lot contributed to the stability of democratic Athens to the extent it made verdicts of chance, not economic or social privilege, the means of assigning governmental positions.

Political Clubs

The ancient Greeks had a saying, *koina ta ton philon*, "all things are common among friends." This emphasis on sharing also included enemies; the enemies of my friends automatically became my enemies as well. This logic is very ancient and can be found at least as far back as the Iliad (9.615) where in the famous embassy scene Achilles reminds his aged tutor, Phoenix, that as a friend, it is unfitting for him to side with Achilles' adversary, Agamemnon. Sentiments such as these did not diminish over time. In fact, they assumed a semi-institutionalized form in associations known as *hetaireiai*.* The term refers to a group of "comrades" and is often

---

* There were a wide variety of *hetaireiai* among the Greeks. There were clubs for dining, gambling, drinking, and apparently, there were even clubs dedicated to religious irreverence (see Athenaeus, Deipnosophistae 551e-f). Historically speaking, however, the most important clubs were the political *hetaireiai,* which played a significant role in civic affairs at Athens.

translated as "club." At Athens where there was nothing approximating the modern political party, these fellowships often became something much more than instruments of recreation.

Typically, the Athenian *hetaireiai* were secretive, tightly knit groups of aristocratic colleagues (Calhoun 24). The association was normally quite small, perhaps twenty members, with meetings taking place at private homes. Attachment to these societies was apparently a matter of great significance to members, which explains the fierce loyalties the *hetaireiai* were able to command from affiliates. We have a sense of this from Andocides' confessions where considerable time and energy are spent attempting to justify the testimony he offers against his former associates (see On the Mysteries 54-69). The spirit of his remarks also suggests that even the general public viewed disloyalty in these matters with considerable contempt, irrespective of the crimes attributable to the clubs.

What were the motivations that led citizens to join the *hetaireiai*? Aristotle notes that membership was based on a variety of interests, including financial gain, entertainment, and religious devotion (see N. Ethics 8.9.4-6). But there is no doubt that politics and the specific political welfare of the membership were important reasons for forming clubs. At Athens one might reasonably assume that *hetaireiai* were part of an oligarchic response to the democratic regimes of the late 6th and 5th centuries. In fact, political clubs at Athens precede the democracy by many years[*] and simply seem to be part of a larger, pervasive instinct on the part of the Greeks to affiliate for political purpose. But there were also some very specific reasons for joining political clubs, particularly in light of the often bitter struggles associated with the Athenian assembly

---

[*] Our first concrete evidence for a political club at Athens is the group associated with Cylon (c. 630 B.C.), the would-be tyrant of Athens.

and courts. The *hetaireiai* frequently provided a variety of supports for members without which the unallied individual might find himself at a distinct disadvantage. These services included money, witnesses, bribes, suppression of incriminating evidence, and the public abuse of opponents. Among some groups, orchestrated perjury on behalf of *philoi* was common and there is even evidence of club-sponsored violence, ranging from disruptions of public meetings to political assassination (e.g., Ephialtes?)-- all done on behalf of protecting the interests and objectives of members.

The methods employed by political clubs leave little doubt about their destabilizing potentials. Yet, as problematic as the *hetaireiai* were in principle, there was another form of these associations that was far more virulent—the *synomosia*. The term refers to a group of citizens bound by oath and dedicated to conspiratorial purpose. Thucydides uses the term to distinguish this radical form of club from the less extreme *hetaireiai*, and with good reason. There is ample evidence to suggest that the profanation of the mysteries and the desecration of the Hermae were tied to clubs and that the latter act in particular was a kind of promissory gesture undertaken by members of a *synomosia* aimed at irreversibly committing them to their seditious cause.[*] It is also clear that the oligarchic clubs were intimately involved in the revolutions of 411 and 404 at Athens.

Despite the unquestioned authority exercised by the *demos* during most of the classical period, the clandestine network of aristocratic clubs must have been a source of continuous anxiety at Athens. These concerns over a potential fifth column received infa-

---

[*] In the absence of anything remotely constitutive of textual evidence, I find Kuels' (387-392) hypothesis that the Hermae-choppers were actually Athenian women rebelling against their male tormentors impossible to accept.

mous validation with the butchery of Critias and his henchmen. No doubt, they explain why the revised legal code of the 4th century included specific provision against subversive *hetaireiai*.[*]

Sycophancy[†]

In Aristophanes' Acharnians (905-910) there is a well known scene in which a Boeotian merchant visiting Athens wants to trade for something that he cannot get at home. Dicaeopolis has just the thing—a sycophant named Nicarchus![‡] The practice of sycophancy represents one of the more sordid sides of popular sovereignty at Athens. It arose in response to two conditions unique to the Athenian democracy—the absence of a public prosecutor and the formal responsibility of all citizens to prosecute wrongdoers, even in cases where they had no personal interest. These features of the judicial system at Athens created a fertile ground for what is called "malicious prosecutions" brought by a class of professional scoundrels who routinely engaged in blackmail, pettifoggery, false witnessing, and paid advocacy (Lofberg x).

The laws governing prosecution at Athens lent themselves to sycophantic abuse by providing lucrative opportunities for those prepared to engage in unprincipled litigation. In particular, prosecu-

---

[*] Given his political sentiments, Plato might have been expected to endorse these secret societies, but in fact, he condemns them in the harshest terms, branding them the greatest enemies of the state, or at least his Cretan state (Laws 856b).

[†] In Greek, the term sycophant literally means "revealer of figs." Plutarch (Solon 24) claims the etymology refers to a period in Athenian history when the exportation of figs was illegal. Those reporting violations were called sycophants. But Athenaeus (74e) argues that the term refers to the theft of fruit from a sacred fig tree during a famine. Reporters of the sacrilege came to be called "sycophants."

[‡] Aristophanes makes a similar point in his Birds (39-40), "…the cicadas chirp on the branches for a month or two, the Athenians chirp away at lawsuits continually all their lives long."

tions such as those concerned with the commercial laws, those involving misrepresentation of citizen status, and those relating to properties owed the state (*apographe*), created a kind of bounty system in which a large portion of any assessment was granted the initiator of the suit (MacDowell 62).[*] In some sense, of course, the prosecutions brought by sycophants achieved legitimate ends; violators were brought to justice and revenues were generated for the state. These points have led some to argue that sycophancy was not only a practice to which Athens became reconciled, but was positively essential for the operation of the democracy itself (see Osbourne in Cartledge 1993). Still, the abuses associated with this institution[†] cannot be so easily denied on the basis of certain unintended benefits; this was not an instance of private vice conducing to public virtue. The great (infamous) sycophants of Athens, men like Agoratus, Callimachus, Aristogeiton, and Theocrines, played a depraved and divisive game involving extortion, threat, and intimidation, none of which contributed in the least to the civic well being of the city. Indeed, our sources speak not only of the domestic discord engendered by the sycophants (Demosthenes, Against Aristogeiton 50, and Aristotle, Politics 5.4.1), they also tell of how malicious lawsuits evoked hatred from Athens' allies (Lysias, Subverting the Democracy 19 and Isocrates, Antidosis 319).

---

[*] A successful prosecutor in the first category received one-half of the fine; in the second class of cases involving violations of the laws governing citizen status, the prosecutor again received one-half of the assessed penalty; the *apographe* must have been particularly attractive to sycophants because here three-quarters of the amount received by the state was remitted to the prosecutor.

[†] The evidence suggests it is indeed appropriate to speak of Athenian sycophancy as an "institution." It seems that the skills of this disreputable profession were actually passed on from father to son (Aristophanes, Birds 143ff), and according to Demosthenes (Against Boeotus I and II), there were even sycophantic societies such as those organized around Mnesicles and Menicles.

A variety of counter measures, some official others unofficial, did exist against sycophancy. Under the Tyranny of The Thirty, Critias and his colleagues made elimination of sycophants part of state policy, a move met with enthusiasm by many Athenians (Xenophon, Hell. 2.3.38 and Aristotle, Ath. Const. 35.2-3). There were also methods by which a person accused by a sycophant might fight fire with fire. In his Memorabilia, Xenophon speaks of an honest and trustworthy man named Archedemus who becomes Crito's "watchdog," protecting his master against sycophantic assault by filing counter-litigation. We know too of specific legal devices which could be invoked against sycophants. During the sixth *prytany* (January), on the occasion when the vote was taken regarding ostracism, an opportunity to move against sycophants called the *probole sycophanton* became available. Up to six individuals (three citizens and three metics) could be charged and brought to trial on the grounds that their barratry constituted a public deception. In addition, Athenian law sought to discourage sycophancy by punishing those who initiated lawsuits and subsequently abandoned them (presumably after having received a bribe), as well as those who failed in their prosecution to receive a least one-fifth of the total votes cast. The penalty in each instance was a fine of 1,000 drachma and may also have included a partial suspension of citizen rights (*atimia*).

Despite efforts to curb the chicanery of the sycophants and despite the fact that such practices must have seriously eroded public confidence in the state's judicial mechanisms, we know of only two instances in which individuals were formally condemned (see Demosthenes, Against Aristogeiton 19 and Lysias, Against Agoratus 67). The infrequency with which penalties were assigned suggests that sycophancy was a deeply entrenched feature of the Athenian state, one that the *demos* was willing to tolerate as part of the cost of maintaining its conception of a democratic society.

Ostracism

The practice of ostracism[*] involved the expulsion of some member of the community, typically someone of note, for ten years without forfeiture of properties or income. Here again, we have an institution firmly linked in popular imagination to democratic Athens, but in truth the procedure was also used in a variety of other Greek cities including Argos, Megara, Miletus and Syracuse.[†] The precise moment the Athenians began to employ ostracism remains uncertain; Aristotle (<u>Ath. Const</u>. 22) attributes the institution to Cleisthenes, but the first application did not occur according to the philosopher until twenty years later with the expulsion of Hipparchus. Androtion, a mid 4th century Atthidographer (historian of Athens), claims on the contrary, that the establishment of ostracism coincided with its first use in 488-487 B.C.[‡] In any event, our record of confirmed ejections remains remarkably low; only ten instances have been identified with certainty, although many others must have been sent packing during the roughly seventy years[§] of the institution's use.

---

[*] The term "ostracism" is derived from the Greek word *ostracon* or potsherd upon which the names of those slated for expulsion were recorded.

[†] At Syracuse the procedure was called *petalismos* from *petala* (leaves), because instead of potsherds, olive leaves were inscribed with the names of those to be banished (see Diodorus Siculus 11.86-7).

[‡] For a discussion of the chronological issue regarding ostracism, see Rhodes 1993, 268.

[§] Calculated on the assumption that 488-487 was the first use of ostracism at Athens and that the ostracism of Hyperbolus in 417 constituted the final application.

The Athenian *demos* had an opportunity to initiate the process once each year during the sixth *prytany* where a decision was made whether or not to conduct an *ostrakophoria*, a formal vote of ostracism. If authorized, the vote required a quorum of 6,000 citizens and was taken a few months later during the eighth *prytany*. The individual whose name appeared most often on the *ostraca*, not necessarily a majority of the total, had ten days to get his affairs in order and vacate the city. The physical remains of these proceedings have been found in abundance, in the vicinity of the Ceramicus alone approximately 9,000 inscribed potsherds have been found, most of which remain unpublished (Dillon and Garland 130). Some of these discoveries also indicate that ostracism was sometimes used as part of an organized effort to undo political opponents. In the 1930's a cache of 190 *ostraca* were found in a well on the north slope of the acropolis. The potsherds contain the name of only one man, Themistocles, which suggests that these were prefabricated ballots aimed at securing the expulsion of the famous statesman.[*]

There remains the important issue of motivation. Why did the Athenians employ ostracism? What did they hope to accomplish by its use? The ancient sources, as well as modern scholars, have responded to this question in a variety of ways. The ready-made *ostraca* targeting Themistocles suggests that ostracism was a weapon of party, a means of "quietly" disposing of political enemies. There is little doubt that the institution did, on occasion, function along these lines. On the other hand, Aristotle (<u>Ath. Const</u>. 22) believed the institution began as a means of protecting the democracy against tyranny but later became a device by which the *demos*

---

[*] Analysis of the handwriting on these *ostraca* suggests that the entire cache was written by 14 individuals.

humbled any man who appeared too great—irrespective of political ambitions. This last point tends to correspond with the explanation offered by Plutarch (Aristides 7.1-8) who saw the real meaning of Athenian ostracism as part of a contest-envy system in which the ouster of eminent men was motivated by a virulent jealousy of their fame and reputation.[*] The roster of confirmed ostracisms tends to bolster Plutarch's position regarding the victimization of luminaries—Cimon, Aristides, Themistocles, Thucydides (son of Melesias), and Alcibiades, all fell victim to this procedure. At Athens, notoriety, in and of itself, seems to have been a precarious asset;[†] between 487 and 482 B.C. alone, five of the city's leading politicians were banished. It has also been suggested that ostracism was a means of forestalling civil strife by avoiding that perennial threat to political stability in the Greek city—stasis. Rather than allow factional animosities to achieve critical mass, ostracism provided the people with an opportunity to contain potentially disastrous polarizations by excising key leaders. According to this view, ostracism was really a kind of public referendum by other means; an assessment of political agendas in which the losing side forfeited its champion.[‡]

The historian Thucydides mentions yet another possible explanation for the use of ostracism, viz., civic cleansing. While describing the intricacies of the oligarchic Revolution of 411 B.C., Thucy-

---

[*] The most famous illustration of this envy-driven resentment comes from Plutarch (Aristides 7) where an unlettered peasant asks Aristides to write the name "Aristides" on his ostracon. When asked what wrong Aristides had done him, the peasant replied none. His only complaint was that he was tired of hearing the man called "the just."

[†] This appears to be the implication in Aristophanes' Knights where Demos speaks of fattening up political leaders and then having them for dinner (1125-1140).

[‡] As M.I. Finley notes (1962, 21), "Athenian politics had an all-or-nothing quality. The objective on each side was not merely to defeat the opposition but to crush it, to behead it by destroying its leaders."

dides mentions the basis upon which Hyperbolus was ejected from Athens. He specifically indicates that this ostracism had nothing to do with any perceived political threat, but was instead based upon Hyperbolus' despicable nature and the fact that he had become a disgrace to the city (8.73).[*]

While the issue of underlying motive remains open to interpretation, there is little debate about one aspect of ostracism—the heavy-handedness of the process itself. From a procedural viewpoint, ostracism was a due-process nightmare. Those who were eventually removed were not charged with wrongdoing, were never given an opportunity to defend themselves, and were afforded no protection whatsoever against purely political expulsions—hardly the sort of thing one normally associates with a democracy. What we see here again is the long and, by modern standards, peremptory arm of sovereign *demos* against which individuals typically had little recourse.[†]

---

[*] Plutarch shares Thucydides' assessment of Hyperbolus (Nicias 11 and Alcibiades 13) but goes on to state that ostracism was intended only for great men, not scoundrels like Hyperbolus and that misapplications such as this one were responsible for the institution's demise (Aristides 7).

[†] One is reminded here of Oscar Wilde's observation, "Democracy means simply the bludgeoning of the people by the people for the people."

Conclusion

Assessing the nature of ancient democracy, and of Athenian democracy in particular, is a difficult and frustrating endeavor. In addition to the perennial problem of lacunary sources, there are also certain vicissitudes of transmission that greatly compound the task. Virtually all of the detailed ancient commentary we possess is presented by those generally hostile to democracy, individuals such as Thucydides, Plato, Xenophon, and Aristotle.[*] It was chiefly their works that were preserved and handed down by Hellenistic, Roman, Byzantine, and Renaissance scholars which helped create the impression that the *demos* was not a robust and vibrant collection of free citizens engaged in resisting the forces of repression and injustice, but rather a kind of ancient canaille,[†] a violent and vindictive throng that for nearly 200 years ruthlessly imposed its tyrannical will upon the community. It was not until the 19th century that these images were seriously revisited by men such as George Grote and a handful of others.

Twentieth century scholarship continued these corrective efforts in a worthy attempt to provide a more balanced view of Hellenic contributions to popular sovereignty,[‡] but in some instances, the

---

[*] A few exceptions include the generally positive view of democracy offered by Herodotus; the words attributed by Plato to Protagoras in the dialogue named after the famous sophist; and various speeches of the 4th century orators.

[†] It is this imagery of the rabble that influenced the Founders of our own republic. James Madison wrote the following with regard to "pure democracy," "Hence it is that such democracies have ever been spectacles of turbulence and contention; have ever been found incompatible with personal security or the rights of property; and have in general been as short in their lives as they have been violent in their deaths" (see *Federalist Paper* #10, 81).

[‡] In this regard the recent work of J. Ober is particularly noteworthy (see Ober 1989, 1996, 1998).

enthusiasm to adjust past misteachings led to an unwarranted general amnesty. Democratic Athens was not without its sins, and it matters not whether these transgressions were recorded by conservative, anti-democratic voices. In offering our paeans to Athenian democracy, we must not neglect the periodic assertions of dictatorial authority on the part of the people. I refer in particular to episodes such as the execution of the *Hellenotamiae*,[*] where nine innocent men were put to death by popular fiat (Antiphon, <u>On the Murder of Herodes</u> 69-71); the appalling mistreatment of the inhabitants of Melos (416 B.C.); and the vindictive abuse of popular authority following the battle of Arginusae (406 B.C.). In these cases, and in a variety of others, the school of Hellas earned failing grades, a fact that no amount of exculpatory exegesis can efface.[†]

At the same time however, we must also acknowledge that there are no immaculate political systems and that the world still anxiously awaits a regime that actually lives up to its ideals. Viewed from this perspective, the Athenian democracy offers much that is commendable, particularly in comparison to the rest of Hellas where politics tended to be played out as a kind of blood sport. To an extraordinary degree the Athenians succeeded in avoiding these upheavals by achieving an equitable symmetry between the prerogatives of the many versus the claims of the rich few. The people refrained from using their weight of numbers to "soak" the rich (archons and jurors took an oath not to cancel debt or redistribute property) while the rich abstained from dedicating their financial

---

[*] The *Hellenotamiae* were a ten-member board of the Delian League in charge of financial administration. The term literally means, "The Greek Treasurers."

[†] One could argue that several of the most serious stains against the democracy occurred under the extraordinary stresses imposed by the Peloponnesian War. One could just as easily argue, however, that it is precisely such stress that reveals a regime's true metal.

resources to the subversion of the people's authority. By means of this *modus vivendi*, the Athenians managed to avoid the bloody tumult experienced by Mitylene, Argos, Syracuse, Miletus and a host of other Greek city-states.[*]

The democracy's willingness to tolerate public criticism of its officials and policies is another important virtue for which the Athenians deserve credit. It is difficult to imagine any other society in the ancient world (or modern society, for that matter) allowing the sort of attacks that were routinely presented on the Athenian stage. Both Aristophanes' lampooning of Cleon in *Knights* and the disparagement of Pericles by the comedic playwright Cratinus are good examples.[†] It is equally remarkable that in the midst of the Peloponnesian War, plays such as Aristophanes' *Babylonians* (426 B.C.), a denunciation of Athenian cruelty against the Samians, and Euripides' *Trojan Women* (415 B.C.), a protest targeting Athenian atrocities on Melos, were allowed to be performed. The willingness to accept, much less broadcast, dissenting views of public policy; to hold up the mirror of self-indictment and to confront the reflections with brutal candor is an act of civic courage rarely seen, even among the most mature modern democracies. Today we use the expression "open society" to indicate a political and social environment where people are free to express their views no matter how unpopular or controversial. The Athenians came closer to this ideal than any other people in antiquity.

---

[*] Perhaps the most savage illustration of *stasis* occurred at Miletus where the common folk gathered the children of the rich exiles and trod them to death with oxen. When the rich once again gained control, they reciprocated by tarring and burning alive many of the poor along with their children (see Athenaeus, <u>Deipnosophistae</u> 12.524a).

[†] Pericles, the uncrowned king of Athens, was referred to by Cratinus as "our squill-headed Zeus."

There remains one episode in the history of democratic Athens that stands above all other measures of the regime's fundamental worth—the amnesty of 403 B.C.. Although the oligarchic tyranny was short-lived, it nevertheless unleashed a torrent of blood the likes of which Athens had never known from civic discord. Few supporters of democracy were left untouched by this reign of terror that was dedicated, it seems, not only to the eradication of popular sovereignty but to the homicidal expression of personal enmity as well. In the end, the democratic forces led by Thrasybulus succeeded in defeating the reactionary faction, but instead of reprisal and blood vengeance, the *demos* chose to dismiss the abominations of their opponents. They extended clemency to all except those most immediately responsible for the violence and then proceeded to declare the matter officially closed. There was little precedent in the Greek world for forbearance such as this. Indeed, one could argue the *demos'* benignity in this matter was positively "un-Greek."[*] Similarly, one must also conclude that such restraint could only occur among a people whose spiritual horizons had been greatly broadened by the democratic experience, a people who had acquired the wisdom and courage to be magnanimous in the face of unspeakable wrongdoing.

How then do the political experiments of ancient Athens relate to the Western tradition of popular sovereignty? To what degree are we entitled to speak of a Hellenic legacy when examining modern democratic institutions? Any suggestion that contemporary democracies are directly indebted to the ancients either structurally

---

[*] Even the traditional opponents of democracy had to concede the incredibly enlightened stance adopted by the people. Aristotle (Ath. Const. 40) states, "...the Athenians appear both in private and public to have behaved towards the past disasters in the most completely honourable and statesmanlike manner of any people in history..." (see also Plato, Seventh Epistle 325b and Xenophon Hell. 2.4.43).

or procedurally is a claim that cannot withstand serious examination. Modern democracy is a world apart from its ancient counterpart; distinctions of size, social structures, economics, cultural norms, and a host of other variables preclude meaningful analogy between ancient and contemporary versions of popular sovereignty. The sources of today's democracies are more profitably sought in the American and French Revolutions and in the liberalism of 17th and 18th century England (Hansen 1989, 26-29).

There is, however, one sense in which we can legitimately refer to Hellenic affinities, notwithstanding the massive interventions of time and circumstance. What we inherited from the ancient Greeks and what continues to lay hold of our hearts and minds is not a specific political institution or some procedural principle, but rather an idea. While the rest of humanity remained politically dormant, as the age-old distinction between rulers and ruled continued without scrutiny or challenge, the Greeks boldly became the world's first politically self-conscious people. This historic awakening was embodied in a variety of precepts—that government must be a deliberative affair; that the law must apply equally and to all; and that self-determination is the necessary condition of all those who would call themselves "free." More than any other idea, it is this last point that constitutes the living legacy of ancient democracy. In Greek hands, the word *eleutheria* (freedom)[*] came to mean something more than the mere absence of tyranny; it became a normative ideal, a prescriptive vision of the only political arrangement worthy of human loyalty. The impact of this ideal is impossible to calculate because even now, 2,500 years after its initial articulation,

---

[*] The uniqueness of the Greek notion of freedom is reflected by the incapacity to translate the term "eleutheria" into any of the near eastern languages, including Hebrew (see M.I. Finley 1973, 28).

its revolutionary implications continue to alter the political and social landscape the world over. We can however say at least this
much with certainty. The ideal of freedom has become a global article of faith, and while it is true our modern understanding of the
term denotes an inclusiveness the Greeks would never have acknowledged, the idea of a masterless political existence, of the fundamental desirability and propriety of a life lived in liberty, is at its
core a Greek conception. And it is in this sense that we are entitled
to look upon all those who marched at Selma, protested before the
Berlin Wall, and bled at Tiananmen Square as the spiritual descendants of an audacious little people who first dared to lift the yoke
of servitude from the neck of man.

Chapter VII

What's A Sophist?

"The word is a mighty despot"—Gorgias

Introduction: Obstacles to Identity

In the opening scene of Plato's <u>Protagoras</u> we learn of young Hippocrates, son of Apollodorus, who is eager to become the acolyte of the noted sophist for whom the dialogue is named. His enthusiasm in this matter is so unbridled, that he has neglected propriety and awakened Socrates in the small hours of the morning seeking an introduction to the distinguished wise man. In addition, he announces a willingness to not only exhaust his own personal finances in this matter but if need be, is prepared to borrow from his friends as well, all in the hope of acquiring some share of Protagoras' famed wisdom.

The ever affable Socrates patiently suggests to his young comrade that it is too early to go calling and that they should pass the time waiting for sunrise engaged in conversation. In the ensuing discussion Socrates points out to Hippocrates that since Protagoras is a sophist, the discipleship he seeks would make him a sophist as well. This realization not only dampens the would-be student's ardor, it brings a blush to his cheek, visible now as the first glimmer of dawn approaches (312a).

Who were these thinkers of the second half of the 5th century B.C. we have come to call the sophists, and what were their teachings? How were they capable of simultaneously generating such passion and fervor on the one hand and a stinging sense of shame on the other? The answer to these questions might at first seem no more distant than a good encyclopedia or dictionary. In truth, the matter of both the sophists' identity and their instruction is far more elusive than the facile definitions of a reference work would suggest. Proof of this point is seen in the chorus of expert voices that have yet to sing in harmony on many of the most basic issues of the sophistic movement. What we have after generations of scholarly assessment is an ongoing debate, some of it loud and much of it labored, on the meaning, purposes, and motivations of the sophists. About the only area in which anything close to agreement has been reached concerns these thinkers' significance. No one maintains that these men were unimportant or that their methods and views did not mark a critical transition in Greek cultural history. But beyond these meager and highly generalized zones of consensus, scholarly contention remains high.

A good illustration of the complexities I am suggesting is seen in the figure of Protagoras, the greatest and most highly regarded of all sophists. To this thinker is ascribed the saying that became the anthem of the entire sophistic movement—the so-called *homo mensura* statement:

> Of all things the measure is man, of the things that are, that they are, and of the things that are not, that they are not (Diels Fr. 1).

At first reading, this declaration may seem simple enough, particularly for some one moderately conversant with the history of

Hellenic thought. Protagoras is asserting that the focal point of all knowing is ultimately man himself. Unlike the earlier *physiologoi* or natural philosophers (e.g., Thales, Anaximander, Anaximenes, etc.) who sought grand principles (*arche*) from their scientific investigation of nature, Protagoras is asserting that the key to understanding rests first and foremost within the subjective knower. Truth and meaning, to whatever degree attainable by man, lie here and not in vaporous theorizing about "the heavens above and the earth below." For these reasons, Cicero's famous accolade (Tus. Disp. 5.4.10) accorded Socrates for having redirected philosophy toward human concerns could just as easily have been extended to Protagoras.

The vast majority of scholars would concur with most, if not all, of the preceding analysis—as far as it goes. But beyond these points, univocality ends and we are confronted with a withering assortment of issues and interpretive disparities. For instance, what is meant by the term "man"? Is Protagoras speaking generically indicating mankind, or is he referring to the individual? Is Protagoras advocating a form of subjective relativism and if so, how far does this relativism extend? Does the subjectivism implied here respect certain socially determined limitations or does it inevitably gravitate toward solipsism (the idea that only the self exists)? Does this premise tacitly accept Heraclitus' notion of *panta rhei* (flux and change as the nature of all reality) and correspondingly constitute an implicit criticism of Eleatic reasoning (reality as unitary and immutable)? What is it that man measures? Are the items gauged limited to sense perception or are values and morality also part of this measurative formula?

All of these questions and potentially many more, from a single observation of one of the best known and most frequently discussed sophists. How and why is this possible? Are the complexities indicated here chiefly synthetic; are they simply the product of academe's love for sententious hairsplitting or are there more substantive explanations? Although scholarly zeal for contest and display has undoubtedly complicated this matter, the fact remains that there are a number of real impediments that prevent any easy explication of the sophist movement.

For one thing, the sophists were not a "school" in any conventional sense of that term and as a result there are few consistently espoused doctrinal links between these thinkers. The ideas expressed by men such as Protagoras, Gorgias, Hippias, Prodicus, and Antiphon reflect highly independent minds with widely divergent interests. In short, beyond chronological proximity and a very general allegiance to certain broad themes, the sophists represent a group of moving targets upon whom the fixing of labels remains extremely difficult.

A related complexity concerns the fundamental issue of sophist identity. Where do the lines demarcating sophist ideas and methods begin and end? The ambiguities here are considerable, so much so that we can legitimately pose a rather startling question, viz., Was Socrates a sophist? For the self-respecting Platonist, this query borders on blasphemy, particularly in light of Plato's fervent efforts to distinguish what he viewed as the frothy pseudo-wisdom of the sophists from the profound depths of philosophy. The fact remains, however, that Plato's metaphysical citadel against the sophists (i.e., the Theory of Ideas), a key feature of his delineative effort, is not a genuine Socratic position. Furthermore, the dialectical method ascribed to Socrates in the dialogues is not the peculiar technique of Plato's master (see Protag. 335a-b and Diogenes Laertius 9.53). Indeed, Plato himself provides illustration of a sophistical dialectic in the Euthydemus. In addition, the portrait of Socrates offered in Aristophanes' Clouds, as well as certain statements in the Apology

(191), suggest that in the popular imagination there was no fundamental difference between a Socrates and a Protagoras. This explains how Aeschines, more than fifty years after Socrates' trial and death, could still refer to him as a sophist without any hint of irony (Against Timarchus 173). Even Plato late in his career admits that the Socratic elenchos, the critical cross-examination technique for which Socrates was famous, was a kind of sophistry (Sophist 230d and 231b). It would seem then that Socrates and the sophists were at least in part "fellow workers," making the lines of demarcation between philosophy and sophistry a more fluid boundary than typically conceived (Robin 134).[*]

Perhaps the most severe limitation we face in attempting to recapture the content and spirit of the sophistic movement lies with the status of the surviving sources. To describe these materials as incomplete or "untidy" is to seriously understate the situation. Almost without exception, our source material is thin, late, and dubious. As a result, scholars are faced with the often intolerable burden of having to piece together fragments in an effort to arrive at reasonably accurate reconstructions. Protagoras again provides a good illustration. Here is a thinker who enjoyed a highly successful career spanning some forty years (Meno 91e). He was a prolific author, publishing at least fifteen books on a variety of subjects from mathematics to religion (Diogenes Laertius 9.55). The entire extant record of his life's work, however, is a frustratingly meager eight lines!

---

[*] There are even identity questions regarding those conventionally acknowledged as sophists. For years experts have contested the true identity of Antiphon. The controversy has centered on whether Antiphon, the orator from Rhamnus mentioned approvingly by Thucydides (8.68), is in fact also the sophist/seer. The discovery in 1906 of the Oxyrhynchus Papyrus convinced many scholars that the orator and sophist were separate individuals, although there are still some who remain unconvinced of the dual personage thesis (e.g., Morrison 1961).

In addition to the volume of surviving material, there are also qualitative issues. There is no real guarantee that the literature we do possess actually constitutes the *ipsissima verba* of the sophists themselves. Much of what we have has come to us via the doxographers who are not "historians" in our sense of the term but rather "collectors of opinions" who typically conducted their work centuries removed from their subject matter. It may well be, then, that the scant gleanings we do possess are of limited worth, having been heavily paraphrased, interpreted, and otherwise altered to reflect the views and attitudes of these later day chroniclers.[*]

Finally, a related word about the Greek language. Any attempt to distill ancient Greek into English, even under the best of circumstances, entails some severe challenges.[†] Unlike most modern languages, ancient Greek displays a rich, multi-dimensional quality that is generally lacking in our own. In fact, these subtleties have been specifically identified as an important factor underlying the Greek achievement, i.e., the Greek language itself facilitated the sort of abstract reasoning that led to the birth of both science and philosophy (see Snell, Chapter 10, and Lloyd 174-5). Ironically, these same linguistic assets compound difficulties for translators. In order to apprehend the sophists properly, we must not only translate their words, we must also bring back to our own linguistic shores the meticulous shadings and exacting nuances of an ancient language that is in many respects more complex than ours (see

---

[*] Much of the doxographical tradition is traceable back to Aristotle and Theophrastus. Other leading figures of later times include Diocles of Magnesia, Diogenes Laertius, Arius Didymus, and Aetius.

[†] As F.M. Cornford noted, "Translation from one language to another is impossible, from an ancient to a modern language grotesquely impossible, because of (the) profound differences of collective representation, which no 'translation' will ever transfer" (1957, 45).

Kahn 1966). In addition, given the fragmentary nature of our sources, we are asked to perform these translational tasks without benefit of contextual compass. All of which implies that identifying sophists is a highly conjectural and often contentious enterprise that demands caution, if not humility.[*]

Sociopolitical Evolution: Setting the Stage

Historical accuracy demands that we not ascribe the origins of the sophistic movement to an isolated handful of novel thinkers of the late 5th century. In truth, the bold new instruction of men like Protagoras and Gorgias did not arise from some spontaneous outpouring of innovative energies but occurred as a result of a larger environment created by centuries of sociopolitical evolution. In a general sense, the transformations to which I allude are a direct concomitant of Hellas' historic progress toward democracy. At Athens the process beings as early as the late 7th century with the legal reforms of Draco and continues with the dramatic revisions of the legendary Athenian lawgiver and reformer, Solon. In 594 B.C. Solon assumed constitutional authority, having rejected an offer of tyrannical powers. One of his first moves was to initiate the *seisachtheia* or canceling of debts that granted much needed financial relief to the poor. Related measures included the abolition of the debtor-slave system in Athens and the prohibition of usurious interest. In addition, the Solonian reforms altered the social struc-

---

[*] Today the term sophist bears a strongly pejorative connotation, but this was not always the case. Prior to the late 5th century the word simply indicated a wise or skilled individual—Pindar, for instance, has no difficulty with a poet being called a sophist (Isth. 5.28). Plato's criticisms represent the major source of negative transformation (Grote 8:434-550), but there is evidence attacks were already being made upon the new teachers prior to his indictment (Guthrie 3:32-33).

ture of the city by allowing *thetes,* or the lowest class of citizens, to participate in the popular jury courts whose authorities were expanded to include a review of *archon* (senior state officials) decision making.

Reforms such as these greatly enhanced the claims of the common man in the political affairs of cities like Athens. They were augmented further by the innovations of Cleisthenes who revised the Athenian *deme* (parish) system in a fashion designed to de-emphasize the significance of high birth and family connections. Also at this time (late 6th century), the institution known as "ostracism" was introduced which enabled the people to take expulsory action against anyone menacing the new democracy.[*]

The 5th century saw additional democratic advancements including Ephialtes' stripping of power from the Areopagus and a corresponding expansion in the popular assembly's authority. Increasingly, an expanded lottery system was used to fill key administrative posts and in the 440's, Pericles begins compensating jurors, a practice which encouraged working class citizens to attend court sessions. By the close of the century, members of the popular assembly were also remunerated.

Perhaps the most significant reform of all however, pertained to the popular privilege known as *isegoria,* which granted the right of speech before the assembly to all citizens, regardless of citizen rank or financial status. This measure had a series of wide-ranging effects particularly relevant to the sophistic movement. For one thing, it instantly created a market for a new form of education emphasizing the power of words. As a result, a historic union was forged between democracy and rhetoric (Ober 78-79). No longer would Athenian citizens be satisfied with the traditional learning

---

[*] See Chapter V, "Government By The Bean."

imparted by *grammatistes* (teacher of letters), *kitharistes* (teacher of music), and *paidotribes* (teacher of physical education). The old aristocratic education, based chiefly upon the poetic paradigms of ancient bards (e.g., Homer, Hesiod, Theognis, Simonides, Pindar, etc.) was increasingly supplemented by the new language arts advanced by the sophists (Jaeger 1945, 1:296). This innovative curriculum proved to be ideally suited to the sociopolitical transformations culminating in the Athenian democracy in the 5th and 4th centuries. Without these democratic reforms the sophist revolution might never have occurred. As reliant as sophistry was upon the rise of the demos, however, there was one critical element of sophist teaching that was fully contributory to the popular cause; one aspect that not only mirrored the spirit of the age but actually contributed to the peoples' victory itself, viz., the sophistic redefinition of *arete* or virtue. Prior to the sophist revolution, the term *arete* referred to the moral worth of an individual understood primarily in terms of character. Significantly, these qualities of character were seen as variables of blood lineage; a man was virtuous because his father had been virtuous. Aristocratic presumptions such as these were challenged by the sophists on two levels. First, instead of abstract notions of character, the sophists defined *arete* in terms of "political virtue," meaning the practical efficacy of the individual in public affairs. Secondly, *arete* was conceived by the sophists in terms of acquired, not genetic characteristics. They argued emphatically that virtue was not a matter of birth, but rather a practical asset that could be taught. In so doing, they helped democratize the meaning of *arete*, a message conveyed by the famous myth of Protagoras where Zeus orders the distribution of the civic arts in a decidedly democratic fashion (Protag. 322e-323a).

Had the sophists done no more than amend Hellenic notions of "virtue," their place in the cultural history of the West would have been secured. In truth, their impact was far broader—so much so, that we can legitimately speak not simply of a sophistic movement, but of a sophistic revolution.

Sophist Revolution

It is important from the outset not to artificially delimit these men or their achievements by simply describing them as teachers of rhetoric. The aspiration of *eu legein*, or speaking well, was certainly a major aspect of their instructional agenda, but the intellectual frontier they opened for the Greek world was far wider.

Protagoras, for example, was the earliest thinker in recorded history to treat language itself as an object of scientific study. Specifically, he was the first to articulate the tenses of verbs, to divide speech into various modes or voices, and to analyze the gender of verb endings—for which he is lampooned by Aristophanes (*Clouds* 659).

Gorgias was a master stylist and the founder of the epideictic (praise/blame) form of rhetoric whereby Hellenic prose was elevated to the level of poetry. He is also described as having a broad range of scientific interests as well (Meno 76c and Sprague 47). Hippias was a renowned polymath with expertise in such diverse fields as astronomy, music, painting, sculpture, history, mythology, and genealogy (Protag. 315c and Hipp. Maj. 285c). He was also famous for having developed an impressive system of mnemonics and for his mathematical investigations. Both he and Antiphon are remembered for their work in attempting to "square the circle" (Heath 1:221 and 225-6; see Aristotles' criticism Sop. Ref. 172a and Phy. 185a).

In short, the sophists were more than rhetoricians, they were intellectual omnivores with a wide range of scholarly appetites. If there is any common element in their activities, it involves a certain boldness, a penchant (if not love) for heterodoxy. As a group, they tended to challenge received opinions and traditional perspectives on everything from social theory to politics, law, morality, and religion. Not surprisingly their iconoclasm was hardly endearing to the more conservative elements of Hellenic society. There is little doubt, however, that their intolerant probing of conventional wisdom liberated and empowered the Greek imagination as never before. What were the specific components of sophist teachings?

There were four banners under which the sophistic revolution marched. First and foremost, there was the humanistic declaration of Protagoras—"Man is the measure of all things." A good way to conceive of this decree's significance is to view it as the cultural equivalent of a Copernican Revolution. Not only did it dramatically alter the conceptual orientation of the Greeks, it also served as the fount from which flowed the other three major themes of sophistry—a radically new ontology/epistemology, a pragmatic/utile approach to life, and a highly irreverent secularism.

Prior to the mid 5th century the object of Greek speculation had been to grasp the reality behind the visible universe; to penetrate the awesome mysteries that nature loved to hide. There are no such aspirations guiding Protagoras. In fact, the sophists rebel against such speculation and shift the emphasis instead to a concrete, common sense anthropology (Havelock 34). In particular, the sophists appear committed to demolishing the highly counter-intuitive monism of Parmenides and his followers who defined "Being" as a finite, spherical, motionless, corporeal plenum.[*] Protagoras and his

---

[*] The key statements of Parmenides include the following: "Being has no coming into being and no destruction, for it is whole of limb, without motion, and without end. And it never Was nor Will be, because it is now, a Whole all together, One, continuous;...Nor shall I allow you to speak or think of it as springing from Non-Being...it

colleagues declared grand ontological pronouncements such as these irrelevant and meaningless. All hypotheses about "things-in-themselves" and immutable first principles were ultimately super-fluous to genuine human experience. The new point of departure was not some absolute existence, but rather relative existence, i.e., man, because all reality is experienced through the mechanisms of human perception (see Versenyi 182). The new center, therefore, of all efforts to comprehend the world must be man himself.

A correlative dimension of Protagoras' human-centered reasoning includes the doctrine known as relativism. If man is the measure of all things, if in some sense each individual stands at the center of his own private universe, then reality itself becomes "privatized." Accordingly, the only version of *aleitheia* (truth) that can exist is the subjectively conditioned verity of the individual.[*] In other words, man as percipient creature "textures" all truth, making it uniquely his own with the result that no absolute truth, no truth with an upper case "T" can exist. Significantly, Protagoras does not limit this relativism to matters of perception but broadens it to include questions of value and morality—thereby projecting his premise beyond the individual into the sociopolitical domain as well (Theaet. 167c-d).

A further dimension of the *homo mensura* precept are the para-doxical corollaries that 1) all beliefs are equally true and 2) the in-dividual is incapable of uttering falsities. If indeed there is no global standard beyond the individual to which appeal can be made in gauging personal perspective, then the opinion of the individual

---

must Be absolutely or not at all...It is motionless in the limits of mighty bonds, with-out cease, since Becoming and Destruction have been driven very far away...it is decreed by divine law that Being shall not be without boundary..." (Diels 7-8).

[*] The influence of this Protagorean logic proved widespread and can even be detected in the Hippocratic Corpus (see On Ancient Medicine 9.18).

comes to enjoy a special sovereignty all its own. This implies that widely disparate beliefs can be equally true for those espousing them (see Aristotles' criticism – Meta. 11.7.1-19). By extension, it also suggests that falsehood or contradiction cannot occur because what is true for the individual is indeed true for him. This last point was advanced further by a clever adaptation of Eleatic logic, viz., that since "untruth" is a form of non-being and one cannot discuss or propose that which is not, man in incapable of uttering falsehood (see Craty. 429d-e).

As fantastic as these propositions may seem, they are tame by comparison to the radical assertions proffered by Gorgias. The famous lines in question are as follows:

> Nothing exists. If anything exists, it is incomprehensible. If it is comprehensible, it is incommunicable (Diels fr. 3).

Assuming these lines were offered seriously, i.e., if they are presented as genuine philosophical statements as opposed to mere rhetorical display, then Gorgias can legitimately be deemed a nihilist—both ontologically and epistemologically (Guthrie 3:25).

There is little doubt that this denial of man's ability to discover, comprehend, and communicate truth is a direct attack upon Eleaticism and perhaps a specific assault upon Melissus (Hays 330). What in effect Gorgias does here is hoist the Eleatics on their own petard by reversing the polarity of their ontological proposition (Rankin 31 in Kerferd 1981). In essence, he uses the Eleatic logical form to demolish Eleatic reasoning. The result is a premise far more extreme than anything propounded by Protagoras who merely sought to reduce the universal truth claims of his predecessors to a more modest and relative human standard. By contrast, the implication of Gorgias' account of reality is that all truth is in principle beyond the grasp of man. This may explain why Gorgias, unlike other sophists, does not profess an ability to teach virtue (Meno 95c). To do so might imply the possession of some substantive body of knowledge, which Gorgias generally denies.

What Gorgias espouses instead is the alternative logic of his denial, viz. the heightened significance that *pistis* and *doxa* (belief and opinion) assume under such conditions. They fill the void left by the absence of factual reality and as a result it is the emotive side of life, not the cognitive, that determines human events in Gorgias' world. This explains the almost mystical reverence he ascribes to persuasive speech (Diels Helen 8, 9, 11, 13, 14 and Gorgias 452d)—speech being the specific method "...that can make any impression it wishes on the soul" (Helen 13). It also accounts for the spectacular poetic elements reflected in Gorgias' oral exhibitions. These were not simply embellishments for aesthetic purpose. The novel combination of words, the balanced constructions, the ingenious concoction of sounds were all part of the Gorgian incantation designed to mold the soul and make it more receptive to the argument (see de Romilly 1975). Gorgias appreciated the virtue of lining his cup with oratorical honey (to use Lucretius' image), and he did so with consummate skill.[*]

Again, truth is not a necessary ingredient in these attempts at soul crafting because there is no truth beyond personal belief. As such, truth is a movable feast for the orator. It is something the skilled speaker conjures in his listener by specifically tailoring his words to a given audience and circumstance. Rhetoric, in short,

---

[*] When Gorgias appeared in Athens in 427 B.C. as an ambassador representing his native city of Leontini, the Athenians were absolutely smitten with his oratorical style. The reception of the Thessalians was similarly exuberant (Philost. 1.521).

does not attempt to instruct or inform; for Gorgias it merely seeks to manufacture certain psychological states (Sesonske 220). Only the garlanded word has meaning here, truth content is fundamentally irrelevant and always negotiable. Evidence of truth's superfluity in these matters is seen by the ease with which the pure device of words can overwhelm those possessing genuine insight and experience (Gorgias 456b)—the implication of which suggests the fundamental futility of the philosophic enterprise (Philebus 58a and Phaedra 267a). In Gorgias' world where there are no credible notions of reality and truth, the Socratic quest becomes a pointless exercise. Here, persuasion is everything and rhetoric, the pseudo-art dismissed by Plato as mere "knack," is king (Helen 8).

A third aspect of the sophistic orientation is its pragmatic/utile approach to life. As a group, these thinkers display a consistent "anti-idealistic" concreteness, a preference for things practical, useful, and tangible (Untersteiner xvi). Much of this perspective is related directly to the epistemology examined above. The "good" enjoys no absolute status for the sophist. It is instead, something complex, relative, and manifold, and here too, man remains the measure. The good is above all the meaningful for man with the result that any endeavor claiming a value or status transcendent of, or superior to, the concrete needs of humanity is rejected by the sophists as vain and otiose. It is for these reasons that Protagoras criticizes the arts and sciences and why he stresses the practical virtues of his own program where students are not asked to squander their energies engaging in theoretical studies. Under Protagoras' guidance an individual is immersed immediately in the more substantial business of learning to manage personal affairs and in acquiring the skills necessary for making a man powerful in public life (Protag. 318d-e). As Isocrates, a student of Gorgias, said in one of his display speeches:

It is much better to form probable opinions about useful things than to have expert knowledge of useless things (Helen 209; also Antidosis 261-2, 266, 269).

A related pragmatism operates in the sophist's portrait of truth. As we have noted, abstract and metaphysical notions of truth are generally dismissed by the sophist masters in favor of more relativistic concepts. In addition, these thinkers tend to view truth with the same instrumental lens employed in their assessments of the "good," i.e., truth is what works, and more specifically, it is what works for the majority. These are the implications of the remarks attributed to Protagoras in the Theaetetus where he notes that consensus is the means by which truth is certified by and for the community (172d). By so arguing, Protagoras not only delimits the anarchic potentials of his relativism to socially determined bounds he does so while remaining faithful to his practical and anti-metaphysical creed. Under these terms truth becomes a seminal coincidence of pragmatically impelled opinions—a conception that would have won for the sophist the sympathy of modern thinkers such as Hume, James, and Dewey.

Not surprisingly, the sophists see persuasive speech as a key player in this consensus building enterprise. Not because it bestows some luminous understanding or ultimate wisdom, but because rhetoric assists men at arriving at "better" judgments regarding matters of utility (Theaet. 166d). In this sense rhetoric helps enhance human decision making resulting in more productive and, in an instrumental sense, "truer" opinions. What rhetoric cannot do, and what the sophists never sought for it to do, was grant the axiomatic insights demanded by philosophers like Plato and his followers.

A final dimension of the sophist revolution involves their strong secularism that increasingly leads to challenges of traditional religious orthodoxies. In broadest terms, this opposition was not initiated by the sophists but was rather a natural by-product of Greek rationalism in general. Accordingly, one could argue that the sophists were merely continuing a process of de-mystification begun earlier by the likes of Xenophanes and Heraclitus. There are, however, important differences. For one thing, the sophist critique is driven by a humanism conceived in doctrinal, almost ideological terms. Aggressively, man is made the focal point of the universe with the result that the gods are left little room on the pedestal. Furthermore, this dislocation carried with it a tacit assumption that man was capable of improving his own life without divine intervention (Jarrett 107). In addition, sophist reproofs of established pieties carried with them a latent radicalism that was truly unprecedented in Hellenic thought. Some sophists were inclined to temper these radical elements by limiting their statements to agnostic theorizing. Others were for less restrained resulting in some audaciously atheistic pronouncements.

Regarding agnosticism, the classic statement is a surviving fragment of a lost work attributed to Protagoras entitled, <u>On the Gods</u>:

> About the gods, I am unable to know whether they exist or do not exist, nor what they are like in form; for the factors preventing knowledge are many: the obscurity of the subject, and the shortness of human life (Diels Fr. 4).

By modern standards, these observations do not appear particularly provocative—if anything, they seem rather reasonable. Protagoras legitimately points to the many complexities precluding definitive knowledge about the gods. According to tradition, however, the Athenians viewed these words as something more than merely non-conformist. Apparently the anti-heresy statutes passed earlier through the efforts of an Athenian soothsayer named Diopeithes were invoked against Protagoras (Plutarch, Pericles 32). Diogenes Laertius claims there was a public burning of Protagoras' books (9.52) and Philostratus reports that from this time on the famous sophist became a marked man continuously pursued by Athenian naval forces (1.494).

Prodicus is also an important figure in this context to the extent he advanced a scheme of divine origins that was entirely naturalistic. According to his view, the traditional Hellenic pantheon originated from a series of beneficial objects that men "divinized" over time (Diels Fr. 5). These origins are still reflected in the various "gifts" associated with certain deities. For example, the god Hephaestus originated with fire, Poseidon from water, Demeter from bread, Dionysus from wine, etc.. This line of reasoning anticipates the views of Euhemerus (c. 300 B.C.) who similarly attributes the foundation of theology to benefactions. According to him the gods were really magnified human figures, great kings and heroes who had performed important services for the benefit of man.

The deification process described by Prodicus implies a procedure remote from conscious decision-making—something that occurs over a long period of time as part of that vague unfolding known as cultural evolution. The hypothetical origins of religious practice put forth by Critias were entirely different. Critias was, to say the least, a controversial figure in Greek history. Significantly, the bulk of his infamous reputation does not stem from his sophistical activities but from his role in the political history of late 5th century Athens. As a key member of the oligarchic party, Critias played a leading role in the infamous "Tyranny of the Thirty" established in Athens at the conclusion of the Peloponnesian War (404-403 B.C.). It seems he also wrote a number of philosophical and rhetorical treatises plus several poems and plays. It is specifically the remains of one of his satiric plays entitled, "*Sisyphus*" that concerns us. In this work, the following lines regarding the origins of religion are found:

> There was a time when the life of man was unordered, bestial and the slave of force...Then, I think men devised retributory laws, in order that justice might be dictator...
>
> Then, when the laws forbade them to commit open crimes of violence, and they began to do them in secret, a wise and clever man invented fear of the gods for mortals, that there might be some means of frightening the wicked, even if they do anything or say or think it in secret...(Diels Fr. 25).

In other words, religion is pure artifice, an invention of some shrewd politician aimed at manipulating the minds and hearts of the credulous masses. Its power lies entirely in fear. By persuading that the gods detect and punish all evil, even that which is conceived or acted upon in private, the lawlessness of men is quenched.[*] Here, Critias not only displays the pragmatism so characteristic of the sophists, he also expresses an atheism worthy of Karl Marx. For both men, religion was indeed a kind of opiate.

---

[*] Critias' distinction of public v. private crimes should be read in conjunction with related points made by Antiphon in the Oxyrhynchus Papyri 11:101 and with Plato's (Critias' nephew) presentation of the ring of Gyges tale in the Republic (359d).

Philosophy's Retort

In presenting the philosophic response to sophistry offered by thinkers such as Plato and Aristotle, certain qualifications must be made. First, it is important we remain clear about the nature of the critique. The philosophers were not simply, as some critics have alleged, reactionary rivals splashing bile at their sophist opponents. Any attempt to reduce philosophy's response to a kind of Thermidorian reaction against sophistry's revolutionary liberalism is highly misleading because it tends to trivialize the profound intellectual disparity between the philosophic and sophistic temperaments. The difference between a philosopher and a sophist, as Aristotle notes, is nothing less than the selection of a different path in life (Meta 4.2.20).

Secondly, we must carefully distinguish the targets of philosophy's critique, i.e., which thinkers are accused of transgression and what specifically are the intellectual misdeeds attributed in each case. Historically speaking, a real separation can and must be made between the first or "Great" generation of sophists and their 4th century disciples (Robin 137). Both Plato and Aristotle did in fact assess these groups differently. Protagoras, Hippias, and Prodicus were not seen by them in the same light as Polos, Lycophron, and Polyxenos. While it is true Plato may occasionally cast one of the major sophists in an unflattering light—Hippias is boastful and prone to bombastic posturing (Protag. 337d and Greater Hippias 283e) and Prodicus is a bit silly in his pedantic displays of lexical minutiae (Protag. 337a and 358b)—the fact remains that interludes such as these in the dialogues are offered as little more than dramatic hue. They are not intended as indictments of character. Indeed, venality is a charge rarely leveled by Plato or Aristotle against the early sophists. Their complaints against these thinkers tend to be strictly intellectual. This is not the case however, with the later sophists who interpret and apply the original teachings in a manner both philosophers deem morally and socially erosive.

With these points in mind, we can proceed to the criticisms themselves. Although there are numerous zones of contention separating the philosophic and sophistic world-views, there is one area of conflict in particular that best summarizes the antagonism, viz., the epistemological contest between *doxa* (opinion) and *aleitheia* (truth). As we have seen, the sophists as a group believe that truth, understood as an abiding, universal body of insight, does not exist. Instead, they bring a Heraclitean logic to all such questions; truth, by its very nature, is protean because the exclusive foundation of *aleitheia* is human opinion. By extension, this reasoning also implies that no viewpoint, however well-grounded in logic or experience, can claim any special adjudicative authority. Implicit here too, is the further notion that there can be no false logos; falsehood implying the existence of some objective evaluative standard is denied by the sophists who acknowledge only the subjective assessments of the individual.[*]

Despite their own substantial methodological differences, Plato and Aristotle share at least two convictions regarding these views. First, sophistry's unholy trinity of phenomenalism, relativism, and subjectivism presented a false view of reality and truth. Second, sophist arguments to the contrary notwithstanding, objective/scientific truth does exist and man is capable of grasping it. Aristotle presses his case against sophist casuistry by dissecting

---

[*] The rejection of objective truth was apparently an acknowledged aspect of sophist instructional technique as indicated by the text known as the <u>Dissoi Logoi</u> (See Sprague 279-293) where both sides of various issues and themes are argued. Exercises such as these were presumably based on the <u>Antilogiae</u> of Protagoras (Diogenes Laertius 9.51).

them with his new and scalpel-like logic. An example is found in the <u>Metaphysics</u> where Aristotle notes the laws of contradiction pointing out that the consequence of denying falsehood to human assertions implies that every opinion has the potential of being simultaneously true and false (4.5.1).

Plato's rebuttal, on the other hand, takes a very different approach and in the end comes to constitute the definitive rejection of sophist thought. I refer of course to Plato's metaphysically based epistemology, the so-called Theory of Ideas, where he asserts the existence of an authoritative truth standard that is at once immutable and everlasting. In this scheme, Being and Value exist as closely intertwined, objectively real essences. As a result, Plato's epistemology must ultimately be seen normatively, i.e., reality for Plato is at once descriptive and prescriptive. Accordingly, dialectic becomes a quest for the ontological insights that distinguish "truth" from the arbitrary and preferential constructs offered by the sophists (<u>Republic</u> 533a). Among other things, this approach allows Plato to reinstate the notion of falsehood; the good, the just, and the beautiful are no longer matters of opinion but rather the final results of a long and toilsome ascent out of darkness (<u>Republic</u> 515e and <u>Phaedrus</u> 274a). In short, Plato's epistemology allows him to demonstrate that truth and value are not invented by men, but rather discovered by them. And for this reason too, no tongue, however nimble or mellifluous, can substitute for the supreme insights afforded by grasping the "Ideas."

Plato's position may seem like an obscure cogitation, a metaphysical musing remote from the realities of this world. But for Plato, the Theory of Ideas was a concretely remedial formula. For one thing, this theory was designed to rescue reason from the nihilistic darkness of the sophist's cave. Instead of the false beacons of *eikasia* (images) and *pistis* (belief), Plato offered imagery of a dazzling reality that ensured the integrity of truth and wisdom. Specifically, Plato was keenly interested in negating the despair and frustration associated with a sophist-induced misology: the idea that there is no order, truth, or logic by which to chart the course of human existence (Phaedo 89d-91c; cf. Republic 538d-c and 539c). The Theory of Ideas is at least in part designed to restore human confidence in the sovereign utility of reason.

On the sociopolitical level too, Plato's metaphysical realism was intended to have a curative effect, the need for which was well demonstrated by the menacing overtones of the *nomos* (man-made law) versus *phusis* (natural law) controversy. Some of the earliest manifestations of this dispute showed promise of a new and benign understanding of the human condition. Several thinkers, including certain sophists, dichotomized these legal categories in a way that highlighted the common bonds of humanity. The epitome of this perspective was captured in an observation attributed to Antiphon:

> ...we are all by nature born the same in every way, both barbarians and Hellenes...we all breathe into the air through mouth and nostrils, and we all eat with hands...(Diels 44).

There was also, however, a potentially dangerous counter-perspective in this debate, one that seems to have been encouraged, at least indirectly, by sophistic teaching. In the view of some, *phusis* seemed to sanction aggressive and self-serving conduct. All around us we see examples of how the strong assert themselves "by nature" against the weak: the hawk against the nightingale (Works and Days 203-212), the wolf against the lamb (Iliad 22.263). Does not *phusis* ordain the same conduct between men? Is not the naturally superior man entitled to exercise his preeminence and to disregard the artificial constraints imposed by conventional law (*nomos*)?

Thinking such as this had already gained considerable currency by the late 5th century as we see in the pages of Thucydides, e.g., the Melian dialogue and the Mytilean debate (5.84-114 and 3.40-41). It appears also in dramatic guise in Plato's Gorgias where Callicles argues brutally for the prerogatives of the mighty at the expense of the inferior many (483c-d).

Obviously, the impact of these views upon the integrity of man-made law was potentially devastating. Not only did the alleged superiority of *phusis* tend to denigrate and trivialize human legislation, conventional law was denounced further as a mere contrivance of the mob aimed at fettering the naturally superior "young lions" of society (Gorgias 483e). The "higher" justice of *phusis* thus interpreted, not only encouraged violation of the city's mandates, it tended to certify force as the sole foundation of law and justice.

Plato correctly surmised that a Darwinian conception of *phusis*, the idea that "might makes right," would render civilized existence impossible. In order to avoid the moral amnesia advocated by men such as Callicles, Plato advanced the notion of a rational cosmos in which the supersensible realities contained in the Realm of Ideas nourish and support human legislation. Properly formulated, the laws of man need not conflict with the laws of nature.* Indeed, a truly enlightened law-maker might formulate legislation that participated in the perennial Truths represented by the Ideas. By grounding the city's *nomoi* in Being itself, by making conventional law the earthly manifestation of paradigms that are at once rational

---

* On this point, Plato expresses views reminiscent of Heraclitus—"For all human laws are nourished by one, which is divine" (Diels Fr. 114).

and moral, Plato restores dignity to *nomos,* obedience to which now becomes the obligation of every well-reasoned citizen.

At the same time, Plato's vision of a moral cosmos rejects any and all claims put forth by the Calliclean strongman; the philosopher-king alone, not some violently conceived *ubermensch,* becomes the exclusive judge of legality. Above all, the Platonic solution to this largely sophist-inspired controversy speaks directly to Protagoras. It is not man per se who is the measure of all things; only the wise and the just are worthy of serving in that mensurative capacity.[*]

Conclusion

Space restrictions make even a summary analysis of sophist influences impossible given the fact that any treatment along these lines, however cursory, would entail nothing less than a cultural history of Europe and the Near East. Suffice it to say that the sophists were intellectual, social, and moral adventurers who radically altered the substance of Greek culture, and by extension, established the new modes and orders that subsequently determined much of the course of Western civilization.

There is one area of sophist achievement however, that merits special attention in light of its incalculable significance as a cultural force, viz., rhetoric. In truth, the Greek fascination with "logos" was evident long before the sophist revolution. Pausanias tells us that Theseus, the mythical hero and unifier of the Athenian people established a cult at Athens in honor of the goddess Peitho (persuasion) in most ancient times (1.22.3). Related testimony is offered in the Iliad, where the ideal man is described as both a doer of deeds and a "speaker of words." Those with particular proficien-

---

[*] Ultimately for Plato it is God, not man, that is the measure of all things (Laws 716c).

cies in this regard are honorifically noted by Homer. Nestor, for instance, is termed, "...the lucid speaker of Pylos, from whose lips the stream of words ran sweeter than honey" (1.247-8) and Odysseus is described as uttering words that, "...came drifting down like the wintry snows" and against which no man could stand (3.220-3). There are even proto-rhetorical elements to be found in the Iliad's famous "Embassy Scene" in Book IX (see also Athanassakis, *Hymn to Hermes*, 369-386).

Sophistic rhetoric then, is not without its antecedents. Yet there is an unprecedented quality about sophist contributions in this area to the extent that they were the first to approach language in a rational, scientific manner, the first to make language conscious of itself. This does not mean that no other people in antiquity had any familiarity with rhetoric. The Old Testament does in fact contain a kind of rhetoric, but it involves an instinctive or reflexive use of words that never achieves anything approaching a "science" of language (Kennedy 1980, 120), and it is precisely these scientific and self-conscious qualities that allow us to credit the sophists with creating the world's first system of metalinguistics (Solmsen 55-56 and de Romilly 1992, 73).

As we have noted, many sophistic achievements, including rhetoric, were not universally accepted or acclaimed. The political and social implications of rhetoric were bitterly resented by the old aristocracy (see Xenophon, On Hunting 13.1-9) and the philosophers, with similar acrimony, condemned the new art on both epistemological and moral grounds. During the 4th century a fierce contest raged between rhetoric and philosophy personified respectively by Isocrates and Plato. Given the latter's status in the pantheon of Western speculation, it comes as a surprise to learn of an Isocratean victory in this matter (Jaeger 3:104 and Marrou 194). Still, the fact remains that the views advanced by Isocrates in works such as the

Nicocles (e.g., 1-10) and the Antidosis (e.g., 261-268) emphasizing the practical benefits of eloquence against the barren subtleties of philosophy, convince the majority that the long steep path prescribed by Plato was best left untrodden. Accordingly, it is Isocrates' conception of culture and learning that carries the day prompting Cicero to liken him to a Trojan Horse from whom emerged numerous honorable and illustrious men (De Or. 2.94) and modern scholars to proclaim his influence upon European prose style as second to none (Hadas 171).

Significantly, it is the Isocratean conception of *paideia* with its strong emphasis on sophist linguistic methods that Alexander the Great exports throughout Asia in the late 4th century. With this introduction of the Greek tongue, the Asian peoples came to participate in a whole new world of metaphors, concepts, and logical categories (Jaeger 1961, 6). The impact was widespread and deeply felt. By the mid 3rd century B.C., the Buddhist decrees of Asoka, an Indian king, were being published and circulated in Greek (Conley 29) and by the 1st century A.D., Jewish scholars, such as Philo, had become so thoroughly assimilated to Greek they were no longer capable of reading Hebrew—a fact that had earlier necessitated the publication of the Septuagint (the earliest Greek translation of the Old Testament).

By far the most important effect of this sophistic diaspora, perhaps the point beyond all others that testifies to the historic significance of the sophists, is the relationship between rhetoric and Christianity. During the time of the primitive church's nascent growth and development, schools of rhetoric flourished throughout the Greco-Roman world (Kennedy 1972, 553). Not surprisingly, the church employed rhetoric from the outset as a means for disseminating the "good news" of salvation and eternal life. Specifically, rhetoric allowed the early Christian fathers to effectively promote their evangelical agenda among the gentile populations.

The definitive illustration of these activities is seen in the career of St. Paul. As a Hellenized Jew, Paul was fully conversant with both the philosophical and literary conventions of Greek thought (Kennedy 1980, 130). Above all, the apostle to the gentiles displayed a thorough knowledge of and considerable proficiency in the rhetorical arts. Paul not only uses each of the three rhetorical forms described by Aristotle (Rhetoric 1.3)—deliberative, forensic, epideictic—he also employs an impressive array of tropes, i.e., the artful use of word patterns designed to make a powerful impression upon a reader or listener.[*] Given his rhetorical dexterity it is reasonable to assume that Paul was a formally trained practitioner of the "Greek wisdom," something the Babylonian Talmud suggests was not an uncommon practice among rabbinic students of Paul's era (Forbes 23-24). Most would agree that Christianity's dissemination, perhaps even its very survival, was directly related to the proselytizing of St. Paul. What is not generally appreciated is the degree to which the apostle called upon his considerable rhetorical skills to advance his mission.

Later, after the church's foundations were more firmly established, rhetoric continued to play an important role doctrinally by providing the persuasive logic and polished forms that helped crystallize many key tenets of the Christian faith. Developments along these lines are easily noted by comparing the stylistic and conceptual distinctions between a declaration such as the Sermon on the Mount and the Nicene Creed (Hatch 1).

---

[*] Among the many tropes used by Paul in his letters are antonomasia, asyndeta, polysyndeton, metonymy, erotema, anaphora, antanaclasis, etc.

Again, during the 4th century A.D. when the Church was plagued by heretical dissension, rhetoric was successfully employed to help establish and serve the orthodox cause. Evidence for this is found in the careers of the Cappadocian Fathers (Basil, Gregory of Nyssa, and Gregory of Nazianzus), each of whom was a skilled rhetorician having sat at the knees of such great rhetorical masters as Himerius and Libanius (Pelikan 15-16). In short, the record shows that much of the early Church's history is directly indebted to the linguistic techniques developed centuries before in pagan Greece, so much so that it is not inappropriate to view the early fathers as "Christian sophists" (Anderson 42).

But the story of sophist influence does not end there. Rhetoric remains very much alive and well today. Indeed, it seems words in the modern era have become more heavily measured than ever before; the casual utterance and spontaneous response having been replaced by carefully guarded tones and expertly embroidered phrases. No dimension of contemporary society has proven immune to this penchant for "manufactured" communique. Rhetoric has become mainstream, it is now a ubiquitous and firmly rooted aspect of our cultural idiom. Thus, when the lawyer attempts to throw dust into the eyes of jurors, when the Madison Avenue executive promotes his client's product with silken words, when the elected official employs double-speak as a routine feature of public discourse, each in his own way demonstrates that Gorgias lives and that the Greek tongue continues to wag.

Chapter VIII

The Midwife's Son

"We cannot fail to see in Socrates the one turning
point and vortex of so-called world history"
—*F. Nietzsche*

Introduction:
Seeking the Historic Socrates

There is no doubt that together, the life and philosophic activity of Socrates constitute a major historical event in Western culture; that his is a voice that speaks across the centuries as few others have. Indeed, it has been argued that with the exception of Jesus, Socrates is the single most influential figure in Western civilization (Livingston v and Stone 4). This being said however, there are troublesome questions and controversies surrounding the man. Despite an abundance of Socratica,[*] not to mention an ocean of modern analysis and commentary, Socrates remains sphinx-like; a flesh and blood riddle, whose life and manner suggest a most peculiar concatenation of disparate elements. Although a familiar and constant presence at the public venues of Athens, there is something

---

[*] Our list of ancient authors composing Socratic apologia is long indeed and includes: Plato, Xenophon, Lysias, Theodectes, Demetrius of Phalerum, Zeno of Sidon, Theon of Antioch, Plutarch, and Libanius.

remote and alien about him. While continually professing ignorance about the commonplaces others take for granted, he displays
Olympian insight about matters of deepest significance. A simple
man of modest means, he nevertheless exerts a magnetism upon the
intellectual, social, and political elite of the city who flock to his
side. How does one begin to grasp the mystery of such a man?

The enigma to which I refer has its roots in the so-called "Socratic Problem." It stems above all from one simple fact, viz., Socrates, notwithstanding several dubious accounts to the contrary
(Phaedo 60c-d, Epictetus, Dis. 2.1.32, and Diogenes Laertius 1.16),
seems to have left us nothing of philosophic substance from his
own hand. In other words, virtually everything we know about this
"demigod" of Western speculation is based upon secondary references, the veracity of which are often in dispute. Needless to say,
many modern scholars despaired of ever accurately decoding the
spirit and method of genuine Socratic philosophy. But in the late
19th century new light was cast upon this problem by Lewis Campbell (1830-1908) who devised a means of dating certain classical
literature based on stylistic analysis. Specifically, Campbell's
"stylometry" allowed us to approximate the dates and sequencing
of Plato's dialogues—perhaps our most important source of Socratic information. This in turn meant scholars were now in a position to begin the complex process of identifying several distinct
chronological units within the Platonic corpus, including an early
period where most experts believe the best portrait of the historic
Socrates can be found (see Lutoslawski, Chapter 3).[*]

---

[*] The so-called "Socratic" or "elenctic" dialogues (referring to the critical cross-
examination Socrates employs in them) are generally seen as the following works—
Apology, Charmides, Crito, Euthyphro, Gorgias, Hippias Minor, Ion, Laches, Protagoras, and Republic I (see Vlastos 1991, 46-7).

This technique and others like it demonstrated that there was indeed an intellectual relationship between Socratic and Platonic doctrine, but that there were also some very significant distinctions. For instance, the testimony of the middle and latter dialogues notwithstanding, it is now clear Socrates was neither an epistemologist nor a metaphysician.[*] These are Plato's beliefs and interests projected upon Socrates who functions in the more advanced dialogues as *dramatis persona*, not as historic personage. Being able to make distinctions such as these, that is, possessing the ability to distinguish Platonic ventriloquism from the "real" Socrates, was vital to the progress of Socratic scholarship, but it hardly eliminated all of the problems surrounding this complex and intriguing figure.

For one thing, the other roughly contemporary ancient sources (Aristophanes, Xenophon, and Aristotle) offer widely varying views of Socrates from those presented by Plato. The Xenophonic Socrates, for example, is a kind of cracker-barrel sage who displays little of the irony and philosophical originality reflected in the Platonic portrait. Similarly, there are significant disparities in the ancient record regarding Socrates' intellectual preparation, his ethical theory, and the role of his *daimonion* (Socrates' internal oracle).

In addition, there are critical distinctions between the ancient and modern biographical traditions, which must be acknowledged as we pursue the "real" Socrates. Unlike modern authors, the ancient biographers did not display any special commitment to historical accuracy. The results were works that vibrate ambiguously between fact and fiction (Mamigliano 46). In the specific case of

---

[*] Although a few scholars such as Burnet and Taylor have argued that Socrates did hold to the Theory of Ideas, the vast majority believe this doctrine to be uniquely Platonic.

Socrates there seems to have been, with the notable exceptions of Aristoxenes and Polycrates,[*] a concerted effort to advance paneygrical imagery designed to promote a portrait of "saint" Socrates. Given the eulogistic agenda attached to so much of the Socratic literature, it is essential not to treat these works as "historical" in any strict sense—something Aristotle recognized clearly when he consigned the Socratic *logoi* to the realm of prose poetry (Poetics 1.8). Further evidence of the non-historic nature of these works is seen in the formulaic elements contained in the various "apologies." Modern scholars have, for example, detected strong similarities between Gorgias' *epideictic* speech known as the *Defense of Palamedes* and the trial dialogues of Plato and Xenophon (see Chroust 216-218 and Reeve 7-8). In turn, it seems Isocrates later incorporated aspects of Plato's Apology in his own display speech known as the *Antidosis*. All of which suggests there were certain literary conventions that helped shape the form and content of our Socratica.

What then do we know of the historic Socrates? There is at least a core of reliable biographical information, derived chiefly from Plato, which most scholars seem willing to accept as reasonably accurate—although even here, these data are by no means entirely free of inconsistency and controversy. In terms of lineage, Socrates was an Athenian, the son of Sophroniscus, a stonemason or sculptor from the deme Alopece (Diogenes Laertius 2.18). His mother, Phaenarete, was a midwife, a service Socrates is also said to have performed although the "children" he helped deliver were of cerebral variety (Theaet. 150b-d). He was married to Xanthippe whose

---

[*] It seems certain that the "accuser" mentioned in the early portions of Xenophon's Memorabilia (1.1.1-1.2.64) is a specific reference to Polycrates who probably composed an imaginary forensic speech traducing Socrates around 393 B.C. which in turn triggered a literary war in defense of the philosopher.

name has become proverbial for female contentiousness and irascibility and with whom he had three sons.

As was customary, Socrates followed the craft of his father and probably achieved a socioeconomic status equivalent to what we might today describe as "middle class." We know this from the fact that during the Peloponnesian War he served as a hoplite, a heavily armed infantryman, who was required to purchase his own armor—a significant expense. Plutarch suggests Socrates was, at least at one point, reasonably comfortable (Aristides 1.9), and Xenophon indicates that even in later life Socrates was not entirely impoverished (Oec. 2.2-4). Still, the most consistent imagery surrounding Socrates during his more mature years is one of general indigence which he himself attributes to the pursuit of his philosophic ministry, a burden taken up in obedience to Delphic dictate (Apol. 23b-c).

The ancient testimony concerning Socrates' physical appearance indicates that he was, to say the least, something of an oddity. Amid a people who virtually worshipped beauty, Socrates was, by all accounts, a singularly unbecoming man. His features included a broad flat nose, thick lips, bulging eyes, and a pot-belly (see Xenophon, Sym. 5).* In addition, he apparently had a most peculiar gait, strange enough to have prompted separate commentary from both Aristophanes and Plato (*Clouds* 362 and Symp. 221b).

All things considered then, what we know of Socrates suggests that he was a most unlikely candidate for cultural stardom. He possessed none of the traditional assets that would normally have marked a man for fame and reputation in Hellenic society—power,

---

* Socrates' facial features apparently bore an uncanny similarity to those of satyrs, the ugly, semi-bestial attendants of the god Dionysus (see Xenophon, Sym. 4.19 and Plato, Symp. 215b).

wealth, physical virtues, etc. Yet the ancient sources consistently speak of certain qualities that elevated him above his contemporaries. In particular, those distinguishing features center upon factors of personality and character. Socrates it seems, was a man of extraordinary righteousness who made morality the focal point of his existence. And it is this moral devotion that may indeed hold the secret to Socrates' magnetism. It may explain why even the likes of an Alcibiades (Plato, Symp. 216b-c and Xenophon, Mem. 1.2.18) felt drawn to his side and why still today, we feel strangely attracted to this peculiar little man.

It seems fitting in what follows, therefore, that we focus primarily on the moral instruction of Socrates—an area in which his thoughts proved to be seminal as well as revolutionary.

Moral Teaching

Unlike many of his philosophical predecessors, the mature Socrates does not evidence much interest in the "things above and the things below," i.e., natural science (Phaedo 98c and Mem. 1.1.11). Instead, the Socrates who appears in most of the extant literature is exclusively concerned with human issues and above all, with matters of morality. Accordingly, the great Socratic question and the center of this man's life was "How ought we to live?" In attempting to answer this question, Socrates devised a new moral compass for the Greeks and an equally innovative method, both of which became indelibly impressed upon the Western mind.

Underlying much of Socrates' moral enterprise is the conviction that virtue can, in some sense, be understood as a craft. In other words, he believes that a proper moral existence requires an expertise analogous to the craft-knowledge of cobblers, carpenters, fullers, etc. In this, Socrates distinguishes himself from the sophists, for unlike Protagoras or Gorgias, he insists that ethics is not a matter of opinion or persuasion but instead involves a series of closely examined premises for which rational and authoritative justification can be offered (Laches, 189e-190b and Gorgias 465a, 500e-501b). In view of this orientation, it is not surprising to find Socrates continuously posing the "What is x?" question throughout the early dialogues of Plato's corpus.* In so doing, Socrates seeks to arrive at rigorously consistent definitions that do more than merely list examples of the respective virtues (Euth. 6d-e, Laches 190e, H. Major 287e-289d) but rather reflect the common element or universal quality that all things deemed virtuous share (Meno 72b, Euth. 11a, etc.). Here it seems Socrates was unable to attain his objective, at least as indicated by the relevant dialogues which typically end in *aporia*, i.e., doubt or perplexity.† But by the logic of the Socratic method (see below), these efforts were by no means fruitless because a healthy, mind-expanding doubt is always superior to a complacent, self-satisfied ignorance. It should also be noted that the latent metaphysic behind Socrates' demand for "universal" definitions served as a conceptual stimulus for Plato's own

---

* What is piety (Euthyphro)? What is temperance (Charmides)? What is justice (Republic I)? etc.

† Doubt and confusion are very much part of Socratic imagery. In the Platonic dialogues Socrates is often heard to disclaim knowledge of the "What is x" questions he puts to others (Apology 21b-d, Euthyphro 5a-e, Charmides 165b-c, Laches 186b-c, Lysis 212a, Meno 71a, H. Major 286c-e, and Gorgias 509c). Many scholars have dismissed these professions of ignorance as ironic. It may be, however, that Socrates honestly does not possess the kind of knowledge he disclaims (Irwin 39-40 and Kraut 245-247). Socrates does indeed possess certain insights, but they are merely propositional, what might be termed merely human knowledge. Yet what he seeks is something equivalent to craft-knowledge in the moral domain and it is this comprehensive understanding that he lacks and indeed may be beyond the grasp of humanity in general. Significantly, in the Apology (23a-b) Socrates asserts that only the god is wise and that by comparison, human knowledge is a small and paltry thing.

attempt to arrive at universal essences (Jaeger 2:67; Guthrie 33; Ross 12 and 17).

Explicitly, Socrates' search for the "good" reflects a strong cognitivism that directly identified knowledge and virtue. That is to say, Socrates believed knowledge was not only necessary for moral agency, it was also sufficient; "knowing that" ensured "knowing how" (cf. Ryle, Chapter 2). This position led Socrates to certain conclusions regarding morality and human motivation that are patently inconsistent with modern perspectives. As a result, these views are often referred to as the "Socratic paradoxes" which can be summarized in the following manner: 1) no one desires evil things and those who pursue them do so involuntarily (Meno. 77b-78b, Protag. 358c, Gorgias 468c), and 2) virtue is knowledge and all who do injustice do so involuntarily from ignorance (Gorgias 460b-d, Protag. 354e, 360d, Meno. 87, 89, Laches 198, Charm. 173).

Now the Greek love of paradox did not begin with Socrates, but his views regarding knowledge and virtue certainly represent an important innovation within established tradition (O'Brien 108-109). What in particular is new and paradoxical in the Socratic position is a denial of the possibility of *akrasia*, i.e., moral weakness or incontinence. Specifically, Socrates argued that knowing the good and doing evil was impossible; the truly wise man could never be vicious or immoral nor, in his view, were knowledgeable individuals capable of being overcome or seduced by base instinct (Protag. 355a-b, Xenophon, Mem. 3.9.4, 4.6.6).

How does Socrates arrive at these conclusions? In great measure his reasoning hinges on what one noted authority refers to as the "endaemonistic axiom" (Vlastos 1969, 84), i.e., the idea that all people, irrespective of individual distinctions, seek the "good" in life because they understand it as the key to happiness. There is, of course, a critical difference between what people typically <u>believe</u> is good and what actually <u>is</u> good. But the fact remains no one pursues that which they consciously recognize as bad. Such a move is dismissed by Socrates as entirely contrary to human nature in the same sense that a person would never desire to become ill or injured. So how then do we account for those who seem routinely committed to lives of injustice and wrongdoing? In all such cases the fault lies not with a defective moral will (*akrasia*). Indeed, for Socrates none of this has anything to do with volitional states because all aim at securing the same thing—their own happiness. If a person does travel down the wrong moral path, it is not because he has been overwhelmed by passion, it is rather because he has been misguided by ignorance and denied thereby an accurate view of the true good. Put another way, Socrates argued that well-knowing resulted in well-doing, which in turn ensured well-being (Versenyi 79).[*]

The unity of *episteme* and *arete* as presented by Socrates does enjoy a general credibility provided one is willing to grant several premises regarding human nature. But therein lies a problem; today, we tend to see very little manifest connection between knowing the good and doing the good[†] —in fact, the strongly intellectu-

---

[*] A related dimension of Socrates' moral cognitivism is the idea that the five cardinal virtues (piety, justice, temperance, wisdom and courage) are really a unity tied together by knowledge, e.g., courage is the knowledge of fearful and non-fearful things (<u>Protag</u>. 360d). In addition, Socrates argued for the existence of a superordinate or master knowledge, which he identified as moral wisdom. Only this special category of wisdom is "good in itself." All the other conventional goods, things like wealth, health, and power, are of merely conditional value and without the guidance afforded by moral insight can become positively detrimental to those possessing them (<u>Euthyd</u>. 281e, <u>Apol</u>. 30a, <u>Crito</u> 44d).

[†] The discontinuity between knowing the good v. doing the good was understood clearly by St. Paul, "I do not do the good I want but I do the evil I do not want (Romans 7:14).

alized perspectives of Socrates are particularly inconsistent with modern psychological doctrine where the stubborn opposition of the passions are fully acknowledged if not emphasized. Interestingly, even in his own day the propositions advanced by Socrates did not go unchallenged or uncriticized. From Euripides we have lines that seem aimed directly at Socrates, asserting that reason can indeed be overwhelmed by non-rational forces (see *Medea* 1075-80 and *Hippolytus* 375-88). Plato too, ardent follower that he was, nevertheless cannot, as a mature thinker, accept the strict cognitivism of his mentor. In the middle and late dialogues, Plato rejected both the craft-analogy and the idea that knowledge is somehow sufficient for virtue (see Irwin 101 and 133; Santas 219; Gulley 96). In particular, the psychology presented by Plato in Book 4 of the Republic acknowledged the powerful role of non-cognitive impulses and calls for special measures to train and condition them. Above all, however, it was Aristotle equipped with his impeccable logical skills who most fully revealed the deficiencies of the Socratic thesis. In addition to deeper insights regarding the emotions, Aristotle also appreciated the critical distinction between moral knowledge and moral character. Moreover, he highlighted the differences between a theoretical science (e.g., astronomy) versus a productive science (e.g., morality), all subtleties far beyond the range of Socratic philosophy (N.E. 7.1.6-7.3.17 also Eud. Ethics 1.5.16-18 and Mag. Mor. 1.1.26-27).

As legitimate as these criticisms were, they still should not serve to minimize our appreciation of Socrates' pioneering influences in the history of ethics. When, for instance, Hegel claimed that Socrates should not merely be noted as a teacher of morality but rather as the inventor of morality (269), he expressed a view which, despite its laudatory tone, remains surprisingly near the mark. The reason why Socrates merits such extraordinary acclaim is that he elevated the level of our moral awareness to unprecedented heights. It is with him specifically that we can trace the progress from *sittlichkeit* to *moralitat*; from a merely reflexive/intuitive morality dominated by conventional belief and practice to a rationally conscious morality capable of independent and even heterodox assessments. Simply put, Socrates upped the moral ante of the Greek world and in the process helped awaken Western man from the somnambulism of received opinion.

Moral Tradition and Moral Innovation

In order to more fully appreciate this Socratic achievement, it is necessary to examine in greater detail two crucial aspects of Socratic thought. First, we must be very clear about the ethical pragmatism that underlies so much of Socrates' position—a key point of demarcation between ancient and modern perspectives. Secondly, we must specify the precise manner and degree to which Socrates departed from the prevailing moral precepts of the 5th century B.C..

With regard to the former, we need to recognize the strong prudential elements operating within all Greek morality, including to a considerable degree, the innovations proposed by Socrates. What is conspicuously absent from Hellenic moral belief in general is anything resembling a deontological component, i.e., an ethical orientation based upon notions of duty (Adkins 261). The modern moral horizon has been powerfully influenced by certain religious and philosophic teachings stressing duty, obligation, and sacrifice as the essence of true morality. This is so much the case that it is difficult for us to acknowledge as legitimate other ethical systems that fail to incorporate these dimensions. But Greek morality developed without the benefit of a Jesus or a Kant and as a result there are powerful strains of ethical egoism operating even in the higher morality put forth by Socrates. If, for example, Socrates were asked why an individual should conduct himself in a morally responsible fashion he would not have responded, "Because it's the right thing to do." Not only would such a response never have occurred to Socrates, such an answer would have made little or no sense to any Greek. For Socrates, as for all Hellenes, a moral agent is always prompted into action by the prospect of some practical benefit promised by the ethical equation itself. The foundation therefore of Socratic morality is not some abstract, "pure ethic" but rather the self-interest of the individual. The "good" is good precisely because it contributes to the well-being of those who act morally—in other words, virtue pays. What distinguishes Socrates' version of ethical pragmatism from typical ancient belief is his understanding of genuine "self-interest." As we shall see, the real advantages Socrates saw accruing to the virtuous person have nothing to do with power, reputation, or wealth but rather with the proper maintenance of our most precious possession—the soul.

With regard to Socrates' suggested alternative to conventional moral standards, there are two dialogues in particular that merit special attention—Crito and Gorgias. In these works Socrates unveils a sweeping revision of Hellenic moral foundations. In fact, his suggestions are so bold, so unexampled, they constitute in the realm of ethics something comparable to what Thomas Kuhn termed a "paradigm shift."[*] The ethos from which Socrates advocated departure had its roots in the vendetta psychology of heroic times (see Chapter I), which included a particularly virulent version of the *lex talionis* and a shame-based honor code in which personal

---

[*] See T. Kuhn, The Structure of Scientific Revolutions. Chicago: University Press, 1970.

worth and status were a matter of public assessment. The governing principle of this highly competitive and often violent world was well summarized by the admonition, "Help friends and harm enemies" (see Iliad 9.613-15, Isocrates, To Demonicus 26, Pindar, 2 Pyth. 83-5, Meno. 71e, etc.).

In direct contrast, Socrates attempted to convince his contemporaries that the good life was somehow directly related to justice and that morality paid a greater dividend than wrongdoing. Here again, we must be clear about what Socrates means by terms such as "good life" and "justice." Traditional commitments to honor, shame, and reprisal are entirely abandoned.[*] In the Crito, for example, Socrates insisted that it is wrong to repay evil with evil (49c-d) and that the assessments of an unenlightened public are generally worthless (47a). Similarly in the Gorgias he argues that it is better to be the victim of injustice than the evildoer (469c) and then goes on to offer the outrageous view that wicked men should aggressively seek their own punishment (480d)! To Greek ears, these suggestions must have implied something much more than mere innovation, they must have seemed like a radical transvaluation of a five hundred-year-old tradition and to this extent Callicles' observation that Socrates' position would turn the whole world upside down was substantially correct (Gorgias 481c). Few men have dared oppose the spiritual current of their times in such as aggressive and categorical fashion. Indeed, Socrates' dedication to these new moral rhythms is so pronounced, as evidence particularly by his rejection of the *talio*, that he legitimately invites comparison with the manner and teachings of Jesus.[†] Both men, each in

---

[*] In Xenophon's portrait, Socrates remains attached to the *talio* (Mem. 2.6.75).

[†] But this comparison should not be pressed too far. If assaulted, Socrates might be prepared to depart without retaliating, but he remains too Greek to turn the other

their own way, were revolutionaries and both received from their respective societies similar treatment.

The Scalpel Tongue

Socrates was a man on a divinely appointed mission (Apol. 23a-b). The task he had been assigned involved helping people recognize the scope and limitations of human understanding. This objective was intimately related to the moral life and human happiness because, as we have seen, Socrates associated knowledge with virtue, which was in turn the key to *eudaemonia*. But what Socrates discovers in the course of his endless interrogations—in the marketplace, the gymnasia, at private homes—is that a terrible obstacle exists which prevents people from attaining the insights they require in life. Here again, the impediment in question has nothing to do with insufficiencies of wealth, power, or status. The great hindrance diagnosed by Socrates was instead a peculiar form of ignorance; a conceited, presumption of knowledge that precluded any possibility of attaining genuine understanding.

For Socrates, the implications of this self-induced blindness were clear. No one can be virtuous, and therefore no one can be happy, unless he has a clear, consistent, and accurate grasp of what virtue really entails. But virtue so conceived inevitably eludes those who arrogantly assume they possess moral wisdom from the outset. They suffer from a compounded ignorance; they know nothing, but think they know everything. This, as Socrates says, is the most disgraceful form of ignorance (Apol. 29a-b) and he might have added the most tragic because if the "unexamined life is not worth living" (Apol. 38a), people such as these are by definition living worthless

---

cheek, much less love his enemies. These are sentiments no Hellene would ever endorse or even comprehend.

lives. Moreover, according to the testimony Socrates offers in Plato's Apology, there is even an element of impiety attached to such an existence. The Oracle of Delphi enjoins the individual to "know thyself" which Socrates interpreted as an injunction to humbly acknowledge the limits of human cognition. But those who suffer from this double ignorance defy the Delphian dictum by remaining pretentiously self-satisfied with their specious views. Socrates is superior to such people, intellectually and morally, not because he possessed some god-like overview of the human drama, but because he accepts his human limitations with pious humility and recognizes himself as merely another pilgrim seeking light.

Socrates' response to the self-inflicted stupidity he encounters at every turn is the critical cross-examination known as *elenchos*. The operational premise here is that a person who truly understands something should be able to offer a rational account of his insight (Laches 190c and Mem.4.6.1). Invariably, however, those scrutinized by Socrates prove to be sadly deficient in this regard, their claims of wisdom notwithstanding. Thus, one of the most important aspects of *elenchos* lies in its cathartic and purifying function. The aim is to strip away the conceit of knowledge and to expose the ignorance for what it is—an absolute obstacle to virtue and happiness. As it turns out, the unenlightened cling stubbornly to their mistaken notions necessitating an acid tone on Socrates' part. Plato's descriptions of Socrates as a "gadfly" or "torpedo fish" bespeaks the stinging exchanges sometimes employed to rescue the misguided (e.g., Apol. 30e and Meno. 80a-b). In addition, Socrates often seems to employ irony with his interlocutors, denying that he himself possesses knowledge while demolishing their arguments with an ease indicating profound insight.[*] It is this sort of thing that infuriates Thrasymachus in the Republic (337a) and no doubt earned Socrates a good deal of ill will among his fellow citizens (see below). Still, for all its acerbity, Socratic scrutiny remained something very different from the eristic combats engaged in by the Sophists. Unlike the latter, Socrates does not aim at verbal victory. His objective is nothing less than the acquisition of moral truth, to whatever degree human beings were capable of attaining it.

As indispensable as the deconstructive phase of the *elenchos* was, Socratic method aspired to do more than merely disconcert and perplex. There was also a constructive side to the "elenctic ministrations" offered by Socrates. For one thing, *elenchos* was a proving ground for the moral assumptions commonly held by Socrates' contemporaries. It provided a means of carefully separating the conceptual dross from potentially precious insights and generally helped the individual arrive at a better understanding of the challenges imposed by the demands of a moral existence. It is in this context too that Socrates likens himself to a midwife; a facilitator who helped bring forth and test the embryonic truths necessary for virtue. It should also be noted that in the process of performing these mental obstetrics, Socrates helped establish the foundations

---

[*] The precise nature of Socratic *eironeia* or irony has stirred considerable controversy. Some have argued that there really is no such thing, that the Socratic disavowal of knowledge represents genuine puzzlement (Irwin 39-40 and Kraut 10). Others have pointed out the irony was a necessary and consistent dimension of Socratic method used to shock those who wallow in ignorance (Robinson 92, in Vlastos 1971). Another position advanced by Vlastos argued that here too Socrates was an innovator proffering a new form of *eironeia*. Traditionally, irony among the Greeks implied deceit and swindle (see Theophrastus, Characters 1; Aristophanes *Wasps* 174 and *Clouds* 449; Plato, Symp. 216e and 218d). But Socrates introduced what Vlastos called "complex irony," which is not intended as sham but rather is meant to be true in one sense and false in another (1991, 25-32).

of logic—specifically the methods of inductive argumentation and the general rules of definition (see Aristotle, Meta. 1.6.2, 13.4.3, and 13.9.22; also Santas 135; Robinson 1966, 46; Grote, 8:586; Ross 22; Danhauser, 105-110).

But the elenctic awakening also entailed something beyond an opportunity for intellectual reassessment. Although there was often pain and embarrassment experienced by those undergoing the Socratic exorcism, the end result was something of inestimable value—a new self-awareness. The rigorous intellectualism espoused by Socrates included the belief that personal psychology was largely determined by cognitive state; that being was a direct reflection of knowing. In other words, we are what we believe and as a result, the *elenchos* allowed one not only to gauge the worth of one's convictions but also to take stock on the level of personality and character. *Elenchos* therefore was not simply a mental exercise, it was also a form of *therapeia,* a source of self-revelation as well as an opportunity for psychic enhancement, all of which directly complied with the Delphic admonition to "know thyself."

Finally, a word about what was perhaps the most important gift of the elenctic experience—a spirit of discovery and openness. If there was one habit of mind that best captured the essence of Socraticism, it was a willingness to examine, sift, and analyze every premise, every value, and every inferred bit of knowledge. Throughout the Platonic dialogues we continuously hear Socrates declare his willingness to follow the argument wherever it leads, no matter how discomforting or self-deflating that journey may prove to be (Euthyp. 14c, Gorgias 527e, Phaedo 82d, Repubic 365d, 394d, etc.). By its very nature, the *elenchos* fostered this kind of mental hygiene. It specifically encouraged the sort of critical spirit that alone can liberate a person from the fetters of ignorance. If, as Aristotle said, philosophy begins in wonder, then the *elenchos* can be seen as the source of that wonder. In short, *elenchos* was the indispensable pre-condition of the philosophic life and as such it constituted the most sacred of all "purifications" (Sophist 230d-e).

The Psychic Revolution

In terms of long-range historical significance, one of the most important accomplishments of Socrates was his dramatic expansion of the concept of "soul." With the exception of a few scholarly experts, his contributions in this area are generally under-appreciated or hardly recognized at all. The fact remains, however, the provenance of our notion of soul, an idea that has dominated European religious and philosophic speculation for 2,400 years, is to a significant degree, Socratic (see Burkert 300-301).

Prior to Socrates, Greek views of the soul were of the sort typically offered in the epic poetry of Homer, where the term functioned as something analogous to a "life-force" (Onians 96 and Autenreith 294). At death, this life principle fled the body and took up residence in Hades as a shade (*eidolon*), an existence Homer made clear no mortal should rush to embrace (Ody. 11.490-4). Slowly, these images began to evolve along more rationalistic lines and under the specific inspiration of scientific-medical theorizing the soul increasingly came to be seen as the center of perception, thought, and feeling. What is significant in all this is the general absence of any detailed conception of what might be called the "ego" soul, i.e., the soul as "self" or the soul conceived as the center of personality and character. This is not to suggest there were no intimations along these lines prior to Socrates.[*] A careful reading of certain pre-Socratic thinkers such as Heraclitus and Pindar reveals impor-

---

[*] Jaeger correctly notes that the soul doctrine reaches it fullness with Socrates but was not his invention per se (1:279).

tant antecedents, as do the plays of Sophocles and especially Euripides (see Solmsen 1983 and Claus 1981). To argue then that the soul as comprehensive personal self was the *ex nihilo* creation of Socrates would be to overstate the case.* Still, Socrates did greatly extend the idea of soul beyond what had come before so that by the close of the 5th century Hellenic views of *psuche* were vastly different than the "life-stuff" conception of archaic times (Bremmer 14).

Among the several Socratic innovations was a tendency to greatly sharpen the division between *soma* and *psuche*—between body and soul. The extent of this differentiation can be seen more clearly by comparing it with Biblical conception. The Hebrew word for soul is *nephesh* and it is consistently used in a fashion suggestive of unity with the body. There is no hint of any dualism here, no suggestion of psychic exclusivity. Nor is there any special status or value assigned the soul such as an assertion of immortality or divinity (cf. Mem. 4.3.14). For the Hebrew, a person did not really "possess" a soul, a person simply was a living soul (Genesis 2.7). All of this stands in marked contrast to Socratic perspectives. For Socrates there is a radical distinction between body and soul, both in substance and quality. In his view, the soul was the exclusive repository of everything we would today imply by the term "psychological." It was the center of personal consciousness, the true "I" behind our identity and self-concept (Xenophon, Sym. 8.4). Moreover, the Socratic soul was also the locus of cognitive and moral activity and as such was vastly superior to the body which in comparison was best understood as the natural servant or tool of the soul (Protag. 326b, Rep. 353d-354a, and Tim. 69c).

---

* As John Burnett did in his much cited article, "The Socratic Doctrine of the Soul" (1919).

In addition to these premises, Socrates also insisted that the soul's special status as our true and most precious self made it worthy of extraordinary attention and care. Here, Socrates' views may have been influenced in part by Orphic-Pythagorean traditions, an idea that has prompted some to speculate that perhaps Socrates was himself a *mystes* (initiate) of such groups.* In any event, Socrates urged that our well-being necessitated making the soul the primary consideration in life; that its proper tendance was of far greater importance than acquiring the things feverishly sought by the many (Apol. 30a-b). But more important still, was Socrates' bold attempt to fuse his prescriptions for a pneumatic-hygiene with his moral and eudaemonistic theories. The significance of this move cannot be overstated either for the history of Greek morality or for that matter, Western civilization, because now in addition to an unprecedented assessment of man as "soul creature," we also have a moral code that identified virtue as a kind of spiritual nourishment and conversely, viewed vice and wickedness as forms of psychic defilement.

By making morality a matter of the inner life, Socrates distinguished himself as the author of a new truth—one for which there were only limited precedents in 5th century Greece. In summary terms, the meaning of this innovation is contained in the following equation: Knowledge equals virtue; virtue is the food of the soul; the well-nourished soul ensures the life worth living (*eudaemonia*). Here, one must be clear about what Socrates means by the term "knowledge." He is not referring to some encyclopedic, factual

---

* A good example being A.E. Taylor (Varia Socratica, Oxford, 1911). Specific grounds for such speculation can be found in several Platonic dialogues. The "Myth of Er" in Republic 10, for example, is heavily indebted to Orphism and the Phaedo offers strong intimation of a Pythagorean-Socratic connection, particularly given the prominence in that dialogue of the two Pythagoreans, Simmias and Cebes.

proficiency. Knowledge for Socrates was above all a matter of psychic self-assessment. In other words, Socrates takes the Delphic admonition to "know thyself" and internalizes it. In his hands, it becomes an introspective mandate; one must strive to understand the true self, i.e., the soul, and on the basis of the insights afforded by this knowledge, pattern one's existence accordingly. It is in this sense that "the unexamined life is not worth living" (Apol. 38a) because without a clear understanding of the soul's primacy, as well as an accurate diagnosis of one's own psychic status, we risk engaging in activities that not only injure the soul but also preclude all prospects for felicity.

Given the fact that the issue of psychic well-being was such a crucial aspect of Socratic morality, its unsparing treatment in several of the early dialogues (e.g., Crito and Gorgias) comes as no surprise. But the message itself must have been rather shocking for those reared under the competitive, retaliatory logic of works such as the Iliad and Odyssey. How could Socrates possibly suggest that it was wrong to requite injustice with further injustice (Crito 49c); what possible support could he offer for the view that it was better to suffer evil than to do evil (Gorgias 482b)? Did not Achilles have a right to seek revenge for the humiliation he suffered through the loss of Briseis? Were not Odysseus' bloody reprisals against the suitors condign and proper? By every measure of Hellenic convention, the position advanced by Socrates was not simply another dubious novelty of 5th century speculation, it was a moral earthquake that threatened the very foundations of traditional beliefs—beliefs by which the Greeks had for centuries assigned worth, defined probity, and established personal reputation.

The basis of Socrates' challenge to customary moral practice lay in his conviction that they were diametrically opposed to the needs of a properly nurtured soul—indeed, they were guaranteed to ensure psychopathology. Again, the true "self" for Socrates was the *psuche*, and in his view injustice was a kind of poison for the soul. Every time a person engaged in an act of wickedness, he in essence inflicted damage upon himself. In other words, the commission of evil was a form of self-mutilation (Gorgias 469b, 477-479a, 508a-e, 509c, 512a, and 527c-d). Contrary to popular belief, assaults against our dignity and even violence against our person leave the true self unscathed. We, and we alone, are the agonizers of our souls—a point lost on the likes of men like Meletus and Anytus[*] who mistakenly assume they have benefited themselves by bringing down a death sentence upon their opponent, Socrates (Apol. 30d). This is why Socrates is prepared to argue that no evil can befall a good man, i.e., one who has solicitously cared for his soul by abstaining from wickedness (Apol. 41d). It also explains the remarkable aplomb with which Socrates awaits his own execution (Phaedo 117b), as well as the blithe manner with which he discusses his own burial.[†] The message of these Platonic dialogues is clear—as a man of unblemished soul, Socrates has nothing to fear.

If then, evil and injustice are malignant to the soul, virtue must be a tonic that guarantees health and vitality. Activities that aim at promoting goodness and justice not only benefit the lives of others they also reward the doer, in an almost medicinal sense, by enhancing psychic well-being. Medical analogy is one of Plato's favorite literary devices and in the Gorgias he expands it to incorporate both political and judicial elements relevant to Socratic psychology. The true statesman, for example, must act as a physician for

---

[*] The lead prosecutors of Socrates at the trial in 399 B.C..

[†] Phaedo 115c-d. Here, Socrates responds to Crito's question about burial by stating that he may bury him any way he wishes, but that he must first "catch" him, meaning that the true Socrates, i.e., the soul, will not stand about waiting for the disposal of the flesh.

the souls of those he governs—a standard by which Pericles, Cimon, Miltiades, Themistocles, and all the other political luminaries of Athenian history fail (Gorgias 517). Similarly, a wrongdoer who escapes punishment places himself in psychic jeopardy because with each act of evil he augments the sickness within. Accordingly, such individuals must seek corrective justice for themselves, i.e. they must solicit punishment appropriate to their crimes, up to and including exile and death (Gorgias 480d). Only in this manner can a wicked person prevent injustice from becoming an incurable, inner cancer destructive of one's human essence.[*]

The Fate of Gadflies

There are a handful of dates in human history, a few pivotal events, the mere mention of which evokes a sense of gravity and awe, accompanied by a corresponding tendency to ask, "What if?". What if the Normans had not been victorious in 1066; what if the British colonies had not declared their independence in 1776; what if Gavrilo Princip had not discharged those fateful shots at Sarajevo in 1914? Although the trial and death of Socrates did not result in a military cataclysm or in the birth of a new nation, we are nevertheless entitled to add the year 399 B.C. to any roster of portentous episodes in world history because it was here that Socrates apparently displayed that lofty and courageous manner that not only ensured his status as a cultural icon but also infused his message with a normative energy enabling it to materially influence the course of Western civilization. The year 399 B.C. is, therefore, a cultural milestone of undeniable significance.

---

[*] Herein lies one of the stronger comparisons between Socrates and Jesus. Both figures insist that gaining the whole world means nothing if in the process one loses his soul (Apol. 30a-b and Mark 8:36). For Jesus' rejection of the *talio*, see Matt. 5:44.

All of this being said, however, there remains one very obvious and puzzling question: If, in fact, Socrates was the sort of man indicated by the encomiastic portraits of Plato and Xenophon, why was he brought to trial in the first place? Why, if as Plato says, he was the bravest, wisest, and most righteous man of his day, was he put to death? There is no simple answer to this question, but over the years scholars have proposed a number of possible explanations.

One theory stems directly from the nature of the accusations leveled against Socrates. Here, we are on firm ground because virtually all of the key sources agree on the content of the charges. In fact, Diogenes Laertius (2.40) reports that the actual affidavit was still on file in the Metroon (the temple where the Athenians kept their official archives) as late as the 1st century A.D.. The three accusations were 1) a failure to worship the state deities, 2) introduction of new deities into the state (a reference to Socrates' *daimonion*), and 3) corruption of the city's youth (Plato, Apol. 24 and Xen., Apol. 11, 12, and 19). On the surface then, it seems a good portion of the complaint against Socrates involved an alleged violation of religious convention and there are those who have argued that this was indeed the cause of Socrates' prosecution and death (Smith and Brickhouse 1994). This view merits serious consideration for several reasons. First, there is some evidence the Athenians were not above persecuting those they deemed guilty of impiety. The Decree of Diopeithes, passed sometime in the 430's, allowed for the prosecution of "atheists" which may have specifically targeted scientist-philosopher types such as Anaxagoras, who was, according to tradition, prosecuted under this statute (see Plutarch,

Pericles 32.1; MacDowell 200-201; and Apol. 26d).[*] Clearly, Aristophanes' *Clouds* portrayed Socrates as directly tied to the secular traditions of Ionian naturalism as does a fragment of Theophrastus, which suggests Socrates was at one time a close associate of Archelaus, the Athenian disciple of Anaxagoras (see Winspear and Silverberg 36). Even Plato acknowledges that Socrates once studied natural philosophy (Phaedo 96a-99d), although his view appears to conflict with Socrates' testimony in the Apology (18b-23c; see also Mem. 4.7.5-6). In addition, the fact that Plato seems at great pains to deny that Socrates was an atheist—on at least thirteen separate occasions in the Apology he stressed Socrates' divinely appointed mission[†] —also tends to lend credibility to the view that the religious issue was a key aspect of the prosecution. What all of this suggests for some, is that the public perception of impiety could indeed result in prosecution and that in the popular imagination Socrates was one of those irreligious free-thinkers who merited indictment.

In a clearly related argument, it has also been alleged that Socrates was tried because of an increasingly hostile reaction toward all those seen as part of the sophistic "enlightenment" (e.g., Ehrenberg 274). From a purely intellectual perspective, this period was truly one of the most remarkable in Greek history, but it must also be noted that many of the ideas and approaches proffered during this Hellenic *Aufklarung* were incompatible with customary attitudes and practices. As a result, men such as Protagoras and Gorgias were probably not seen by the average Athenian as intellectual pio-

---

[*] The Decree of Diopeithes probably lapsed with the reinscription of the laws associated with the Amnesty of 403 B.C.. It is, therefore, unlikely that Socrates was charged under this specific provision.

[†] Apology 21c, 22a, 23b, 23c, 28e, 29d, 30a, 30d-e, 31a, 33c, 35d, and 37e. Also, see Xenophon, Mem. 1.1.2.

neers but rather as dangerous subversives who threatened traditional notions of honor, truth, and decency. In addition, the typical Athenian probably made little or no distinction between these perceived extremists and Socrates. Didn't he practice the same verbal knavery as they? Wasn't he also a "mighty prattler" (Plutarch, Cato 23) capable of making the worse appear better, and the better appear worse? Viewed through this lens, a work like Aristophanes' *Clouds* is not merely a comedy but a conservative manifesto in defense of the *mos majorum* (ancestral traditions). What Athens needed according to this logic were teachers capable of producing the sort of men who had stood at Marathon, not a radical, "Socratified" youth that was nimble of tongue and wanting in virtue.* In brief, Socrates may have become for the Athenians a living symbol of all that was wrong with contemporary Athens and as such, was swept up in a kind of reactionary fervor aimed at all those insidious agitators menacing the revered foundations of society.†

Another possible reason for the indictment of Socrates relates to his divinely appointed mission. Plato makes this a central theme in his Apology, depicting Socrates as a soldier of Apollo engaged in elenctic warfare, the purpose of which was the improvement of men's souls through the disabuse of their unfounded claims to knowledge. The combative nature of these Socratic ministrations merit special note because while it is true Socrates often displays a gentle, conciliatory side (e.g., Laches 195a, Meno 75c-d, Phaedo 89a, etc.), the fact remains, Mr. Chips also had fangs. When scrutinizing those most swollen with pride, Socrates displayed an in-

---

* Xenophon notes that during the tyranny of the Thirty a law was passed specifically aimed at Socrates forbidding the instruction of the young in the art of technical speaking (Mem. 1.2.29).

† The issue of an Athenian witch-hunt has been analyzed by Stone (231-247), who rejected the idea, and by Burnett (1964, 90-91).

quisitorial vehemence that was anything but tender. In addition, this acerbity tended to fall most heavily upon people of substance and station—the rich, the powerful, and the reputedly wise (Apol. 22a-23a and Xen., Mem. 4.2.40). These exchanges were also of a sort that tended to deny a victim the face-saving benefits of private discourse. More often than not, they were conducted in the agora, palaestra, or gymnasium, etc., which meant those undergoing Socratic examination were subjected to varying degrees of public humiliation—this, in a culture where loss of face demanded reprisal (see Vlastos 1991, 296-97, Santas 5, Libanius 6 in Ferguson). Over the years then, Athens must have come to see Socrates as something more than an eccentric old quibbler.* He may have been perceived instead as a public nuisance and pernicious sower of discord who deservedly amassed an immense reservoir of ill will,† particularly from those best able to "swat" the gadfly. Seen in these terms, the resulting trial was all too predictable.

It has also been suggested that "politics" may have been behind the prosecution of Socrates. This should come as no surprise to anyone with even a modest knowledge of the ancient Greeks who, by the late 5th century, if not well before, had elevated political intrigue and violence to the level of high art.‡ The specific situation in which Socrates may or may not have been involved, concerned

---

* The idea of Socrates as quibbler is well expressed by Aristophanes in the *Frogs* where the following lines appear, "Life is bliss when you are not sitting next to Socrates, running off at the mouth..." (1491-1495).

† Diogenes Laertius claims that the elenctic sessions would sometimes result in physical assaults against Socrates (2.21).

‡ I am persuaded that politics was the real reason for Socrates' prosecution. As R. K. Sinclair notes, "Any assessment of Athenian justice must...take full account of the fact that public suits were commonly political in character, and that the stated terms of the charge were not necessarily the only question, or indeed the main question, in the minds of the Athenian citizens" (172; see also Calhoun 98).

the inveterate enmities between popular and oligarchic factions in classical Athens. Although Athens had begun its historic journey toward democracy as far back as the 6th century with the reforms of Solon and Cleisthenes, powerful anti-democratic forces remained viable and active. Indeed, these elements had erupted violently on several occasions during the closing years of the 5th century, the most notorious example being the revolution of 404 B.C. which resulted in the short lived but murderous Tyranny of the Thirty. Led by the likes of the infamous Critias, a former "student" of Socrates, this government distinguished itself in just a few short months as one of the bloodiest regimes in Greek history. Not only did it decimate the commons, killing an estimated 1,500 people, it also directed the same appalling violence toward moderate elements of its own class, as the fates of Niceratus, Antiphon, and Theramenes demonstrate (Xen. Hellen. 2.3.39-40 and 54-56). The terror came to an end as a result of a successful counterrevolution led by a group of exiled democrats known as the "men of the Piraeus"—notable among whom was Anytus, the same man who in 399 B.C. would lead the prosecution against Socrates.

In an effort to finally end the city's internecine strife, the *demos* took the remarkably enlightened step of instituting a general amnesty in the year 403 B.C.. Under the terms of that indemnity, the laws of Athens were to be recodified and more importantly for our purposes, no one was to be prosecuted for crimes committed during the oligarchic dictatorship.[*] Proof of the restored democracy's resolve in this matter is furnished by Aristotle who tells of the execution of a democrat who challenged the terms of the amnesty in an attempt at political reprisal (Athen. Const. 40.2).

---

[*] The exceptions being members of the Thirty, the Eleven (the state police serving the Thirty), and the Ten (the magistrates who controlled the Piraeus during the tyranny). Even these, however, were extended the right to offer an accounting of their actions.

What if any bearing did these events have on Socrates? While there is no evidence to indicate Socrates actively supported either faction in the tumult of 404-403 B.C., there are at least two circumstantial aspects of his life and thought that may have fostered the impression that Socrates was a *misodemos* (hater of the people). First, there was the matter of his philosophic circle. It is undeniable that several of the democracy's greatest despoilers had spent their youth at Socrates' knee. As their teacher, wasn't Socrates responsible for the likes of Critias and Charmides? Hadn't Alcibiades, Socrates' turncoat disciple, contemptuously disparaged democracy as "an admitted folly" (Thucydides 6.89.6)? On these grounds alone, there must have been an irresistible temptation among the people to assign guilt by association.* This tendency was no doubt reinforced by various references from the comedic stage linking Socrates to pro-Spartan (i.e., oligarchic) sentiments. References to Socratic "laconizing" were made not only by Aristophanes (*Clouds* 103, 175, and 362; *Birds* 1281-4), but can also be found in fragments of Eupolis and Ameipsias.

In addition to the issue of pedagogic culpability, there are numerous statements ascribed to Socrates in the works of Plato and Xenophon that indicate anti-democratic attitude. Interestingly, the basis for many of these critical remarks lie with the same craft-analogy employed by Socrates in his moral theory. Politics, according to Socrates, was a craft like any other and as such required practitioners of special aptitude and training (Protag. 319b-d, Mem. 3.9.10 and 4.2.3-7). In other words, Socrates argued that good government necessitated specialized expertise because just as the un-

---

* Xenophon (Mem. 1.2.12) says Socrates' association with Alcibiades was a key factor in the prosecution, while Aeschines identifies the relationship with Critias as the cause of Socrates' condemnation (Against Timarchus 173).

trained person could not perform the functions of a carpenter, so too, the unskilled "many" were incapable of arriving at a sound political order. The *basiliki techne* (kingly art) was therefore, by its very nature, inconsistent with the majoritarian principles of democracy (Mem. 4.2.11). Well-crafted laws and wise officials were not arrived at, according to Socrates, by drawing beans from an urn or by tabulating the number of outstretched arms attached to mindless assemblymen (Mem. 1.2.9 and 3.7.5-6). The good state is attained only through the talent and energies manifested by the knowledgeable expert. Accordingly, his hand alone should wield the sceptre.

Needless to say, these observations on popular government leave very little room for compromise since they challenge the core assumptions of democracy by explicitly denouncing the logic and worth of popular sovereignty. If factual, views such as these must have earned Socrates considerable hostility from democratic authorities, enough perhaps to supply the real motivation for the prosecution. The same opinions have also prompted certain scholars to conclude that Socrates really was a seditious supporter of the oligarchic camp. In fact, some have gone so far as to depict him as a fifth columnist anxiously awaiting the demise of the *demos* (Winspear and Silverberg, esp. 54 and 58; Wood and Wood, 82-3, 105, 115). But others have argued that Socrates belonged to no party and that his message of psychic conversion inherently transcends the narrow limits of partisan politics. They point to the fact that he condemns all of the great political darlings of Athenian history— oligarch and democrat alike (Gorgias 515b-517c)—and that he personally defied both regimes when they ordered him to participate in their unjust schemes (Apol. 32b-d). In addition, Socrates' friendship with well-known democrats like Chaerephon and Lysias provides further evidence against his alleged enthusiasm for partisan cause (Vlastos 1994, 87 and 108). Thus, the degree to which Socrates was himself a "political" figure and the extent to which public perception along these lines contributed to his trial and execution remain open questions.

Finally, a word about the manner in which Socrates conducted himself during the trial. From the outset, Plato's Socrates assumed a provocative, even remonstrative, tone toward the jury; a posture Cicero would later describe as "noble obstinacy" (Tus. Disp. 29.71). Xenophon believed he would have been acquitted easily had he been willing to engage in the maudlin theatrics for which the Athenian courts had become notorious (Mem. 4.4.4). But Socrates explicitly refuses to demean himself by resorting to such chicanery (Apol. 34c). Instead, he does precisely what he has done habitually since becoming the deputy of Apollo; he takes the five hundred jurors to school rebuking them for their ill-gauged priorities and above all, for the neglect of their souls (Apol. 29d-30c). In the process he presents a defense conspicuous for its lack of "plea." Indeed, there are moments in Plato's dialogue where one could argue that Socrates positively thirsts for the hemlock,[*] e.g., when he declared himself unwilling to accept any limitations on his ministry (29d), irrespective of court instruction, and his proposal that he be fed at public expense as an alternative to the death sentence (36d-37a).[†] Xenophon viewed such inflammatory conduct as no accident, insisting that Socrates had every intention of putting the cup to his own lips. Specifically, he maintains that Socrates' *megalegoria* (boastful speech) was part of a premeditated suicide strategy

---

[*] Brickhouse and Smith (1989) argue otherwise. See especially Chapter 5.

[†] There are two votes taken in a trial such as this: One to establish guilt or innocence and the other to determine penalty where appropriate. The vote for guilt had succeeded by a margin of sixty jurors. After Socrates' flippancy regarding public maintenance, the call for death succeeded by a majority of one hundred and ten votes.

aimed at avoiding the indignities of old age (Apol. 1.2, 1.9, 1.32 and Mem. 4.8.1).

Plato, on the other hand, employs his literary genius to promote a more nuanced portrait of Socratic belligerence. For him, the defiance displayed by Socrates seems to be an expression of heroic temperament.[*] Just as Achilles chose to die rather than live a life without honor (Iliad 9.4.10-15), Socrates elects to die rather than live in disobedience to his divinely appointed mission. By associating Socrates with the immemorial paradigms of the archaic past,[†] Plato's Apology pours new wine into old bottles. The ancient imagery is summoned to the cause of advancing a new moral and spiritual protocol. In Plato's hands, the trial of Socrates becomes something more than a judicial proceeding. It is an Iliadic episode transformed, an *aristeia* without spear or sword in which the hero no longer seeks martial glory or honor but a principled victory over ignorance and injustice.

Conclusion

Assessing the Socratic legacy is no easy task. His impact was so massive that any comprehensive analysis of his influence would undoubtedly result in a multi-volumed study. Suffice it to say that Socrates was the philosophic equivalent of the humble mustard seed of scripture; from dubious beginnings there sprang forth a mighty growth in whose limbs we find firmly perched Cynic, Cyrenaic, Megarian, Stoic, and Skeptic alike (see Zeller 1962 and

---

[*] On the heroic imagery of Plato's Socrates, see Knox 58 and Whitman 39.

[†] Plato does this specifically by directly comparing Socrates with the likes of Achilles, Palamedes, and Ajax (28b-d and 41a-b).

Vander Waerdt 1994).[*] But how are we to account for this remarkable fountain of progenitive energy, particularly from so implausible a source? Surely, the answer cannot rest entirely with the gifted apologists who rushed to Socrates' defense after 399 B.C.. The fact that Socrates became a universally acknowledged seismic event in the history of philosophy must, in good measure, relate to the content and spirit of his message.

There are certainly many strands to Socrates' genius, but as we have seen, he was first and foremost a moral theorist. More than anyone else before him, Socrates offered a new meditation on the life worth living insisting that we must divorce ourselves from the vanities most people prize if we are to gain the happiness all people seek. In particular, he demonstrated that the art of proper living was a moral art and that it necessarily included reverence for and care of the soul. In a word, he elevated the standards of Greek morality from the foothills of conventional belief to the peaks of systematic ethical insight.

As important as these moral realignments were, however, they must not be understood in isolation from a larger, and in some sense more fundamental aspect of Socratic teaching, viz., the passion for truth. The words ascribed to Socrates, as well as the manner and style in which he apparently lived his life, all suggest that for him truth, no matter how inconvenient, disquieting, or perilous, was an indispensable precondition of the good life. It should be noted the term "truth," as used here, suggests something more than the satisfaction of academic curiosity. It implies making truth a kind of reflex in our lives capable of informing and conditioning

---

[*] For a roster of Socrates' immediate disciples, see Phaedo 59b and Diogenes Laertius 2.47. For an explanation of the proliferation of Socratic schools, see Cicero DeOratore 3.16.61 and Tus. Disp. 5.4.11.

one's entire existence. Socrates knew well the ease with which shadow and apparition masquerade as reality in human affairs. He correctly understood that negligence with regard to truth indentures us to darkness and places the higher morality he advocated beyond our grasp. For these reasons, he believed we must become truth-lovers because only then would we be able to avail ourselves of the redemptive powers inherent in such devotion.

Lessons such as these, if they do in fact reflect his actual thinking, reveal the reason why Socrates became an object of cultural veneration. The values he espoused, and the authentic manner in which he lived in accordance with his convictions, projected Socrates beyond the particular circumstances of 5th century Athens. His message transcends the boundaries of time, locale, and race precisely because it speaks to something essential in the human spirit—the cherished belief that reason can liberate us from the ancient bonds of ignorance, deceit, and violence. This, above all, was the glad tiding of Socrates, an enigmatic little man who, in his relentless pursuit of truth, became the West's perduring symbol of the enlightened existence.

Chapter IX

The Sons of Abraham and the Sons of Javan[*]

"What has Athens to do with Jerusalem?"
                                    —Tertullian

One of the ways in which we can sharpen our understanding of Hellenic culture is by comparing the Greeks with other ancient peoples. In this regard, a comparison with the Hebrews is particularly instructive for at least two reasons. First, as Matthew Arnold observes, "...between these two points of influence (Hebraism and Hellenism) moves our world" (130). In other words, the foundations of Western culture are in great measure an amalgam of Jewish and Greek genius: the moral/religious elements are traceable to the sons of Abraham, the rational/scientific features, what Arnold calls "sweetness and light," attributable to the Hellenes. By assessing these facts of our cultural identity, we not only cast light upon the contributors but upon ourselves as the descendants of that rich syncretism known as Western civilization.

A second revelation of the comparative analysis of Jews and Greeks is the profoundly different world-views espoused by each people. There is no better way to comprehend who the Greeks were

---

[*] The "Sons of Abraham" refers to the Hebrews. The descendants of Javan suggest the Greeks as indicated by the table of nations contained in <u>Genesis</u> 10:1-4.

than to recognize who they were not. In this regard, the Hebrews, beyond all the other ancients, are the perfect foil, for in virtually every major cultural endeavor, the Jewish life discipline represents a dramatic antinomy to the Grecian.

For literary economy the analysis that follows is restricted to three areas: the essence and function of God, the nature and proper activity of man, and the scope and limitations of human reason. By assessing the belief systems surrounding these and related questions, we gain additional insight into "Hellenism."

Yahweh and Zeus

The most consistent feature of Hebraic culture is unquestionably its theocentric orientation. What was said of Spinoza by Novalis, viz., that he was "God-intoxicated," can appropriately be said of his people from the outset of their history. Even the most casual scrutiny of the Jewish Bible continuously conveys the primacy of divine category for the Jews. God is the universal center of Hebraic existence; every blessing, every tragedy is linked directly to the will of Yahweh. Secular history of the sort we find in Thucydides is a conceptual impossibility for the ancient Jews. God is the universal and continuously operative presence behind all their experience—from the triumph over Pharaoh to the disaster of the Babylonian captivity. The search for other explanations is neither necessary nor appropriate.

Perhaps the most definitive feature of the God of Abraham is his awesome power. His authority and might are unlimited; nothing is beyond his capacity. He can deliver the hopeless and lay low the mightiest of kings as he chooses. There is no necessity or restraint operating on him of any kind. Creator of the universe, maker of man, author of history, he is pure, numinous potency on an unfathomable scale. Even his name, Yahweh, is indicative of this power. Stemming from the Hebrew verb, *hawah*, "to be," the name implies that he is the point of origin of all existence (Ex. 3:14-15). Historically speaking, most of our modern understanding of a "supreme being" is ultimately founded upon these Hebraic conceptions of a single, all-pervasive divine force operating ubiquitously in the world. And it is precisely this rigorously conceived monotheistic scheme that is the source of one of Judaism's greatest legacies to world culture.

In addition to his might, the Jewish God is also the authoritative source of law and justice for man and the universe. All things function in accordance with divine legislation and it is above all a stern legalism that characterizes God throughout most of the Old Testament. The *agapastic* or loving qualities of Yahweh are not systematically developed until late in Jewish tradition and will not achieve full fruition until the Word was made flesh. But for the most part, God is the irascible, judgmental father who makes his anger weigh heavily upon the disobedient. Throughout most of Jewish history, therefore, religion is not primarily an affair of the soul but rather a matter of the law. One need only consider the substance and spirit of Old Testament books such as Leviticus and Numbers to appreciate this point. The legalistic zeal of these works is astonishing by any standard. In particular, the normative sweep of Hebraic sacramentalism is remarkably comprehensive addressing everything from religious and ethical practices to food, clothing, and medicinal procedures. In all, the Pentateuch (the first five books of the Jewish Bible) contains, it is said, six hundred and thirteen laws, definitive and binding upon the faithful. It offered the Jewish people a comprehensive, divinely inspired life code promising the dutiful practitioner a raft of blessings in exchange for ritual purity and loyalty to the commandments:

If you live in accordance with my precepts and are careful to observe my commandments, I will give you rain in due season, so that the land will bear its crops, and the trees their fruit; your threshing will last till vintage time, and your vintage till the time for sowing, and you will have food to eat in abundance, so that you may dwell securely in your land. I will establish peace in the land, that you may lie down to rest without anxiety. I will rid the country of ravenous beasts, and keep the sword of war from sweeping across your land. You will rout your enemies and lay them low with your sword. Five of you will put a hundred of your foes to flight, and a hundred of you will chase ten thousand of them, till they are cut down by your sword.... (Lev. 26:3-8).

In addition, the law supplied something much more important than material comfort and security. It furnished a spiritual solidarity unique in human history. Torah was more than simply a method or approach to life. It was also the centerpiece of Jewish existence, the source of national identity, and in great measure, the explanation for the Jews' remarkable survival as a distinct people in what was frequently an overwhelmingly alien and hostile world. Bereft of land, temple, and king, the Jews nevertheless survived by clinging to the Law. Without this religious mucilage, the Jews would almost certainly have suffered cultural extinction, i.e. assimilation. Instead, they endure every challenge and agony by returning again and again to the Law supplied them by the living God.

Israel was, in the fullest sense of the term, a theocracy in which every facet of life was saturated by the continuous presence of an omnipotent God. No aspect of Jewish life functioned independently of this theistic perspective. At every turn, the will of Yahweh and the content of his law was made the determining consideration for both the community and the individual. In short, Hebraic consciousness can never be appreciated apart from the drama at Mount Sinai—this was the definitive moment of the Jewish people.

And what of the Greeks? In what form and manner do they understand the divine? How does Zeus' role and authority in human affairs compare to that of Yahweh's? To begin with, there is little in the Greek mythological statement to indicate any conception of divine omnipotence, omniscience, or omnipresence. Divine powers are conceived of by the Greeks as limited—superior to man certainly, but nevertheless limited. Zeus can be tricked by the other gods (Iliad 14.160), and there are forces at work in the universe that the father of the gods cannot control. In the Iliad (8.70) Zeus laments the impending death of his son, Sarpedon, but *moira* (fate) has ordained his demise at the hands of Patroclus, and Zeus seems incapable of altering the flow of events (cf. Euripides, *Hecuba* 800).

Similarly, from the very outset of their theological speculation, the Greeks recognized their gods as being incapable of certain things. A prime example being ex nihilo creation, the very notion of which offended the tenets of Greek rationalism. This explains Aristotle's insistence (On the Heavens 2.1.26-30) that the universe is a temporally infinite organism and why Plato is careful to note in Timaeus (32b-c) that the *demiurgos* merely "organizes" the preexisting material substratum; he creates nothing. In short, there is no Hellenic Genesis because the gods were not capable of such awesome displays of power.

With regard to human origins, we again encounter significant restriction on divine potency. Unlike the Hebrews, the Greeks lack any single, coherent tale regarding the inception of mankind. Hesiod tells us that both gods and man have the same point of origination in Gaia, the all-fecund earth-Mother described in Works and Days (107-8).* Later, mythology ascribes the creation of man to a benignly inclined Titan, Prometheus, who assumes the role of ombudsman on behalf of humanity against the Olympians (see below). The Orphics also present a separate scheme of human derivation employing mythological motifs associated with the god, Dionysus. The Greeks conceive of no single divine figure as responsible for the race of man, and, as one should note from Hesiodic testimony, there is even a tendency to see men and gods springing from a common source.

It should be clear at this stage in our analysis that considerable differences exist between Hebraic and Hellenic theology.† No doubt a significant portion of the disparity is ascribable to what has been called the "severe" anthropomorphism brought to religious understanding by the Greeks (Kirk 1974, 51). The influence of these man-centered perspectives is far-reaching indeed and constitutes one of the hallmarks of Greek culture in general. With regard to impact upon Hellenic conceptions of the divine, this anthropomorphism is pivotal. The Old Testament tells us (Genesis 1:26, 1:27, 5:3, 9:6) that God fashioned man in his own image.‡ In a

---

* Pindar (Nemean 6.1) makes the same point, "There is one race of men, another of gods; but from one mother (Gaia) we both draw our breath."

† Strictly speaking, it is inaccurate to speak of a "Hebraic theology" because as Anselm said, "Theology is faith seeking understanding," but for the Hebrew all proper understanding lay in faith itself.

‡ One could interpret these references to God's image as evidence that the Hebrews viewed man in an elevated, if not divine, light. But there are significant difficulties with this view. First, the idea of man having been created in God's image is not a consistent theme in Jewish thought, occurring exclusively in the chapters of Genesis cited. Next, the rabbinic tradition displays considerable discomfort with any attempt to link man too closely with God and consequently speaks of man having been made "after" the image of God in the sense of a Platonic arch-type. Later Jewish tradition

sense, the Greeks proceeded in obverse fashion; they fashioned their gods in the image of man. And herein lies the explanation for many of the peculiarities associated with the Hellenic pantheon. It explains, for example, the limited powers wielded by the Greek gods. The Hellenes saw their gods more as older, stronger brothers, than as categorically superior beings. The true point of demarcation between man and god was not power per se, but rather human finitude, i.e., immunity to death was the great preeminence enjoyed by the Olympians.

Again, anthropomorphism sheds light on the questionable morality we find presented in many of the Greek myths. Unlike Yahweh who, as author of the Law, is the essence of moral probity in Jewish thought, Zeus is a vice-laden Lothario of unrivaled proportions. His penchants for fraud, gratuitous cruelty, and sexual exploit reveal human, all too human, passions. Homer gives us a long roster of his conquests (Iliad 14.317-27). Later, mythographers tallied the amorous adventures of this divine Casanova and recorded at least one hundred and fifteen separate conquests (Burkert 128). Nor were his children to be outdone in these matters. One is reminded of the famous adultery scene in the Odyssey where Ares and Aphrodite are apprehended by the cuckold Hephaestus' snare (8.266-326). The moral tone of Greek theology does progress over time, but a genuine morality, something approximating Hebraic notions, does not appear on the Hellenic horizon until the advent of the Orphic mysteries (6th cent. B.C.). In the meantime, we have

---

also attempts to distance the relation between man and God by translating the word *elohim* (a plural form) not as God but as "divine beings," i.e., man was fashioned after angels. Perhaps most important of all there is a critical distinction between image and essence. The Greeks will not only argue that men share a common image with the gods, they will also view themselves as the earthly embodiment of divine essence.

deities that are anything but virtuous exemplars—Boccaccio makes for poor moral theology (Dix 10-11).

It remains to examine what the Greeks expected of their gods. As we have seen, the Hebrew understood Yahweh as the ultimate source and explanation for virtually every major event in Jewish experience. David's victories in Canaan, the assaults of Sennacherib, the use of Cyrus in the restoration of the Israelites—these were not simply phases in some mechanical ebb and flow of history. These and all other chapters in Israel's history are divinely appointed episodes. David's enemies become his "footstool" because Yahweh has decreed so (Psalms 110.1-2). Israel is reestablished through the mechanism of Persia because Cyrus is the chosen instrument of Yahweh (Isaiah 45.1-7). What the Jews expect and believe they receive from their God is simply everything: everything from the most joyous benefactions to the most grievous misfortunes. Yahweh is the all-encompassing source of Jewish existence.

Greek expectations regarding the gods reflect well the fundamental divergence of Hebraic and Hellenic theological perspectives. In a manner of speaking, it can be said the Greeks had a "love-hate" relationship with their deities. The idea of "love of God" does not appear in Greek thought until Aristotle who specifically denies the possibility of such a relationship (Magna Moralia 2.11.6-7 and N.E. 8.7.5). This all stands in marked contrast to the passionate ardor felt for God by the Jew. At best, Hellenic attitudes toward the divine remain deeply ambivalent. For example, the notion of "goodness" implied by the concept of divinity is far from absolute in the Greek imagination. Some gods are occasionally well-disposed toward certain human favorites—Athena is the aggressive patron of Odysseus and Artemis cares deeply for Hippolytus—but none of the gods is consistently gracious or merciful

(Greene 47). Indeed, some gods seem to conduct particularly malignant vendettas against certain individuals. Hera's persecution of Heracles prior to his apotheosis is a prime example. Odysseus lamenting the agonies inflicted upon him by the "Lord of Thunder" voices common Greek sentiment: "Father Zeus, none other god is more baleful than thou; for thou hast no pity on men when thou has begotten them, but dost give them fellowship with evil and bitter pains" (Odyssey 20.201-3).

Beyond general displays of Olympian malice, the Greeks also recognized a specific, highly virulent form of divine antipathy. It involved what the Greeks called *phthonos theon*, or divine envy. In great measure, this conceptualization stems from what might be termed "anthropomorphic projection." The Greeks believed all men were, by nature, jealous of the success of others—even the success of friends and neighbors could engender secret animosities deep within the bosom of those unblessed. Aristotle discusses this matter in some detail in both the Rhetoric (2.9) and the Nicomachean Ethics (2.7.15). In the latter work he notes there is such a thing as righteous indignation in the face of undeserved good fortune. But there is also a tendency to lapse into sheer, rancorous jealousy leading to an even more passionate state of animosity called *epichairekakia* in which a man rejoices over the calamities of others (see Knox 42).

Such is the malicious nature of man and these same instincts are mirrored in the actions of the Greek gods. It should be noted that Yahweh, too, is a jealous God, but there is a key distinction between Hebraic and Hellenic notions of divine grudgingness. The God of Abraham is jealous of other gods; his malice is directed toward the Jewish people in response to infidelity. He does not envy them their successes as human beings. Such sentiments would be entirely misplaced in this context because whatever blessings the

Jews enjoyed were in fact gifts bestowed by God himself. In addition, given Yahweh's might, it would be absurd for God to feel envy toward such puny creatures as men. Indeed, such sentiments would tend to diminish his stature.

But none of this logic applies to the more limited deities of the Hellenic pantheon. Given their anthropomorphic affinities, the Greek gods display all of the same spiteful pettiness of man, but with one obvious qualification: they enjoy an enhanced ability to vent their jealous rages. This means the Greeks see their gods as a continuous source of menace: it is unsafe in life to be too happy, to achieve extraordinary success, or to even conceive of oneself as achieving such success. Regarding the latter case, the Greeks even had a specific term to convey this danger—*agaasthai*—meaning "to think too greatly."

There are numerous illustrations of divine displeasure available in surviving Greek literature. It is, for instance, a favorite theme in Herodotus' Histories. The well-known story of the fabulously wealthy king Croesus is punctuated with an ominous observation, "Often enough God gives a man a glimpse of happiness, and then utterly ruins him" (1.32). The tyrant Polycrates is warned of the dangers attached to his astonishing good fortune by his fellow potentate Amasis:

> "It is pleasure to hear of a friend and ally doing well, but as I know that the gods are jealous of success, I cannot rejoice at your excessive prosperity. My own wish, both for myself and for those I care for, would be to do well in some things and badly in others, passing through life with alternate success and failure; for I have never yet heard of a man who after an unbroken

run of luck was not finally brought to complete ruin." (3.40).

Similarly, the disasters awaiting the Persians in their attempts to conquer Greece are inspired by divine envy (7.10). The gods have no intention of allowing a single man, the Great King, to be master of both Europe and Asia.

When the Greek gods were not busy visiting their divine wrath upon men, they displayed an insouciance toward humanity indicative of callous condescension. Mortal men, those mere "eaters of bread," do not merit any special exertions on the part of the gods. In the Iliad, Hera advises Hephaestus to cease his assaults on the river god, Xanthos because, "…it is not fitting to batter thus an immortal god for the sake of mortals" (21.380). Similarly, Apollo tells his uncle, Poseidon, that he will not contest against a fellow god, "…for the sake of insignificant mortals, who are as leaves are, and now flourish and grow warm with life, and feed on what the ground gives, but then again fade way and are dead" (21.463-5). All of this stands in marked contrast to Yahweh's active solicitude for this beloved child, Israel.

Statements such as these indicate the Greeks did not envision their gods as fulfilling any consistent salvational role in this world or the next. Despite his epithet as "soter" (savior), the son of Chronos does not seem particularly willing to extend his aegis for the benefit of man. By contrast, the Old Testament is a running commentary on the continuous efforts of Yahweh to preserve and protect his chosen people and, significantly, the Israelites acknowledge that all of their fortunes rest ultimately with these soteriological activities. There is no attempt on the part of the Jewish people to "go it alone," i.e., to chart their own course in life, to fashion their own fate. The existence of Israel is inextricably tied to the will of Yahweh.

This is clearly not the case for the Greeks. Their relationships with the gods lacked the intimate quality of Jewish religious experience. As we have seen, in most instances about the best the typical Greek could anticipate was the Olympian equivalent of benign neglect. Only in the rarest of instances do we find the Greek gods actively rendering service to human beings. The effect of this was to throw the Greeks back upon their own resources; what the gods would not do for man, man must do for himself. This spirit of self-reliance is expressed consistently throughout Greek history. Time and again we hear of individuals struggling to attain their purpose without appeal to divine shortcuts. The names of various deities are often invoked during moments of serious trial, but there is rarely any substitute sought for human endeavor. When, for example, Ajax prays to Zeus to lift the mist shrouding the battlefield prior to the struggle for Patroclus' body, he does not ask the father of the gods to underwrite a positive outcome (Iliad 17.645). Human courage will determine that aspect of the situation. He only requests that those who are about to die be accorded the dignity of doing so in broad daylight.*

A similar point is found in Hesiod's Works and Days where in the process of lecturing Perses, his indolent brother, the poet observes, "That man is all-best who himself works out every problem and solves it..." (293-94). He does not propose that the problems of life are remediable through the offering of rich sacrifice or

---

* The identical point is made by Hector, the Trojan hero, who rejects portents and signs and instead declares, "One omen is best, to fight for one's country." In a sense then, the Greeks view humanity in auto-messianic terms; they seek no parting of the seas or trumpet blasts to facilitate their endeavors.

prayer. Discipline and hard work are the keys to human success proffered by Hesiod.

Related evidence is also found in the testimony offered by the Greek stage. In *Seven Against Thebes* the chorus of women flock to the shrines seeking protection from the besiegers. The reaction from Eteocles is revealing. He advises the women, "For protection pray that our towers hold off the enemy's spears." In other words, god favors those with the biggest battalions or, in this case, the strongest fortifications (217-18). He continues by reminding the women that obedience to civil instruction is the mother of success and success is the mother of rescue (223-25). Conspicuously absent at this moment of crisis is any mention of or appeal to the gods.

Reliance upon human enterprise is expressed again in Sophocles' *Ajax*. Before proceeding to battle, the hero's father bids him to go forth and win "with God's help." Ajax's response reveals the autonomous spirit of the Greeks vis-à-vis their gods. He answers, "I propose, without that help, to win my prize of fame" (168-9). In reaction to these "graceless words," the goddess Athena visits madness upon the hero. Still, boastful though these sentiments may be, they are reflective of an important cultural attitude, to wit, men should assume responsibility for their own fates to whatever extent that is humanly possible; a man waits in vain for Olympian largess.

A final display of the Hellenic penchant for seeking life's remedies within, as opposed to divinely subsidized solutions, is seen in the spirit and practice of Greek sacrifice. Much of the vocabulary in the Old Testament, particularly the so-called "P" or priestly source material, is heavily weighted toward atonement sacrifice. This is particularly true of works such as <u>Leviticus</u> and <u>Numbers</u>. Now, the subject of ancient sacrifice is highly complex and Jewish practices are certainly no exception. We know, for instance, that the Hebrews had a series of separate rituals, including burnt offerings, peace offerings, purification offerings, and reparation sacrifice. Despite this apparently wide range, it can be argued that the underlying spirit of Jewish sacrificial practice is essentially penitential with the ultimate objective being the restoration of God's active agency on behalf of the Jewish people.

The spirit of Greek sacrifice is significantly different. To begin with, atonement sacrifice implies a violation of some divinely sanctioned code or standard; the rules have been broken and compensation must be offered up to restore God's assistance. As we shall see below, the Greeks have no divinely inspired "system" of regulations from which to stray. The Olympians are not legislative authorities; the Greeks lack both covenant and Decalogue. Accordingly, Hellenic sacrifice lacks much of the atonement quality found among the Hebrews.

Moreover, given the fact that the Greeks do not tend to look to their gods as a source of salvation but instead rely upon their own energies, the supplicative essence of Hebraic sacrifice is clearly less prominent among the Greeks. In fact, it makes sense to draw a distinction here between sacrifice aimed at supplication versus sacrifice aimed at placation; the former applying to Jewish practice, the latter to Greek. When the Hellene offered savor to the gods, a good portion of the intent seems to have been to stem the malice emanating from either Mt. Olympus or from some chthonic deity. In other words, much of Greek sacrificial practice was apotropaeic, i.e, designed to immunize against evil, a primary source of which was the gods themselves.[*] This is specifically the purpose of festivals such as the Diasia and the Anthesteria (Murray 13-16). The chief aspiration behind Greek sacrifice, therefore, is not to secure

---

[*] As Sewall notes (26), "...a Greek's fondest wish was that the gods would leave him alone."

the active support of the gods but rather to forestall divine tendencies for impairing human enterprise.[*] In largest terms, these sentiments bespeak the humanistic orientation of Greek civilization. They indicate a proto-secular confidence in the ability of man to craft his own existence when left unmolested by the gods. Accordingly, sacrifice for the Greek constitutes a ritual "white flag;" it is an attempt to mollify, appease, and pacify deities that all too often delight in disrupting the ventures of men.[†]

The Nature of Man

We now turn to an examination of how the ancient Jews and Greeks conceived of the nature and worth of man. As one would expect from the preceding analysis, the Hebrews approach this question from a God-centered perspective. The nature of man and his status in life are ultimately assessed against the supreme standard—Yahweh. By this measure, mankind is viewed in a highly subordinate light. As created being, the gap separating God and man is fundamentally unbridgeable. This distance is a characteristic feature of all the west-Asian theologies where men were viewed

---

[*] This point is illustrated by a comparison of what are perhaps the two most famous sacrifices in Western culture, viz., those of Isaac and Iphigenia. The former is a test of faith imposed upon Abraham whose unquestioning obedience saves his son's life. The sacrifice of Iphigenia has nothing to do with divine interest in Agamemnon's fidelity. It is the price that must be paid to advance human enterprise, i.e. the conquest of Troy.

[†] It has also been observed that the spirit of prayer is markedly different between Hellene and Hebrew. The Jew rarely demands recompense from his God; he is not inclined to say, "Give, because I gave." But Greek prayer is almost always expressed in the imperative mood, i.e., the Greeks tend to demand reciprocity from their gods in an almost contractual sense (Pulleyn 150-151). Similarly, when things go amiss, the Greeks tend not to pray for refuge or rescue, instead they upbraid the gods for neglecting their reciprocal obligation (Nilsson 163). These sentiments are also reflected in the physical posture of the Greek worshiper who almost never kneels or prostrates himself when addressing heaven (VonStraten 161).

"as slaves and manual workers of the gods" (Kirk 1974, 266). This tendency is probably less pronounced among the Hebrews than it is among the other semitic peoples of the region--Yahweh is an imperious monarch, but he also displays genuine affection and care for his people, including a continuous capacity to forgive their transgressions. Still, the general tenor of Jewish statements in this matter tends to reduce humanity to an unequivocally inferior status (e.g., Levit. 25:25).

This is the message conveyed consistently throughout the Jewish sapiential literature—works such as Proverbs, Ecclesiastes, Ecclesiasticus, Job, Psalms, etc. In these works human distance from and inferiority to God are presented as central aspects of the Jewish "wisdom." In Job, for instance, the splendor and loftiness of God are stressed at the direct expense of human worth. In the speech of Bildad we are told, "Behold, even the moon is not clean in his (God's) sight. How much less man, who is but a maggot, the son of man, who is only a worm?" (25:4).

Human submission is another key feature of Jewish teaching on this question. When Job learns of the death of his children, he accepts without quarrel or lament, "The Lord gave and the Lord has taken away; blessed be the name of the Lord" (1:21). Later, when the voice from the whirlwind responds assertively to Job's protests (38:4), he is instantly reduced to a quivering, self-rebuking shell, "Behold, I am of little account; what can I answer you (God)?" (40:4-5). Similarly, Ecclesiasticus admonishes that men must submit to the yoke of God (51:25-26) and receive his teaching submissively without question or protest (6:25).

Along these same lines, humility is a prime virtue extolled in Jewish thought. Proverbs promises the humble man "riches, honor, and life" (22.4 cf. 19.8 and 24:5) and assures that he who travels through this world with humility is granted wisdom (Proverbs 11:2, also 15:33). A related point concerns the issue of human self-reliance. A man that is wise in his own eyes, someone who believes that human resources alone can solve the riddle of life, is a fool (Proverbs 3.5, 26:12, 28:26). The appropriate approach by contrast, is to develop an attentive and receptive ear (Ecclesiasticus 3:27) and to "Leave it to the Lord" (Psalms 37:7). The truly wise man is further advised to speak little and fear the Lord (Ecclesiastes 5.6). He must be willing to accept "correction" (Proverbs 12:1-2, 12:15) if he is to be deemed wise and good, and only he who willingly embraces "discipline" finds God (Ecclesiasticus 32.14).

Obedience, submission, dependence, humility—these are the central premises regarding the proper conduct of man according to Jewish tradition. These points follow naturally from a conception of humanity that views man as radically inferior to his maker and links man inseparably to an all-embracing divinely inspired code of law. Under these conditions, virtually any form of autonomous self-expression runs the risk of violating Torah and offending its divine author. The good man assimilates to a highly prescriptive environment in which religious authority functions as the *ex cathedra* source of value and conduct. Conceptually, this compliance is fully appropriate given the subservient nature of man relative to his omnipotent maker.

Things are very different on the Hellenic side of this question. To begin with, there is no definitive legal text and no authoritative priestly caste to define and structure the proper activities of man. The Greeks have no Veda, no Pyramid Texts, and no priestly brotherhood. About the closest the Greeks come to a sacred literature is the Iliad and the Pythian priestesses at Delphi are hardly equivalent to those in charge of the Temple's ritual. The Greeks would develop a life code for man, but they would do so in a manner largely devoid of the restrictive weight of religious authority. In great measure, Hellenic conceptions of the good man and the good life would receive their ultimate articulation through secular reasoning, i.e., philosophy (see below).

Of far greater importance to our question of human nature is the issue of relative distance separating man and God. The Jews see the gap as fundamental and proceed to conceptualize man's essence based on this discontinuity—the essence of man, the essence of God are categorically distinct in Hebraic thought. In contrast, the Greeks perceive man as an interstitial being; a creature living on the cusp between things human and divine.* With the narrowing of this aperture, man is accorded an elevated status that he lacks under Judaism. Man is not seen by the Greeks as merely some debased shadow of divine majesty. Man possesses his own dignity and worth. To appreciate the point, one need only compare the statement cited above from <u>Job</u> (25.4) with one offered by Sophocles, "Many are the wonders, none is more wonderful than what is man" (*Antigone* 367). Significantly, the chorus offering these lines does not make god the supreme wonder, but focuses instead upon the ingenuity and craft of humanity as a fitting subject of paean.

Greek mythology also illustrates this tendency to lessen the disunion between god and man. In his <u>Works and Days</u>, Hesiod describes a "golden age" in which mortals "lived as if they were gods" and were "on friendly terms with the blessed immortals" (109-120). During this period, men not only feasted with the gods, they even took goddesses as their brides as we see in the examples of Peleus and Thetis and Cadmus and Harmonia.

The mystery religion known as Orphism also relays an important tale about the elevated status of man. The child god Dionysus

---

* In describing Homer's portrait of man, Longinus (9.7) observes, "Homer has done his best to make the men in the <u>Iliad</u> gods and the gods men."

is killed by the Titans and his dismembered body is then devoured by the murderers. In response, Zeus smites the Titans with a thunderbolt reducing them to ash. Mankind is eventually fashioned from the charred remains which explains our dualistic nature; from the Titans man has inherited a black side, but from the flesh of Dionysus all men contain an element of the divine (see Plato, Laws, 701c). The objective of Orphic discipline is to purge the Titanic components of our being and to purify the godly. The successful *mystes* (initiate), upon traveling to the next world, is addressed by the mistress of the infernal realm (Persephone) in the following terms, "Blessed and fortunate being, you shall be a god instead of a mortal. You have fallen as a kid into milk" (Diels, *Orpheus* fr. 18, cf. Pindar fr. 137).

This same orientation is seen in Greek hero worship, which at Athens became part of official cult practice in the late 7th century B.C. under Draco (Rhode 114). Here, we have men formally elevated to the rank of gods and subject to the same devotions and honors extended full-fledged deities. This logic is eventually transferred to living political figures in the Greco-Roman world as signified by the title "Epiphanes," meaning a god made manifest. Alexander's deification at the Siwah oasis, the status accorded the Diadochi, and the "August" nature of Roman emperors are all related to this Hellenic penchant for the ascension of man. What must be born firmly in mind here is the fact that any parallel activity on the part of a Jew would have collided directly with the canons of Hebraic monotheism (Ex. 20:3) resulting in death by stoning as prescribed by law (Deut. 27:2-7).

It is not only the mythic-religious testimony of the Hellenes that affirms this aggrandized view of man, the same affirmation is made by the philosophers. Greek philosophy in general, and Plato and Aristotle in particular, tend to analyze things from a teleological perspective, i.e., they begin their investigations by focusing on the natural "ends" or "purposes" governing a given subject matter— mankind being no exception. According to this logic, the natural telos of man is *eudaemonia* (happiness) and the means of achieving it involved the "perfection" of human essence, meaning man's rational and moral capacities (Politics 7.1). Reasoning such as this is not to be found among the Hebrews. Proper activity for the ancient Jew had little to do with the self-actualization of human potentials. The concern instead lay with an all-absorbing devotion to religious prescription. Moreover, the ancient Hebrews would have been deeply troubled with any theorizing about man's autonomous capacity to "self-perfect." For the Hebrew, man is by nature a dependent being who is forever reliant upon the merciful dispensations of God. Perfection is the unique attribute of Yahweh and to suggest that men can somehow participate in this ideal state and do so by their own agency is the stuff of scandal and blasphemy. Yet, this is precisely what Greek philosophy proposes. This is not to suggest that the Greeks had no conception of human deficiency; the relevant literature often speaks of "violating the mean," "missing the mark," "disturbing the proper proportion." But the Greeks seem not to have any consistent notion of "sin" or limitation suggestive of a continuous impediment to human development (see Parker, esp. Chapter 8). Thus, Plato, who is fully aware of man's dark side, nevertheless admonishes his reader on numerous occasions to strive for godliness (Tim. 90c, Theat. 176b, Phaed. 253b, Rep. 500c-d. cf. Plotinus, Ennead. 1.2.6). Aristotle too, argues that a human form of divinity is achievable by all those who participate in the unalloyed joys of *theoria*. He asserts, "...we must not follow those who advise us, being men, to think of human things, and, being mortal, of mortal things, but must, so far as we can, make ourselves immortal..." (<u>N.E.</u> 10.7). By Hebraic standards, Greek philosophy comes perilously close to self-idolatry.

As scandalous as these Hellenic encroachments upon god's domain may seem, they are tame by comparison to other aspects of Greek thought regarding the nature of man. We have already observed that the Greeks had a "love-hate" relationship with their gods. In fact, the term "love" probably overstates the positive side of this relationship. There is nothing, for instance, in Greek literary records analogous to the fidelity and sacrifice offered by a Jewish mother and her seven sons portrayed in the <u>Fourth Book of Maccabees</u>. The story describes the persecutions of Antiochus IV in which Jews were compelled to adopt Greek ways at the expense of Torah. Rather than taste pork, the mother and her sons sacrifice themselves in loyalty and devotion to God. It is difficult to conceive of a Hellenic analogy; a Greek might die for his city or to preserve his reputation and honor, but no Greek dies for Zeus. The intensity of religious sentiment found among the Hebrews, their "love" of God and law, is unparalleled in Greek culture.

Another point for which there is little or no corollary among the two peoples is the element of insolence and challenge aimed directly at the gods by the Greeks. We are not speaking here of mere disobedience to religious precept but rather overt expressions of disrespect and audacity toward the gods themselves. Indeed, stories emphasizing human-divine antagonism enjoy an unusual prominence in Hellenic thought (Burkert 121). These tales are conceptually possible for the reasons already described—limitations on divine authority, anthropomorphism, and the elevation of human stature. They result in myths whose imagery and spirit are entirely inconsistent with the idiom of Old Testament teaching.

The Greek hero is a prime illustration of these rebellious tendencies. One of the defining characteristics of a Hellenic hero is his willingness to tread dangerously close to the great divide separating things mortal and immortal. The heroic figures of Greek myth continuously probe and test the limits of human achievement with an eye toward blurring the distinction between profane and divine. The exploits of heroes such as Perseus, Theseus, Cadmus, Jason, Bellerophon, and Heracles are indicative. One need only recall Bellerophon's attempt to ride Pegasus directly into heaven or Heracles' battle with the god Apollo for control of the oracular tripod at Delphi to appreciate the peculiar frictions the Greeks believed operated between men and gods.

The Iliad is also a rich source for such imagery. During the *aristeia* (a sort of adrenaline episode for warriors) of Diomedes, the Greek warrior actually engages Aphrodite in combat, inflicting serious wounds necessitating her tearful withdrawal from battle (5.335). As the battle progresses, Diomedes also attacks Ares (5.855-860) and even challenges Apollo in his frenzied attempt to put Aeneas to the sword (5.437-8). A similar confrontation occurs later as Apollo impedes the fury of Achilles' vengeful rampage allowing many Trojans to reach the safety of their walls. In response, Achilles addresses this major deity of the Greek pantheon as "most malignant of gods" (22.15) and threateningly observes, "I would punish you, if only the strength were in me" (22.20). These, of course, are words and deeds unthinkable to the Hebrew. Even if these myths lacked the heuristic weight they in fact bear among the Greeks,[*] even if they were seen merely as fanciful tales, the Jews would never have tolerated such disrespect and defiance toward

---

[*] The significance of mythology for the Greeks is not to be denied. Kirk (1970, 250) notes that, "In a sense the history of Greek culture is the history of its attitudes to myth; no other important Western civilization has been so controlled by a developed mythical tradition." For us then, the Greek myths represent a kind of psychic archaeology where the encoded values of the culture are both presented and prescribed.

their God. One could argue, of course, that the sin of Adam constitutes a powerful counterpoint to this statement, but as Leo Strauss observes, "...they (Adam and Eve) did not rebel high-handedly against God; they rather forgot to obey God; they drifted into disobedience..." (Strauss 1967, 12). The point is the Greeks need no serpent to prompt their insurrection, they challenge their gods as near equals challenge those enjoying only marginal superiority.

There is one additional figure in Greek mythology that merits our examination as a model for the antipathies we are considering—Prometheus. Technically, Prometheus is not a mortal, he is a Titan, which means he enjoys a precarious status somewhere above man but below the Olympians. Significantly, the word Titan comes from the term *titainein* which means "to overreach oneself." From earliest times, the Greeks seem to have acknowledged Prometheus as a symbol of rebellion against divine authority (Hamilton 73). His relationship with mankind was particularly intimate.[*] Indeed, according to some traditions, it was he who first fashioned man from potter's clay using the gods themselves as his model. In addition, the beneficent Titan was responsible for equipping man with the accouterments needed to not only ensure survival but to lessen human dependence upon the Olympians. These generosities were bad enough in the eyes of father Zeus who saw them as direct affronts to this authority. But Prometheus is guilty of an additional mischief that summarizes well the tension we have examined between man and god. It involves the legendary establishment of Greek sacrificial practice at Mekone. By its nature, sacrifice involves ritual designed to honor the gods, but the procedures set down by Prometheus reflect instead a conscious intent to deceive and cheat the gods of their fair share. Prometheus prepares a great

---

[*] Kerenyi (78) suggests that Prometheus is best understood as mankind's double.

ox and divides the carcass into two parcels; one containing all the edible meat carefully hidden beneath hide and entrails, the other containing bones overladen with layers of "shining fat" (Hesiod, Theog. 535-555). Zeus is invited to choose the portion he wishes offered in sacrifice. Selecting the latter, he is outraged to learn of the ruse.

It has been argued that myth is a powerful barometer of cultural perspective, a kind of philosophizing not yet aware of itself (Levi-Strauss 47). If this is so, then the Promethean tale bears a significance that should not be underestimated. The alimentary fraud at Mekone says much about a fundamental strife between man and god that stands at the center of Greek religious belief. More, it conveys an important message about Hellenic cultural attitudes concerning human status, and the contrast with Hebraic thought reflected in this message is as obvious as it is categorical. In Leviticus (10.16-20) we are told of another sacrifice offered by Eleazar and Ithamar, the sons of Aaron, who voluntarily submit to Yahweh the portion of meat they were entitled to eat because they felt themselves lacking in sufficient sanctity to consume the flesh. The spirit underlying this gesture is a telling counterpoint to that behind the Promethean subterfuge.

Zeus' reaction to the Promethean swindle is to have the Titan chained to a rock and suffer continuous torture from an eagle who feeds upon his liver daily. The story of Job offers an Old Testament analogy to this scene of torment. Prometheus and Job are blood brothers in suffering, but there are important distinctions. For one thing, the wrath of Zeus is condign; Prometheus' deceit earns him his agony. Job, by contrast, is an innocent, god-fearing man who is gratuitously afflicted as part of a divine loyalty check. How the two figures respond to their torments is revealing. Job, the innocent man, repents (for what?) "in dust and ashes" before God (Job

42:6). Prometheus, however, remains defiant, "He is a monster…I care less than nothing for Zeus. Let him do as he likes" (*Prometheus Bound* 937-40).*

The evidence for man-centered acerbity toward the gods is clear in Greek culture. Time and again we learn of men defiantly rejecting the gods' edicts and belligerently attempting to efface the demarcations between humanity and divinity.† But what of the Olympian response? How do the Greek gods react to this recalcitrancy? There is one member of the Hellenic pantheon in particular who plays a special role in checking the obstreperous advances of men and in reminding humanity of the penalties for such ambition. Above all, this function belongs to Apollo.

The lord of Delphi is a complex, multi-faceted figure as indicated by his many appellations—*Loxias* (the oblique), *Mousagetes* (leader of the muses), *Parnopius* (grasshopper), *Iatros* (healer), *Lykeios* (wolf), and *Akersekomas* (with unshorn hair). In addition, Apollo is frequently described as the "God of Afar," i.e., he is distant, apart, separate from the rest. It is precisely this separateness that concerns us because the maintenance of "distance," specifically between man and god, is a chief responsibility of this deity. His role in this regard is reflected in the famous Pythian admonition, "Know thyself" (*gnothi sauton*) which does not encourage the acquisition of knowledge per se, but rather specific recognition of

---

* These lines from Aeschylus illustrates the point well, viz., no people in antiquity were more inclined to shake their fists at heaven than the Greeks.

† The Greek stage is a rich source for these belligerent tones. In the comedies of Aristophanes, for example, the gods are routinely represented as inferior to their human counterparts (e.g., Dionysus in *Frogs* and Zeus in *Birds*). The same impudence can also be found in the tragedies where Zeus is portrayed as an evil tyrant (Aeschylus' *Prometheus Bound*); where we are advised the gods are often shameful in their conduct (Sophocles' *Women of Trachis*); and where we are told that men are entitled to curse the gods given their injustices (Euripides' *Hippolytus*).

one's limitations as a human being; in other words, "know" that you are merely human. It is also seen in a large number of incidents in which Apollo punishes any creature who would encroach in word or deed, upon the boundaries of heaven. We hear of the famous music competition between Marsyas and Apollo in which the former is flayed for his audacity in challenging a god to contest. Niobe and her twelve children are slain because she indiscreetly claims procreative superiority over Leto, the mother of Apollo and Artemis. The son of Achilles, Pyrrhos (Neoptolemos), is killed by Apollo because he protests the division of sacrificed meat assigned him by those officiating at Apollo's oracle (Pindar, Paean 6 and Nemean 7). The Iliad presents a similar portrait of Apollo as guardian of things divine. It is he who warns Diomedes during his furious *aristeia*, "Think, son of Tydeus and shrink, and desire not to match thy spirit with gods, since there is nothing common to the race of the immortal gods and to the men who walk upon the earth" (5.440-442). Patroclus also experiences the sting of Pythian justice awaiting those who would breach the line (16.816-822). And in the end, it is Apollo too who will eventually orchestrate the death of Achilles in response to his becoming "something more than a mortal" (20.493). A major theme of the epic seems to be the necessity of reminding listeners that the "man who fights the immortals lives for no long time" (5.407).

Divine vengeance along these lines is typically triggered by human excess. The word commonly employed to describe this prideful imprudence is *hubris*. It entails an instinct for trespass; a tendency to violate the orderly limits (*moira*) of human existence (see Fisher 1992). The Greeks were not unaware of the dangers associated with such immoderacy. Pindar, perhaps the most Hebraic of Greek poets, continuously reminds his victors during their "epinikian" moment not to seek that which is more than human

(Pythian 2.88 and 10.24, Olympian 5.24, Nemean 6.1-9, Nemean 11.13-16).

Significantly, what was for the Greek a continuous and pervasive source of cultural tension, was for the Jew a non-issue. There is no Apollo among the ancient Hebrews because there was no need for such a figure. As the testimony of the prophets makes clear, the center of spiritual discord among the Jews is not *hubris*, it is guilt, guilt stemming from infidelity to Almighty God and his edicts. Among the Greeks, gods and men are cast in very different roles. The consistent religious enthusiasm of the Hebrew is without parallel in Hellas. What the Greeks display instead is a conviction in man's ability to transcend his mortal essence;[*] to elevate his own being to heights rivaling those of the Olympians, notwithstanding the limitations and hazards such aspirations entail.

Two Wisdoms: Hokma v. Sophia

Careful analysis of the manner in which a people define, apply, and delimit a word like "wisdom" can yield important cultural insights. This is so because the conceptual field surrounding such key terms often provide a rich and surprisingly detailed view of the major ideals and attitudes operating in a society. Word images such as these can function as a sort of cultural cross-section of larger belief systems allowing for new revelations in areas as diverse as politics, morality, religion, and social theory. Thus, by answering a question such as, "Who is the wise man?" among Israelites and Hellenes respectively, we shed additional comparative light upon the unique qualities of each group and clarify further the heterogeneity of Jerusalem and Athens.

---

[*] As Goethe correctly noted, "The purpose and goal of the Greeks is to deify man, not to humanize deity. This is not anthropomorphism but theomorphism."

Perhaps the most ubiquitous admonition in the entire Old Testament is the notion that "Fear of the Lord" is the foundation of all wisdom. The frequency with which this observation is made affirms its status as a cultural imperative among the Hebrews. In addition to being found in <u>Job</u> (e.g., 28.28) and <u>Proverbs</u> (e.g., 1:7, 2:6) it is cited sixty-three times in <u>Ecclesiasticus</u> and seventy-nine times in <u>Psalms</u>.

What is being suggested by the phrase? Here again we encounter the characteristic imagery of Yahweh as the all-powerful, universal agent. Respect for and submission to God is the indispensable first step in the acquisition of wisdom. The wise man is he who has come to understand his own insignificance in the face of divine grandeur. He appreciates the fact that any human understanding, as frail and limited as it is, begins with a recognition of human inferiority and the necessity of submission. Awe and dedication to Yahweh is both generative and constitutive of wisdom, i.e., fear of God is both the method of attaining and the substance of wisdom. These points are, not unexpectedly, consistent with our previous analysis. Hebraic piety elevates Yahweh's stature to heights unimagined by the Greeks; he is the fount of all things including whatever sagacity can be claimed by man.

Beyond this foundational premise, the Hebrew recognizes an indissoluble relationship between wisdom and scripture. The attainment and expansion of knowledge is not a secular exercise for the Jew—wisdom is a matter of belief not discovery. The pivotal instrument, the code by which the proper parameters of human intellection are established, is the Law. Torah marks the limits of inquiry for man; it is the definitive expression of all that is salient and necessary for the pious life. Accordingly, knowledge of, and obedience toward the Law is the essence of wisdom. The point is made frequently in the Jewish sapiential literature. <u>Psalm</u> 119 (97-

98 and 19:8-11) links wisdom and knowledge to the commandments of God; the Book of Wisdom (6:17-19) argues that love of
wisdom is demonstrated by keeping the Laws; and in Ecclesiasticus, Sirach fuses wisdom and Torah into an indivisible holy union
(1:23, 15:1-3, 17:9-10, 24:22). In sum, the Law represents the flaw-
less light of Yahweh. He who is in any way estranged from the
Law is like a boat tossed in a storm (Ecclesiasticus 33:2). Such a
man is a "fool" and he lives a life that is worse than death (Book of
Wisdom 13:1, Ecclesiasticus 22:10). Wisdom is reserved for the
true believer; the good life is bounty from the Lord.

To this point we have observed that Jewish religious tradition
links "wisdom" to a comprehensive obedience toward God and
more concretely, devotion to God's mandates. In addition to these
positions, there is a tendency in Hebraic thought to impose absolute
limits upon what men can ultimately know about God himself and
upon the degree men are free to speculate beyond the boundaries
established by sectarian authority.

With regard to the former limitation, there is a substantive distinction between knowing and obeying God's laws and actually
"knowing God." The essence of God not only involves awesome
powers, it includes mystery and distance as well (Job 36:26 and
37:23). There are no analogies between the ways of Yahweh and
the ways of man; the incommensurability between divine and human realms is absolute and unalterable. Accordingly, there is no
attempt among the Jews to analyze the metaphysical nature of
God's being (see Kung 300). To do so would have constituted a
presumptuous affront from the perspective of Hebrew piety.

In addition, Jewish teaching tends to place absolute limits upon
man's cognitive horizons in general. Not only is man incapable of
penetrating the shroud of mystery surrounding the inscrutable
Yahweh, he is also unable to obtain certain categories of under-

standing which remain the exclusive province of God. In <u>Ecclesias-ticus</u> we are reminded that, "All wisdom comes from the Lord and with him it remains forever" (1.1). The point is made also during the rhetorical questioning of Job by God, "Where were you when I founded the earth? Tell me, if you have understanding" (38:4). In some sense then, Yahweh enjoys an epistemological monopoly that cannot be shared with finite creatures. There is an ultimate wisdom beyond our comprehension that bespeaks the inner sanctum of divine will and mind. What men call "wisdom" is something entirely secondary, a sort of refracted insight laden with demands of faith and discipline. The truly wise man recognizes these restrictions and limits and acknowledges his station in the ordained scheme without question or complaint because God owes no man an accounting (<u>Job</u> 37:23).

There are also severe injunctions leveled against secular speculation. The learned and wise man is not expert in profane knowledge; he is neither an encyclopedist, scientist, nor philosopher. He is a master of Torah as reflected in both his words and his deeds, a man of faith and devotion whose life priorities are entirely dictated by the decrees of God. Intellectual pursuits as an end in themselves, speculation committed to the "life of the mind" as freestanding activity, is entirely alien to Hebraic thought. Expenditures of time and effort along these lines are not only wasteful, they can also lapse into self-aggrandizing exercises. The <u>Wisdom of Solomon</u> warns that "worldly" knowledge is often a source of sin and folly (1:12-15) and <u>Ecclesiastes</u> advises not to become too wise, "lest you be ruined" (7:16). There is a tendency then in the Judaic tradition to radically undervalue the significance of secular learning. For the Jew, a man's cognitive energies are claimed by the faith; learnedness is synonymous with knowledge of the Law. This makes Jewish wisdom a form of metaphorical understanding, a revealed insight devoid of the instincts and methods associated with science and philosophy. These same orientations are, *mutatis mutandis*, continued in Judaism's daughter religion, Christianity, where the devoted are asked, "…what concern to us are such things as genera and species?" (Thomas a Kempis 1.3, cf. 1.4, 1.7, 1.14, 3.31).

It is fair to say then, that the intellectual horizons of the Jewish sage are narrowly predefined.[*] His activities as a scholar are limited to a continuous conjugation of religious precept, i.e., his task is not to invent, discover, or innovate but rather to lend supportive illustration and logic to the law of God. In the historic polarity between faith and reason, that fiery dispute animating Western culture for the last two thousand years, the Hebrews make faith the essence of their life code—the rational impulse is the legacy of Hellas.

In his first letter to the Corinthians, Paul observes that the "Jews require a sign and the Greeks seek after wisdom" (1:22). This terse, but insightful, summary touches the very core of Judaeo-Hellenic contrast. As we have noted, the Greeks lack a definitive sacred literature, a priestly class, and many of the normative restraints upon

---

[*] To the extent philosophy involves judging and choosing, it must be observed that there was no philosophy among the Hebrews because they had nothing to choose. They had received the Law once and for all and for them to engage in critical assessment now would have rendered them something other than Jewish (Castoriadis 87). Thus, when the Hebrew "studies" Torah, he does not do so in a manner consistent with philosophy. His is not a quest for supposition-free truth. It is rather an exercise pre-armed with conviction whose ultimate purpose is to confirm belief already held. This mentality is powerfully conveyed by the following commentary on <u>Genesis,</u> "Why was the world created by the letter Beth?" (Beth is the first letter of the first word in the Torah, Bereshith, 'In the beginning'). Just as the shape of the letter Beth is closed on three sides and open toward the front, so you do not have permission to be concerned with that which is below or above the earth, nor with what happened before this world came to be (Genesis Rabbah 1:10 in Hertzberg 55-56).

mind and spirit common to the ancient cultures of western Asia. This allowed for a certain "spontaneity of consciousness" (Arnold 134) among the Greeks that is generally absent in the heavily prescriptive atmosphere of Judaism. It has been said that the Talmud is the fence around the Law. It might also be argued that the Law itself constituted a powerful delimiting force. The point is, there were no such enclosures circumscribing the Hellenic imagination. It is not a coincidence that the dawn of "science," i.e., a naturalistic explanation of the world largely devoid of theological elements, appears first among the Greeks. They were free to speculate, to question, to investigate along lines the Hebrew could not pursue without becoming disloyal to the faith. Indeed, one of the fundamental premises of the Old Testament is an implicit rejection of philosophy (Strauss 1953, 81) because for the ancient Jews the "first questions" are answered before they are asked. The authoritative essence of Torah is all-encompassing; everything worth knowing is contained within the Law. Under these conditions, philosophy is an unbidden and unwelcomed guest. This is necessarily the case because by its very nature, philosophy is a subversive thing. Articles of faith, received opinions, hallowed traditions—all of these become the object of critical assault beneath the lens of philosophic speculation. Even God himself is not safe under such circumstances because if, as Plato and Aristotle argue (Laws 891c and Meta. 1.1.17), philosophy is the systematic attempt to ascertain "first principles," then God becomes a concept, an object of critical theorizing. It is this investigative impulse, this unrestrained analytical spirit that the Hebrew finds unacceptable and it is for this reason, too, that the spirit of Judaism's response to Greek philosophy during the Hellenistic era is, "Thou shalt not know" (e.g., Ecclesiasticus 2:12-14, 3:17-20, and 9:22-30).

In addition to lacking the doctrinal restraints of a revealed religion, the Greeks were also justified in pursuing their rationalism by a distinctive theory of man. Reason, for the Greek, was not simply a peripheral dimension of the human composite. Man was, in essence, the "rational animal" for whom the development of reason was a natural imperative. Indeed, there is much to indicate the Greeks viewed this development as part of a teleological scheme; in order to achieve fulfillment and happiness in life, human beings must actualize their rational potentials to the fullest extent. Significantly, there is no divine prohibition associated with man's cognitive journey. In fact, by the 4th century B.C. both Plato and Aristotle are prepared to argue that the expansion of rational essence establishes a unique bond between man and God. This is what Plato alludes to when he describes reason as "a golden link to heaven" (Laws 644e) and what Aristotle means when he explains how the truly cultivated mind makes its possessor the "friend" of God (N.E. 10.8.30).

Here again, we mark an important departure from Hebraic thought. The "closeness" to God achieved by rational development implies more for the Greek than simply a clearer understanding of God's nature or of his authoritative plans for the universe. Presumably making oneself expert in Torah and following its instruction brings the Hebrew closer to God, but Greek thought connotes something more. The ripened logic of Greek philosophy argues that God's essence too is reason and that the human mind when properly developed constitutes a microcosm of the divine mind. In a sense, this is a philosophical expression of that continuous Hellenic inclination to impose anthropomorphic imagery upon the gods or God; man is rational, therefore, God is rational. Implicit here as well is that second Greek tendency, viz., to apotheosize man, to narrow the gap between earth and heaven. The human microcosm described in Greek philosophy is not offered as metaphor—man is in substance a miniature of the divine. In other words, man's mind is understood as a fragment in kind of the Supreme Mind itself, the same essence and quality functioning on a sublunary scale. These ideas would exert a powerful influence on later philosophical (e.g., Stoicism) and religious thought. For the Hebrew, of course, all of these ideas amount to an outlandish expression of self-veneration.

As Greek rationalism continued to evolve, the Hellenic wise man adopted increasingly heterodox views concerning the religious traditions of his culture. These tendencies were latent in the rationalist revolution begun by the Ionian scientists of the 6th century B.C. and continued in the next century with the de-mystifying speculation of thinkers such as Anaxagoras (see Plutarch, Life of Pericles 6.2). By the middle and latter portion of the 5th century we encounter an unprecedented religious skepticism operating among the Greeks that issues shortly in full-blown atheism (see Cicero, DeNatura Deorum 1.117-20), as we see in the statements attributed to men such as Diagoras of Melos and Critias of Athens. Significantly, while the Greeks seemed willing to practice a kind of "deicide" via their secularistic scrutinies, they were not prepared to question the dignity of man (Whitman 225).

All of these examples illustrate a world-view radically distinct from Hebraic practice and attitude. In the end, no aspect of Greek civilization is granted immunity from the searing rays of reason; no belief, no ritual, no institution is spared. All facets of the supernatural are dragged before the altar of reason and offered up to the gods of rational inquiry and it is specifically this rationalistic holocaust that distinguishes the Hellenes most from all other ancient peoples.[*]

Conclusion

The gap between Hebrew and Greek is powerfully illustrated by the Talmudic instruction of Rabbi Eleazar who cautions his students:

> Now then, even though you study the teaching of the Gentiles in order to know how to answer them, beware lest any of these teachings enter your heart (Goldin 113-114).

The spirit of this statement suggests that philosophy as understood by the Greeks could not take root in Jewish soil. It shows that Jerusalem was a city that could produce neither a Thales nor a Socrates because there, truth was not sought out by the mind but was rather impressed upon it; a city where homiletic precluded dialectic and where the yearning for "God" progressed restrictively along predetermined lines.

To the contemporary mind this kind of religious fervency appears incarcerative. It suggests a powerful network of intellectual

---

[*] Of course, Greek rationalism should not lead us to conclude that the "man in the street" viewed religion in anything other than conventional terms—here one is reminded of Jacob Burckhardt's observation, "Reason for the few, magic for the many." These traditional perspectives no doubt explain why Anaxogoras and Protagoras were both allegedly indicted for impiety and why Diagoras the Atheist carried a price on his head (*Birds* 1074). Moreover, it should also be noted that the Greeks were never arid cerebralists insensitive to the ecstatic side of life. In addition to the brilliant light of Apollo, they also embraced shadowy figures such as Hecate, Cybele, and above all, Dionysus. In short, the vertiginous revel of the mystic was also part of the Greek way—Phoebus' tripod was entwined with ivy.

constraints conducive of uncritical contentment with received opinion and the unexamined life. By comparison, the Greeks, who launched Western man on his critical-secular journey, seem strangely modern in message and spirit and because ours is an age in which "faith" has been transferred from the altar to the laboratory, we are naturally drawn to the Hellene and are inclined to dismiss the Jewish wisdom as antique and unserviceable. However, while it may be true that the Hebrew suffered inordinately from what J.S. Mill called, "the deep slumber of decided opinion" and while it may also be true that the horizons of Jewish life were severely delimited by an all-embracing religious legalism, the fact remains that in one area their insights and sensitivities were unprecedented and supreme, viz., the moral domain. Here, it must be admitted the Hebrews registered achievements every bit as revolutionary and world historic as the Hellenic accomplishments in science and philosophy.

Where, for example, in the literature of the ancient Greeks are we instructed to show merciful concern for the *anawim*; to leave a portion of the harvest behind for the stranger, the orphan, and the widow (Deut. 24:19)? Where are we advised to extend food and drink to our enemy because such deeds are pleasing to God (Prov. 25:21-22)? Above all, where are the Hellenic equivalents to the prophetic voices of 8th century Judah and Israel?[*] Who among the Greeks ever admonished his brethren that compassion, not burnt offerings, was what God really sought from his people (Hosea 6:6 and Isaiah 19)? And where among the sons of Javan do we encounter a message of divinely sanctioned brotherhood advocating the unity of humankind—Hebrew, Ethiopian, Philistine, and Syrian alike (Amos 9:7)? The answer to all these questions is that the an-

---

[*] Teiresias foretells the future, he is not a moral pedagogue.

cient Greeks can offer nothing comparable to such winged moral sentiments and the reason why is not far to see. By comparison to the Jewish faith, Greek religion was shallow and perfunctory; it never evolved beyond a kind of mechanical piety where ritual observance alone, not spiritual commitment, was the measure of religiosity. But unlike Zeus, Yahweh was not some remote figure peering down from Mt. Olympus. He was an omnipresent Father who saw deeply into the hearts of his children and demanded something more of them than mere orthopraxy. The dutiful sons of Abraham were required to devote themselves on the level of conscience to a life of inner discipline whose rigors included charity, forgiveness, and compassion. No people in the ancient world, including the Greeks ever approximated the loftiness and insight of this imaginative moral vision.[*] Simply put, while the rest of the world continued to venerate mindless cultic formalisms, the Jews proceeded to write a profound and unprecedented chapter in the history of man's moral evolution. Morally speaking, had the Hebrews not existed, it would have been necessary for Western civilization to invent them.

We must conclude then, that while it may be true that Jerusalem was incapable of producing a Thales or a Socrates, it was equally the case that Athens was incapable of producing the likes of an Amos or an Isaiah. In the end, however, despite enormous divergencies of life strategy and spiritual outlook, Jerusalem and Athens became sister cities in a remarkable cultural fusion whereby the moral genius of the sons of Abraham was wed to the audacious rationalism of the sons of Javan. Much of what we prize most, much

---

[*] As Bowra notes (30-31), "The Greeks never thought it possible or desirable to love their enemies, and forgiveness is a rare word in their vocabulary except for trivial or involuntary offenses. More often they found a positive pleasure in hating their enemies and enjoyed the prospect of revenge."

of what has indelibly determined the course of human history, is directly attributable to this momentous bonding of Jew and Greek.

Bibliography

Chapter I

Adkins, W. H. A. <u>Merit and Responsibility- A Study in Greek Values</u>. Chicago: U of Chicago P, 1975.

Apollodorus. <u>Library</u>. Trans. J. G. Frazer. Vol. 2. Cambridge: Harvard UP, 1990.

Arendt, H. <u>Between Past and Future</u>. New York: Viking, 1961.

Aristophanes. <u>Aristophanes</u>. Trans. B. B. Rogers. Vol. 2. Cambridge: Harvard UP, 1992.

Aristotle. <u>Aristotle</u>. Trans. H. Rackham, et al. 23 vols. Cambridge: Harvard UP, 1926-91.

Arrian. <u>The Campaigns of Alexander</u>. Trans. Aubrey De Selincourt. Middlesex, Eng.: Penguin, 1981.

Blundell, M. W. <u>Helping Friends and Harming Enemies</u>. Cambridge: Cambridge UP, 1990.

Bowra, C. M. <u>The Greek Experience</u>. Cleveland: World, 1957.

Burckhardt, J. <u>History of Greek Culture</u>. Trans. Palmer Hilty. New York: Ungar, 1963.

Bury, J. B. <u>The Ancient Greek Historians</u>. New York: Dover, 1958.

Cairns, D. L. <u>Aidos</u>. Oxford, Eng.: Clarendon, 1993.

Demosthenes. <u>Demosthenes</u>. Trans. J. H. Vince. 7 vols. Cambridge: Harvard UP, 1986.

Dodds, E. R. <u>The Greeks and the Irrational</u>. Berkeley: U of California P, 1984.

Dover, K. J. <u>Greek Popular Morality in the Time of Plato and Aristotle</u>. Berkeley: U of California P, 1974.

Faraone, C. A. and **D. Obbink**, eds. <u>Magika Hiera</u>. New York: Oxford UP, 1991.

Finley, M. I. <u>Politics in the Ancient World</u>. Cambridge: UP, 1991.
—. <u>The World of Odysseus.</u> Middlesex, Eng.: Penguin, 1979.

Fister, N. R. E. <u>Hybris</u>. Warminster, Eng.: Aris, 1992.

Frankel, H. <u>Early Greek Poetry and Philosophy</u>. Trans. M. Hadas and J. Willis. New York: Harcourt, 1975.

Gouldner, A. W. <u>Enter Plato</u>. New York: Basic, 1965.

Greene, D. and **R. Lattimore**, eds. <u>The Complete Greek Tragedies</u>. 4 vols. Chicago: U of Chicago P, 1992.

Grote, G. <u>History of Greece</u>. 12 vols. London, Eng.: Murray, 1854.

Hands, A. R. <u>Charities and Social Aid in Greece and Rome</u>. London, Eng.: Thames, 1968.

Hanson, V. D. <u>The Western Way of War</u>. New York: Oxford UP, 1990.

Harris, W. V. <u>Ancient Literacy</u>. Cambridge: Harvard UP, 1989.

Havelock, E. A. <u>The Concept of Justice</u>. Cambridge: Harvard UP, 1978.
—. <u>Preface to Plato</u>. Cambridge: Harvard UP, 1963.

Hegel, G. W. F. The Phenomenology of the Mind. Trans. J. B. Baille. London, Eng.: Allen, 1964.

Herodotus. The Histories. Trans. Aubrey De Selincourt. Baltimore: Penguin, 1968.

Hesiod. Hesiod, the Homeric Hymns and Homerica. Trans. H. G. Evelyn-White. Cambridge: Harvard UP, 1982.

Homer. The Iliad. Trans. R. Lattimore. Chicago: U of Chicago P, 1967.
—. The Odyssey of Homer. Trans. Robert Fitzgerald. Garden City: Doubleday, 1963.

Horace. Odes and Epodes. Trans. C. E. Bennett. Cambridge: Harvard UP, 1968.

Isocrates. Isocrates. Trans. LaRue Van Hook. Vol. 3. Cambridge: Harvard UP, 1986.

Jaeger, Werner. Paideia: The Ideals of Greek Culture. Trans. Gilbert Highet. New York: UP, 1945.

Kirk, G. S. The Nature of Greek Myths. London, Eng.: Penguin, 1974.

Knox, Bernard. The Oldest Dead White European Males. New York: Norton, 1993.
—. "Silent Reading in Antiquity." Greek, Roman and Byzantine Studies 9 (1968): 421-35.

Logan, R. K. The Alphabet Effect. New York: St. Martin's, 1968.

Long, A. A. "Morals and Values in Homer." Journal of Hellenic Studies 90 (1970): 121-39.

MacCary, T. W. Childlike Achilles- Ontology and Phylogeny in the Iliad. New York: Columbia UP, 1982.

MacIntyre, A. After Virtue. South Bend: Notre Dame UP, 1984.

Maclachlan, B. The Age of Grace. Princeton: Princeton UP, 1993.

Marrou, H. I. A History of Education in Antiquity. Trans. George Lamb. New York: Sheed, 1956.

Nietzsche, F. The Portable Nietzsche. Ed. and Trans. W. Kaufmann. New York: Viking, 1982.
—. Twilight of the Idols. Trans. R. J. Hollingdale. Middlesex, Eng.: Penguin, 1971.

Ovid. Metamorphoses. Trans. F. J. Milller. 2 vols. Cambridge: Harvard UP, 1984.

Parker, R. Miasma. Oxford, Eng.: Clarendon, 1990.

Parry, M. The Making of Homeric Verse- The Collected Papers of Milman Parry. Ed. Adam Parry. New York: Oxford UP, 1987.

Plato. The Dialogues of Plato. Trans. B. Jowett. 4 vols. Oxford, Eng.: Clarendon, 1967.

Plutarch. Plutarch's Lives. Trans. B. Perrin. Cambridge: Harvard UP, 1914-26.

Scott, J. A. Homer and His Influence. New York: Cooper, 1963.

Snell, B. The Discovery of the Mind. Trans. T. G. Rosenmeyer. Cambridge: Harvard UP, 1953.

Sophocles. Sophocles. Trans. F. Storr. 2 vols. Cambridge: Harvard UP, 1981.

Svenbro, Jesper. Phrasikleia. Trans. Janet Lloyd. Ithaca: Cornell UP, 1993.

Thucydides. The Peloponnesian War. Trans. Rex Warner. Baltimore: Penguin, 1966

Van Nortwick, T. Somewhere I Have Never Traveled. New York: Oxford UP, 1992.

Vitruvius. De Architectura. Trans. F. Granger. 2 vols. Cambridge: Harvard UP, 1983.

Walcot, P. Envy and the Greeks. Warminster, Eng.: Aris, 1978.

Weil, S. Simone Weil Reader. Ed. G. A. Panichas. Mt. Kisko: Moyer, 1977.

Wood, M. In Search of the Trojan War. New York: New American, 1985.

Xenophon. Xenophon. Trans. C . L. Brownson, et al. 7 vols. Cambridge: Harvard UP, 1914-25.

Chapter II

Aristotle. <u>Aristotle</u>. Trans. H. Rackham, et al. 23 vols. Cambridge: Harvard UP, 1926-91.

Athenaeus. <u>Deipnosophists</u>. Trans. C. B. Gluck. Cambridge: Harvard UP, 1969.

Bacon, F. <u>The Great Instauration and New Atlantis</u>. Ed. J. Weinberger. Arlington Heights: ARM, 1980.

Barnes, J. <u>The Presocratic Philosophers</u>. 2 vols. London, Eng.: Routledge, 1979.

Beardslee, J. W. <u>The Use of Phusis in 5th Century Greek Literature</u>. Chicago: U of Chicago P, 1918.

Burckhardt, J. <u>History of Greek Culture</u>. Trans. Palmer Hilty. New York: Unger, 1963.

Burnet, J. <u>Early Greek Philosophy</u>. London, Eng.: Black, 1963.

Cherniss, H. <u>Aristotle's Criticism of Presocratic Philosophy</u>. New York: Octagon, 1976.

Classen, C. J. "Anaximander and Anaximenes: The Earliest Greek Theories of Change." <u>Phronesis</u> 22 (1977): 89-102.

Cohen, M. R. and **I. E. Drabkin**, eds. <u>A Source Book in Greek Science</u>. Cambridge: Harvard UP, 1958.

Cornford, F. M. <u>From Religion to Philosophy</u>. New York: Harper, 1957.

—. "Greek Natural Philosophy and Modern Science." <u>Background to Modern Science</u>. Ed. J. Needham and W. Pagel. New York: Macmillan, 1938. 3-22.

—. <u>Principium Sapientiae</u>. Cambridge: Cambridge UP, 1952.

—. <u>The Unwritten Philosophy</u>. Cambridge: Cambridge UP, 1967.

Davies, J. C. "Mythological Influences on the First Emergence of Greek Scientific and Philosophical Thought." <u>Folklore</u> 8 (1970): 23-36.

Dicks, D. R. <u>Early Greek Astronomy to Aristotle</u>. Ithaca: Cornell UP, 1970.

Farrington, B. <u>Greek Science</u>. Baltimore: Penguin, 1966.

Finkelberg, A. "Anaximander's Conception of the Apeiron." <u>Phronesis</u> 38 (1993): 229-56.

Fritz, Kurt Von. "Ancient Greek and Roman Philosophy." <u>The New Encyclopedia Britannica</u>. 15th ed. 1993.

Gall, S. L. and **J. T. Plumberger.** <u>NASA Spins Off - 30 Years Commemorative Edition</u>. Washington: NASA, 1992.

Gibbon, E. <u>The Decline and Fall of the Roman Empire</u>. 3 vols. New York: Modern, 1932.

Gomprez, H. "Problems and Methods of Early Greek Science." <u>Journal of the History of Ideas</u> 4 (1943): 161-76.

Guthrie, W. K. C. "Aristotle as Historian." Studies in Pre-Socratic Philosophy. Ed. D. J. Furley and R.E. Allen. 2 vols. New York: Humanities, 1970. 239-54.
—. The Greek Philosophers. New York: Harper, 1975.

Hack, R. K. God in Greek Philosophy to the Time of Socrates. Princeton: Princeton UP, 1969.

Havelock, E. A. "The Linguistic Task of the Presocratics." Language and Thought in Early Greek Philosophy. Ed. K. Robb. LaSalle: Monist, 1983.
—. Origins of Western Literacy. Toronto, Can.: Inst. for Studies in Educ., 1976.
—. Preface to Plato. Cambridge: Harvard UP, 1963.

Heath, T. Aristarchus of Samos- The Ancient Copernicus. Oxford, Eng.: Clarendon, 1959.

Heidel, W. A. The Heroic Age of Science. Baltimore: Williams, 1933.
—. "Qualitative Change in Pre-Socratic Philosophy." The Pre-Socratics. Ed. A. P. D. Mourelatos. Princeton: Princeton UP, 86-95.

Hippocrates. Hippocrates. Trans. W. H. Jones, et al. 7 vols. Cambridge: Harvard UP, 1923-95.

Jaeger, W. The Theology of the Early Greek Philosophers. Oxford, Eng.: Clarendon, 1952.

Kahn, C. H. Anaximander and the Origins of Greek Cosmology. New York: Columbia UP, 1960.
—. "The Greek Verb `to be' and the Concept of Being." Foundations of Language 2 (1966), 245-65.

Kirk, G. S. The Nature of Greek Myths. London, Eng.: Pelican, 1974.

—. J. E. Raven, and M. Schofield. The Presocratic Philosophers. Cambridge: UP, 1987.

Kuhn, T. S. "The Relations between History and History of Science." Daedalus 100 (1971): 271-304.

Lalumia, J. "From Science to Metaphysics and Philosophy." Diogenes 5 (1974): 1-35.

Landels, J. G. Engineering in the Ancient World. Berkeley: U of California P, 1978.

Lloyd, G. E. R. Early Greek Science: Thales to Aristotle. New York: Norton, 1970.

—. Magic, Reason, and Experience. London, Eng.: Cambridge UP, 1979.

—. Polarity and Analogy. Indianapolis: Hackett, 1992.

—. The Revolutions of Wisdom. Berkeley: U of California P, 1989.

—. "The Social Background of Early Greek Philosophy and Science." The Classical World. Ed. D. Daiches and A. Thorlby. London, Eng.: Aldus, 1972. 381-95.

Logan, R K. The Alphabet Effect. New York: St. Martin's, 1986.

Majno, G. The Healing Hand. Cambridge: Harvard UP, 1975.

Needham, J. The Grand Tradition. London, Eng.: Allen, 1969.

Ong, W. J. Orality and Literacy. London, Eng.: Routledge, 1988.

Onians, R. B. The Origins of European Thought. Cambridge: UP, 1954.

Plutarch. "Dinner of the Seven Wise Men." <u>Moralia</u>. Trans. F. C. Babbitt. 16 vols. London, Eng.: Heinemann, 1971.

Popper, K. "Back to the PreSocratics." <u>Studies in Pre-Socratic Philosophy</u>. Ed. D. J. Furley and R.E. Allen. 2 vols. New York: Humanities, 1970. 130-53.

Robin, L. <u>Greek Thought and the Origins of the Scientific Spirit</u>. New York: Knopf, 1928.

Sambursky, S. <u>The Physical World of the Greeks</u>. Trans. M. Dagut. New York: Macmillan, 1956.

Schibli, H. S. <u>Pherekydes of Syros</u>. Oxford, Eng.: Clarendon, 1990.

Scott, A. <u>Origin and the Life of the Stars</u>. Oxford, Eng.: Clarendon, 1991.

Snell, B. <u>The Discovery of the Mind</u>. Trans. T. G. Rosenmeyer. Cambridge: Harvard UP, 1953.

Taran, L. "Anaximenes of Miletus." <u>Dictionary of Scientific Biography</u>. Ed. Charles C. Gillispie. Vol. 1. New York: Scribner's, 1970. 151-52.

Vlastos, G. <u>Studies in Greek Philosophy</u>. Ed. D. W. Graham. 2 vols. Princeton: Princeton UP, 1995.
—. "Theology and Philosophy in Early Greek Thought." <u>Studies in Pre-Socratic Philosophy</u>. Ed. D. J. Furley and R. E. Allen. 2 vols. New York: Humanities, 1970. 92-129.

West, M. L. <u>Earl Greek Philosophy and the Orient</u>. Oxford, Eng.: Clarendon, 1971.

Chapter III

Aristotle. Poetics. Trans. W. F. Fyfe. Cambridge: Harvard UP, 1991.

—. Politics. Trans. H. Rackham. Cambridge: Harvard UP, 1990.

Ashmole, B. The Classical Ideal in Greek Art. Cincinnati: UP, 1964.

Bernal, M. Black Athena. Vol. 1. New Brunswick: Rutgers UP, 1987.

Boardman, J. The Greeks Overseas. London, Eng.: Thames, 1988.

—, ed. The Oxford History of Classical Art. Oxford, Eng.: UP, 1993.

Bowra, C. M. The Greek Experience. Cleveland: World, 1957.

Bruno, V. J., ed. The Parthenon. New York: Norton, 1974.

Buitron-Oliver, D., ed. The Greek Miracle. Washington: National Gallery of Art, 1992.

Burkert, W. The Orientalizing Revolution. Trans. M. E. Pinder. Cambridge: Harvard UP, 1992.

Buschor, E. On the Meaning of Greek Statues. Trans. J. L. Bensen. Amherst: U of Massachusetts P, 1980.

Butler, E. M. The Tyranny of Greece over Germany. Boston: Beacon, 1958.

Carpenter, R. The Aesthetic Basics of Greek Art. Bloomington: Indiana UP, 1965.

Diodoros Siculus. Library of History. Trans. C. H. Oldfather. 12 vols. Cambridge: Harvard UP, 1989.

Fairbanks, A. Greek Art. New York: Longmans, 1933.

Finley, M. I., ed. The Legacy of Greece. Oxford, Eng.: Clarendon, 1981.

Fowler, B. H. The Hellenistic Aesthetic. Madison: U of Wisconsin P, 1989.

Gardner, E. A. Six Greek Sculptors. London, Eng.: Duckworth, 1910.

Getz-Preziosi, P. Sculptors of the Cyclades: Individual and Tradition in the Third Millennium B.C. Ann Arbor: U of Michigan P, 1987.

Goodyear, W. H. Greek Refinements. New Haven: Yale UP, 1912.

Grube. G. M. A. "Plato's Theory of Beauty." The Monist (1927): 269-88.

Heath, T. H. A History of Greek Mathematics. 2 vols. New York: Dover, 1981.

Herodotus. The Histories. Trans. A. D. Godley. 4 vols. Cambridge: Harvard UP, 1990.

Higgins, R. Minoan and Mycenean Art. New York: Praeger, 1967.

Hyde, W. W. Ancient Greek Mariners. New York: Oxford UP, 1947.

Kantorowicz, G. The Inner Nature of Greek Art. Trans. J. L. Benson. New York: Caratzas, 1922.

Kitto, H. D. F. The Greeks. Middlesex, Eng.: Penguin, 1975.

Kuels, E. C. Plato and Greek Painting. Leiden: Brill, 1978.

Lessing, G. E. Laocoon. Trans. E. Frothingham. New York: Noonday, 1965.

Lullies, R. Greek Sculpture. Trans. M. Bullock. New York: Abrams, 1960.

Moon, W. G. Polykleitos, Doryphoros, and Tradition. Madison: U of Wisconsin P, 1995.

Pausanias. Description of Greece. Trans. W. H. S. Jones. 5 vols. Cambridge: Harvard UP, 1993.

Penrose, F. C. An Investigation of the Principles of Athenian Architecture. Washington: McGrath, 1973.

Plato. The Dialogues of Plato. Trans. B. Jowett. 4 vols. Oxford, Eng.: Clarendon, 1967.

Pliny. Natural History. Trans. H. Rackham. 10 vols. Cambridge: Harvard UP, 1984.

Plotinus. Enneads. Trans. A. H. Armstrong. 7 vols. Cambridge: Harvard UP, 1989.

Pollitt, J. J. Art and Experience in Classical Greece. Cambridge: UP, 1972.
—. The Ancient View of Greek Art. New Haven: Yale UP, 1974.

Renehan, R. "The Greek Anthropocentric View of Man." Harvard Studies of Classical Philosophy 85 (1980): 239-60.

Renfrew, C. The Cycladic Spirit. New York: Abrams, 1991.

Richter, G. M. A. A Handbook of Greek Art. London, Eng.: Phaidon, 1987.
—. Korai-Archaic Greek Maidens. New York: Hacker, 1988.

Ridgway. B. S. <u>Fifth Century Styles in Greek Sculpture</u>. Princeton: Princeton UP, 1981.

Scranton, R. L. <u>Aesthetic Aspects of Greek Art</u>. Chicago: UP, 1964.

Seneca, <u>Epistles.</u> Trans. R. M. Gummere. Cambridge: Harvard UP, 1991.

Stewart, A. <u>Greek Sculpture</u>. 2 vols. New Haven: Yale UP, 1990.

Thucydides. <u>History of the Peloponnesian War</u>. Trans. C. F. Smith. 4 vols. Cambridge: Harvard UP, 1919-23.

Tobin, R. "The Canon of Polykleitos." <u>American Journal of Archeology</u> 79 (1975): 307-21.

Winckelmann, J. J. <u>The History of Ancient Art</u>. Trans. C. H. Lodge. 4 vols. Boston: Osgood, 1872.

Chapter IV

Anderson, W. D. Music and Musicians in Ancient Greece. Ithaca: Cornell UP, 1994.

Andocides. Minor Attic Orators. Trans. K. J. Maidment. 2 vols. Cambridge: Harvard UP, 1982.

Aristophanes. Aristophanes. Trans. B. B. Rogers. 3 vols. Cambridge: Harvard UP, 1992.

Aristotle. Aristotle. Trans. H. Rackham, et al. 23 vols. Cambridge: Harvard UP, 1926-91.

Athenaeus. The Deipnosophists. Trans. C. B. Gluck. 7 vols. Cambridge: Harvard UP, 1969.

Burkert, W. "Greek Tragedy and Sacrificial Tragedy." Greek and Byzantine Studies 7 (1966) 87-121.

Cornford, F. M. The Origin of Attic Comedy. Ann Arbor: U of Michigan P, 1993.

Csapo, E. and **W. J. Slater.** The Context of Ancient Drama. Ann Arbor: U of Michigan P, 1998.

Demosthenes. Demosthenes. Trans. J. H. Vince. Vol. 3. Cambridge: Harvard UP, 1986.

Else, G. F. Aristotle Poetics: The Argument. Cambridge: Harvard UP, 1963.
—. The Origin and Early Form of Greek Tragedy. Cambridge: Harvard UP, 1965.

Euben, J. P., ed. Greek Tragedy and Political Theory. Berkeley: U of California P, 1986.

Fairman, H. W., ed and trans. The Triumph of Horus. Berkeley: U of California P, 1974.

Frazier, J. The New Golden Bough. New York: Mentor, 1959.

Gellrich, M. Tragedy and Political Theory- The Problem of Conflict Since Aristotle. Princeton: Princeton UP, 1988.

Golden, L. "Minesis and Katharsis." Classical Philology 64 (1966): 145-53.

Gregory, J. Euripides and the Instruction of the Athenians. Ann Arbor: U of Michigan P, 1997.

Greene, D. and **R. Lattimore,** eds. The Complete Greek Tragedies. 4 vols. Chicago: U of Chicago P, 1992.

Haigh, A. E. The Attic Theatre. Oxford: Clarendon, 1907.

Harrison, J. E. Themis. Cleveland: World, 1962.

Harsh, P. W. A Handbook of Classical Drama. Stanford: UP, 1944.

Hegel, G. W. F. Aesthetics- Lectures on Fine Art. Trans. T. M. Knox. 2 vols. Oxford: Clarendon P, 1975.
—. The Philosophy of History. Trans. J. Sibree. New York: Willey, 1900.

Herodotus. Herodotus: Trans. A. D. Godley. 4 vols. Cambridge: Harvard UP, 1900.

Homer. Iliad. Trans. R. Lattimore. Chicago: U of Chicago P, 1967.

Jaspers, K. Tragedy is Not Enough. Trans. H. A. T. Reiche, H. T. Moore, and K. W. Deutsh. Hamden: Archon, 1969.

Jebb, R. C. The Growth and Influence of Classical Greek Poetry. New York: Gordian, 1970.

Kitto, H. D. F. Greek Tragedy. London: Routledge, 1990.

Knox, B. Essays on the Ancient Theatre. Baltimore: John Hopkins UP, 1986.
—. The Heroic Temper- Studies in Sophoclean Tragedy. Berkeley: U of California P, 1983.
—. Oedipus at Thebes. New Haven: Yale UP, 1957.

Krook, D. Elements of Tragedy. New Haven, Yale UP, 1969.

Lesky, A. Greek Tragedy. London: Benn, 1965.

Lysias, Lysias. Trans. W. R. M. Lamb. Cambridge: Harvard UP, 1988.

Meier, C. The Political Art of Greek Tragedy. Baltimore: John Hopkins UP, 1993.

Moorhead, J. K., ed. Conversations of Goethe with J. P. Eckermann. Trans. J. Overnford. New York: DeCapo, 1998.

Murray, G. Aeschylus- The Creator of Tragedy. Oxford: Clarendon, 1968.

Nietzsche, F. Beyond Good and Evil. Trans. W. Kaufmann. New York: Vintage, 1966.
—. The Birth of Tragedy. Trans. W. Kaufmann. New York: Vintage, 1967.

Nussbaum, M. C. The Fragility of Goodness. New York: Cambridge UP, 1986.

Pickard-Cambridge, A. <u>Dithyramb, Tragedy, and Comedy</u>. Oxford: Clarendon P, 1997.

—. <u>The Dramatic Festivals of Athens</u>. London: Routledge, 1973.

Pindar. <u>The Odes of Pindar</u>. Trans. J. Sandys. 2 vols. Cambridge: Harvard UP, 1989.

Plato. <u>The Dialogues of Plato</u>. Trans. B. Jowett. Oxford: Clarendon, 1967.

Plutarch. <u>Plutarch's Lives</u>. Trans. B. Perrin. 11 vols. Cambridge: Harvard UP, 1914-26.

Raphael, D. D. <u>The Paradox of Tragedy</u>. Bloomington: U of Indiana P, 1961.

Rees, B. R. "Aristotle's Approach to Poetry." <u>Greece and Rome</u> 28 (1981): 23-39.

Ridgeway, W. <u>The Origin of Tragedy</u>. New York: Benjamin Bloom, 1966.

Schopenhauer, A. <u>The World as Will and Representation</u>. Trans. E. F. F. Payne. 2 vols. New York: Dover, 1966.

Silk, M. S. and **J. P. Stern.** <u>Nietzsche on Tragedy</u>. Cambridge: UP, 1981.

Snell, B. <u>The Discovery of the Mind</u>. Trans. T. G. Rosenmeyer. Cambridge: Harvard UP, 1953.

Solon. <u>Elegy and Iambus</u>. Trans. A. D. Godley. 2 vols. Cambridge: Harvard UP, 1982.

Taplin, O. <u>Greek Tragedy in Athens</u>. London: Routledge, 1993.

Theognis. <u>Elegy and Iambus</u>. Trans. J. M. Edmonds. 2 vols. Cambridge: Harvard UP, 1982.

Vernant J. P. and **P. Vidal-Naquet.** <u>Myth and Tragedy in Ancient Greece</u>. New York: Zone, 1990.

Vitruvius. <u>On Architecture</u>. Trans. F. Granger. 2 vols. Cambridge: Harvard UP, 1983.

West, M. L. <u>Ancient Greek Music</u>. Oxford: Clarendon, 1994.
—. <u>Introduction to Greek Meter</u>. Oxford: Clarendon, 1987.

Whitman, C .H. <u>Sophocles- A Study of Heroic Humanism</u>. Cambridge: Harvard UP, 1966.

Winkler, J. J. "The Ephebes Song: Tragoidia and Polis." <u>Nothing to Do With Dionysos</u>. Ed. J. J. Winkler and Zeitlin. Princeton: UP, 1992. 2-62.

Chapter V

Abbott, G. F. Thucydides- A Study in Historical Reality. London: Routlege, 1925.

Aeschylus. Aeschylus. Trans. H. Weir. Cambridge: Harvard UP, 1992.

Armstrong, A. H., and **R. A. Markus.** Christian Faith and Greek Philosophy. New York: Sheed, 1960.

Aristophanes. Aristophanes. Trans. B. B. Rogers. 3 vols. Cambridge: Harvard UP, 1992.

Aristotle. The Poetics. Trans. W. F. Fyfe. Cambridge: Harvard UP, 1991.
—. Politics. Trans. H. Rackham. Cambridge: Harvard UP, 1990.

Barnes, H. E. A History of Historical Writing. New York: Dover, 1963.

Bury, J. B. The Ancient Greek Historians. New York: Dover, 1958.
—. The Idea of Progress. New York: Dover, 1960.

Calhoun, G. M. Athenian Clubs. New York: Franklin, 1970.

Castoriadis, C. Philosophy, Politics, Autonomy. New York: Oxford UP, 1991.

Cicero. DeLegibus. Trans. C. W. Keyes. Cambridge: Harvard UP, 1988.
—. De Oratore. Trans. E. W. Sutton and H. Rackham. Cambridge: Harvard UP, 1988.

Cochrane, C. N. Thucydides and the Science of History. New York: Russell, 1965.

Cogan, M. The Human Thing. Chicago: U of Chicago P, 1981.

Collingswood, R. G. The Idea of History. New York: Oxford UP, 1956.

Cornford, F. M. Thucydides Mythistoricus. London, Eng.: Routlege, 1965.

de Rommily, J. The Rise and Fall of States According to Greek Authors. Ann Arbor: U of Michigan P, 1977.
—. Thucydides and Athenian Imperialism. Trans. P. Thody. Salem: Ayer, 1988.

de Ste. Croix, G. E. M. The Origins of the Peloponnesian War. London, Eng.: Duckworth, 1989.

Diels, H. Ancilla to the Pre-Socratic Philosophers. Trans. K. Freeman. Cambridge: Harvard UP, 1957.

Dionysius of Halicarnassus. Critical Essays. Trans. S. Usher. Cambridge: Harvard UP, 1974.

Ehrenberg, V. "Polypragmosyne: A Study in Greek Politics." Journal of Hellenic Studies 67 (1957): 46-67.

Erasmus. The Education of a Christian Prince. Trans. N. S. Chestine and M. J. Heath. Cambridge: Harvard UP, 1997.

Finely, J. H. Three Essays on Thucydides. Cambridge: Harvard UP, 1967.

— . Thucydides. Cambridge: Harvard UP, 1942.

Finely, M. I., ed. The Greek Historians. London, Eng.: Chatto, 1959.

Gomme, A. W., A. Andrews, and **K. J. Dover.** A Historical Commentary on Thucydides. 5 vols. Oxford, Eng.: Clarendon, 1950-81.

Greene, D. Man in his Pride. Chicago: U of Chicago P, 1950.

Hadas, M. A History of Greek Literature. New York: Columbia UP, 1950.

Herodotus. Herodotus. Trans. A. D. Godley. 4 vols. Cambridge: Harvard UP, 1990.

Hesiod. Works and Days. Trans. H. G. Evelyn-White. Cambridge: Harvard UP, 1982.

Hobbes, T. Leviathan. Oxford, Eng.: Blackwell, 1946.

Hornblower, E., ed. Greek Historiography. Oxford, Eng.: Clarendon, 1966.

Iggers, G. G. The German Conception of History. Middletown: Weslyn UP, 1968.

Jaeger, W. Paideia. Trans. G. Highet. 3 vols. New York: Oxford UP, 1945.

Johnson, L. M. Thucydides. Hobbes and the Interpretation of Realism. Dekalb: N. Illinois UP, 1993.

Isocrates. Isocrates. Trans. G. Norlin. 3 vols. Cambridge: Harvard UP, 1991.

Kagan, D. The Fall of the Athenian Empire. Ithaca: Cornell UP, 1991.

—. The Outbreak of the Peloponnesian War. Ithaca: Cornell UP, 1994.

Lucian. "How to Write History." Trans. K. Kilburn. Lucian. Vol. 6. Cambridge: Harvard UP, 1990. 3-73.

Machiavelli, N. Machiavelli- The Chief Works and Others. Trans. A. Gilbert. 2 vols. Durham: Duke UP, 1965.

Mamigliano, A. Studies in Historiography. London, Eng.: Weindenfeld, 1966.

Marinatos, N. "Thucydides and Oracles." Journal of the Hellenic Studies. 101 (1981) 138-40.

Orwin, C. The Humanity of Thucydides. Priceton: Princeton UP, 1994.

Palmer, M. Love of Glory and the Common Good. Landham: Rowman, 1992.

Plato. The Dialogues of Plato. Trans. B. Jowett. Oxford, Eng.: Clarendon, 1967.

Plutarch. "On the Malice of Herodotus." Trans. L. Pearson. Moralia. Vol. 11. Cambridge: Harvard UP, 1970. 9-129.
—. "Pericles." Trans. B. Perrin. Plutarch's Lives. Vol. 3. Cambridge: Harvard UP, 1984.

Polybius. The Histories. Trans. W. R. Paton. 6 vols. Cambridge: Harvard UP, 1992.

Pouncey, P. R. The Necessities of War. New York: Columbia UP, 1980.

Shrimpton, G. S. History and Memory in Ancient Greece. Montreal, Can.: McGill-Queens UP, 1997.

Starr, C. G. The Awakening of the Greek Historical Spirit. New York: Knopf, 1968.

Strauss, L. The City and Man. Chicago: U of Chicago P, 1978.

Tod, M. N., ed. Selection of Greek Historical Inscriptions. Oxford, Eng.: Clarendon, 1951.

Thucydides. The History of the Peloponnesian War. Trans. Thomas Hobbes. 2 vols. London: Bohn, 1843.
—. History of the Peloponnesian War. Trans. C. F. Smith. 4 vols. Cambridge: Harvard UP, 1919- 23.

Westlake, H. D. Individuals in Thucydides. Cambridge: Harvard UP, 1968.

Wilcken, U. Alexander the Great. New York: Norton, 1967.

Woodhead. A. G. Thucydides on the Nature of Power. Cambridge: Harvard UP, 1970.

Chapter VI

Aeschines. The Speeches of Aeschines. Trans. C. D. Adams. Cambridge: Harvard UP, 1988.

Andocidies. Minor Attic Orators. Trans. K. J. Maidment. Cambridge: Harvard UP, 1982.

Antiphon. Minor Attic Orators. Trans. K.J. Maidment. Cambridge: Harvard UP, 1982.

Arendt, H. The Human Condition. Chicago: U of Chicago P, 1989.

Aristophanes. The Comedies of Aristophanes. Trans. A. H. Sommerstein. 7 vols. Wittshire, Eng.: Aris, 1987.

Aristotle. Aristotle. Trans. H. Rackham, et al. 23 vols. Cambridge: Harvard UP, 1926-91.

Athenaeus. Deipnosophists. Trans. C. B. Gulick. 7 vols. Cambridge: Harvard UP, 1927-93.

Bowra, C. M. The Greek Experience. Cleveland: World Publishing, 1957.

Burkert, W. Greek Religion. Trans. J. Raffan. Cambridge: Basil; Harvard UP, 1985

Calhoun, G. E. Athenian Clubs in Politics and Litigation. New York: Burt, 1970.

DeCounlanges, F. The Ancient City. Trans. W. Small. Boston: Lothrop, 1901.

Demosthenes. Demosthenes. Trans. J. H. Vance, et al. Cambridge: Harvard UP, 1930-89.

Dillon, M. and L. Garland. Ancient Greece: Social and Historical Documents from Archaic Times to the Death of Socrates. New York: Routledge, 1994.

Diodorus Siculus. Library of History. Trans. C.H. Oldfather, et al. Cambridge: Harvard UP, 1933-89.

Ehrenberg, V. Aspects of the Ancient World. Oxford, Eng.: Basil, 1946.

—. The Greek State. New York: Norton, 1964.

Finely, M.I. The Ancient Economy. Berkeley: U of California P, 1973.

—. "Athenian Demagogues." Past and Present 21 (1962) : 3-24.

—. Economy and Society in Ancient Greece. Ed. B.D. Shaw and R.P. Saller. New York: Viking, 1982.

—. Politics in the Ancient World. Cambridge: UP, 1991.

Forrest, W.G. The Emergence of Greek Democracy. New York: McGraw, 1966.

Fritz, K. Von. The Theory of Mixed Constitution. New York: Columbia UP, 1954.

Garlan, Y. Slavery in Ancient Greece. Tran. J. Lloyd. Ithaca: Cornell UP, 1988.

Glotz, G. The Greek City and Its Institutions. London, Eng.: Routledge, 1950.

Gomme, A.W. The Population of Athens in the Fifth and Fourth Centuries B.C. Oxford, Eng.: Basil, 1933.

Greenidge, A.H.J. A Handbook of Greek Constitutional History. London, Eng.: Macmillan, 1920.

Hammond, B. E. The Political Institutions of the Ancient Greeks. Chicago: Argonaut, 1970.

Hansen, M. H. "Demos, Ecclesia, and Dicasterion in Classical Athens." Greek, Roman and Byzantine Studies 19 (1978) : 127-46.

—. Eisangelia. Vol. 6. Odense, Den.: Odense UP, 1975.

—. "How Many Athenians Attended the Ecclesia." Greek, Roman and Byzantine Studies 17 (1976) : 115-34.

—. "Seven Hundred Archai in Classical Athens." Greek, Roman and Byzantine Studies 21 (1980) : 151-73.

Harris, V. W. Ancient Literacy. Cambridge: Harvard UP, 1989.

Harrison, A. R. W. The Laws of Athens. 2 vols. Indianapolis: Hackett, 1998.

Headlam, J.W. Election by Lot at Athens. Cambridge: UP. 1933.

Herodotus. Herodotus. Trans. A. D. Godley. 4 vols. Cambridge: Harvard UP, 1920-25.

Hiebel, F. The Gospel of Hellas. New York: Anthroposophic, 1949.

Hignett, C. A History of the Athenian Consitution. Oxford, Eng.: Clarendon, 1962.

Homer. The Iliad. Trans. R. Lattimore. Chicago: U of Chicago P, 1967.

—. The Odyssey. Trans. R. Fitzgerald. Garden City: Doubleday, 1963.

Jones, H. W. The Law and Legal Theory of the Greeks. Oxford, Eng.: Clarendon, 1956.

Kuels, E. The Reign of the Phallus. Berkeley: U of California P, 1993.

"Law and Procedure, Athenian." The Oxford Classical Dictionary. 3rd ed. 1995.

Lloyd, G. E. R. The Revolutions of Wisdom. Berkeley: U of California P, 1989.

Lofberg, J. O. Sycophancy in Athens. Chicago: Ares, 1976.

Lysias. Lysias. Trans. W. R. M. Lamb. Cambridge: Harvard UP, 1988.

MacDowell, D. M. The Law in Classical Athens. Ithaca: Cornell UP, 1978.

Madison, J. , Alexander Hamilton, and **John Jay.** The Federalist Papers. Ed. I. Kramnick. London, Eng.: Penguin, 1987.

Munn, M. The School of History. Berkeley: U of California P, 2000.

Ober, J. The Athenian Revolution. Princeton: Princeton UP, 1996.
—. Mass and Elite in Democratic Athens. Princeton: Princeton UP, 1989.
—. Political Dissent in Democratic Athens. Princeton: Princeton UP, 1998.

Osborne, R. "Vexatious Litigation in Classical Athens: Sykophancy and The Sykophant." Nomos- Essays in Athenian Law, Politics and Society. Ed. Cartledge, P. Millet and S. Todd. Cambridge: UP, 1993. 83-102.

Ostwald, M. Nomos and the Beginning of the Athenian Democracy. Oxford, Eng.: Clarendon, 1969.

Phoca, I. and **P. Valavanis.** Architecture and City Planning. Athens, Gr.: Kredos, 1999.

Plato. The Dialogues of Plato. Trans. B Jowett. 4 vols. Oxford, Eng. Clarendon, 1967.
—. Plato's Epistles. Trans. G. R. Morrow. Indianapolis: Bobbs, 1962.

Plutarch. Plutarch's Lives. Trans. B. Perrin. 11 vols. Cambridge: Harvard UP, 1914-26.

Rhodes, P. J. A Commentary on the Aristotelian Athenaion Politeia. Oxford, Eng. : Clarendon, 1993.

Roberts, J. T. Accountability in Athenian Government. Madison: U of Wisconsin P, 1982.

Sagan, E. The Honey and the Hemlock. New York: Basic, 1991.

Sealey, R. A History of the Greek City States: 700- 338 B.C. Berkeley: U of California P, 1976.
—. The Justice of the Greeks. Ann Arbor: U of Michigan P, 1999.

Sinclair, R. K. Democracy and Participation in Athens. Cambridge: UP, 1989.

Solon. Greek Elegy and Iambus. Trans J. M. Edmonds. Vol. 1. Cambridge: Harvard UP, 1982.

Stockton, D. The Classical Athenian Democracy. New York: Oxford UP, 1990.

Thorley, J. Athenian Democracy. London, Eng.: Routledge, 1996.

Toynbee, A. R. Greek Political Thought. Boston: Beacon Press, 1950.

Thucydides. History of the Peloponnesian War. Trans. C. F. Smith. 4 vols. Cambridge: Harvard UP, 1919-23.

Whitman, C. H. The Heroic Paradox. Ithaca: Cornell UP, 1982.

Xenophon. Xenophon. Trans. C.L. Brownson. 7 vols. Cambridge: Harvard UP, 1914-25.

Chapter VII

Aeschines. The Speeches of Aeschines. Trans. C. D. Adams. Cambridge: Harvard UP, 1988.

Anderson, G. The Second Sophistic. London, Eng.: Routlege, 1993.

Aristophanes. Aristophanes. Trans. B. B. Rogers. 3 vols. Cambridge: Harvard UP, 1992.

Aristotle. Aristotle. Trans. H. Rackham, et al. 23 vols. Cambridge: Harvard UP, 1926-91.

Athanassakis, A. N., trans. The Homeric Hymns. Baltimore: John Hopkins UP, 1976.

Cicero. De Oratore. Trans. E. W. Sutton. 2 vols. Cambridge: Harvard UP, 1988.
—. Tusculan Disputations. Trans. J. E. King. Cambridge: Harvard UP, 1989.

Conley, T. M. Rhetoric in the European Tradition. Chicago: Chicago UP, 1990.

Cornford, F. M. From Religion to Philosophy. New York: Harper, 1957.

de Romilly, J. The Great Sophists of Periclean Athens. Oxford, Eng.: Clarendon, 1992.
—. Magic and Rhetoric in Ancient Greece. Cambridge: Harvard UP, 1995.

Diels, H. Ancilla to the Pre-Socratic Philosophers. Trans. K. Freeman. Cambridge: Harvard UP, 1957.

Diogenes Laertius. Lives of Eminent Philosophers. Trans. R D. Hicks. Cambridge: Harvard UP, 1991.

Forbes, C. "Comparison, Self-Patience and Irony: Paul's Boasting and the Convention of Hellenistic Rhetoric." New Testament Studies 32 (1986): 1-30.

Grenfell, B. P., ed. The Oxyrhynchus Papyri. Vol. 11. London, Eng.: Hunt, 1915.

Grote, G. History of Greece. 12 vols. London, Eng.: Murray, 1854.

Guthrie, W. K. C. A History of Greek Philosophy. 6 vols. Cambridge: Cambridge UP, 1962-81.

Hadas, M. A History of Greek Literature. New York: Columbia UP, 1950.

Hatch, E. The Influence of Greek Ideas on Christianity. Gloucester: Smith, 1970.

Havelock, E. A. The Liberal Temper in Greek Politics. New Haven: Yale UP, 1957.

Hays, S. "On the Skeptical Influence of Gorgias' on Non-Being." Journal of the History of Philosophy 283 (1990): 327-37.

Heath, T. H. A History of Greek Mathematics. 2 vols. New York: Dover, 1981.

Hesiod. Hesiod. Trans. H. G. Evelyn-White. Cambridge: Harvard UP, 1982.

Hippocrates. Ancient Medicine. Trans. W. H. S. Jones. Vol. 1. Cambridge: Harvard UP, 1984.

Homer. The Iliad. Trans. R. Lattimore. Chicago: U of Chicago P, 1967.

Isocrates. Isocrates. Trans. G. Norline and L. R. Van Hook. 3 vols. Cambridge: Harvard UP, 1991.

Jaeger, W. Early Christianity and Greek Paideia. Cambridge: Harvard UP, 1961.

—. Paideia: The Ideals of Greek Culture. Trans. G. Highet. 3 vols. New York: UP, 1943-45.

Jarrett, J. L., ed. The Educational Theories of the Sophists. New York: Columbia UP, 1969.

Kahn, C. H. "The Greek Verb 'to be' and the Concept of Being." Foundations of Language 2 (1966): 245-65.

Kennedy, G. A. The Art of Rhetoric in the Roman World. Princeton: Princeton UP, 1972.

—. Classical Rhetoric and its Christian and Secular Tradition from Ancient to Modern Times. Chapel Hill: U of North Carolina P, 1980.

Knox, B. The Oldest Dead White European Males. New York: Norton, 1993.

Lloyd, G. E. R. The Revolutions of Wisdom. Berkeley: U of California P, 1989.

Marrou, H. I. A History of Education in Antiquity. Trans. G. Lamb. New York: Sheed and Ward, 1956.

Morrison, J. S. "Antiphon." Proceedings of the Cambridge Philological Society 7 (1961): 49-58.

Myers, P. A History of Greece. Boston: Ginn, 1900.

Ober, J. Mass and Elite in Democratic Athens. Princeton: Princeton UP, 1989.

Pausanias. Description of Greece. Trans. W. H. S. Jones. 5 vols. Cambridge: Harvard UP, 1992.

Pelikan, J. Christianity and Classical Culture. New Haven: Yale UP, 1993.

Philostratus. The Lives of the Sophists. Trans. W. C. Wright. Cambridge: Harvard UP, 1989.

Plato. The Dialogues of Plato. Trans. B. Jowett. 4 vols. Oxford, Eng.: Clarendon, 1967.

Plutarch. Plutarch's Lives. Trans. B. Penin. 11 vols. Cambridge: Harvard UP, 1914-26.

Rankin, H. D. "Ouk estin Antilegin." The Sophists and Their Legacy Ed. G. B. Kerferd. Wiesbaden, Ger.: Steiner, 1981. 25-37.

Robin, L. Greek Thought. Trans. M. R. Dobie. New York: Knopf, 1928.

Schiappa, E. Protagoras and Logos. Columbia: U of South Carolina P, 1991.

Sesonske, A. "To Make the Weaker Argument Defeat the Stronger." Journal of the History of Philosophy 6 (1966): 217-31.

Snell, B. The Discovery of the Mind. Trans. T. G. Rosenmeyer. Cambridge: Harvard UP, 1953.

Solmsen, F. Intellectual Experiments of the Greek Enlightenment. Princeton: Princeton UP, 1975.

Sprague, R. J., ed. The Older Sophists. Columbia: U of South Carolina P, 1972.

Thucydides. History of the Peloponnesian War. Trans. C. F. Smith. 4 vols. Cambridge: Harvard UP, 1919-23.

Untersteiner, M. The Sophists. Trans. K. Freeman. Oxford, Eng.: Basil, 1954.

Versenyi, L. "Protagoras' Man-Measure Fragment." American Journal of Philology 83 (1962): 178-84.

Xenophon. Scripta Minora. Trans. E. C. Marchant. Cambridge: Harvard UP, 1984.

Chapter VIII

Adkins, A. W. H. Merit and Responsibility. Chicago: UP, 1975.

Aeschines. The Speeches of Aeschines. Trans. C. D. Adams. Cambridge: Harvard UP, 1919.

Angus, S. The Mystery Religions and Christianity. New York: Carol, 1966.

Aristophanes. Aristophanes. Trans. B. B. Rogers. 3 vols. Cambridge: Harvard UP, 1992.

Aristotle. Aristotle. Trans. H. Rackham, et al. 23 vols. Cambridge: Harvard UP, 1926-91.

Autenrieth, G. The Homeric Dictionary. Trans. I. Flagg. Norman: U of Oklahoma P, 1979.

Bremmer, J. The Early Greek Concept of the Soul. Princeton: UP, 1983.

Brickhouse, T. C. and **N. D. Smith.** Plato's Socrates. New York: Oxford UP, 1989.
—. Socrates on Trial. Princeton: UP, 1989.

Burkert, W. Greek Religion. Trans. J. Raffan. Cambridge: Harvard UP, 1985.

Burnet, J. Greek Philosophy- Thales to Plato. London, Eng.: Macmillan, 1964.
—. "The Socratic Doctrine of the Soul." Proceedings of the British Academy 7 (1919): 235-59.

Calhoun, G. E. Athenian Clubs in Politics and Litigation. New York: Franklin, 1970.

Chroust, A. H. <u>Socrates- Man and Myth</u>. South Bend: U of Notre Dame P, 1957.

Cicero. <u>De Oratore</u>. Trans. E. W. Sutton and H. Rackham. 2 vols. Cambridge: Harvard UP, 1988-92.
—. <u>Tusculan Disputations</u>. Trans. J. E. King. Vol. 18. Cambridge: Harvard UP, 1989.

Claus, D. B. <u>Toward the Soul</u>. New Haven: Yale UP, 1981.

Danhouser, W. J. <u>Nietzsche's View of Socrates</u>. Ithaca: Cornell UP, 1964.

Diogenes Laertius. <u>Lives of Eminent Philosophers</u>. Trans. R. D. Hicks. 2 vols. Cambridge: Harvard UP, 1991.

Ehrenberg, V. <u>The People of Aristophanes</u>. Cambridge: Harvard UP, 1951.

Epictetus. <u>Epictetus</u>. Trans. W. A. Oldfather. 2 vols. Cambridge: Harvard UP, 1989.

Ferguson, N. <u>Socrates: A Source Book</u>. London, Eng.: Open U, 1970.

Grote, G. <u>History of Greece</u>. 12 vols. London, Eng.: Murray, 1855.

Gulley, N. "The Interpretation of 'No One Does Wrong Willingly' in Plato's Dialogues." <u>Phronesis</u> 9-11 (1965): 82-96.

Guthrie, W. K. C. <u>Socrates</u>. Cambridge: UP, 1990.

Hegel, G. W. F. <u>The Philosophy of History</u>. Trans. J. Sibree. New York: Willey, 1900.

Homer. The Iliad. Trans. R. Lattimore. Chicago: U of Chicago P, 1967.

—. The Odyssey of Homer. Trans. R. Fitzgerald. Garden City: Doubleday, 1963.

Irwin, T. Plato's Moral Theory: The Early and Middle Dialogues Oxford, Eng.: UP, 1977.

Isocrates. Isocrates. Trans. G. Norlin and L. Van Hook. Cambridge: Harvard UP, 1991.

Jaeger, W. Paideia. Trans. G. Highet. 3 vols. New York: Oxford UP, 1943-45.

Knox, B. Heroic Temper- Studies in Sophoclean Tragedy. Berkeley: U of California P, 1983.

Kraut, R. Socrates and the State. Princeton: UP, 1984.

Kuhn, T. S. The Structure of Scientific Revolutions. Chicago: UP, 1970.

Livingston, Sir Richard. Portrait of Socrates. New York: Oxford UP, 1966.

Lutoslawski, W. The Origin and Growth of Plato's Logic. London, Eng.: Longman's, 1897.

MacDowell, D. M. The Law in Classic Athens. Ithaca: Cornell UP, 1978.

Momigliano, A. The Development of Greek Biography. Cambridge: Harvard UP, 1993.

O'Brien, M. J. The Socratic Paradoxes and the Greek Mind. Chapel Hill: U of North Carolina P, 1967.

Onians, R. B. The Origins of European Thought. Cambridge: UP, 1954.

Pindar. Pindar. Trans. J. Sandys and W. H. Race. Cambridge: Harvard UP, 1989; 1977.

Plato. The Dialogues of Plato. Trans. B. Jowett. Oxford, Eng.: Clarendon, 1967.

—. Plato's Epistles. Trans. G. R. Morrow. Indianapolis: Bobbs, 1961.

Plutarch. Plutarch's Lives. Trans. B. Perrin. I 1 vols. Cambridge: Harvard UP, 1993.

Reeve, C. D. C. Socrates in the Apology. Indianapolis: Hackett, 1989.

Robinson, R. "Elenchus." The Philosophy of Socrates Ed. G. Vlastos. Garden City: Doubleday, 1971.7-24.

—. Plato's Earlier Dialectic. Oxford, Eng.: Clarendon, 1966.

Ross, W. D. "The Socratic Problem." Proceedings of the Classical Association 30 (1933): 7-24.

Ryle, G. The Concert of the Mind. New York: Barnes, 1949.

Santas, G. X. Socrates. London: Routledge, 1979.

Senior, D., ed. The Catholic Study Bible. New York: Oxford UP, 1990.

Sinclair, R. K. Democracy and Participation in Athens. Cambridge: UP, 1989.

Solmsen, F. "Plato and the Concept of the Soul: Some Historical Perspectives." Journal of the History of Ideas 44 (1983): 355-67.

Stone, I. F. The Trial of Socrates. New York: Doubleday, 1989.

Taylor, A. E. Varia Socratica. Oxford, Eng.: Parker, 1911.

Theophrastus. Characters. Trans. J. Rusten. Cambridge: Harvard UP, 1993.

Thucydides. History of the Peloponnesian War. Trans. C. F. Smith. 4 vols. Cambridge: Harvard UP, 1991.

Vander Waerdt, P. A., ed. The Socratic Movement. Ithaca: Cornell UP, 1994.

Versenyi, L. Socratic Humanism. New Haven: Yale UP, 1963.

Vlastos, G., ed. The Philosophy of Socrates. Garden City: Doubleday, 1991.

—. Socrates- Ironist and Moral Philosopher. Ithaca: Cornell UP, 1991.

—. "Socrates on Acrasia." Phoenix 23 (1969): 7-88.

—. Socratic Studies. Ed. M. Burnycat. Cambridge: UP, 1994.

Whitman, C. H. The Heroic Paradox. Ithaca: Cornell UP, 1982.

Winspear, A. D. and **T. Silverberg.** Who Was Socrates?. New York: Russell, 1960.

Wood, E. M. and **N. Wood.** Class Ideology and Ancient Political Theory. New York: Oxford UP, 1978.

Xenophon. Xenophon. Trans. C. L. Brownson, et al. 7 vols. Cambridge: Harvard UP, 1992.

Chapter IX

Aristophanes. Aristophanes. Trans. BB. Rogers. Vol. 2. Cambridge: Harvard UP, 1989.

Aristotle. Aristotle. Trans. H. Rackham, et al. 26 vols. Cambridge: Harvard UP, 1926-91.

Arnold, M. Culture and Anarchy. Cambridge: Cambridge UP, 1954.

Bowra, C. M. The Greek Experience. Cleveland: World, 1957.

Burkert, W. Greek Religion. Cambridge: Harvard UP, 1985.

Campbell, J. Myths to Live By. Toronto: Bantam, 1988.

Castoriadis, C. Philosophy, Politics, Autonomy. Ed. D.A. Curtis. New York: Oxford, 1991.

Cicero. De Natura Deorum. Trans. H. Rackham. Vol. 19. Cambridge: Harvard UP, 1979.

De Romilly, J. The Great Sophists in Periclean Athens. Trans. J. Lloyd. Oxford, Eng: Clarendon, 1992.

Diels, H. Ancilla to the Pre-Socratic Philosophers. Trans. K. Freeman. Cambridge: Harvard UP, 1957.

Diordorus Siculus. Library of History. Trans. C. H. Oldfather. Vol. 5. Cambridge: Harvard UP, 1979.

Diogenes Laertius. Lives of Eminent Philosophers. Trans. R. D. Hicks. Vol. 2. Cambridge: Harvard UP, 1991.

Dix, D. G. Jews and Greeks. New York: Harper, 1953.

Dodds, E. R. The Greeks and the Irrational. Berkeley: U of California P, 1984.

Faraone, C. A., and **D. Obbink,** eds. Magika Hiera. New York: Oxford UP, 1991.

Fisher, N. R. E. Hyrbis. Westminster, Eng.: Aris; Cambridge: Harvard UP, 1991.

Goldin, Judah, ed. and trans. The Living Talmud. New Haven: Yale UP, 1957.

Greene, W. C. Moira- Fate, Good, and Evil in Greek Thought. New York: Harper, 1963.

Greene, D. and **Lattimore,** R. eds. The Complete Greek Tragedies. 4 vols. Chicago: U of Chicago P, 1991.

Hadas, M. ed. and trans. The Third and Fourth Books of Maccabees. New York: Harper, 1957.

Hamilton, E. Mythology. New York: New American, 1969.

Herodotus. The Histories. Trans. Aubrey de Selincourt. Baltimore: Penguin, 1968.

Hertzberg, A. ed. Judaism. New York: George, 1962.

Hesoid. Hesoid. Trans. H. G. Evelyn-White. Cambridge: Harvard UP, 1982.

Hippocrates. Hippocrates. Trans W. H. S. Jones. Vol. 2. Cambridge: Harvard UP, 1981.

Homer. The Odyssey of Homer. Trans R. Fitzgerald. Garden City: Doubleday, 1963.

—. The Iliad. Trans. R. Lattimore. Chicago: U of Chicago P, 1967.

Kerenyi, C. Prometheus- Archetypal Image of Human Existence. Trans. R. Manheim. Princeton: Princeton UP, 1997.

Kirk, G. S. Myth. Berkeley: U of California P, 1970.

—. The Nature of Greek Myths. London: Penguin, 1974.

Knox, B. The Oldest Dead White European Males. New York: Norton, 1993.

Kung, H. On Being a Christian. New York: Doubleday, 1976.

Lattimore, R. trans. The Iliad of Homer. Chicago: U of Chicago P, 1967.

Levi-Strauss, C. From Honey to Ashes. Trans. J. & D. Weightman. New York: Harper, 1973.

Longinus. On the Sublime. Trans. W. Hamilton. Cambridge: Harvard UP, 1927.

Lucian. The Passing of Peregrinus. Trans. A. M. Harmon. Vol. 5. Cambridge: Harvard UP, 1972.

Luck, G. Arcana Mundi. Baltimore: Johns Hopkins P, 1985.

Murray, G. Five Stages of Greek Religion. Garden City: Doubleday, 1955.

Nilsson, M. P. A History of Greek Religion. Trans. F. J. Fielden. Oxford, Eng.: Clarendon, 1925.

Parker, R. Miasma. Oxford, Eng.: Clarendon, 1990.

Pindar. The Odes of Pindar. Trans. Sir John Sandys. Cambridge: Harvard UP, 1989.

Plato. The Dialogues of Plato. Trans. B. Jowett. 4 vols. Oxford, Eng.: Clarendon, 1967.

Plotinus. Enneads. Trans. A. H. Armstrong. Vol. 1. Cambridge: Harvard UP, 1989.

Plutarch. Plutarch's Lives. Trans. B. Perrin. Vol. 3. Cambridge: Harvard UP, 1984.

Pulleyn, S. Prayer in Greek Religion. Trans. F. J. Fielden. Oxford, Eng.: Clarendon, 1997.

Rhode, E. Psyche. New York: Harcourt, 1925.

Senior, D. ed. The Catholic Study Bible. New York: Oxford UP, 1990.

Sewall, R. B. The Vision of Tragedy. New Haven: Yale UP, 1960.

Straten, F. T. Van. "Did the Greeks Kneel Before Their Gods?" Bulletin Antieke Beschaving: Babesh 49 (1974) :159-189.

Strauss, L. The Natural Right of History. Chicago: U of Chicago P, 1953.

Thomas A. Kempis. The Imitation of Christ. Trans. Leo Sherley-Price. New York: Dorset, 1986.

Whitman, C. H. The Heroic Paradox. Ithaca: Cornell UP, 1982.

ക•ക